Frameworks of World History

Volume Two: Since 1350

Stephen Morillo

New York   Oxford
OXFORD UNIVERSITY PRESS

Oxford University Press is a department of the University of Oxford.
It furthers the University's objective of excellence in research,
scholarship, and education by publishing worldwide.

Oxford   New York
Auckland   Cape Town   Dar es Salaam   Hong Kong   Karachi
Kuala Lumpur   Madrid   Melbourne   Mexico City   Nairobi
New Delhi   Shanghai   Taipei   Toronto

With offices in
Argentina   Austria   Brazil   Chile   Czech Republic   France   Greece
Guatemala   Hungary   Italy   Japan   Poland   Portugal   Singapore
South Korea   Switzerland   Thailand   Turkey   Ukraine   Vietnam

For titles covered by Section 112 of the US Higher Education Opportunity
Act, please visit www.oup.com/us/he for the latest information about
pricing and alternate formats.

Published by Oxford University Press
198 Madison Avenue, New York, NY 10016
www.oup.com

Library of Congress Cataloging-in-Publication Data
Morillo, Stephen.
  Frameworks of world history / Stephen Morillo, Wabash College.
     pages cm
  Includes bibliographical references and index.
  ISBN 978-0-19-998779-5 (combined volume); ISBN 978-019-998780-1 (volume 1);
  ISBN 978-019-998781-8 (volume 2). 1. World history-—Textbooks. I. Title.
  D21.M85 2013
  909—dc23
                                                                      2013016872

Printing number: 9 8 7 6 5 4 3 2 1

Printed in the United States of America
on acid-free paper

Brief Contents

○ Contents

PART I. Formations: To 600 BCE

Note: All volumes include the Introduction. Volume 1 ends with Chapter 14; Volume 2 begins with "Frameworks of World History to 1500: A Summary," followed by Chapter 14.

PART III. Traditions: 400 to 1100

PART VI. Convulsions: 1750 to 1914

PART VIII. Modernity: Since 1970

Issues in Doing World History

1. What Is "Natural"?
2. "Progress," Teleology, and Contingency
3. The Meaning of the Word "Civilization"
4. The Impact of Ideas
5. "Western Civilization"
6. Science, Evidence, and History
7. The Connection of Past and Present
8. Oceanic and National Histories
9. Slicing Up a Vast Topic
10. Archival Survival
11. Romanticizing the Past
12. Cultural Frames and "Holy War"
13. Evolution and Historical Evidence
14. European Exceptionalism
15. "Late Agrarian" versus "Early Modern"
16. The "Military Revolution"
17. Science and Religion
18. The Meaning of the Word "Revolution"
19. "Great Men"
20. Nationalism and Academic History
21. Post-Colonial Theory
22. "Modern," "Western," Historical Processes
23. Marxism and History
24. World War II and Video Culture
25. The Problem of Contemporary History
26. The Textbook Industry
27. Is a Global Perspective Possible?
28. Languages, Knowledge, History

Images on the Screen

Preface

This book has been a long time in the making. I've developed its approach over the course of more than twenty years of teaching world history. My general intellectual inclination is toward generalization and seeing broad patterns and comparisons, so world history has always appealed to me. This book emerged as I gradually tried to synthesize various ideas that I have tried out in class to help students understand the broad sweep of global development. In the process, I came to new understandings myself. This is therefore, I hope, more than just a textbook. It is an interpretive history of our human species. Read it, think about it, and as I say in all my syllabi, have fun!

Acknowledgments

World history is a vast topic, and writing a book is a vast undertaking. I could not have accomplished this task by myself. My first thanks go to several generations of students at Wabash College for their questions, insights, and enthusiasm for the subject. Classes at Loyola University in New Orleans, where I first taught world history, and Hawaii Pacific University in Honolulu also contributed to my thinking. I must also thank my world history colleagues in the Wabash History Department, Rick Warner and Michelle Rhoades, for productive conversations over the years. Rick constantly reminded me of the importance of networks, and Michelle suggested how to build gender into the model of Agrarian hierarchies. Further thanks go to Ken Hall and Jim Connolly, who run the Small Cities conference at Ball State University. They have invited me to several of their conferences, asking me to comment on and tie together a fascinating range of papers on various topics, especially pre-industrial Indian Ocean networks. These challenges helped me to develop my model significantly. More immediately, Nadejda Popov (University of West Georgia), Evan Ward (Brigham Young University), Ras Michael Brown (Southern Illinois University, Carbondale), Eric Nelson (Missouri State University), Tim Keirn (California State University, Long Beach), Roger Kanet (University of Miami), Robert Carriedo (US Air Force Academy), Kevin Lawton (Northern Arizona University), Andrew Devenney (Mid-Michigan Community College) as well as ten anonymous reviewers made valuable and insightful comments on the entire manuscript. Their careful readings saved me from several embarrassing errors, as well as contributing a number of fascinating interpretive points. The team at Oxford University Press was terrific: Francelle Carapetyan, photo researcher, Keith Faivre, production editor, George Chakvetadze, cartographer, Michelle Koufopoulos and Jennifer Campbell, editorial assistants, and Michele Laseau, design director.

Three people deserve special thanks. First, my editor at Oxford University Press, Charles Cavaliere, has believed in this project from its conception. He has shepherded it through the byzantine byways of contracts and production, contributed terrific ideas about presentation and a plethora of suggestions about illustrations, and in general he has been as much friend as editor. The book is a better book because of him.

Second, my mother, Carolyn Morillo, read every chapter as I finished writing each one. She provided intelligent comments and reactions and all the enthusiasm and encouragement a son could hope for.

Finally, this book would not have been possible without the love, support, and intellectual partnership of my wife Lynne Miles-Morillo. A specialist in Early New High German linguistics and culture, she has been a sounding board for ideas and an invaluable editor of my prose. She has kept me on track and has been generous beyond what I could reasonably ask for. She has taken on the twin tasks of compiling, with me, the sourcebook that accompanies this text and writing the Instructor Resource Manual for it. She has done all this while we took care of three wonderful children, Robin, Dione, and Raphael. I dedicate this book to her.

About the Author

Stephen Morillo received his AB in History from Harvard College, where he graduated Magna cum laude and Phi Beta Kappa. He did a DPhil in History at Oxford University, which he attended as a Rhodes Scholar. Originally trained as a specialist in medieval European history, he has spent his career broadening his scope to encompass the world from the Big Bang to the present.

He has held appointments at Loyola University in New Orleans, where he first taught world history, the University of Georgia, and Wabash College, where he currently chairs the Social Sciences Division. He was for a year the NEH Distinguished Visiting Scholar in Diplomacy and Military Studies at Hawaii Pacific University. At Wabash he has held the Jane and Frederic M. Hadley Chair in History. He has won both the McLain-McTurnan-Arnold Research Fellowship and the McLain-McTurnan-Arnold Excellence in Teaching Award. Morillo has authored numerous books and articles, including *War in World History: Society, Technology and War from Ancient Times to the Present* (McGraw Hill, 2008), a military world history. He co-edited *Encounters in World History: Sources and Themes from the Global Past* (McGraw Hill, 2005), a world history sourcebook, and edited ten volumes of *The Haskins Society Journal*. He is President of De Re Militari: The Society for Medieval Military History and serves on several editorial boards.

He currently lives in Crawfordsville, Indiana, with his wife Lynne Miles-Morillo, his three children, Robin, Dione, and Raphael, and two rambunctious cats. In addition to history, he enjoys painting, cartooning, playing music, and cooking.

Introduction

Maldives 2009. Women on a ferry.

Welcome to a different sort of world history text. This is a text whose presentation of the past relies on an explicit analytical model (that's the first difference), a model that allows some specific arguments to be made about why world history followed the path it did (that's the second difference). To understand the function of this model and why it matters, let's think metaphorically about doing world history.

The Model

Memorize all this art! The conventional museum tour approach to studying world history: visitors encounter a whirl of impressions, but they do not probe beneath the surface to acquire a deeper understanding.

Imagine the past as a vast mansion made up of many different rooms. Most world history textbooks take students in through the front door and give them a room-by-room tour of the mansion, pointing out the shape of each room, the furniture, and all the art on the walls. Some rooms lead to others, some are shaped similarly to still others even though they are not connected, and the tour guide may occasionally point such things out. But the great variety of rooms and the furniture and art that each contains remain the main focus until finally we exit out another door.

By the end of such a tour, students are likely to have "art object fatigue." Some especially interesting pieces may stand out to them, and they may remember roughly what their route through the mansion was. (The tour guide almost always takes them from the oldest rooms to the most recent.) But they probably cannot explain why the mansion was arranged the way it was, nor understand in what other ways the mansion might have been built.

This book conducts a similar tour. The chronological route is roughly the same, though perhaps divided up a little differently. But the tour is conducted, in effect, with a blueprint of the mansion in hand. The book's analytical model is the blueprint—the conceptual framework of the mansion—and it lets us think about the layout of the rooms in a more abstract way: about engineering and construction techniques and about the plumbing and wiring that connects the rooms. That information places the artwork of the mansion in a different context, as well. The following section makes the elements of this "mansion metaphor" more explicit by introducing the major components of our model. Those components consist of two sorts of structures, networks and hierarchies, and the cultural frames and cultural screens that arise from, shape, and give meaning to the structures. These words are central to our model and have a specific meaning in this book.

Networks and Hierarchies

The rooms of the mansion can represent hierarchies, or what are more commonly referred to as states, countries, kingdoms, empires or even nations. Thus, many tours of world history pass through a room called "Han China," which was built around the same time as a room called "Roman Empire," and so forth. These rooms

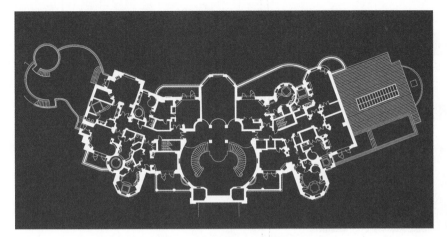

Frameworks of World History: A Blueprint. The Frameworks approach: understand the underlying structure of the mansion.

and their furnishings are the standard topics of world history. The standard tour of the mansion is often organized into what can be called "regional tours," visiting, one at a time, sets of rooms built around the same time. There are a lot of rooms, and since historians tend to specialize in particular rooms, the aggregate demand coming from all tour leaders is for a guidebook that is as comprehensive as possible so that nobody's room gets left out. The problem is that the guidebook then gets so large that nobody wants to carry it around.

Meanwhile, the standard guidebooks that spend most of their effort describing each room and its furnishings don't pay much attention to another vital aspect of the framework or architecture of the mansion: each room connects to a set of networks that we can think of metaphorically as the plumbing and wiring of the mansion. These represent the connections of trade, migration, cultural exchange, and so forth that linked historical hierarchies together, such as the copper pipe called "the Silk Road" that ran from the Han China room to the Roman Empire room. Early rooms might have had little more than some primitive clay pipe plumbing, but as time went on, the mansion came to include gas lines, central air and heat, electrical wires, and phone and cable hookups. And now that the mansion has a wireless LAN and Wi-Fi, the most recent rooms have become so connected that one can begin to question whether the walls of the different rooms really divide the mansion much at all. The rooms themselves threaten to become virtual.

This guidebook includes blueprints of the mansion that show the different construction techniques of rooms from different periods, as well as all the wiring and other systems that connect the rooms. Indeed, it focuses on such issues, including the problems that room builders faced in trying to incorporate all those network connections into the workings of a room. In other words, this is a book about networks, hierarchies, and their complex intersections: the framework in which the mansion was built. We will visit many of the familiar rooms, but partly in order to show how the "blueprint" worked in practice, we will do so with a focus on the common construction features of sets of rooms, rather than a focus on the room for its own sake. This is because the story that our blueprint tells is not the aggregated stories of all the rooms, but a more unified story of the construction of

Shifting Cultural Frames. Kansas and Oz: different colors, different cultural frame values. (Top: Mary Evans Picture Library/Everett Collection. Bottom: Courtesy Everett Collection.)

the entire mansion. It is a framework for understanding the mansion as a whole.

Still, no matter how similar the construction techniques of the Han China room and the Roman Empire room, each is decorated in different ways that make them not only look and "feel" different from each other, but actually function differently as rooms, in the same way that a room divided up by a bunch of decorative screens will function differently from one with a single large futon in the middle of the floor. How do we account for this in a model of networks and hierarchies? How, in other words, do we account for culture in a structural model?

Cultural Frames and Screens

In the 1939 MGM classic *The Wizard of Oz,* Dorothy Gale and her little dog Toto find themselves hurtling through a tornado in their small Kansas farmhouse. When the house lands and Dorothy steps out, she says to her pet, "Toto, I have a feeling we're not in Kansas anymore!" Now how does she (and we the audience) know this?

Well, some of the issues that the people are talking about seem a bit strange. There's apparently a dead witch, and an angry green evil witch related to her, and even a good witch. But then, there was an angry woman on a bicycle in Kansas who wanted to send Toto to the pound. We don't have to squint much to see the similarity between her and the angry green witch. Maybe the woman on the bicycle has a sister and we've simply landed in another town in Kansas near Dorothy's. But no, Dorothy is certain that we're not in Kansas, and we the audience are not inclined to disagree with her. Why?

Because she's stepped out into a *Technicolor* world! We've already experienced Kansas—it was a sepia-colored monochromatic place. The color shift in *Wizard of Oz* is a visual symbol of the division between two worlds with very different cultural frames, that is, different fundamental assumptions about how and why the world works the way it does. We know that the color of each world is a frame value (or a visual symbol of a frame value, at least) because nobody in either place mentions it. Nobody in Kansas said, "Dang, sure is looking sepia-colored today. Wonder when we'll get some green folks around here? Brighten the place up a bit." Nobody in Oz says to Dorothy as she steps out of her house, "I reckon you notice all the color here. Right purty, ain't it, young lady?" They don't mention it because they take it for granted: that's how their world always looks to them.

The color shift in *Wizard of Oz* shows us how cultural frames work. The people in any particular room of our mansion, such as the Han China room, create their own cultural frame. It's like the background color of the room. They may have inherited major parts of their frame from the people who lived in the earlier room next to theirs without even thinking about it. Of course, the Han China room is red, because it's connected to the Warring States and the Qin China room, which was also reddish. The color may be influenced by the shape or function of the room, but it also affects how the room functions, how the people see it, and what kind of art they want to put on the walls. Most of the people in the room will probably assume that all rooms are that color, just naturally. Only people who move between rooms—people who work in the networks connecting rooms, like merchants, or accidental travelers like Dorothy, or people like us taking a retrospective tour of lots of rooms—notice the differences. And for most of those people, the differences often look strange and un-natural because they're different from the color of the room where they grew up.

As we noted, arguments arise within each room. What art should go on that wall? Several different paintings might fit, given the background color. Such issues involve conscious disagreement, even if there's a significant majority opinion. In our model, we will refer to positions about such issues as cultural screen images to show that they're being projected intentionally onto a cultural screen. Some issues might, in their fundamental form, show up in several different rooms. For example, angry older unmarried women might seem dangerous, and people in many rooms might therefore call them "witches." But in one world they're sepia colored and ride bicycles, and in another they're green and ride brooms, and the differences matter as much as the similarities. And if we visit Oz through the frame provided by Gregory Maguire in *Wicked,* we might see Elphaba Thropp, the "Wicked Witch of the West," differently again, and wonder about calling people witches at all.

Are there universals in human culture, things that look the same no matter what cultural frame we see them through? Possibly. Dorothy makes friends in both Kansas and Oz. Friendship, or making people angry, might be universal. But we have to be very careful about what we think is universal. Something that looks universal may just be colored in harmony with our own frame. The fact of friendship or anger might mean very little without being put into appropriate action, and the appropriateness of the action is colored by the cultural frame within which it occurs. We'll leave the existence of universals as an open question, because the task of our model is to identify the crucial frame elements coloring various rooms, as well as to highlight some of the screen issues that the room's inhabitants thought were important given the color of their room. This is how we account for culture in this structural model.

The Use of Models in History

Accounting for culture is vital because culture, in the form of both frames (invisible from within the culture) and screens (how cultures view themselves), provides much of the motivating force for change, making the model dynamic. And the model must capture the dynamism of history. Models would be easier to build (but also less interesting) if what they modeled were static. The tendency of models to portray fixed rather than fluid structures is one reason that many historians are suspicious of models. The other is that models focus on commonalities across cases, and historians are trained to look for the interesting differences that make each historical case unique. Models, in this view of the discipline of history, are for sociologists, economists, and other social scientists.

Models: Advantages and Uses

The problem is that everyone uses a model of some sort when they write history, because a model is simply an explicitly worked out idea of causation, of what makes things change in history. A model is a theory. This book operates on the assumption that making the explanatory model behind its account of world history explicit has several advantages. First, explicit models or theories, because they are consciously developed and open to inspection, are likely (not certain, but likely) to be more sophisticated and nuanced than implicit assumptions about how the world works. Another way of putting this is that every historian has his or her own cultural frame through which he or she views history, a frame that colors his or her view of the past. Making one's model explicit is a way of trying to be more consciously aware of the potential distortions that one's frame imposes. Furthermore, if the model is out there for everyone to see, others can adjust, correct, or modify it so that it works even better, since the distortions imposed by individual cultural frames can often cancel each other out.

Making a model or theory explicit has another advantage. It allows the model to be tested against new evidence. This book cites plenty of evidence in support of its view of the past, giving examples from a wide range of cultures and societies. It is not, however—and cannot be—exhaustive. But it doesn't need to be. It provides a model, a conceptual framework, that in theory applies to any evidence. Thus, teachers and students can bring their own examples, their own special interests, to the table, not simply as another interesting example of what has happened in the past, but as evidence that can be used to test the model (Does this new case fit? Do we need to modify the model to account for this case?) and that can be interpreted in terms of the model, illuminating similarities and contrasts with other cases.

So explicit theories or models allow for collective self-correction and for testing against evidence. This is the way science works, in fact. Thus, in a way, the explicit model that shapes this text makes it more like a science textbook than a typical world history text.

Doing History

We won't press this claim about history as a science too hard. It's not that the methods of history and the sciences are fundamentally different. (It's true that historians can't run repeatable experiments, but then neither can paleontologists, cosmologists, or any other practitioner of the "historical sciences," the sciences that examine past natural events.) Rather, two factors complicate the historian's task. First, historians' subject matter—humans and their actions, intentions, and thoughts—is so complex that no theory or model could capture it all, and so historians' individual interpretations will always enter into the equation. Second, those interpretations will often be aimed not at establishing basic facts, but at deciding what they, and the larger story they are part of, *mean*. History is a form of storytelling. Storytelling is one of the most basic and pervasive ways in which humans make their world meaningful. As storytellers and makers of meaning, historians are allied with their colleagues in the humanities.

Subjectivity is therefore involved in doing history. This is inevitable and not necessarily bad, but it does raise issues about "doing history." Since students of history are, ideally, doing history (something our explicit model encourages, we hope), this book highlights some of these issues. Each chapter contains a box called

Issues in Doing World History that discusses a philosophical or methodological problem raised by the content of the chapter.

Overview

Although the method, the analytical model, employed by this book is different from the methodology of other world history textbooks, the model is deployed within a basically chronological framework for examining world history that should look familiar to those who have looked at the topic before. The chapter divisions within the chronological periods are not determined by geography, as is usual in the "regional tour" model of world history textbooks, but are instead thematically focused and global (or at least very broadly trans-regional) in perspective. Some chapters range much more broadly and thematically than others. Since the issues and developments in world history are continuous and proceed at different paces in different places, the chronological divisions of the eight main parts of the book and their constituent chapters sometimes overlap. They are, furthermore, built around a periodization, or chronological division, of this book that is explained further in Chapter 1 and which is summarized in the chart below.

The eight parts are divided into two volumes as follows. Volume 1 starts with *Part I, Formations: To 600 BCE*, which traces the foundations of human history and of the human communities that form the main "actors" in the story of world history. It therefore covers the Hunter-Gatherer Era and part of the Early Agrarian Era. *Part II, Transformations: 600 BCE to 700 CE*, covers the rest of the Early Agrarian Era and analyzes the changes and developments that took place as those communities became more complex—changes that resulted in the emergence of cultural and political traditions still recognizable today. Those traditions and the many societies that embodied and elaborated them are the subject of *Part III, Traditions: 400 to 1100*. The growing interaction of those communities produced the exchange and conflicts analyzed in *Part IV, Contradictions: 1100 to 1500*. Parts III and IV together cover the High Agrarian Era.

Volume 2 starts with the Late Agrarian Era, in which the increasing influence of connections and exchanges between different human communities becomes more visible, an era covered in *Part V, Connections: 1500 to 1800*. Eventually, those exchanges produced a major period of transformation whose contours are traced in *Part VI, Convulsions, 1750 to 1914*. Those transformations produced a tumultuous century described in *Part VII, Crises: 1914 to 1989*. In the overlap between the Parts, we shift from the Early Industrial Era to the High Industrial Era. A final section, *Part VIII, Modernity: Since 1970*, applies the analytical model to the major issues and developments of the world in the last forty years and continues our coverage of the High Industrial Era.

Features and additional Resources

Each chapter of the book includes a number of features designed to make the book more useful:

- Framing the Argument. A short list, placed with the opening story of each chapter, of the central ideas presented in the chapter.

Frameworks of World History: Periodization

Era	Sub-era	Dates	Networks	Hierarchies	Cultures
Hunter-Gatherer	**Early**	To 70,000 BCE	None	Simple bands	Pre-symbolic
	High	70,000 to 20,000 BCE	Emergent	Bands	Cognitive-Linguistic Revolution
	Late	20,000 to 4000 BCE	Short-range connections	Bands, tribes	Status markers
Agrarian	**Early**	8000 BCE to 700 CE	Emergent long-distance	Chiefdoms, states, empires	Philosophical-religious foundations
	High	400 to 1500	Multiple circuits	Chiefdoms, states, empires	Major cultural traditions
	Late	1500–1800	Emergent global	Maritime empires	Increasing encounters
Industrial	**Early**	1750–1945	Powerful global	Modern states, global empires	Isms, esp. Nationalism
	High	Since 1914	Pervasive global	Regional unions	Globalization
	Late		?	?	? ?

Frameworks of World History: Periodization.

- Framing the Chapter. A global map, placed just after the opening story, that highlights the key places discussed in the chapter and includes visual images from each place that illustrate the themes of the chapter.
- Principles and Patterns. In the course of each chapter, two or three key ideas are highlighted in the margin. These are basic tendencies—not quite rules, but close—of human societies (principles) or long-term trends of world history (patterns).
- Images on the Screen. A page of photographs of cultural artifacts from different places, which are thematically related and which illustrate the role of such artifacts in how people constructed their identities.
- Frame it Yourself. A brief thought problem, placed at the end of each chapter, that asks you to apply the conceptual tools of the model. There are three types. *Frame Your World* asks for comparisons between the past and the world today. *Extending the Frame* asks you to apply the model to a society that the chapter does not have room to talk about. *Changing the Frame* asks you to play "What if?" with history.

- Further Readings. At the end of each chapter is a brief list of books that provide more information about the main topics of the chapter.
- Sources for Frameworks of World History. A separate book that provides 4–6 primary sources per chapter, with introductions and questions, specifically chosen to go with Frameworks.
- Instructor's Resource Manual. Provides outlines, key terms, content review questions, and varied classroom activities.

A Note about Dates

As the reader will have noted in reading the outline above, this book uses the standard BCE/CE dating system. This is, frankly, a nod to convention that this author has made somewhat reluctantly. The original intent was to give the book its own convention for conveying the difference between dates falling before or after Year 1 in the calendar used in much of the world today. Dates before that year, which are usually referred to with the abbreviations BC (Before Christ) or BCE (Before Common Era), would have been shown with a minus sign as negative numbers. For example, the Battle of Marathon took place, in such a system, in −490 (rather than 490 BC or 490 BCE). Dates after the Year 1, which are usually referred to with the abbreviations AD (Anno Domini) or CE (Common Era), would have been designated either with a plus sign if they need to be distinguished from minus dates, or with no sign. Thus, the Han Dynasty lasted, in such a system, from −202 to +220; the Tang Dynasty from 618 to 906.

This admittedly idiosyncratic system seemed preferable for reasons of clarity and typographical simplicity. The designations BC and AD make explicit the Christian origins of this system of dating. Many historians and other writers adopted the BCE/CE system as a way of making the system less culturally exclusive. But the attempt has struck others as less than completely successful—after all, the numbers are still the same and their origins still pretty clear—at the expense of clarity, for the meanings of the designations BCE and CE are not always obvious to students, especially since "CE" contains a "C" just as "BC" does. And "BCE" adds an extra letter to the typographical mix. While acknowledging the attempt to be more culturally inclusive, we wanted to adopt our system of plusses and minuses mainly because it struck us as typographically cleaner and conceptually clearer. But for the sake of making an already different book more accessible, we went with convention. See the "Issues in Doing World History" box in Chapter 26 for more on such issues. Perhaps in a second edition.

Using the Model: Key Terms

The periodization and the model used in this book entail the use of some specialized terms. The following list presents a thematic grouping of the key terms employed in this book's analysis of world history. The terms are defined briefly in the Glossary at the end of the book.

Periodization Terms

- Hunter-Gatherer Era (before 8000 BCE) Chapter 1
- Early Hunter-Gatherer (before ca. 70,000 BCE)
- High Hunter-Gatherer (ca. 70,000 BCE to ca. 20,000 BCE)
- Late Hunter-Gatherer (ca. 20,000 BCE to 4000 BCE)
- Agrarian Era (8000 BCE to 1800 BCE)
- Early Agrarian (8000 BCE to 700 CE) Chapters 2–7
- High Agrarian (400 to 1500) Chapters 8–14
- Late Agrarian (1500 to 1800) Chapters 15–18
- Industrial Era (after 1800)
- Early Industrial (1800 to 1945) Chapters 19–24
- High Industrial (1914) Chapters 23–28
- Late Industrial (the future?)

Cognitive-Linguistic Revolution
  (ca. 70,000 years ago)
Agricultural Revolution
  (ca. 8000 BCE)
Industrial Revolution
  (ca. 1800 CE)

Hunter-Gatherer societies
Agrarian societies
Pastoralist societies
Industrial societies

The Model: General Terms

Model
Structures
Networks

Hierarchies
Culture
Cultural screen

Cultural frame
Low and slow

Network Terms

Network flows
Network circuits

Inner circuit Eurasia
Outer circuit Afro-Eurasia

Dense local network
Network crisis

Hierarchy Terms

Simple societies
Bands
Tribes
Complex societies
Chiefdoms
State-level complex societies
Agrarian Pyramid
State
Society
Unitary political leader
Elites

Commoners
Class power
Top and bottom layers of the Pyramid
Gender power
Front and back faces of the Pyramid
Industrial hierarchy
State
Social sphere
Corporate sphere
Conquest societies
Fragment societies

Nomad-Sedentary cycle
Warfare
Intracultural warfare
Intercultural warfare
Subcultural warfare
Reactions to imperialism
Traditionalist resisters
Westernizers
Modernizers
Identerest
Kleptocracy

Terms Relating to the Intersection of Networks and Hierarchies

Merchant dilemma
Cores
Peripheries
Wise practitioners
Informed officials

Worldly travelers
Spheres of maritime activity
Naval sphere of maritime activity
Merchant sphere of maritime activity
Pirate sphere of maritime activity

State-private dichotomy
War-peace dichotomy
Official-unofficial dichotomy
Navies of imperial defense
Predatory sea peoples

Cultural Frame and Screen Terms

Frame values

Cultural screen images

Great Cultural Divide

Color Code

Finally, when we present variations on the Agrarian Pyramid, we use the following color code to represent different sorts of people, especially elites, and their place in the society.

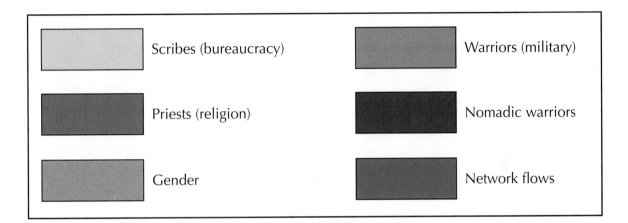

Frameworks of World History to 1500: A Summary

The tour of the mansion so far . . .

Introduction

Studying world history starting around 1500 means that you are coming in somewhere in the middle of an ongoing story. So imagine that you have just turned on your Frameworks TV and a disembodied voice is telling you, "Previously on *Frameworks of World History . . .*"

Following the principles of organization that inform this book and that are laid out in the Introduction, this brief overview comes in two parts. First, we will run through a chronological overview of global developments. This will take us from the emergence of modern humans as a species, in the context of a much longer natural history of the universe, through the Hunter-Gatherer Era and to the end of the High Agrarian Era. Second, we will summarize the central themes and long-term developmental patterns that underlie that chronology, in a section called "Models, Principles, and Patterns." This section will introduce and fill out the key analytical concepts of our model of networks, hierarchies, and cultural frames. These are the tools that this book uses to analyze world history.

Chronological Overview

The universe is about 13.6 billion years old. The earth is about 4.6 billion years old. Life on earth is about 3.8 billion years old. Complex multicellular life is around 600 million years old. Human life, even counting our most distant ancestors after our evolutionary line split from chimpanzees around 6 million years ago, is thus a tiny fraction of universal history. It is, however the fraction we're most interested in. Our chronology begins, in effect, when early hominins, the members of our family of species, began using stone tools more than 2 million years ago. They had been gathering food all along. They started hunting animals perhaps 1.8 million years ago. The Hunter-Gatherer Era had begun.

The Hunter-Gatherer Era

Evolution produced *Homo sapiens,* the modern human species, about 200,000 years ago. But the extremely slow change in early human tool kits indicates that our earlier ancestors and even our cousin species that existed when our species emerged, including Neanderthals, did not think the way we do. Even the earliest modern humans living before about 70,000 years ago seem still to have seen the world differently from us. The Early Hunter-Gatherer Era was inhabited by people who seem to have been much less self-conscious than we are.

The Cognitive-Linguistic Revolution and the High Hunter-Gatherer Era

Then, around 70,000 years ago, modern humans stopped being a tiny, isolated species in East Africa. They spread all over the globe in the next 60,000 years (see Figure S.1). What changed? This book posits that this was when humans shifted from older, non-symbolic forms of communication to our modern use of word-and-syntax language and, as a result, symbolic and metaphorical thought: a Cognitive-Linguistic Revolution. This shift created the foundation for the quintessentially human activities our model captures. Unlike earlier forms of communication, modern language, though it changes and divides constantly, can be translated from one version to another and so creates the capacity for humans to create networks across which they exchange goods and ideas. Language and symbolic thought make people see the world in terms of symbolic status and so create the capacity for people to construct complex hierarchies, societies that rank people according to attributed status. Finally, language and symbolic thought cause people to interpret themselves and to seek meaning in the world. Constructing identity and making meaning are the activities represented by the cultural frames and screens of our model. The Cognitive-Linguistic Revolution made humans culturally inventive and therefore capable of adapting to a far broader range of climates than before. The result was the global spread of humanity. (See Figure S.1.)

The Late Hunter-Gatherer Era

By the time humans occupied nearly the entire globe between 20,000 and 15,000 years ago, the Ice Age was coming to an end. A warming climate benefited some regions but created challenges for some of the most densely occupied parts of the hunter-gatherer world, where some people had already largely abandoned the nomadic life of most hunter-gatherers and had settled in permanent locations. This

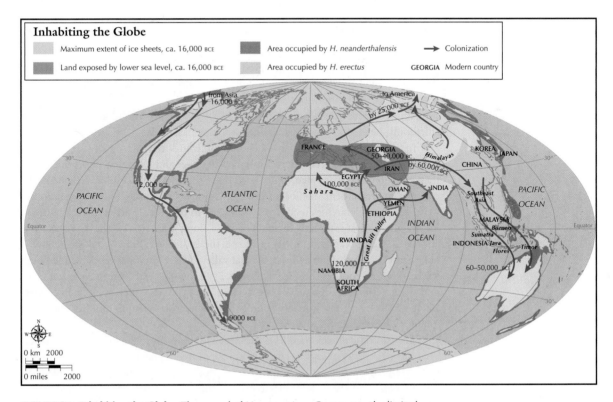

FIGURE S.1 Inhabiting the Globe. The spread of *Homo sapiens*. Compare to the limited range of *Homo erectus*.

was one element in a complex set of factors that led to the invention of agriculture. From around 10,000 years ago, some human communities began growing their own crops and, in fewer places, raising their own domesticated animals. This happened independently in a number of places around the globe. Agriculture spread slowly from those original centers and the Agrarian Era began.

The Agrarian Era

The word "agrarian" denotes societies whose main form of subsistence is agriculture. Although some peoples continued to practice hunting and gathering right through the Agrarian Era and into the Industrial Era, many more lived by agriculture, which can support more people than hunting and gathering. (Individually, many of those people ended up less well off than under hunting and gathering, however.) This justifies our seeing a new era with the multiple inventions of agriculture beginning about 10,000 years ago.

The Early Agrarian Era

For several thousand years after the invention of agriculture, the people practicing agriculture lived in small villages. But the ability of agriculture to support larger numbers of people while creating storable surpluses of food meant that Agrarian societies, unlike their Hunter-Gatherer predecessors, could begin to build more complex hierarchies. Hunter-gatherer bands became tribes in villages. In some places, even larger, more complex societies called chiefdoms emerged. These societies featured leaders who had become hereditary (the chief) supported by a small portion of the population that achieved hereditary elite status. The same conditions that encouraged the invention of agriculture had also led to the invention of warfare between human communities around the same time, and the spread of war now accompanied the spread of agriculture. Thus, some early chiefdoms were warrior chiefdoms, headed by a war leader and a warrior-based elite.

In a few places, starting around 4000 BCE in lower Mesopotamia, state-level complex societies appeared. They featured even larger and more stratified populations than chiefdoms. They tended to be based politically in a new form of settlement, the city, and to create demands for information storage that resulted in the invention of writing. These hierarchies tended not, however, to be led by warriors, at least at first. Rather, the earliest state-level hierarchies arose along great rivers—the Tigris and Euphrates in Mesopotamia, the Nile in Egypt, the Indus in Pakistan, and the Yellow in northern China—that created rich alluvial valleys whose exploitation demanded high levels of social cooperation (see Figure S.2). Religious and bureaucratic elites, or priests and scribes, seem to have been better able to convince their subjects to cooperate at a new level than warriors could, though warriors would come to rule many state-level hierarchies as time went on.

The earliest complex state-level societies existed, from their point of view, as isolated islands of order in a sea of chaos. Nature appeared threatening, as did surrounding non-state peoples. But nature and non-state peoples also presented fairly simple challenges for early state-level hierarchies to manage culturally. Such societies grew and spread, however, because their greater numbers and levels of sociopolitical cooperation let them outcompete their less organized neighbors. (They also hosted greater concentrations

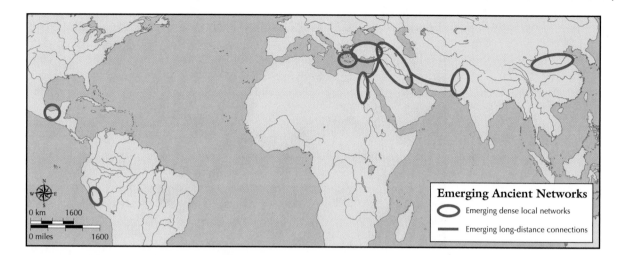

FIGURE S.2 **Emerging Ancient Networks.** Areas of growing network density in the ancient world. Note that they correspond with the locations of the most complex hierarchies.

of diseases that their neighbors found deadly.) As state-level organization spread, so did contact with other states across network connections that grew along with the population of the Early Agrarian Era. This was especially true across the temperate swathe of Eurasia running from China to Spain and including North India, Southwest Asia, and the Mediterranean, with the central Asian steppes acting as a crucial region of connection. By 600 BCE, this swath contained probably 90% of the world's population. Eventually, the challenges posed by this more complex world threatened the ability of its early states' cultures to maintain social and political stability. (In regions where network connections were weaker and more isolated and populations were less dense, such as in the Americas, this challenge developed much more slowly.)

The challenge of a more complex world was the background to what historians refer to as the Axial Age. This was a period from about 600 BCE to 300 BCE when world (or at least Eurasian) history seemed to turn on an axis and head off in a new direction. In concrete terms, this was the period of great thinkers such as Confucius, the Buddha, and Plato. In other words, this period saw the birth of great philosophical and religious traditions. Four stand out: first, the Chinese traditions of secular philosophy that included Confucianism, Daoism, and Legalism; second, the Indian religious traditions that included Hinduism, Buddhism, and Jainism; third, the Southwest Asian religious traditions that included Zoroastrianism and Judaism; fourth, the Greek secular traditions of philosophy that coalesced less around specific schools of thought than around a method of inquiry. (See Figure S.3.)

Though existing largely at the elite level of culture, these Axial Age philosophies proved to be effective as technologies of social control. Put another way, they allowed rulers to construct more sophisticated and flexible hierarchies capable of uniting more diverse peoples across larger regions than ever before. They therefore laid the foundations for the subsequent Age of Empires that lasted roughly from 400 BCE to 400 CE. The Persian Empire, the Chinese Han Empire, the Roman Empire, and the Indian

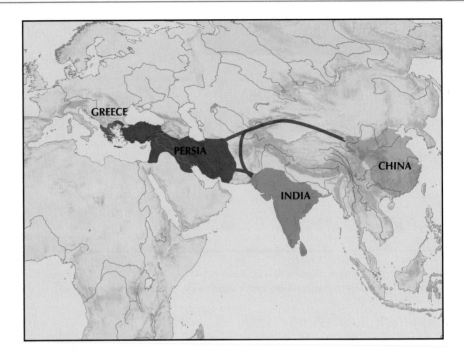

FIGURE S.3 Axial Age cultural regions.

Mauryan Empire created classical, or pattern-setting, models of political organization for huge regions of the world. Although all of the great empires broke up, some sooner than others, their successor states followed the precedents the earlier empires had established. The Chinese empire actually reemerged in unified form and established an effectively permanent presence that lasted through several changes of ruling dynasty. (See Figure S.4.)

These empires created the context for the last major development of the Early Agrarian Era, the rise of the salvation religions. Unlike most of Axial Age philosophical and religious thought, which existed among and appealed primarily to elites, the salvation religions aimed their messages at everyone, especially the poor, women, and other marginalized folk. They also claimed to apply equally to all places. These appeals to universalism made the religions attractive to many rulers as ways to bolster their legitimacy and appeal to their populations. The four major salvation traditions were Mahayana Buddhism, Devotional Hinduism, Christianity, and Islam. They spread across network connections to dominate the Afro-Eurasian religious landscape.

The High Agrarian Era

When the new salvation religions had blended with the established Axial Age traditions in the (mostly) more politically fragmented world after the Age of Empires, the result was the establishment of fairly stable cultural and political traditions in many places that are still recognizable today. The history of the High Agrarian Era between roughly 400 and 1100 is the story of the gradual growth and elaboration of these traditions and of their equally gradual divergence from each other. But just as the slowly

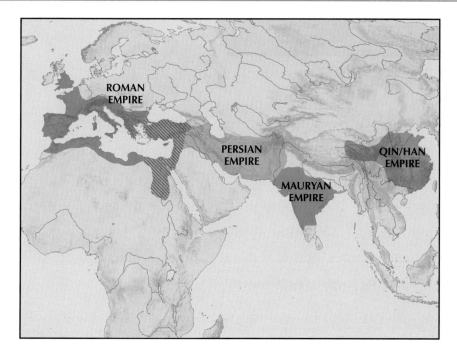

FIGURE S.4 The Age of Empires.

expanding capacity of network connections had brought the earliest state-level societies into contact with each other and complicated their world, the continued expansion of networks of cultural and economic exchange in the High Agrarian brought some hierarchies and their traditions into greater contact with each other and introduced further contradictions and conflict. Between 1100 and 1500, the movements of nomads, Crusaders, and merchants highlighted this process in Afro-Eurasia.

Punctuating this era of growing exchange between different cultural traditions was a twin calamity for much of the Eurasian world. First, beginning in 1206, the Mongols under Chingiz Khan conquered a vast area of Eurasia, creating the largest land empire ever (See Figure S.5.). In the process, they did incalculable damage to many different societies and rearranged the pattern of network connection tying this world together. Starting in the 1330s, that network carried a deadly plague, the Black Death, to many of the most populated regions of this world. Most of the hierarchies affected by either or both of these calamities recovered over the course of the fifteenth century. They rebuilt their cultural traditions by looking back to earlier models. Damaged networks reconnected and even expanded as maritime pathways reached farther. By 1500, they had reached around Africa, connecting the Indian Ocean trade circuit with that of the Afro-European Atlantic coast. They also reached across the Atlantic to the Americas, two continents previously unknown to Afro-Eurasians. The world's separate networks united into a single global network, and the Late Agrarian Era began. This second volume of *Frameworks of World History* picks up this story in Chapter 14 (which also ended Volume 1). Chapter 14 analyzes continued reactions to the calamities of Mongols

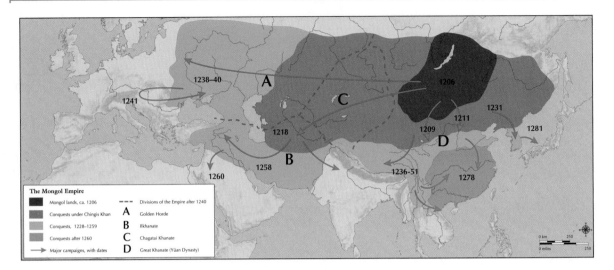

FIGURE S.5 The Creation of the Mongol Empire.

and plague, focusing on western Europe's somewhat idiosyncratic way of viewing the consequences of these events. It continues with the maritime expansion that globalized network flows. This summary and Chapter 14 lead us into the Late Agrarian world, where this volume starts.

Models, Principles, and Patterns

This book does far more than tell a chronological story. It attempts to analyze the path of world history by making a model of world history dynamics. It uses that model to highlight some of the fundamental principles at work in the operation of human societies and to identify the long-term patterns into which the development of those societies fell. It is to the model and the principles and patterns of world history to 1500 that we now turn.

The Model

Our model starts from some basic facts about human population. It then has three principal parts: networks, hierarchies, and cultural frames and screens. These parts are linked, and it is the combination of them that models historical processes.

Demographics

We can start with two graphs of total human population since the emergence of our modern species. The first plots population against time on a standard arithmetic scale. The second converts both population and time to a logarithmic scale so as to compare the rates of change in more detail. (See Figure S.6.)

The first doesn't seem to tell us much except that only about 10% of all the people who have ever been alive lived in the Hunter-Gatherer Era down to 10,000 years ago,

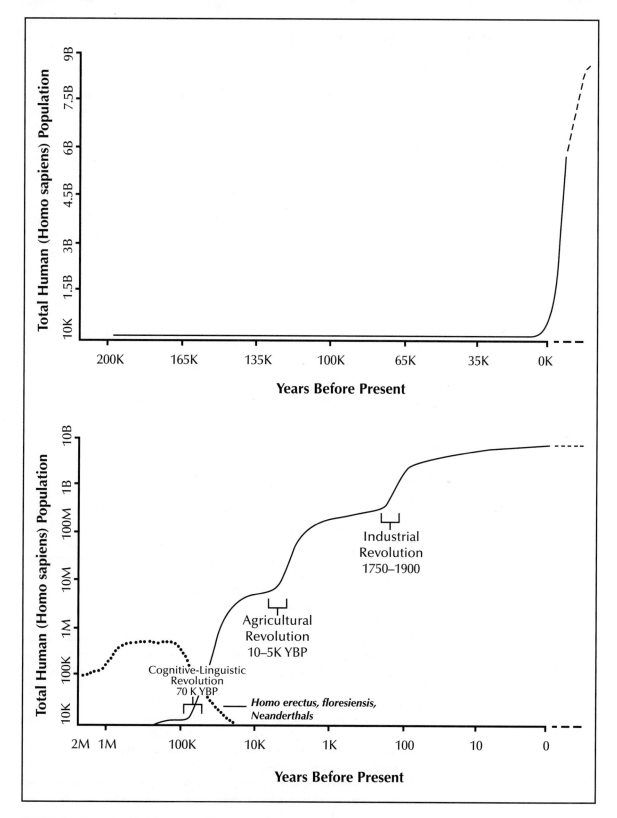

FIGURE S.6 Demographic History. Total human population since 200,000 years ago. (Top) Arithmetic scale. (Bottom) Logarithmic scale.

though that era takes up 95% of the time the species has been around. By contrast, nearly 20% have lived in the brief 200 years of the Industrial Era, and almost 8% of all the people who have ever lived are alive today—nearly as many as during the entire Hunter-Gatherer Era. About 65% lived in the Agrarian Era between 10,000 and 200 years ago, though that stage doesn't show up well at this scale.

But the second graph reveals different details from the first. Here, three revolutions in the relationship of humans to their environment dominate the story. First, the Cognitive-Linguistic Revolution launches population upward until the limits of the hunter-gatherer mode of existence are approached and numbers level off. Second, agriculture initiates another increase, not quite as steep or as high as the first (again, in terms of rates of change, not absolute numbers), which again levels off as the limits of agrarian modes of production are approached. Third, industrialization allowed a final (and from this perspective, least significant) increase, which is already leveling off (demographers expect world population to stop growing around 2050, at which point there will be roughly 10 billion of us). This graph is the basis for our periodization of world history outlined above.

This demographic story also drives other aspects of the model. Rising population led to the rising interconnectedness of separate human communities in material and cultural terms, that is, to the emergence and growth of networks. It also led to the rising complexity of the sociopolitical organization of individual communities, that is, to the emergence and growth of hierarchies. It is to these structures that we now turn.

Networks

The spread of modern humans across the globe was accomplished by the slow but steady migration of small groups of people, but these individual small communities generally retained ties to nearby groups or created new connections as founder groups grew, split, and migrated farther. By sometime between 20,000 and 11,000 years ago, the continents except for Antarctica and most major islands, except Madagascar and those in the Pacific, were covered by networks of hunter-gatherer communities. The term *networks* refers to the horizontal structures of connections that linked different human communities. The density and intensity of network connections varied with the concentration of population, and for most of history there were many separate networks.

Goods were exchanged in a variety of ways along these networks. Some were traded in essentially economic ways, bartered for other goods that both sides agreed were of roughly equal value. But networks from their earliest stages carried more than just material artifacts. Things came from a cultural context, were thus imbued with cultural meanings, and were received in a different cultural context within which individuals reinterpreted the meaning (and sometimes the function) of material goods. Thus, cultures and ideas traveled across networks, and divisions between networked areas were sometimes geographic but were also often cultural. In other words, network frontiers were often defined by shared cultural values and types of goods. Finally, people moved across networks as individual traders and travelers and as entire migrating groups. As networks developed, important nodes on the network could develop into cities, and some areas developed dense local networks with rich and varied

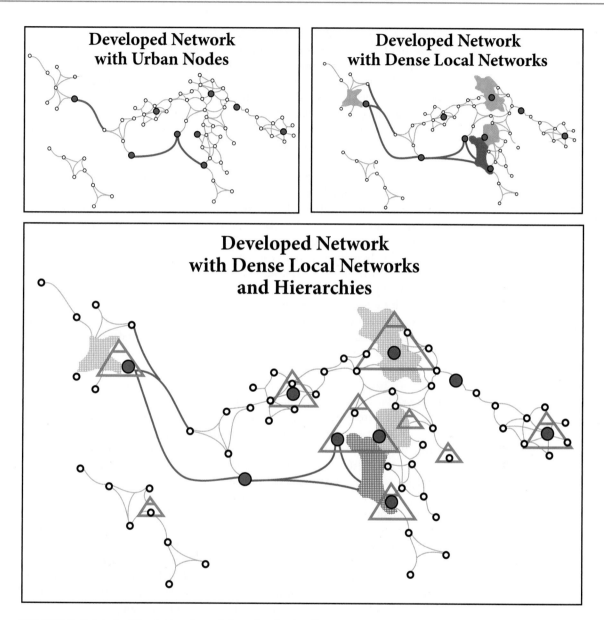

FIGURE S.7 Network with urban nodes and dense local networks.

connections. Figure S.7 shows a network with urban nodes and regions of dense local networks.

Hierarchies

The term *hierarchies* in our model refers to the vertical structures of power that shaped individual human communities, that is, their social and political organization.

This book will divide societies into four widely accepted basic types. The first two of these four types, bands and tribes, are simple, while the second two, chiefdoms and states, are complex. The total population and the density of settlement encompassed by a single community, as well as the community's network connections and the political organization of neighboring communities, all influenced what sort of structure a hierarchy developed. Population size and density were crucial because these factors affected the ability of communities to resolve disputes, redistribute economic goods efficiently, and make collective decisions, especially ones that had to be made quickly.

Bands consisted of under about eighty people. A band could sometimes be as small as a single nuclear family, but in any case all or almost all members of a band tended to be closely related. Bands were egalitarian in terms of decision making, with few if any permanent distinctions of status, except perhaps by age, and without any pattern of gender dominance. Bands settled internal disputes informally, though not always non-violently: interpersonal violence was undoubtedly unavoidable even in the most cooperative of communities. The members of a band acted economically as a unit, with all the members contributing and supporting each other. This was probably the product of cultural strictures as well as necessity, and codes of sharing would also have helped to inhibit any aggrandizement of any one individual's status. There probably was a differentiation of gender roles, with males doing most of the hunting and females the gathering. But differentiation did not produce dominance, in part because gathering almost always provided significantly more of a band's nutrition than hunting did. Since most hunter-gatherers lived in bands and most bands were hunter-gatherers, they tended to be nomadic.

Tribes were larger than bands, consisting of up to several hundred people: still few enough that everyone in a tribe knew every other person in the tribe. Tribes are often divided into clans, or extended family groups (which independently would have been bands). Decision making, dispute resolution, and economic exchanges were still informal and were handled by meetings within what remained a relatively egalitarian community, though some tribes had "big men," or recognized leaders whose influence was greater than others'. Such positions were based on practical achievements or personal qualities and thus were not (generally) heritable. In addition, tribal leadership could be exercised by women, especially in tribal areas without much warfare, and gender relations generally were not characterized by consistent patterns of male dominance. While many tribes since the invention of warfare have engaged in chronic conflict with neighbors, this was by no means the rule. Furthermore, some networks of tribes have managed to "govern" fairly vast areas without any recourse to complex hierarchical organization. Most tribes differed from bands in that they lived in a single fixed village: tribal organization was normal for village agriculturalists. But some tribes (and even chiefdoms, the next category) were nomadic, especially among pastoralists.

Chiefdoms tended to arise when the number of people in a single community exceeded several thousand, ranging into tens of thousands in size. Chiefdoms thus encompassed one or more fixed villages, one of which might emerge as a central village, ruled by a hereditary chief supported by a small group of elite families with hereditary noble status. Thus, chiefdoms are the level of sociopolitical organization at which complexity in the form of class stratification appears. And while female chiefs were not unknown, they were rarer than matrilineal tribes, and gender relations generally tended more toward patriarchy. This was probably related to the common role of chiefs as war leaders and the consequent militarization of elite status. The chief managed decision making, conflict resolution, and aspects of economic exchange that were handled informally in bands and tribes. But chiefs tended to have very few coercive tools at their disposal. Their status and ability to manage communal action depended instead on powers of moral persuasion, often backed by some form of religious legitimation, which we will discuss further in the section on cultural frames. Chiefdoms, however, varied widely in their level of organization, depending mostly on their size: some were barely more than tribes whose "big man" inherited his position, while some were close to being states, with simple bureaucracies and some public buildings. The more sophisticated the organization of the chiefdom, the greater the potential for coercive power to accrue to the chief. We can represent these levels of social organization with simple diagrams (see Figure S.8).

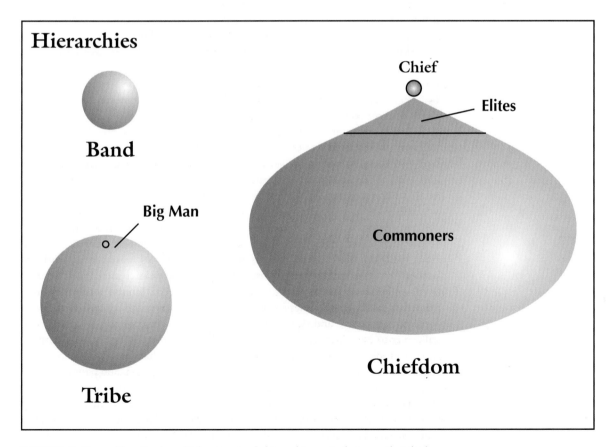

FIGURE S.8 Hierarchies. Bands and tribes are simple hierarchies: note that even if a tribe has a "big man" he is part of the group, not really above it. Chiefdoms (and states) are complex.

States, or state-level complex societies, were the most complex form of hierarchy. To understand the shape of Agrarian Era state-level hierarchies, we must see the basic contexts in which they existed. And here we need to think about such contexts not in contrast to the much simpler world of the Hunter-Gatherer Era of hunting and gathering bands, but in contrast to our own modern age. The conditions that all of us alive today have grown up with are radically different from those that obtained throughout the Agrarian Era, so we must work hard to think ourselves out of the expectations generated by our own context.

The two fundamental constraints shaping the networks and especially the hierarchies of the Agrarian Era were *low productivity* and *slow communications*. "Low and slow" will be a constant refrain in our explanations of the patterns of the Agrarian Era. What does "low and slow" mean?

Low productivity means that there was very little surplus wealth. Individual farming families often grew barely more than enough to feed themselves, so only a tiny percentage of the population could engage in non-food-producing activities. Manufacturing had to happen by hand ("manufacture" is from the Latin roots for "hand" and "make"), so there were many fewer things in the world than today, even if some of them were of very high craftsmanship. Sources of power for doing work were limited to wind, water, and above all muscle, animal or human.

Slow communications meant that the things that did exist, as well as ideas, moved only as fast as wind, water, and muscle could carry them. This made transport expensive as well as slow. Most people lived out their lives within the confines of a very local world. People, commodities, and ideas that moved long distances were the exception.

These constraints had important results. By our standards, population was low and sparsely scattered. Cities were small: though the largest urban concentrations could occasionally reach a million or more, even the largest cities were usually only about 200,000, and most were barely in the tens of thousands. Cities of under 10,000 were common. There was not really what we call a "middle class." There were elites and commoners, with distinctions of wealth and status among them: a top and bottom with no middle. Finally, "low and slow" meant that "the market," that abstract realm of buying and selling that is made real in particular market locations and that in our world permeates nearly our entire lives, was relatively weak and limited. Limited numbers of goods and limited transport created this, but commonly imposed political constraints further reinforced limited markets. Things treated as basic commodities in our world—land, labor, and money—were often ruled out for buying and selling because they were too important as bases of political power to be exchanged in the market. (This made merchants politically suspect, a crucial topic to which we shall return repeatedly.) Exchanges of such goods were more likely to occur politically, through taxes, rents, extortion, and plunder.

These conditions shaped the space of possibilities for political structures. Mass democracy of the modern sort was impossible under such constraints, for example. While there were exceptions, we can model the basic sociopolitical structure of Agrarian states as a sort of pyramid (see Figure S.9).

At the top of the pyramid was a single political leader, commonly a king or emperor, whose rule usually was claimed to be sanctioned by divine forces. Below

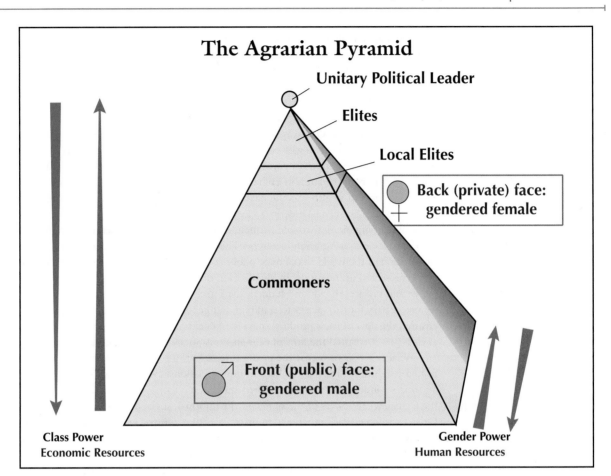

FIGURE S.9 The Agrarian Pyramid. The sociopolitical pyramid shape of Agrarian Era state-level societies.

the king were the elites who supported him, some more prominent than others, who might only be elite at a local level. Elites came in three kinds: priests, or specialists in managing the society's relationships with the forces of the cosmos; scribes, or specialists in the tasks of administration and record-keeping that kept the society organized and running; and warriors, who specialized both in defending the society from external threats and even more in providing force, the ultimate insurance for the position of the elites and the demands of the state. Politics in such a world was personal and involved elite competition for access to or control over the king, while the chief job of the king was elite building, or attempting to keep all the elites happy and ideologically unified so as to prevent factional conflict that could tear a state apart.

The role of force was vital in running hierarchies, however distant its actual use remained, because the entire structure was built to extract resources from the society. One way to see the basic two-part division between elites and commoners was as a division between specialists in the use of force and its justifications, on one hand, and specialists in the production of wealth on the other. This was theoretically a mutually beneficial arrangement: in exchange for a share of their wealth, commoners received protection from nature, chaos, and human enemies. But it was an asymmetrical relationship, as the specialists in force could enforce an unfair level of exchange that the producers of wealth had trouble resisting.

The two main sorts of wealth produced by commoners account for further aspects of the structure. One was food, or agricultural produce more generally, including primary products such as wool, wood, flax, and so forth. Thus farmers in states everywhere found themselves paying taxes and rents, and often giving up their freedom to move from the land, in exchange for "protection." Farmers became peasants. The other form of wealth was the next generation of workers, produced by the labor of the society's women. Thus, in a close analogy to the subjugation of farmers by elites, the subjugation of women by men, especially elite men, cemented patriarchy as a normal element of Agrarian hierarchy. This was almost always framed, culturally, by the division of the world into a male public sphere and a female private sphere, a division represented in the model by the division of the pyramid between front and back, public and private, shown and hidden, male and female. Both halves of the pyramid were necessary for the society to stand up, but gender power kept women in place and ensured the flow of their production to the benefit of the elites and the state as much as class power ensured the flow of economic resources to the same end.

What this tells us is that the pyramid represents a sociopolitical structure, shaped from top to bottom and front to back by power relationships. It was not, in other words, a socioeconomic structure managed by a state, as modern societies tend to be. Instead, the formal, legal powers of the state and the informal, social powers of the elites overlapped, reinforced each other, and in many cases were inextricably linked. One result of this was that power (over people) was the surest path to wealth, the reverse relationship from our world in which the acquisition of wealth is the surest path to power. In Agrarian societies, politics took precedence over economics. Two further corollaries of the dominance of politics over economics are important. First, the surest way to demonstrate that one had power in Agrarian hierarchies was to give things away. Second, labor shortages in Agrarian hierarchies led to declines in labor freedom. They did not lead to rising wages, as we might expect from our market-based frame of reference.

The state's limited resources and lack of information, however—the direct effects of low productivity and slow communications—meant that the state was both fragile (easily disrupted) and had limited reach into the everyday lives of the people outside the visits of tax collectors. For the most part, the tasks of the state were limited to maintaining an army for defense of the state (and the privileges of the elites); keeping internal order, partly through policing by the army and partly through a system of courts; and vaguely providing for the welfare of the people, a function often fulfilled by the building of temples to keep the gods happy. In fact, Agrarian states leaned heavily on symbolism in place of real functionality. Law decrees were often meant to encourage people to settle their own disputes; public works symbolically displayed the power and authority of the ruler.

Thus, Agrarian states were forced to rely on the operation of social organizations that continued to exist beneath the state, including families, religious associations, guilds, and so forth. States therefore had trouble limiting revenge violence ("self-help") because they lacked adequate policing and legal systems. And ultimately, all Agrarian states had both inadequate policing and legal systems and very high levels of daily violence by modern standards. Because the balance between state power and the power of other forms of social organization was delicate, and because elites aimed above all at keeping themselves in power, Agrarian Era state-level hierarchies were built to resist change.

Cultural Frames and Screens

The final element of our model is *cultural frames* and *screens*. As social animals who see the world in terms of symbolism and metaphor, humans inevitably live in communities that generate collective understandings of the world. Aggregate or communal cultures become powerful, indeed central, elements in the cultural identity of the individuals in the community. We must be careful not to think of these cultures as static or as having an existence independent of the people whose individual perceptions add up to the collective. Cultures are always under construction and reconstruction as the individuals in a community interpret—and contest the interpretations of—new events, discoveries, and so forth. Furthermore, there are always divisions, or subcultures, within cultures (and further subdivisions of subcultures). Nor are cultures exclusive. Individuals can think of themselves as belonging to different groups depending on the context. No such imagined group is any more real than any other, and many may overlap.

But collective understandings, because they form the basis for the education of new generations, can exert a powerful and historically significant, though not deterministic, influence on how the individual members of a community see themselves, others, and the world they live in. Thus, as long as we bear in mind the collective, contested, and constantly reconstructed nature of cultures, and as long as we pick out collectives that really did each have a coherent cultural view, it is useful to think in terms of, say, "Tang Chinese culture" or "the culture of colonial New England."

We can represent this aspect of the existence of human communities by imagining that each society projects a sort of picture of itself and its place in the world onto a screen visible to the whole society, as Figure S.10 shows for bands, tribes, and chiefdoms.

As the illustration shows, there are actually two elements to this projection of a cultural self-image or collective identity. The obvious one is the cultural screen itself. This is where contested issues—debates between different schools of thought, competing religious faiths, or political philosophies and factions—all show up. The multiplicity of issues and the emphasis on debates here are the reminders that no culture is monolithic.

The less obvious but more important element is the cultural frame. This is the set of cultural values and assumptions that are so fundamental to that culture's understanding of the world and themselves that they are assumed, usually unspoken, and therefore practically invisible to the members of that culture. They are the ideas considered "natural," or at least morally unquestionable, in a given culture. This frame shapes not only the debates within it, but also ideas that might come from the outside world onto the screen. The frame thus shapes that culture's perception of other cultures and the outside world in fundamental ways. Foreign ideas that don't fit comfortably within a culture's frame will tend to be ignored, misinterpreted, reinterpreted in more fitting terms, or marginalized. (The same will tend to happen to

Cultural Frames and Screens

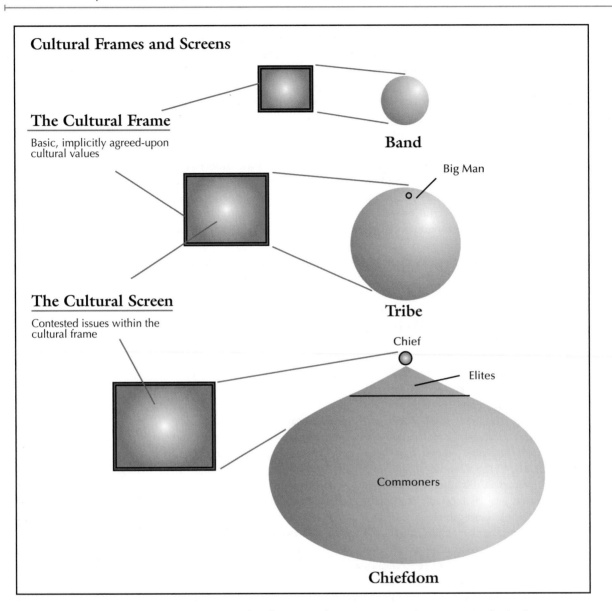

The Cultural Frame

Basic, implicitly agreed-upon
cultural values

Band

Big Man

Tribe

The Cultural Screen

Contested issues within the
cultural frame

Chief

Elites

Commoners

Chiefdom

FIGURE S.10 Cultural Frames and Screens. Every society, no matter what its size or complexity, makes claims about the meaning of the universe and about its own identity. These are the images projected onto a cultural screen. The frame represents the unspoken values that define which screen images are "natural" or acceptable.

the ideas of members of the community who fail to accept the boundaries of the cultural frame. Depending on the culture, those with such ideas may face unpleasant consequences.) We will see many examples of these sorts of cultural dynamics throughout this book, but an immediate example of the difference between the screen and the frame can be drawn from modern US politics. Democrats and Republicans argue about many issues, such as environmental policy or how to run a solvent retirement scheme. Those issues show up on the US screen. But they happen within a frame that assumes that elections and constitutional rules are the proper way to run politics. Serious anarchists or proponents of military rule, by moving outside the frame, are relegated to the "lunatic fringe." Of course, proponents of mob rule ("democracy") were relegated to the lunatic fringe for much of history, since most societies during the Agrarian Era took monarchy to be the natural shape of politics.

Two developments differentiate the structures of culture in state-level societies from those up through chiefdoms. First, the realm of input into the cultural screen is even more restricted than in chiefdoms. In general, rulers and elites exercised disproportionate influence on both the values contained in the frame and on the issues that appeared on the screen. But since the frame of most such societies assumed monarchical government and thus inequality, such disproportionate influence was accepted generally without comment. This is a fine example of the mutual influence of cultural perceptions upon social structure and social structure upon cultural perceptions. (See Figure S.11.)

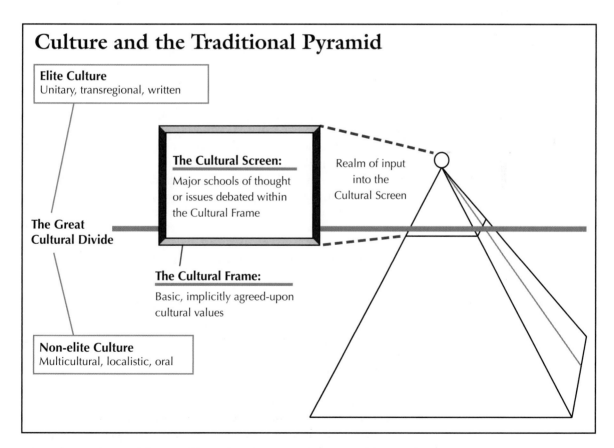

FIGURE S.11 Culture and the Pyramid. Input into the cultural frame and the screen reflect the emergence of the Great Cultural Divide, itself a reflection of the fundamental division of such societies into elites and non-elites.

The cultural influence of rulers and elites reflects the second development, the appearance of a Great Cultural Divide between elites and non-elites. Above the line of the Divide, the elites of a society tended to speak and, crucially, write a single language that acted as a marker of elite status. This was often therefore an archaic language imbued with the prestige of antiquity and prior achievement. Elite culture thus tended to be unitary across a state and society, and even to transcend particular states and so characterize a region of "civilization" in the cultural sense.

Non-elite culture, on the other hand, remained oral, since writing was a difficult, specialized task requiring education that only elites could afford, especially when writing systems were ideographic or syllabic and so contained hundreds or even thousands of characters that had to be memorized. And given slow communications, oral cultures inevitably were also localistic, with dialects constantly diverging, making non-elite culture multicultural to at least some extent.

Rising Population, Growing Complexity

The presentation so far of the elements of our model has emphasized elements that stayed the same across time. But a steady trend is embedded in the different parts of the model. As population rose (rapidly in the High Hunter-Gatherer Era and the Early Agrarian, more slowly at other times), the complexity of each element of the model tended to increase as well. The different models of hierarchy show this explicitly. Bands were at first the universal form of hierarchy. States developed last, but once on the historical stage they began slowly to spread at the expense of all other forms of hierarchy.

Networks, too, became more complex. Cities arose, dense local networks developed. Significantly, over time maritime connections became more important. Because increasingly sophisticated ships, guided by steadily improving navigation techniques, were far more efficient than overland caravans for carrying goods, increasing maritime trade also increased the carrying capacity and thus the influence of the network over time.

Finally, the complexity and sophistication of cultural frame values and screen images increased over time as well. Axial Age inquiries into the nature of the cosmos, the foundations of social order, and individual ethical action are a clear instance of this. We noted earlier that both Axial Age developments and the rise of the salvation religions provided rulers with better technologies of social control, another way of measuring the growing complexity of cultural frames and screens.

Hierarchies and Other Hierarchies

Aside from rising complexity, we can discern several other patterns and trends in the interactions of hierarchies with other hierarchies.

Expansionism, War, and Culture

The first of these is that Agrarian hierarchies tended to be expansionist. This is because "low and slow" restricted the options of a ruler who wanted to expand his economic resources. Grabbing new agricultural territory was virtually the only option. But "low and slow" also set limits to such expansionism, as hierarchies inevitably came to regions that were not productive enough to justify the expense of conquering them or that were so far away as to be almost impossible to govern from the hierarchy's center. Or expansion ran into other hierarchies, which raised the possibility of military conflict. War could be profitable, but it was always expensive and often risky.

Warfare that crossed cultural boundaries could be especially dangerous. Intracultural warfare, war that pitted foes who shared a common cultural understanding of war, was more predictable and thus often more limited. Wars that crossed cultural boundaries came in two types. Intercultural warfare happened when two cultures met with no previous understanding of the other. No rules created largely pragmatic responses on both sides; these could be unpredictable and less limited than intracultural warfare. But intercultural enemies tended to come to know each other and to acculturate, leading back to intracultural war or to subcultural warfare. Subcultural warfare happened when two subcultures of a larger culture fought. In such conflicts, both sides saw the other as the embodiment of evil and tried to annihilate the other. This was the most vicious and destructive form of cultural conflict.

The Nomad-Sedentary Cycle

One of the most important cultural divides in the Agrarian Era was between settled, agriculturally based sedentary societies on the one hand and nomadic, pastoralist societies (which depended on domesticated animals but not plants) on the other. The pastoralists of the central Asian steppes, who domesticated horses and therefore were able to deploy armies of skilled horse archers, were the most important pastoralists in the world. Their interactions with their sedentary neighbors followed a cyclical pattern. Nomadic tribes who lived nearest to sedentary societies usually established regular trade contacts. But their potential military advantage over sedentary armies, combined with their disadvantageous trade position—nomads needed sedentary products more than vice versa—created incentive for them to raid and steal instead, the threat of which could lead to nomads getting what they wanted by tribute. Regular trade, raid, and tribute had two effects on nomadic society. First, the nomads absorbed some of the cultural values of their sedentary neighbors, often in terms of political ideology. Second, since the tribal leader of a successful raiding tribe could use the goods he collected to build up his following by giving it away (the same rules applied on the steppes as in settled hierarchies, in this case), he could build a larger, more dangerous coalition and raise himself to the level of a major chief. One ironic aspect of this dynamic was that the richest sedentary societies—China usually filled this role—often spawned the largest, most powerful steppe coalitions just beyond their borders. The burden of paying tribute could then contribute to a decline in the state's ability to govern effectively. At this point, the powerful nomadic chief could be tempted to solidify his access to the goods produced by the sedentary society by conquering it. The nomadic tribe could, should the campaign of conquest prove successful, essentially replace the top part of the sedentary society's sociopolitical pyramid. The conqueror, now with the resources of both nomadic and sedentary worlds at his disposal, could reinvigorate and expand the society he had conquered. But the fundamental incompatibility of the pastoralist and agricultural economies and the continuing cultural mistrust that incompatibility generated meant that, usually within a generation, the united worlds would split again, and the cycle would restart. The cycle is illustrated in Figure S.12.

This cycle never exactly repeated itself (and the model is an idealization of historical relations that were always complicated in detail) because each iteration of the cycle created new cultural combinations and innovations. Syncretism, the mixing of beliefs and cultures, was in fact one major result of the operation of the cycle. The other was that over the long term, the area under the control of the sedentary

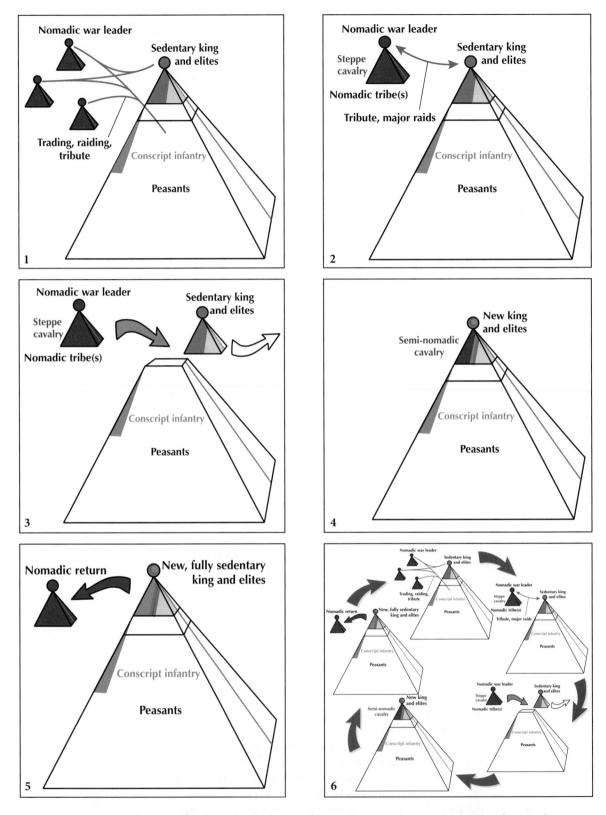

FIGURE S.12 Nomad-Sedentary Cycle. The cycle of nomadic-sedentary interaction. 1. Interaction. 2. Rise of a nomadic coalition. 3. Conquest. 4. Synthesis. 5. Split. 6. The full cycle summarized.

societies gradually expanded, mostly because of the demographic advantage that sedentary societies accumulated over pastoralists, since agriculture could support far more people than herding. But the cycle would not end until the steppes were finally brought under sedentary control in the seventeenth century.

The Intersection of Networks and Hierarchies

The most important theme of this book is generated by the interaction of the separate elements of our model. That theme is that the intersection of networks and hierarchies was a tense and creative meeting place that generated many of the most important developments in world history.

Networks and hierarchies coexisted: every human community had both its own internal organization as well as connections to other communities. In other words, networks and hierarchies inevitably intersected. It was the opposed characteristics of the two structures that made (and continues to make) their points of intersection places of creative tension and sometimes conflict. The two structures emerged as a result of individual actions that aimed at two very different sorts of goals, and so the structures themselves developed around sometimes conflicting purposes. A brief comparison of the fundamental characteristics of each type of structure reveals this tension.

Networks were *horizontal* structures. That is, they connected separate communities or societies without necessarily placing one over the other. This is because they were also *cooperative*. It is clearest in the case of the economic aspect of network connections: trade is by definition a consensual exchange of goods in which each party perceives itself as having received fair value in return for what it gives away. But the cooperative, or at least non-coercive, nature of networks also applies to the other sorts of exchanges that flowed through them. They were *extensive*, connecting communities that could be widely separated geographically and politically. Finally, they were focused on *urban* centers. The tentacles of trade and cultural exchange of course reached into the countryside of farming villages and pastoral lands, but the great centers of exchange tended to be cities.

Hierarchies, on the other hand, were *vertical* structures, as the name implies. The essence of a hierarchy was the ranking of social groups above and below each other. This is because they were *coercive* structures (especially complex hierarchies), which is another way of saying that they were political rather than economic. The coercion might take many forms (it might be well justified, disguised, consented to, and so forth), but the central feature of a state or even the distributed power of a simple community was that it enforced individual compliance with orders, laws, or informal norms. That is, it made cooperation work in an unequal environment. Hierarchies were *intensive*. That is, a hierarchy focused its coercive power over the specific area under its control, and additions to that area tended to be contiguous. Finally, hierarchies were based in *rural* production. They might have urban centers, and indeed cities were central to most (though not all) state-level societies. But the role of cities as centers of exchange in networks differed from the role of cities as centers of the concentration of power and of people who wielded power.

There were synergies between networks and hierarchies. Network wealth could be tapped by hierarchy builders. Strong hierarchies made network flows safer. But as a result of their fundamental differences, networks and hierarchies coexisted uneasily.

The tense intersection of networks and hierarchies was mediated by cultural mechanisms, that is, by the manipulation of cultural screen images by people in both networks and hierarchies. Three types of people operated across the intersections of networks and hierarchies and created such images. Wise practitioners were the merchants and other sorts of people who made a living from operating within networks. Informed officials were the people within hierarchies who were charged with managing network flows. Worldly travelers crossed between networks and hierarchies and made a living telling stories about each.

The Merchant Dilemma

The most important symptom of the tense intersection of networks and hierarchies was the merchant dilemma. The movement not just of goods but of people and ideas accounts for many of the tensions created by the intersection of networks and hierarchies. Hierarchies in the Agrarian Era, again, were built for stability. The kings and elites who led them attempted to fit a fragile structure to a particular environment and had to guard their own privileged position within a coercive, unequal social pyramid both physically and culturally, with ideas that justified their power projected onto their society's cultural screen. The inflow of new people and ideas thus constituted a potential challenge to established elites. And yet the goods and even ideas that merchants could bring into a hierarchy, especially if they were rare and exotic, offered a way for elites with exclusive access to them to further distinguish themselves from non-elites. In other words, the search for stability, expressed in part as competition for social status, at the same time both encouraged and discouraged trade in "foreign" luxury goods and ideas. This contradiction most often expressed itself in elite attitudes toward merchants. The goods that merchants carried might be highly valued. But merchants themselves (domestic as well as foreign) were widely mistrusted by Agrarian elites. Elites often suspected them of harboring foreign subversive ideas, and the wealth of merchants, generated by their exploitation of the mysterious differences in the prices of goods in different places, rather than by "honestly" exploiting farmers attached to land under elite control, aroused suspicion and envy. Merchants, in short, were "bad but necessary people." They created a dilemma that had to be managed.

Management took three common forms. The first was sequestration. Merchants often found themselves restricted to certain quarters of major cities, both in their own hierarchies and especially when they traveled to major foreign trade cities. The second was regulation. Hierarchies often forced merchants to organize in state-regulated associations such as guilds. These two methods reflected hierarchies' use of coercion to manage their network connections. Third and most common was co-opting. Elite-dominated cultural frames channeled or neutralized the potential threat posed by merchant activity by causing merchants to buy into those same elite values.

Maritime Spheres of Activity

With the growth of maritime trade noted above, one final aspect of the network-hierarchy intersection rose in importance: the role of hierarchies in the main spheres of maritime activity. We can model three main spheres of maritime activity as a set of overlapping circles representing the types of people who worked on the water or made use of the expertise of sailors and navigators: navies, pirates, and merchants

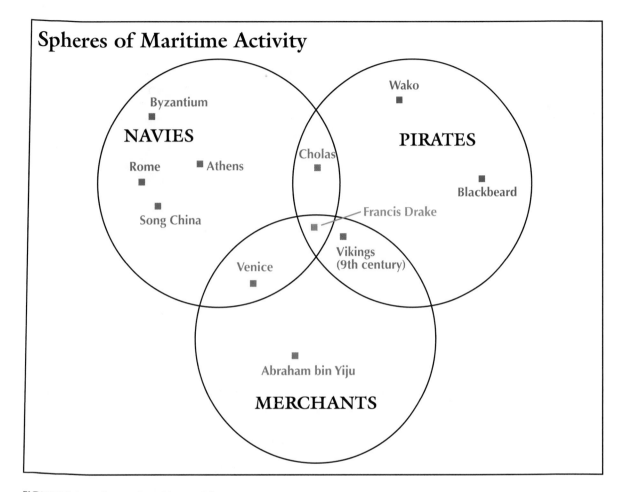

FIGURE S.13 Spheres of maritime activity.

(see Figure S.13). The circles overlap because boundaries were not hard and fast between these types. Merchants and pirates, traders and raiders, although apparently (and often in reality) at odds, were often the same people, whose quest for wealth took different forms depending on opportunities.

We can also view these three spheres in terms of three different dichotomies or oppositions that set one maritime type against the other two. Merchants and pirates were mostly non-state actors, as opposed to navies; navies and pirates conducted essentially military or coercive operations, merchants did not; and navies and (usually) merchants were sanctioned, legal, or officially recognized while pirates operated outside such contexts. (See Figure S.14.)

All three of these dichotomies—state-private, war-peace, and official-unofficial—were (and are) always operating as part of the dynamics of maritime activity. But from early in the history of maritime activity until well after 1500, the primary dichotomy in most places was the first: state-private. This reflects the relationship of

T

Frameworks of
World History

CHAPTER FOURTEEN

Innovation and Tradition: 1350 to 1550

Monument to Prince Henry the Navigator in Lisbon.

Introduction

Prince Henry of the House of Aviz was the third son of King John I of Portugal and his wife Philippa of Lancaster, granddaughter of King Edward III of England. Born in 1394, he accompanied his father in 1415 on an expedition to conquer Ceuta, the Muslim port across the Straits of Gibraltar from the Iberian Peninsula. The success of this expedition seems to have inspired in Henry a deep interest in Africa, especially in finding a way around the Muslim countries that controlled the northern ends of the trans-Saharan trade routes that brought gold and slaves north from the kingdoms of the Sahel and in finding the legendary Christian kingdom of Prester John. When his father appointed him in 1419 as governor of Algarve, the southernmost province of Portugal, and then also as governor of the Order of Christ, the Crusading order that succeeded the Knights Templar in Portugal, in 1420, he had the resources and position necessary to pursue his interest. He would become known as Prince Henry the Navigator.

He established residences in and around Lagos, the port on the southwestern tip of Portugal, and he began to sponsor voyages of exploration. Sailing in caravels—small, fast, maneuverable ships with two triangular lateen (fore-and-aft rigged) sails developed under Henry's patronage—these expeditions rapidly paid off. Two of his captains, blown off course by a storm, discovered the Madeira Islands in 1420. Technically, they rediscovered them, as they had been known to the Carthaginians who had originally created the port at Lagos. Henry settled colonists there and it later became a center of sugarcane cultivation. In 1427, another of his captains discovered (or again, probably rediscovered) the Azores, in the middle of the Atlantic. These too received colonists. In 1434, yet another captain became the first to find a way past the treacherous shoals and currents of Cape Bojador. (Or the first, perhaps, since the Carthaginian Hanno the Navigator did so around 500 BCE!) Within ten years after that, Portuguese ships had reached the Gold Coast, and Portuguese merchants initiated a lively direct trade that brought gold and slaves to Lagos. Henry died in 1460, but the momentum that he had established continued. Bartolomeu Dias reached the Cape of Good Hope, the southern tip of Africa, in 1490; in 1498, Vasco da Gama became the first European captain to sail around Africa and into the trade network of the Indian Ocean.

And in the Indian Ocean, up to a mere seventy years earlier, vast Chinese Treasure Fleets had made periodic voyages that fostered trade and a flow of gifts and tribute to the Middle Kingdom from as far away as East Africa. (The Yongle Emperor kept giraffes and other exotic animals in parks near his palace in Beijing.) Why were the Chinese no longer there? Why did the Portuguese feel the need to come?

The story of Prince Henry the Navigator establishes the key themes of this chapter. It is a story about the expansion of maritime worlds and

Framing the Argument

- The continued growth of maritime networks creates the beginnings of the first truly global network

- The different opportunities, means, and motives that different societies brought to exploitation of the global maritime network

- Further responses to the crises of the Mongols and the Black Death: innovation and tradition within differing cultural frames

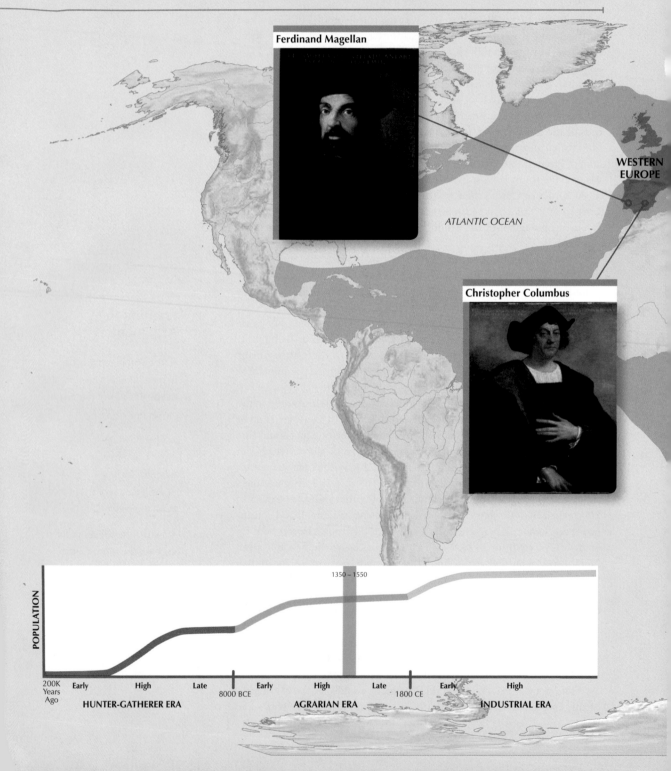

Ferdinand Magellan

Christopher Columbus

WESTERN
EUROPE

ATLANTIC OCEAN

1350 – 1550

POPULATION

200K
Years
Ago

Early   High   Late   Early   High   Late   Early   High

8000 BCE   1800 CE

HUNTER-GATHERER ERA   AGRARIAN ERA   INDUSTRIAL ERA

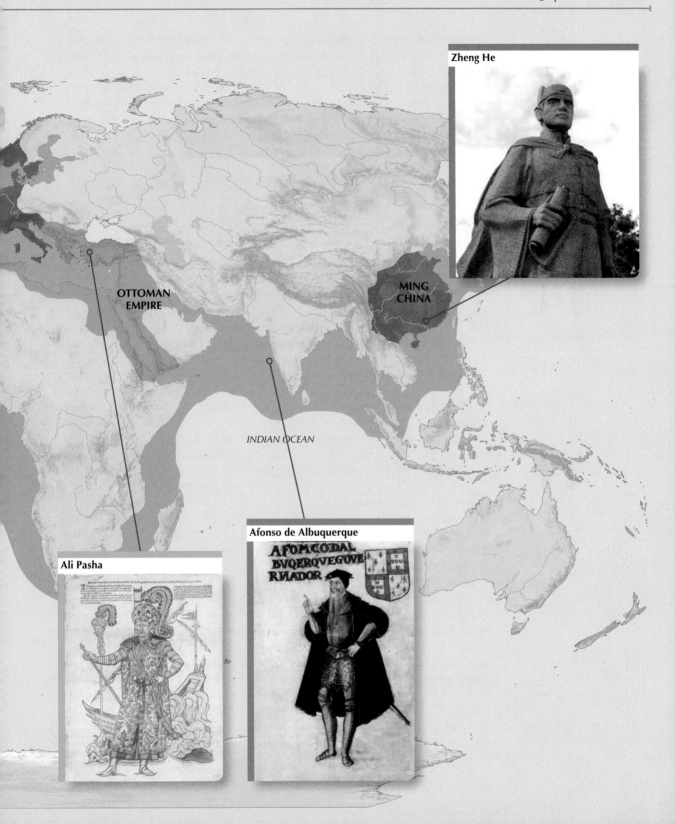

Zheng He

OTTOMAN EMPIRE

MING CHINA

INDIAN OCEAN

Afonso de Albuquerque

Ali Pasha

networks and about the eventual emergence of a truly global network. This expansion had many sources and contributors, of whom Europeans such as Henry were only a minority, as opportunities were everywhere. But it is also a story about the particular means and motives that different societies brought to those opportunities—a story, in other words, of the **cultural frames** through which networks and the world were viewed. And so it is also a continuation of the themes of Chapter 13: namely, of how societies reacted to the Mongols and the Black Death, and thus how they interpreted innovation and tradition.

———— ＊ ————

Broken: Post-Plague Western Europe

We pick up the story of reactions to disasters in western Europe. We saw in the previous chapter that societies drew on key elements of their cultural frames to make their experience of invasion and infection meaningful. Such reactions tended to stress tradition, including a "return to past virtue," and thus at the same time to stress continuity through disruption, even when the actual responses included significant innovations.

The key frame value in western Europe, as we saw in Chapter 12, was militarized law, expressed in terms of social relations through the centrality of contracts. We also noted that such a frame tended to provide a way of settling disputes more than it did a definitive set of answers. It was good for method, but not so much for meaning. What impact did such a frame have when Europeans faced difficult circumstances that cried out for meaning?

Toward Breakdown

Let us approach that question first with an examination of the circumstances that Europe faced in the 1300s, for despite the threat of Mongol invasion in 1240, Europe in fact escaped that calamity. But Europe more than made up for that piece of luck with difficulties both self-generated and imported via the Eurasian network.

To begin with, the global climate, which had gone through a warming phase between 1000 and 1300, now cooled again. This proved favorable in hotter, drier parts of the globe, but in western Europe, as in some other areas, it brought trouble. Shorter, cooler, wetter summers meant that wheat harvests declined. Indeed, disastrous crops in 1310 to 1313 brought widespread famine and generally marked the end of a period of demographic growth that had been going on since 900 or so. That growth had made Europe as a whole probably more populous than any major region except China. Population growth stretched the technologies of food production at the time to their limits, as much marginal land came under cultivation—land that was less productive to begin with and more easily exhausted after several years of cultivation. When the climate changed, the limits tightened, and undernourishment and malnutrition spread, probably making the population more vulnerable to outbreaks of disease.

A growing population and economy, however, had meant a boom in the intra-European network and its connections beyond Europe, which in turn had provided resources for state-building to the most ambitious European princes. This meant that some states could raise larger armies and launch larger, more destructive wars. The most widespread and destructive of these began in 1337 when England and France began a war that would last, off and on, until 1453 and would come to be known as the Hundred Years War. This was conducted, especially on the English side, through *chevauchees,* or campaigns in which English armies would ride through the French countryside burning and pillaging in order to demonstrate the French king's inability to defend his subjects, thus presumably strengthening the claim of Edward III of England (Prince Henry's great grandfather) to the French throne.

Heightened military efforts led to higher taxes and periodic disruptions of trade, in particular between English wool growers and Flemish weaving centers, and they also stretched the capacity of both the English and Flemish hierarchies to maintain internal order. Crime rose. In addition, both England and France proved

FIGURE 14.1 The Battle of Crecy. The English victory in 1346 was part of a long and destructive struggle between the two leading European monarchies.

FIGURE 14.2 Peasant Revolt. Execution of a leader of the Jacquerie, a bloodily suppressed uprising against warrior misrule in France.

more capable of raising armies and starting war than of demobilizing armies and ending war. Periods of truce, as for example between 1360 and 1375, after a string of major English victories, saw not a decrease in warfare but its diffusion. English armies intervened in Spanish and Portuguese dynastic quarrels, for example. More important, bands of soldiers left unemployed by the states that had hired them stuck together under their own leadership and hired themselves to new employers, such as rich Italian city-states, or they simply went "free lance" and lived from further pillaging. This spread the impact of the war informally but just as destructively to other parts of France, Italy, and the Iberian Peninsula. State prestige, generally, suffered.

In the midst of the Hundred Years War, the Black Death struck western Europe in 1348, leaving probably a third of the European population dead within three years, returning periodically afterward for centuries. The initial outbreak disrupted economic production and caused widespread panic, despair, and further reactions detailed later in this chapter. Yet the wars continued, the armies somewhat reduced in size but their depredations and demands for money unabated. The result was increasing levels of social conflict within European hierarchies. In 1358, large numbers of French peasants rose in violent revolt against their lords, the warrior **elite** who were so obviously failing to protect them. The French nobility ruthlessly and bloodily suppressed this "Jacquerie," or revolt of what the knightly class called "Jacques" (roughly, "Joe Shmoes"). Other instances of conflict included the revolt of the Ciompi, the wool weavers of Florence, in 1378 and the English Peasants' Revolt of 1381. The latter, raised in response to a new poll tax to support the war effort, was, interestingly, far less bloody in its aims and in how it was suppressed than the Jacquerie, reflecting the more consensual, less rigidly class-bound nature of English society and politics as compared to the French, a subject to which we will return in the next section.

Finally, laid on top of all this secular conflict, the religious structure of western European society was also falling into crisis. The simmering conflict between the papacy and various secular rulers over the primacy of religious or secular authority reached a new boiling point in the early 1300s. Philip the Fair of France had levied taxes on monastic property in France, a move to which Pope Boniface VIII objected strongly. When diplomacy failed, Philip sent troops to arrest the eighty-year-old Pope in Italy. He died in captivity a week later and a French bishop was elected as his successor, taking the name Clement V. Clement then moved the seat of the papacy from Rome to Avignon, ostensibly to escape the corrupting influence of the Roman nobility. Avignon was a small town in a piece of church-owned territory surrounded by French provinces in southern France, and the justifiable impression of an alliance between the papacy and France left the English and German regions of the church disgruntled, while Italians felt (again, not without justification) that the bishop of Rome should, in fact, reside in Rome. The Catholic Church was clearly becoming, in a sense, less catholic (that is, less universal) and instead a collection of politically based churches.

The Avignon popes made things worse by building a huge papal palace whose opulence stood in stark contrast to the poverty of the town and whose construction costs entailed imposition of higher church taxes. With the papal seat occupied since the time of Innocent III (authorizer of the Fourth Crusade) in the early 1200s by canon lawyers (not actually a surprising development, given the law-based frame values of this society), the spiritual reputation of the papacy sank to new lows, as medieval lawyers were no more likely than modern ones to garner a reputation for holiness.

This bad situation grew worse starting in 1378, when a disputed election resulted in the election of two popes, the "official" one in Avignon, supported by the French and Spanish bishops, and a so-called Anti-Pope in Rome, supported by the English, Germans, and Italians. Since the emperor of Germany opposed the official pope, the pope supported the election of an anti-emperor in Germany. This schism would last until 1415, when a church council elected a "unification" pope, except that the two sitting popes refused to resign, meaning that there were three popes until a new council forced all three out in 1418 and a reunified papacy reoccupied its home in Rome. In the meantime, however, the schism had serious consequences. Perhaps the key power that popes wielded in political battles was excommunication, which removed people from the communion of the church and prevented them from taking the sacraments. With two popes fighting each other, virtually everyone in Europe found themselves excommunicated by one pope or another. So to sum up, material conditions featured famine, war, plague, high taxes, and general unrest and violence, while spiritually Latin Christendom was fractured. As many Europeans at the time must have seen it, life was terrible and everyone was going to hell. (See Figure 14.3.)

How were people at the time to understand this state of the world? Through what frame could they view this mess in such a way as to make it meaningful? Could militarized law and contractual social relationships hold a culture together, especially when the very legalism of the church had contributed to the Schism? If not, were there other frame values on which they could draw to reconstruct stability, continuity, and tradition?

Framing a Breakdown

Let us start to answer this question first by looking at the immediate effect of a militarized legal and contractual frame on the socioeconomic responses to the mortality of the Black Death. As elsewhere, the first consequence of such mortality was widespread shortage of labor, especially for agricultural work. What should we expect of a traditional, Agrarian hierarchy in the face of labor shortages? The answer, as we saw in the previous chapter: assertion of elite coercive power and a decline in peasant freedom, as the elite collectively agree that each shall lock in his share of the available labor.

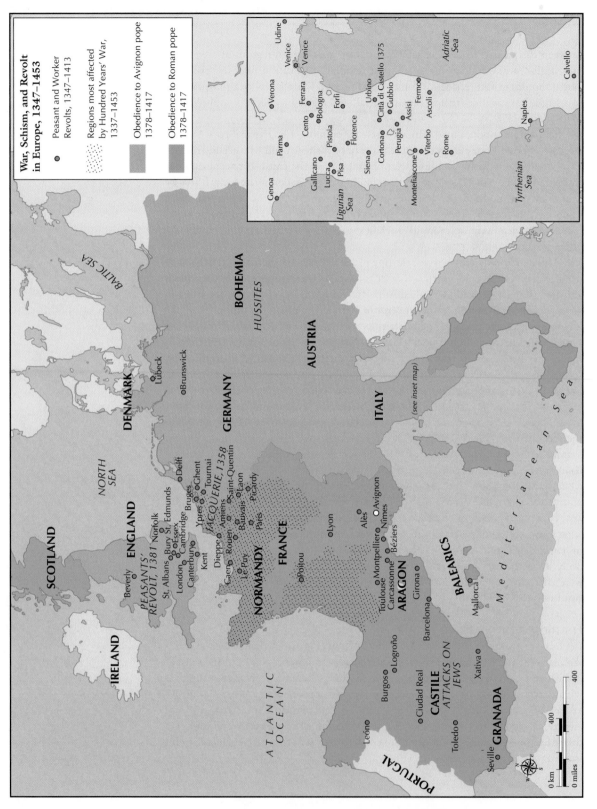

FIGURE 14.3 War and Schism. Europe was fractured along multiple axes in the fourteenth century: military, religious, social, and political.

England provides us a crystal clear illustration of this principle in action in the wake of the plague—and also of the failure of the principle in the context of the western European hierarchy structure and its accompanying cultural frame.

Hierarchy Structure: The Tumor Metastasizes

The plague came to England in 1348 and within a year had killed about a third of the population, a similar proportion as in Europe as a whole. Rural and village populations were hit as hard as cities, according to the available evidence. In some places, whole villages eventually disappeared. After the initial shock and disruption to agricultural production, the lords of manors began trying to restore order. They tried to mobilize the remaining labor force to work their demesne lands, the lands they farmed directly using customary unfree peasant labor or indirectly by hiring wage labor. They also tried to collect the established rents due to them from free peasant tenants on their estates. To their horror, they found that the remaining workforce had some notion of the consequences of the plague's mortality. Serfs, or unfree peasants, demanded lightened labor obligations or to be freed from their serfdom altogether, backed by the threat that they would run away to another estate where better terms might be on offer. Paid laborers demanded substantially increased wages. Renters demanded reduced rents. In themselves, such demands were not necessarily surprising: according to Ahmad al-Maqrizi, grave diggers, reciters of the Qur'an, and body carriers received substantial wages during the height of the plague in Cairo in 1348. But in Egypt, such demands were met only briefly, during the worst of the crisis, and in urban populations. As we have seen, Egyptian agriculture saw an increase in serfdom in the years after the plague as the ruling warrior elite imposed its political will on the Egyptian economy.

The English elite tried to do the same thing. In 1351, they met in Parliament and passed the Statute of Laborers, which decreed that no one should take a job at wages higher than were customarily paid in 1347, before the Black Death, with suitable punishments laid out in the law. In other words, when gathered together face-to-face, the English landowning class conformed to standard Agrarian expectations and asserted the primacy of politics over economics. But when they went back to their individual estates, they cheated on each other as much as they possibly could, stealing labor from each other by offering higher wages and lower rents to attract labor. Operating in a contractually mediated society with a legal structure that made them landowners whose income (and thus social status) depended on professional estate management, they had no choice. They acted as any good merchant would to keep business going and maximize their profits (or, more accurately, to minimize their losses). Wages rose, rents fell, and repeated renewals of the Statute of Laborers had no effect in stopping this trend over the following decades.

FIGURE 14.4 Agricultural Laborers. Labor shortages led to wages that were higher in real terms in 1400 than they would be again until the mid-nineteenth century.

PRINCIPLES AND PATTERNS

The common Agrarian pattern (politics trumps economics, labor shortage leads to declines in labor freedom) highlights the significantly opposite result in western Europe: labor shortage led to higher wages.

Thus, the mortality crisis revealed that western European *hierarchies* had become permeated with *network* values. The result was that economic imperatives trumped political force, exactly the opposite result one would expect from a traditional, Agrarian society.

The English case is particularly clear and legally framed because of the stronger role of Parliament (or medieval constitutionalism) in that country than elsewhere, including the principle that the king himself was subject to the laws of the realm. These were the same factors that mitigated the violence of the 1381 revolt and the response to it. But throughout western Europe, similar trends emerged. Wages rose, rents fell, and as a result, standards of living improved for the mass of the population. This was reflected in prices for commodities. The price of the most basic food, bread, fell, because the vastly smaller population needed less of it, and the land that remained under cultivation was on average more productive, given that it no longer included the marginal land that had been brought under the plow to feed the peak population of the pre-plague years. But the price of more "luxurious" basic goods—meat, butter, eggs—rose, as per capita demand rose with rising wages and falling rents. Thus, the plague had the ironic impact of leaving those who survived it much richer, individually, than they had been before. This in turn encouraged further regional specialization and a more diverse economy.

Let's look at these results in terms of our model, returning again to the broad picture of European hierarchies that we've seen before. (See Figure 14.5.) The key feature here is the sphere of urban, mercantile society, the burgesses, guildsmen, and urban workers, only partially incorporated, who form what looks like a tumor on the pyramid of European hierarchies. Indeed, let's think of this mercantile part of society as a tumor. Before the plague, it had been at least more or less culturally contained (though not rendered harmless) by the strength of competing warrior and priestly values among the elite and by the favorable ratio of people to land from the perspective of those traditional elites. But with warrior-elite states and the church both in disarray, and under the impetus of demographic crisis, the barriers weakened and the tumor metastasized. Its values had clearly already permeated the elite level of society, and although this was unconscious at the level of frame values, it was certainly conscious at the level of cultural screen images espoused by warriors and priests. Further, merchant values had even reached to some extent into the operations of the rural economy, and now its reach expanded rapidly. The tentacles of commercial contractual relationships reached further into both the upper and lower reaches of society. Agriculture became even more commercialized and market oriented (as the various movements of prices show), and so the influence of merchants intruded more strongly into rural society.

Much of this shift took place in the form of market mechanisms, and the consumer demands of cities for food and other goods, demands met by merchant activity. But increasingly, merchants also intervened by buying land from distressed peasants, building up landed estates that, in combination with their mercantile wealth, allowed merchant families to buy their way into noble status, though the old nobility kept their social distance from these *nouveau* aristocrats. At the other end of the scale, we can see the process of change even more clearly in terms of network values. Peasants could only buy and sell land, or enter into other contractual

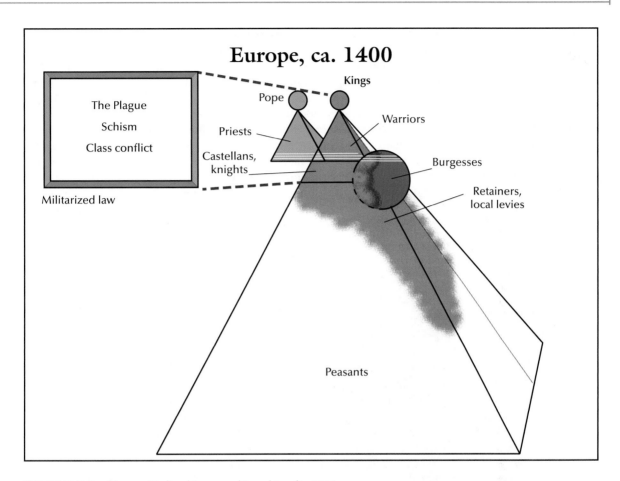

FIGURE 14.5 **Breaking . . .** Medieval European hierarchies after 1100.

relationships with merchants, if they had free status: serfs, unfree subjects of their lords, could not legally sign contracts. Thus, demands for emancipation of serfs came not just from the peasantry themselves, but from merchants. And indeed at times these demands came from landlords, who found it more profitable to free their serfs and enter into rental agreements with them than to continue to demand labor from unfree peasants.

In short, the plague stimulated the already widespread monetization and commercialization of the European economy, rural and urban, and of European society. In purely economic terms, this was not terribly different from the pervasive commercialization of the Chinese economy at the same time. But in China, such commercialization filtered up to and ultimately reinforced Confucian values and the Confucian-led hierarchy. In western Europe, commercialization filtered up to— what? This is to re-ask the question: Through what frame values could Europeans make sense of disruptive times?

Frames and Screens in Pieces Everywhere

To begin answering this question, let us note that some strong frame value was perhaps even more necessary because of a peculiar demographic effect of the plague: it killed the young disproportionately. This resulted in the immediate aftermath in a society with disproportionately many old people. But when they died off naturally, a generation later it left a disproportionately young society with an unusually young leadership class in need of traditional guidance. But because of the pervasive crises in church, state, and society, such guidance was in short supply. The result was a wide range of screen-image responses that reflected both the underlying military-legal-contractual frame values of the society and the inability of those very frame values to provide unified meaning to a society in crisis. Like the other societies that dealt with the crises of this period, western Europe's practical responses showed both continuity and innovation. But unlike societies that framed innovation in terms of continuity, thus downplaying innovation, Europe tended to frame innovation in terms of discontinuity, thus glorifying innovation.

This is clearest in the cultural values proposed by the Italian humanist scholars who invented the Renaissance. While they consciously looked back to classical Greek and Roman models, they claimed that there had been a vast *discontinuity*, a "Dark Ages," between that past and themselves as revivers of that past, thereby emphasizing the newness of what they were doing. Their discontinuous conception of history was so powerful that it has convinced many scholars to this day to divide the world into eras of classical, medieval, and modern (with modern starting at the Renaissance or thereabouts). The patient and productive building of centuries of medieval scholars were elided in one stroke in favor of the image of the New Classicism. New Classicism was put forward as a model for creating (or recreating in new and improved form) knowledge in a variety of areas. The same trick, applied to religious thought, allowed Luther and others after him to be creators of a New Traditionalism, a return to past virtue necessitated not by external interruption, but by internal corruption and discontinuity on the part of a central established institution, the Catholic Church. Thus, the Renaissance of the fifteenth century and the Reformation of the sixteenth framed innovation as righteous responses to discontinuity.

While some invented discontinuity to advertise innovation, some simply advertised innovation as innovation. Gutenberg, "inventor" of the printing press,

Typographus. Der Buchdrucker.

ARte mea reliquas illuſtro Typographus artes,
    Imprimo dum varios ære micante libros.
Quæ prius aucta ſitu, quæ puluere plena iacebant,
Vidimus obſcura noctē ſepulta premi.

Hæc veterum renouo neglecta volumina Patrum
    Atq ſcolis curo publica facta legi.
Artem prima nouam reperiſſe Moguntia fertur,
    Vrbs grauis, & multu ingenioſa modis.
Qua nihil vtilius videt, aut precioſius orbis,
    Vix melius quicquam ſecla futura dabunt.
                    C 3   Char-

FIGURE 14.6 Publishing Innovation. A mid-sixteenth-century printing press. Set in the European cultural frame, printing became an agent for change.

borrowed ideas from traditions both domestic (metallurgy) and foreign. (An "inventor" was a newly claimed category of person who could claim at least some measure of prestige from working with their hands—how wildly non-elite!) Both the idea of movable type printing and papermaking came to Europe from China, the latter via the Islamic world. Gutenberg advertised his creation not as a better version of tradition, but as an invention, at least in part because he was in it to make money. Neither he nor his investors saw much return, but others who borrowed his invention certainly did. They watched the profits roll in as printing became an industry that, unlike in China, spread as many new ideas as old ones. Even the old ideas that it spread were newly packaged: Luther's German translation of the Bible undermined the ability of the Catholic Church to monopolize interpretations thereof, whereas printing Confucius had allowed more people to aspire to the Confucian bureaucracy. It was the cultural frame, not the invention, that differed.

Finally, some innovation and discontinuity came to European culture unbidden and incapable of fitting comfortably into an existing frame or screen value. The prime case of this was the realization that Columbus, rather than having found a way to Japan and China, had instead run into a whole New World. In terms of secular knowledge, it was clear that Aristotle, The Philosopher of medieval Europe, the "man who knew everything," did not know about these continents. In terms of religious knowledge, it was unclear whether the indigenous peoples of the New World were innocents still in the Garden of Eden, souls to be saved, savages to be exterminated, or all three at once: "Noble Savages." It *was* clear that the claims of different European states to parts of the New World had to be established legally, essentially by contracts enforced by military backing. The fundamental European frame value could handle any new development in terms of creating a process to decide ownership (and this even included emergent ideas about ownership of inventions, eventually). What it couldn't do was give those new developments a coherent meaning in terms of the European past.

In short, the plague revealed western European societies as "failed" traditional Agrarian hierarchies. They had failed because they no longer had established, ideologically secure elites or a cultural frame through which new developments could be viewed and incorporated into a stable structure. And they failed in a consequential way: the structure of their hierarchies intersected with networks and the potentially disruptive, subversive values and practices of merchants. Effectively uncontained by either administrative coercion or cultural cooptation, European merchants found themselves freer and freer to exert their subversive influence on the values of Europe's hierarchies. At the same time, the networks in which they operated were about to gain significant new power and reach because they were becoming global. It is to that world of networks—the world in which the European merchants and hierarchies would operate—that we now turn.

Post-Plague Networks

The epidemics of the fourteenth century had significant effects not just on individual societies and hierarchies, but (pretty obviously) on the networks that connected

ISSUES IN DOING WORLD HISTORY

European Exceptionalism

Be alert now, folks! If you've been paying attention, you just saw me lay out one of the basic arguments of this book—in effect, one of my theses. A thesis is, at its heart, an answer to a question, and good history books, including good world history textbooks, should have a thesis (as opposed to bad history books, which just present a compilation of events). Maybe, given the scope of world history, a book should have several theses.

The question I've only just begun to answer is widely considered a Big Question in world history: How do we account for "the rise of the West"? One of the first real world history textbooks, published in 1963 and written by William McNeill, probably the most distinguished world historian of the twentieth century, was titled *The Rise of the West*.

We don't really want to answer the question in this form any longer. First, "the rise of the West" substitutes "the West" (a vague and culturally tendentious term that invites formulations such as "the West and the Rest") for "northwestern Europe and a few of its major colonial offshoots, especially the United States," and even this formulation, as we shall see in the following chapters of this book, is probably far too broad. We'll need to specify some smaller subset of "(western) Europe" to arrive at a plausible answer. Second, we need to qualify the "rise" part of the question, too. It's becoming clearer by the decade that what we're really talking about may well be a temporary (250-year?) interruption of a longer term world history pattern in which China is, as it has often claimed to be, the world's center of gravity, the self-proclaimed Middle Kingdom.

The question we're really trying to answer is as follows. How do we explain why the emergence of the Industrial Era and the end of the Agrarian Era happened first in a part of northwestern Europe and spread from there to the rest of the world? In other words, by contrast with the shift from hunting and gathering to agriculture, industry was essentially invented once, in one place. Why?

And here's where we need to be very careful about formulating not just the question, but an answer. The common formulations to this question assume that industrialization and the "modernity" it created are a good thing. Well, in fact, I share this assumption. I'd define it carefully and qualify it heavily, as the rest of this book will do. But I share it. The automatic assumption that seems to follow, but which I do not share, is that if industrialization is good, Europe must have been *exceptional in some way that was also good* in order to produce it. This assumption is known as "European Exceptionalism." It has taken overtly racist forms. It has taken more carefully argued forms. It has been rejected by others so thoroughly that the origins of industrialization are reduced to an accident (or an inevitability) that might have happened anywhere. None of these answers seems to me satisfactory.

The rest of this book will flesh out the details of my answer to this question, as well as answers to some other major questions raised by doing a history of the entire world. What I want to emphasize in this Issues box is what I am and what I am *not* saying in my answer.

I am saying that Europe was different. I am *not* saying that this difference made Europe better. Europe was different in the way every society on earth was different: it had its peculiarities of social structure and cultural frames. Furthermore, I am *not* saying that something *inherent* in the peculiarity of Europe, by itself, should have produced a significant result. I am *not* saying that this is a story about Europe. I am saying that this is a story in which a particular set of characteristics of certain European hierarchies, set in the context of their place in a global network, all of whose parts mattered, and all of which the actors themselves saw through particular cultural frames, had somewhat unpredictable and certainly unintended but nevertheless explicable consequences. In other words, I am saying that this is a contingent and necessarily a world historical story. If an element of European

Exceptionalism remains, it's imposed by the basic fact that industrialization inescapably originated in Europe (in its global context) and not elsewhere, and that fact must be explained.

Finally, I tell this story using our model of hierarchies, networks, and cultural frames and screens. But the model was *not* designed to answer this question specifically. The model did, in fact, help me see the answer I offer in this book, but it was designed to analyze and explain other characteristics of world history as I saw them. It proved its worth to me (and I hope it will to you) by generating new insights beyond the ones it was designed for, as any productive theoretical framework should.

those societies and over which the plague spread. The crucial effect was a realignment of the Eurasian network, a shifting of the relative weights of some of its components, that weakened the network position of some societies while opening up new opportunities for others.

Probably the key effect of the epidemics was to cause, both directly and indirectly, a decline in the relative importance of the Silk Road as a route connecting the continent from east to west. The direct part of this effect was the disruption of production and consumption in the major sedentary societies at either end of the Silk Road for much of the fourteenth century. The damage that the Mongols and then Timur did to the Iraqi heartland of the Islamic world, one of the major termini of the Silk Road from China via the steppes and northern Persia, was especially severe in this regard. But in many places, production and consumption recovered, at least partially (as well as adapting to smaller but, as in Europe, sometimes richer markets). The problem was that by the time this recovery was under way, the political breakup of the Mongol Empire was far advanced. Competition on the steppes among the successor fragments and steppe peoples made the Silk Road route much less secure, particularly when compared to the thirteenth-century security of the "Pax Mongolica," the unity and security of the early Mongol Empire on the steppes. Timur's attack on the Golden Horde (see Chapter 13) is a key example of this, and the decline of the Silk Road further damaged the economic underpinnings of the Horde's rule in Russia and the western steppes.

Thus, when the volume of trade began to revive in the decades after the plague, the pattern of that trade shifted even more toward the maritime routes that connected Eurasia from east to west along its southern coast. The disruptions of the epidemics therefore accelerated a trend that had been progressing for centuries as improved shipbuilding and navigational techniques made seaborne transport somewhat safer and faster (see Chapter 8). One result of this trend was to emphasize the political shift of Islam's center of gravity away from Baghdad and toward the Mamluks in Egypt and the Ottomans in Asia Minor. Cairo and (after 1453) Constantinople (Istanbul) rose in importance relative to Baghdad because of their maritime connections on the Mediterranean and to the Red Sea and Persian Gulf. This shift benefited Mamluk Egypt and the Ottomans directly in terms of trade with China (for example, by the early 1500s, there were manufacturers in China who made porcelain specifically for the Ottoman market). It also put them in the position of monopolistic middlemen, from the perspective of western European merchants who wished to obtain East Asian and South Asian goods. (See Figure 14.7.) Another

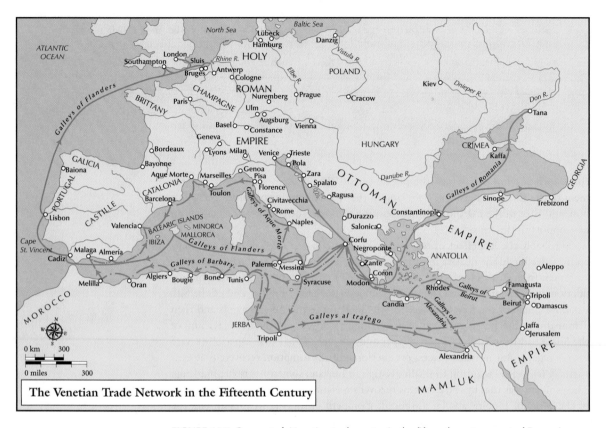

The Venetian Trade Network in the Fifteenth Century

FIGURE 14.7 Connected. Venetian trade routes in the fifteenth century, part of Europe's connections to the Afro-Eurasian network of trade.

result of this shift was to stimulate the general expansion of maritime networks, bringing different maritime worlds into closer contact with each other. It is to this that we now turn in more detail.

Maritime Worlds

The increasing importance of maritime network connections meant that the hierarchies of outer circuit Afro-Eurasia gained importance relative to the core areas of inner circuit Eurasia. They also came into increased contact—and potential competition—with each other and with the inner circuit core areas that connected to the maritime network, such as southeast China. The ability and motivation of each hierarchy to exploit its network connections depended on the means at its disposal, that is, on the maritime technologies available to it, and on the cultural frame values that shaped its goals.

Maritime Technologies

Three major elements went into the suites of maritime technology that allowed hierarchies to take advantage of maritime network connections. Ships, and thus traditions of shipbuilding, were of course foundational. Improving techniques and technologies of navigation further permitted ships to expand the network and to exploit it more efficiently. Finally, the spread of military technologies at sea proved valuable when direct competition arose on the network. It should be noted that the increase of naval (maritime military) activity represents the spread of hierarchy values into network activity, showing that the tense intersection of networks and hierarchies affected both types of structures.

Shipbuilding

Pre-industrial shipbuilding was clearly an art rather than a science and thus heavily dependent on traditions and hands-on received wisdom. One of the basic patterns of pre-industrial shipbuilding was thus that ship construction reflected the resources and demands of local maritime environments. Smaller trade ships in the Indian Ocean, for instance, were constructed from sewn-together planks. Not only was iron for nails in somewhat short supply, especially around the western half of the ocean, including Arabia, one center of maritime trade, but the resulting flexibility of the hulls proved to be a successful way of dealing with the large swells of the open ocean on monsoon-driven direct crossings from Arabia to southern India.

The expansion of maritime networks began in this period to bring different shipbuilding traditions into contact with each other, and the resulting synergies led to improved ship designs. One such instance of this occurred in China with the Yongle Emperor's building of a series of so-called Treasure Fleets (see further discussion later in this chapter). There, shipbuilding traditions from the northern Yellow Sea coasts and the southern South China Sea coasts came together. Sailors in the Yellow Sea had to deal with shallows and shifting sandbanks, so ships there had flat bottoms, shallow drafts, and good maneuverability. The South China Sea was rougher and infested with hidden reefs and pirates, so southern ships featured strong-keeled, deep, V-shaped hulls, and high reinforced prows that protected against hitting reefs and allowed ramming of smaller ships. The new ships of the Treasure Fleets combined features of both traditions, and the biggest of them did so at an unprecedented scale, with multiple masts, stern rudders, and vast cargo capacity.

In western Europe, a similar synergy emerged, without state impetus, between Mediterranean and North Sea designs. Here, too, different sorts of hull construction informed each other. More important, Mediterranean two-masted fore-and-aft sail plans were combined with North Sea single-masted square sail designs to produce the "full-rigged ship," which could sail efficiently with the wind using its square sails and maneuver along coasts and into or out of ports with its fore-and-aft sails. As in China, specialized variants emerged, designed either for cargo (rounder, slower, but with greater capacity) or for war (narrower, faster, and more heavily manned).

In an interesting contrast, the Ottomans also came to control two different shipbuilding traditions: one from their end of the Mediterranean and another based in the Persian Gulf and Indian Ocean. But the difficulty of direct maritime contact

FIGURE 14.8 Galleon. The meeting of shipbuilding traditions in Europe resulted in the "full-rigged ship." The galleon was a version specialized for war.

between these two worlds and the very different environmental demands they created failed to produce productive synergies.

Navigation

Improvements in navigational technology and knowledge diffused more widely than shipbuilding techniques. The main improvement across the Eurasian network came in the form of steadily improved charts and maps, including detailed instructions for entering and leaving the major ports from north China all the way to east Africa, as well as throughout the Mediterranean and North Sea–Baltic regions. Navigation was still, like shipbuilding, largely passed on by oral instruction and apprenticeship, but unlike shipbuilding, navigation was beginning to acquire a significant written component.

That component was stimulated by inventions such as the magnetic compass, first invented in China and perhaps independently reinvented in Europe, and the astrolabe, probably an Arabic invention, which allowed mariners to calculate accurately how far north or south of the equator they were. Both would become gradually more important as open-water navigation, still rare in the fifteenth century, became more common. No reliable way to determine longitude (east-west position) would be devised until the late eighteenth century, but with roughly accurate ways to measure direction, latitude, and speed (measured in Europe, for example, by a rope with knots tied at regular intervals played out behind the boat), a little geometry could go a long way in helping sailors figure out where they were.

Weaponry and Naval Warfare

Specialized ships for warfare remained, down to 1500, in the relatively calm Mediterranean largely the province of the galleys, while in China the imperial Chinese navies of the Song, Yüan, and early Ming dynasties created a whole range of armed paddlewheel riverboats, ships with catapults and gunpowder bombs, and other ingenious designs. But naval warfare remained basically an adjunct of land warfare, since ships could not stray far from their bases for both navigational and, even more crucially, logistical reasons. Methods of killing ships were limited: the ship itself could be used as a weapon by ramming, or ships might be set on fire by fire arrows, by something like the great Byzantine weapon called Greek fire, or by Chinese gunpowder bombs. More likely, sea battles used ships as platforms for fighting men who grappled enemy ships and engaged in hand-to-hand combat. It was only from around 1500 that the potential of gunpowder cannon, mounted in the bows of galleys or along the broadsides of sailing ships, began to be exploited effectively by European

Charting the Waters

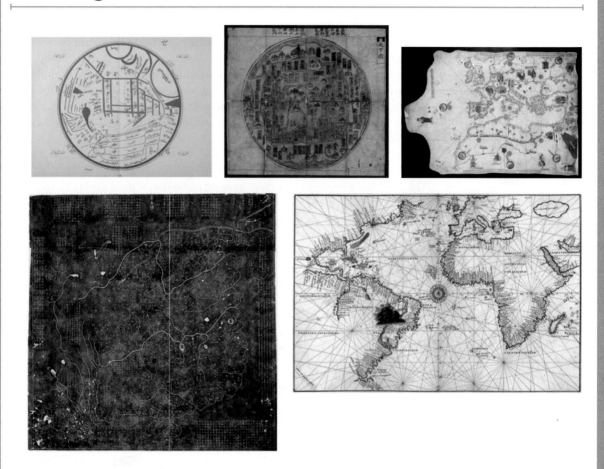

The advance of network knowledge intersected with different cultural frames to produce images of the world. Top left: the earliest known Turkish world map, from the eleventh century CE, centered (naturally) in Central Asia. Top middle: a late medieval Korean world map. Bottom left: a Chinese stone map from ca. 1136 showing the coastline of China and major river systems. Top right: a late fifteenth-century European portolan, designed for navigation, as indicated by the compass lines. Bottom right: a sixteenth-century portolan, which now shows the east coast of the American continents.

mariners: Vasco da Gama showed up in the Indian Ocean with full-rigged ships armed with bronze cannon.

Case Studies in Maritime Organization and Goals

As we have emphasized about other technological developments, maritime technology did not determine maritime activity but was merely a tool, a means, toward the pursuit of goals that were shaped by opportunities. Such opportunities could be opened up by the natural environment (land-locked countries were pretty unlikely to develop large navies!) as well as by competition (or lack thereof), and these opportunities were culturally defined. In order to understand the different paths that the development of maritime networks followed between 1350 and 1550, we should bear in mind our model of **maritime spheres of activity** and their dichotomies from Chapter 8. (See Figure 14.9.)

China and the Treasure Fleets

The third Ming emperor, who took the reign name Yongle (r. 1402–1424), conceived of China's position in the world in aggressive terms modeled on the Tang. He projected an image of Chinese grandeur through projects of massive size: the rebuilding of the northern capital at Beijing, work on the Grand Canal and the Great Wall, and above all in the building of massive Treasure Ships designed to project China's power and majesty throughout the East Asian and Indian Ocean maritime worlds. Six Treasure Ship fleets, under the command of the great eunuch admiral Zheng He, sailed between 1405 and 1421, and a seventh sailed for Yongle's grandson and heir in 1431 (see Figure 14.10). Each expedition of the fleets lasted for nearly two years and reached variously from China's coast to Southeast Asia, through the Straits of Melaka, all across the Indian Ocean, and as far as the Persian Gulf, Arabia, and parts of East Africa.

Maritime Dichotomies

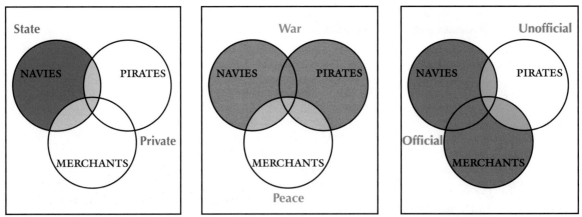

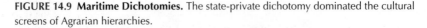

FIGURE 14.9 Maritime Dichotomies. The state-private dichotomy dominated the cultural screens of Agrarian hierarchies.

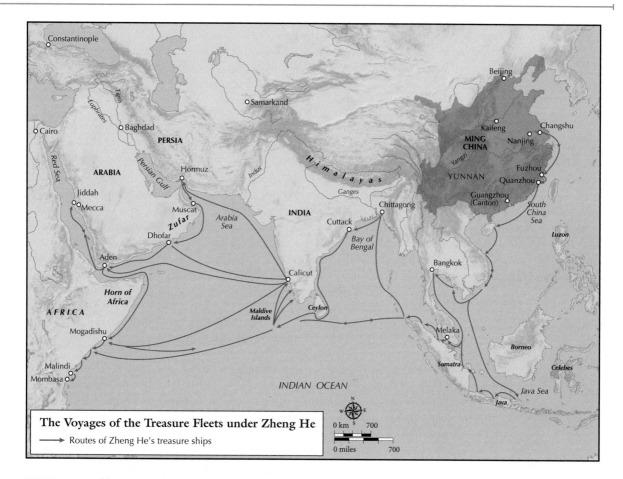

FIGURE 14.10 **China at Sea.** The voyages of the Treasure Fleets under Zheng He.

The Treasure Fleets involved cooperation between the imperial government and Chinese merchants, but the state definitely took control and managed the expeditions, placing them in the overlap between **naval** and **merchant spheres of maritime activity**. But the fleets were undoubtedly still interpreted, especially by the state and its officials, even those friendly to foreign trade, as operating within the **state-private dichotomy**. This was reflected in the fleets' many-sided mission, the most important of which was political. The fleets and the valuable goods they carried advertised the wealth and prestige of the Dragon Throne, with Zheng He acting as an ambassador to multiple kings and princes. The warships of the fleet and the thousands of troops they carried allowed the expeditions to support a Ming

FIGURE 14.11 **Naval Dominance.** The size and sail plan of the largest Treasure Ships, compared to Columbus's biggest ship, the Santa Maria (shown in black).

war in Vietnam, to clear the Straits of Melaka of pirates, and to manage the small states of the region to China's advantage. If the Treasure Fleets—militarily unrivaled at sea—had still been in the Indian Ocean seventy years later, Da Gama's Portuguese galleons would have faced a formidable challenge to their forcible entry into the Indian Ocean network.

The commercial aspect of these expeditions also illustrates the dominance of the state and reveals a cultural frame dominated by state interest. Some of the goods carried by the fleets, especially high-prestige Chinese manufactures such as porcelain, were given away as gifts, which in the Agrarian world was a powerful statement, since giving things away, at the state as much as the personal level, created moral debts and allegiances. Such gifts also drew gifts and tribute in return that flowed to Yongle's court, including the African giraffes that he kept in his private reserves. Much of the cargo was traded directly for foreign goods such as spices and medicines, returning at least some profit to the state, though it is likely that the direct balance sheets for the fleets were in the red, given the massive cost of building and manning them. Such exchanges also stimulated further private trade between China and the rest of Asia, which profited the economy as a whole and brought tax revenues to the state. Even private foreign trade to China, however, was interpreted through the state-dominated cultural frame as "tribute" that implicitly recognized the supremacy of the Dragon throne and the central place of the Middle Kingdom in the world.

Finally, there was certainly an element of what European navigators would have depicted as "exploration and discovery," especially among some of the Chinese scholars who accompanied the fleets. But from within the traditional Chinese cultural frame, such interest was projected as attempts to rediscover and confirm what the emperor ruled, at least indirectly, and how he could bring the benefits of his policies to more of the world's peoples.

The dominance of the state in the Chinese model of maritime organization and indeed the continuing centrality of the state-private dichotomy is also reflected, however, in the cessation of the Treasure Fleet expeditions with Yongle's grandson's premature death in 1435. Not only did no other Ming emperors sponsor fleets, the Ming state increasingly restricted and regulated private overseas trade over the century after 1435. Indeed, Chinese merchants were eventually forbidden from leaving China at all (those who did became exiles, forbidden to return), and Chinese knowledge of how to build oceangoing ships was gradually forgotten. Foreign merchants were still allowed to enter China, but they found themselves restricted to defined quarters in specified ports and faced with growing hostility from the Chinese people.

Why did the Chinese end the Treasure Fleets? Why did they cease to reach out to the network? This is an important question in the context of arguments about European Exceptionalism (see the Issues in Doing World History box), and we will explore the question further later in the chapter. But a few immediate factors may be mentioned.

Interest by individual emperors was crucial given the Chinese hierarchy structure, and this was not forthcoming after the death of Yongle's grandson.

PRINCIPLES AND PATTERNS

He who gives things away is powerful—true at the state level as well as the individual level, and a symptom of the dominance of politics over economics.

Factionalism further discouraged state interest: Confucian bureaucrats, hostile to merchants and trade, opposed new fleets to cut down the power of their rivals the eunuchs, who in turn damaged their own cause through corruption that raised the cost of trade. In short, powerful state control turned effectively from sponsorship to restriction. The fleets were also expensive in direct costs, and new outbreaks of plague in the mid-1400s reduced state land-tax revenue, causing a fiscal crisis. Finally, renewed Mongol pressure in the north, culminating in the capture of the emperor in 1449, focused state efforts elsewhere. Ming China even retreated from the **navies of imperial defense** model (see Chapter 8) pursued by the Song and Yüan dynasties, relying on land-based coastal defenses instead of warships. Thus, China left the seas to foreign merchants, Japanese and Korean pirates, and, from the 1530s, Europeans, all of whom were virtually indistinguishable within the state-private dichotomy under which the Chinese state operated. The disruptive potential of the intersection between the global network and the Chinese hierarchy came to dominate the Ming view of the world.

The Ottomans on Two Seas

Ottoman maritime organization lacked even temporary interest in state-supported commerce and partnership with merchants that the Ming displayed with the Treasure Fleets. The Ottomans, heirs to the fortress mentality of Byzantium in terms of its view of the network-hierarchy intersection, operated purely within the navies of imperial defense model of naval organization and the state-private dichotomy. (Though some of the westernmost North African provinces of the Empire, the Barbary States, which were nominally under Istanbul's rule but effectively independent, pursued a "piracy for state profit" policy in the following centuries that could be seen as expressing the **war-peace dichotomy**.)

This defensive mentality, or cultural frame, expressed itself in several ways in Ottoman policy. In terms of merchant activity, native Ottoman merchants were, like their Byzantine predecessors, strictly regulated and prohibited from leaving the empire. This limited them to internal trade and left the importing of foreign goods to foreign merchants, mostly Italians in the Mediterranean, along with various groups in the Indian Ocean. Though they were recognized as nominal overlords in the mosque prayers of many merchant communities, especially on the west coast of India, this had more to do with those communities managing their political relationships to local powers (which were lesser but closer) than it did with Ottoman trade policy.

FIGURE 14.12 Ottoman War Galley. Such ships were useful in the Mediterranean, but not in the Indian Ocean, where the Ottomans also had maritime interests.

The mentality also led the Ottomans to build up a large war fleet of gunpowder galleys in the Mediterranean, again building on old Byzantine models (see Figure 14.12). With this fleet, they competed on at least equal terms with European naval powers, above all Venice and Spain, through the first half of the

1500s. Galley warfare was then eclipsed by a new style of naval warfare developed in the Atlantic.

Western Europe, the Atlantic, and the World

The world of Henry the Navigator followed a different path from Ming China and the Ottoman Empire in terms of maritime organization. This was a path pioneered in Europe by various Italian city-states such as Venice and Genoa from as early as the 1100s, as we saw in Chapter 8, and it might be called a proto-capitalist model of naval organization. This model depended on the close cooperation between private merchants and states whose interests were dominated by mercantile interests. The Italian city-states were not, in fact, unique in this respect, though they were among the most successful to pursue this path in the world before 1400. But various small, highly networked cities that were not part of a larger land-based Agrarian hierarchy or that existed on the loosely controlled margins of such hierarchies had followed similar political-mercantile paths. Examples could be cited from the east coast of Africa, both coasts of India, Southeast Asia and the region of the Straits of Melaka, and from elsewhere in medieval Europe, including various German towns that even banded together to form the Hanseatic League. The proto-capitalist model was not even unique to maritime network cities, as at times some of the great oasis cities of central Asia, such as Samarkand, can be characterized in this way (except that they had no navies).

Most of the time, however, such cities operated under at least two significant constraints. First, as city-states, they were small hierarchies. Second, their political and cultural influence was limited. Either they were located so marginally that even if they were independent they had little opportunity to use that independence to exert broad political or cultural influence; or they were more centrally located but wealthy enough to attract the attention of major land-powers who took from them their mercantile-based independence, as happened to Samarkand under Timur. The fragmented political map of medieval Europe, however, gave the Italian (as well as German and to some extent Dutch) mercantile cities at least some freedom of maneuver and the ability to survive at crucial locations on the broader network, and thence to exert influence on other European hierarchies that, as we saw at the beginning of the chapter, were becoming more vulnerable to network-based practices and culture.

That Portugal was the first European kingdom to express some of that influence is not surprising. As a land-based Agrarian hierarchy it was small, poor, and isolated on the southwestern-most corner of the Iberian Peninsula, itself a relatively isolated tip of the larger European peninsula of Asia. Confined by the Spanish kingdoms to its east, it looked south and west, to Africa and the Atlantic, for potential network-generated wealth that its poor Agrarian base could not provide. Henry adopted the mercantile, proto-capitalist outlook of the Italians, hired Italian cartographers to map what his navigators (many of them Italian) found, and drew the rest of Europe slowly after him. (See Figure 14.13.)

The rest of Europe followed him because he was successful. His explorations, funded on a shoestring and miniscule by comparison with the Ming Treasure Fleets, returned an almost immediate profit on the investment in terms of gold and

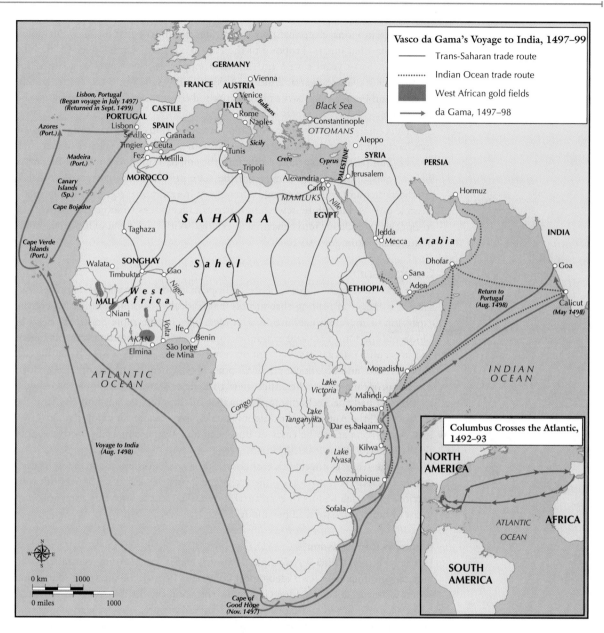

FIGURE 14.13 A New Route. Vasco da Gama's voyage to India, 1497–1499.

slaves, obtained in exchange for woolen cloth and guns. Finding a path around Africa could also be portrayed as part of an ongoing military-religious crusade against the Muslim Ottomans, and this made the concept even more salable in traditional terms, even though it was really the Venetian monopoly on trade to the east through the Ottomans that many wished to bypass. The newly united Aragonese and Castillian monarchies that now constituted Spain, the first to follow, gambled on the somewhat lunatic proposal of the Italian navigator Christopher Columbus, and within forty years a vast and lucrative empire in the Americas (named for yet another Italian navigator, Amerigo Vespucci) had fallen into their laps. Dutch, English, and French state-backed merchants and adventurers began to follow by the mid-1500s.

Thus emerged a growing partnership between various European states and their merchants, located at the intersection of the naval and merchant spheres of maritime activity. This partnership would slowly shift the emphasis in global network-hierarchy intersections, in maritime terms, from the state-private dichotomy to the official-unofficial dichotomy. It was an odd partnership in traditional Agrarian terms, made possible only by the failure of western European hierarchies to successfully coerce or co-opt their merchants into behaving "properly." With the benefit of historical hindsight, it also looks quite successful.

Comparisons

Given the subsequent success of the European model of maritime organization, there is a danger of reading that success teleologically: "of course this is where the expansion of maritime networks was headed." But as the more "normal" cases of China and the Ottomans make clear, European maritime expansion was contingent on the peculiar internal development of western Europe, which was itself contingent, unpredictable, and dependent on developments elsewhere. Furthermore, the style in which Europeans approached their new connections and possessions was equally contingent: had the Pacific been the smaller of the great oceans and the Chinese "discovered" the Americas, the outcome could have been far different in many ways. It is worth comparing the cases of European and Chinese maritime activity more closely in this light.

A large set of connected factors contributed to the different outcomes, as each of these societies was an organic hierarchy and a part of a larger set of network connections, and each had its own cultural frame. We can consider this comparison in terms of those three parts of our model.

Hierarchy Comparisons

In formal terms, China was a single hierarchy, and it was a strong, centralized and bureaucratic hierarchy with ideological coherence because of the Confucian exam system. Confucianism encouraged rule for the good of all subjects of the emperor. These factors allowed and motivated the Chinese hierarchy to manage its network intersection carefully. Whether management meant promotion or restriction of its network connections was the hierarchy's choice. Thus, the norm for Agrarian hierarchies obtained in China: politics ultimately constrained economics.

Western Europe, by contrast, was divided into numerous competing hierarchies, none of which was as sophisticated as China's. Certainly none had the landed resources on which China could draw, and so kings looked to their cities and merchants as a source of income that they could not afford to suppress and that they often had pressing reasons to cultivate. Furthermore, though "the good of the people" was a talking point for European governments, practical necessity made kings estate managers as much as their nobility and the church were, further emphasizing practicality over ideology in policy decisions. Thus, European hierarchies lacked either the motivation or indeed the basic ability to manage their network connections closely or restrictively.

Network Comparisons

China was very well placed in the broad Eurasian network of trade. It was the world's most sophisticated producer of manufactured goods and was a huge, prosperous market for spices, medicines, and exotic prestige items. Trade thus came to China whether the state promoted it or not: the participation of Chinese merchants abroad was not a necessity. Europe, by contrast, was poorer and more marginal, and it had little to offer beyond wool and weapons. European merchants had to pursue foreign trade actively, and so they also actively sought sources of gold and silver to finance a negative balance of trade in manufactures, whereas China imported silver, which helped finance its vast internal network. The geography of the Eurasian network also mattered in a different way, however. It was Europe, not China, that among the Eurasian societies lay closest to the Americas and their potential riches in mineral, agricultural, and human wealth. For Europe, geography was a lucky "accident."

Geography also shaped the respective internal networks of the two societies. For China, essentially a vast circle of land, the seas were secondary to overland and canal-based movement of goods. Europe, a peninsula made of peninsulas and islands, used maritime transport far more extensively and so had more deeply rooted traditions of shipbuilding and sailing expertise that were not as dependent on state sponsorship for their continuation.

Cultural Frame Comparisons

Ultimately, hierarchy structure and network position influenced the differing paths that China and Europe followed, but the crucial difference lay in their cultural frames, the ways they saw and interpreted the world, including both themselves and (often differently) others. As with hierarchies and networks, cultural frames apply in different ways to "us" and "them."

To begin with, deep frame values shaped the more informal aspects of hierarchy structure and power, especially the role of merchants in each society. China was filled with rich merchants, but their lack of theoretical prestige in Confucian ideology, even though they lived far better than peasants or craftsmen, led them to adopt and espouse Confucian values, often quite practically by educating their sons in the Confucian canon so that they might become state bureaucrats. In other words, the state exercised an informal monopoly on the conferring of prestige, but the meritocracy of the exam system opened a path for merchants to assimilate to the gentry class who dominated society and state service.

European merchants, by contrast, were probably less rich, on average, than Chinese ones, and less numerous in absolute terms but more numerous relative to their society as a whole. Furthermore, to the extent that there was a European social theory—the medieval "three orders" of those who pray, those who fight, and those who work—that theory was not hostile to merchants, it just ignored them. European merchants did face a practical hostility from both warrior aristocrats and the church, and the lack of a theoretical framework meant that they could buy their way into informal prestige much less easily than Chinese merchants could, even when they could purchase formal positions in government. They therefore invented their own forms of prestige, built not surprisingly around making more money, and in places such as the city-states of Italy, merchants ruled their own cities and contributed to Renaissance culture. Meanwhile, paradoxically, the legal-contractual frame of European social relations, as we have noted, opened paths for merchant influence on their own terms.

Cultural frame differences also shaped how the two societies constructed their relations to the outside world in what might be called the cultural roots of colonialism. Chinese scholar bureaucrats, as we have seen many times, saw their country as the Middle Kingdom, the center of the world. This had several consequences. First, it fostered an ideology of self-sufficiency: China did not *need* foreign trade, it allowed it as tribute to the Dragon Throne. But looking outward, a Middle Kingdom had no real incentive to conquer or attempt to control distant parts of the networked world when other countries were already sending "tribute" to their (at least nominal) Chinese overlord. This accounts for why the Treasure Fleets used vast military resources to set up friendly subject kingdoms that acknowledged the superiority of the emperor rather than attempting colonial conquest. Direct military intervention remained reserved for vulnerable land borders such as in Mongolia, Tibet, and Vietnam. The aim of spreading the benefits of Chinese civilization peacefully dovetailed with Chinese religious and philosophical beliefs that had a muted missionary impulse at best—and no militancy—in its ideology.

Europe's cultural frame and many of its prominent screen elements, by contrast, encouraged colonialism. Militarized law saw possession as the necessary first step to legal title in land. Crusading ideals arose from the entanglement of a militant missionary religion and the interests of a warrior aristocracy who held this frame value. When the predatory, expansionist nature of capitalist business enterprises signed onto this cultural contract, the result was a powerful set of intermixed motives for colonial expansion. Trade (along with military force and missionary activity) was increasingly seen as a tool of

FIGURE 14.14 Giraffe in China. Sent as symbolic tribute, received as an auspicious omen. The Treasure Fleets and their cargo were political as much as economic.

aggression and domination, shaped first by competition within Europe and then subsequently projected outward. Militarized trade was the motive, largely lacking in China and conceptualized in purely military terms by the Ottomans, that drove European states to exploit the means and opportunities that were available in a number of places for maritime expansion. Indeed, it led Europeans to attempt not just traditional hierarchy-to-hierarchy conquests, but to colonize the network itself.

A Global Network Emerges

The globalization of the world's previously separate networks brought about by the expansion of maritime connections is significant enough that it forms the standard breaking point for world history courses and textbooks, and it is usually linked explicitly to Columbus's accidental collision with the Americas. In terms of the model used in this book, the century from 1450 to 1550 forms the hinge between the High and Late periods of the Agrarian Era, and the growing power of networks relative to individual hierarchies distinguishes the boundary between these two periods. The globalization of the world's networks, not just networks of trade, including the American resources that suddenly flowed into the

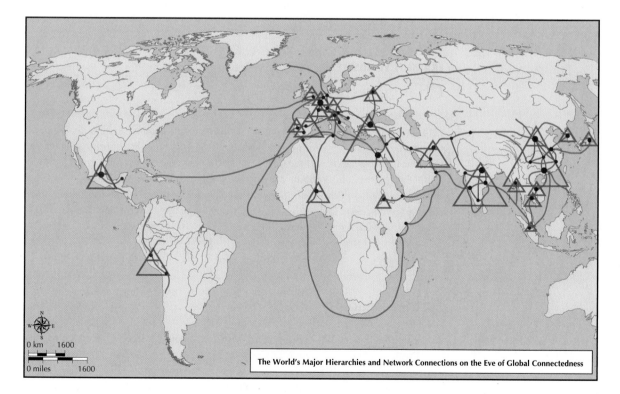

The World's Major Hierarchies and Network Connections on the Eve of Global Connectedness

FIGURE 14.15 The World's Major Hierarchies and Network Connections on the Eve of Global Connectedness.

Afro-Eurasian world, but also networks of diplomatic exchange and interaction among the world's hierarchies, as well as networks of cultural encounter and exchange, all significantly raised the influence of network connections upon hierarchies. This in turn powerfully raised the stakes in network-hierarchy intersections and in the collision of cultural frames. (See Figure 14.15.)

Conclusion

By the mid-sixteenth century, the reorganized shape of a world disrupted by the Mongols and the Black Death was beginning to emerge. It was still a world of traditional Agrarian hierarchies, the pyramids of power with which we have become familiar. These, as always, were built to resist change and promote stability—some hierarchies more successfully than others, perhaps, but the basic intent still held everywhere. The rising influence of a globalized network, however, would pose new challenges, spreading new forces for change, to the world's hierarchies and the cultural frames through which they viewed the changing world. We will take up the patterns of challenge and response that characterized the newly globalized Agrarian world in the next chapter and volume of this book.

FRAME IT YOURSELF

Changing the Frame

Let's play with the counterfactual history hinted at in this chapter. Assume that the only thing different in the world of 1400 is geography: the Atlantic is the size of the Pacific and vice versa, so that China was the major Eurasian hierarchy closest to the Americas. Holding all the other factors as constant as possible (the hierarchy structure, network dynamics, and cultural frames of the major players), write a brief history of the period 1420 to 1620 that starts with one of Zheng He's voyages heading east and "discovering" the west coast of Mexico and the Aztec Empire.

Further Reading

Abu-Lughod, Janet. 1989. *Before European Hegemony.* Oxford: Oxford University Press.

Gottfried, Robert. 1985. *The Black Death: Natural and Human Disaster in Medieval Europe.* New York: Free Press.

Levathes, Louise. 1994. *When China Ruled the Seas: The Treasure Fleet of the Dragon Throne 1405–1433.* New York: Oxford University Press.

Lewis, Archibald, and Timothy Runyon. 1990. *European Naval and Maritime History, 300–1500.* Bloomington: Indiana University Press.

Ozment, Steven. 1981. *The Age of Reform, 1250–1550: An Intellectual and Religious History of Late Medieval and Reformation Europe.* New Haven, CT: Yale University Press. .

Russell, Peter. 2001. *Prince Henry the Navigator.* New Haven, CT: Yale University Press.

For additional learning and instructional resources related to this chapter, please go to www.oup.com/us/morillo

La Malinche.

PART V

Connections

1500 to 1800

The new plumbing systems built in Chapter 14 connected virtually the entire mansion into a single network. The networked Late Agrarian Era rooms of 1500 to 1800 were constructed by architects who took Agrarian Era room-building techniques, network capacity, and decorating schemes to their limits. Part V tours this Late Agrarian section of the mansion, ending in an odd room where network technicians were beginning to take over running the room itself.

Chapter 15 lays out the operations of the mansion's entire plumbing system—a system now developed enough to pose a significant management challenge to even the most well-built rooms. Chapter 16 explains how individual room builders dealt with their room's inhabitants and with each other, negotiating through network connections for space in an increasingly crowded floor plan. Chapter 17 shows how room builders deployed ever more sophisticated decorating schemes to make their rooms livable and indeed how they traded ideas about how to decorate effectively.

Chapter 18, however, shows us a room whose safeguards against overly strong network flows had broken down. The increasing role of network technicians in decorating and even designing the room gave it a peculiar shape, and its inhabitants were acting correspondingly oddly. Their activities would bring the Agrarian Era to a close.

CHAPTER FIFTEEN

The Late Agrarian World I: Networks of Exchange, 1500 to 1800

Indian Collecting Cochineal with a Deer Tail by Jose Antonio de Alzate y Ramirez, 1777.

Introduction

The cochineal is a small insect native to central Mexico whose females live as parasites on cacti. To protect themselves from predation by other insects, they synthesize carminic acid inside their bodies—the acid can constitute one-fifth to one-quarter of the dry weight of the insect. It can also, when extracted and mixed with calcium salts, make carmine dye, which will impart to cloth a range of colors from golden to bright red, depending on the cloth and the dying time.

Before 1500, the use of cochineal for dying was restricted to ceremonial robes among the elites of the Aztec Empire, including their great enemies the Tlaxcallans. The gathering of cochineal was therefore a minor occupation. Then the Tlaxcallans, allying themselves with Hernán Cortés and his band of adventurers, overthrew the Aztecs in 1519; this victory brought them not independence but a privileged position in the new Spanish Empire in Mexico. This in turn brought cochineal, via the global network of which Spanish America became a part, to the attention of a global market. Cochineal was suddenly a valuable commodity, and a great many Tlaxcallans began cultivating cochineal cactus, harvesting cochineal, and selling it to cochineal dealers.

On March 3, 1553, the *cabildo*, or ruling council, of the city of Tlaxcala met to discuss what they saw as a cochineal crisis. Made up of the former ruling elite of Tlaxcala, now working as part of Spanish colonial administration, the council kept minutes that were recorded in Nahuatl, their native language, written in the Roman alphabet. Their concerns were many. "Everyone does nothing but take care of cochineal cactus; no longer is care taken that maize and other edibles are planted." Thus, "famine truly impends." The people devote themselves to the cactus even on Sundays, and so "no longer do they go to church to hear Mass." They sell their cochineal to gain money, often in the form of cacao beans, and then squander their wealth on pulque (an alcoholic drink made from cactus juice) or even Castilian wine. "He who belonged to someone no longer respects whoever was his lord and master, because he is seen to have gold and cacao." Some of the cochineal dealers were women, and in the meetings between growers and dealers, "they make the women drunk there, and there some commit sins." The fabric of society, it seemed to these traditional elite males, was coming apart at its cochineal-dyed seams. Their culture was in danger. "Things are no longer as they were long ago." They decided to suggest to the viceroy in Mexico City that no one should keep more than ten cochineal cactus, and that women should be prohibited from dealing in cochineal.

Translated into the terms of this book's model, what we see is a classic conflict at the intersection between the newly global and ever more powerful network and a particular hierarchy: one that was, in its 1553 form, relatively new, not all that coherent, and whose people had only joined the global network three decades earlier. Especially from the

Framing the Argument

- The major commodities exchanged on the Late Agrarian global network, including, among other things, luxury goods, silver, and human beings, as well as ideas

- The systems of labor that produced the goods and ideas exchanged on the global network, including the rise of joint stock companies as a new form of merchant capitalist organization

- The growing influence of this global network on hierarchies and their interactions, including patterns of colonialism

FRAMING   The Late Agrarian World I:
Networks of Exchange, 1500 to 1800

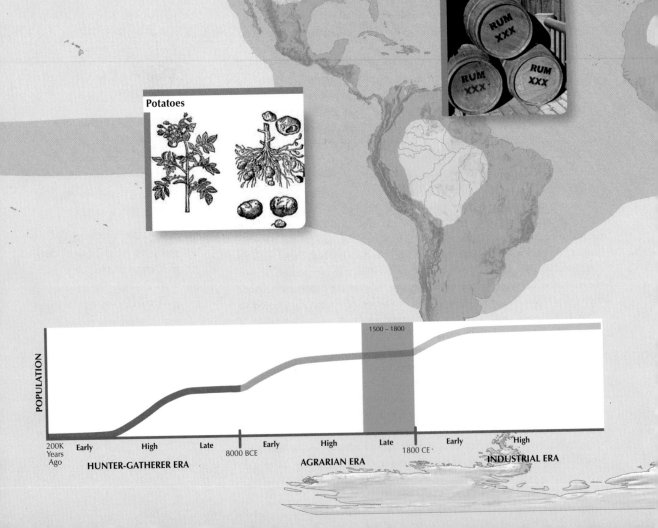

Rum

Potatoes

1500 – 1800

POPULATION

| 200K Years Ago | Early | High | Late | 8000 BCE | Early | High | Late | 1800 CE | Early | High |

HUNTER-GATHERER ERA

AGRARIAN ERA

INDUSTRIAL ERA

Wheat

Rice

Cattle

perspective of the traditional elites of the region, network influences threatened both class power and gender power, the two fundamental bases of societal structure and authority in any Agrarian Era hierarchy. They reacted in a classic Agrarian elite way: by attempting to regulate the scale of trade, thereby reasserting the dominance of politics over economics in order to maintain traditional class divisions; and by banishing women from the public sphere at the front face of their social pyramid to maintain traditional gender roles.

In short, the Tlaxcala *cabildo* meeting of March 3, 1553, is the story of the world's network of trade, cultural exchange, and human movement, and its growing impact on the world's hierarchies after 1500. This is the story of this chapter.

---- ✳ ----

The Connected World of 1500 to 1800

Much of this book up to this point has proceeded chronologically, with chapters covering much of the globe during a particular period. The temporal boundaries between chapters have often overlapped, because chronological divisions in history are a construction imposed upon a seamless past for analytical and narrative purposes. But for the most part, we've proceeded steadily through time.

The next three chapters, however, will all examine the world in the same time period: 1500 to 1800, which this book's periodization calls the Late Agrarian Era (see the Issues in Doing World History box on the naming of this period). We paused in our chronological march once before, in Chapters 9 through 11, to survey the world. But the differences between these two pauses are instructive. When we looked at the world of 400 to 1100, we sliced the topic geographically according to network relationships: an inner circuit Eurasian core, an outer circuit Afro-Eurasian set of regions, and isolated worlds on separate circuits (whose different rates of development stretched our chronological reach to 1500). This scheme reflected the more fragmented nature of the world's network connections down through 1100 and essentially grouped similar hierarchies (or at least hierarchies facing similar network relations) together. (See Figure 15.1.)

Now, looking at the world of 1500 to 1800, we take a different approach that reflects the far greater reach, unity, and influence of the globalized network on the world's hierarchies. We will examine the entire world in each chapter, or at least representative elements of the whole world—again, we can't cover everything, and the aim of this book is to provide a conceptual framework into which examples of societies not covered here can be fit. We will therefore slice the topic up in a different way, looking at the world in terms of the three major elements of our model. This chapter will examine how the world's *network* operated, how it tied the entire world together in ways that justify our taking the entire world as our new unit of analysis. Chapter 16 will analyze the development of the world's *hierarchies*, the states, chiefdoms, and less complex societies in which the people of the world lived, under the

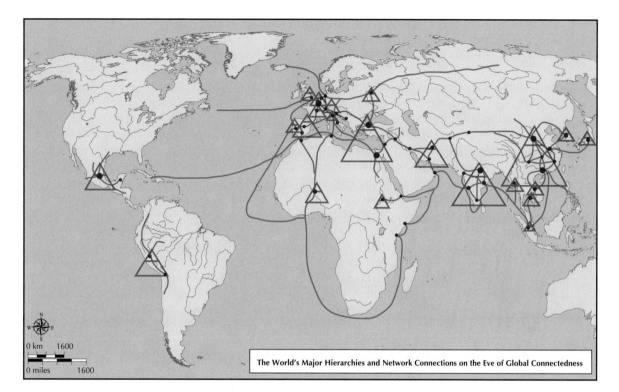

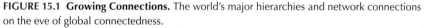

FIGURE 15.1 Growing Connections. The world's major hierarchies and network connections on the eve of global connectedness.

influence of more pervasive, global connections. Finally, Chapter 17 will view the encounters of a globalizing world in terms of *cultural frames* and *cultural screens*: How did the people of the world make sense of this world? The circumstances that brought the Agrarian Era to an end are the topic of Chapter 18.

As the example of the Tlaxcala *cabildo* reminds us, however, this scheme too inevitably imposes artificial divisions on a seamless past, just as periodization does. The world's networks and hierarchies were inextricably bound together, and people's activities within both network and hierarchy contexts were constantly shaped by the cultural frames through which they viewed the world. Their activities and encounters with others in turn influenced those very frames. Analytical convenience, not the unified fabric of reality (dyed with cochineal or not), shapes our chapters.

Commodities

A fundamental rule about networks is that they carry far more than just material goods. Goods inevitably come with ideas and cultural practices attached, and they are received into cultural environments that change their meaning. Furthermore,

ISSUES IN DOING WORLD HISTORY

"Late Agrarian" versus "Early Modern"

This book refers to the period of 1500 to 1800 as the "Late Agrarian Era." This name is based in our division of world history into three main eras, each based on the primary mode of human subsistence prevalent during that era: hunting and gathering, agriculture, and industry (see the graph and periodization chart in the Introduction). This is not the usual name for this period in most historical writing. This period, especially in European history but also in much of world history, is referred to as the "Early Modern" age. Why does this book diverge from common practice?

Well, bluntly, just because something has become widely accepted doesn't make it right, and there are conceptual problems with the old label. It requires, for one, that one define "modernity," so as to identify the characteristics that presumably show up in their "early" form in this period. ("Early," "high," and "late" in our scheme are more simply chronological divisions.) But

modernity is a moving target—everyone has always thought of themselves as living in their own modern times—and the further we get from 1500 to 1800, the less "modern" it looks. And despite attempts to extend the concept globally by some world historians, many of the key characteristics of "modernity" are inevitably European—"early modernity" in the (Western) history of philosophy starts with Descartes, for example. Indeed, modernity as a historical period is a relic of the tripartite division of history into ancient, medieval, and modern, itself a product of the Renaissance Italian humanists' successful self-promotion (see Chapter 14), and "early modernity" is a duct-tape-style fix required when the passage of time rendered fifteenth-century Italian modernity not so modern anymore.

So we'll go with periods defined by broad patterns of subsistence and demography.

PRINCIPLES AND PATTERNS

Commodities always travel the network with ideas attached to them.

ideas are often the main "commodity" exchanged—think of missionary work, for example. We will consider the cultural aspect of the global network more closely in Chapter 17. Here, we start with the exchange of actual material goods.

The Columbian Exchange

When Columbus ran into the Americas, he initiated a vast exchange of microbes, flora, fauna, and people known as the Columbian exchange. (See Figure 15.2.) The most immediate aspect of this exchange—and certainly the most devastating to the indigenous American populations—was the uniting of the Afro-Eurasian and American disease pools. Because crowd diseases originated in human populations from herd animals (see Chapter 2), of which the Americas had, basically, none, almost all of this exchange came to the Americas, spreading immediately and far faster than Europeans themselves. In the century after 1500, Mexican population dropped from perhaps 20 million to around 1 million, Peruvian population from 8 million to under a million. North America was seriously depopulated even before Europeans arrived there. Syphilis may have come back from the Americas (the evidence is disputed), but that was it.

One might count tobacco as part of the American disease return, but of course it was really one of the crops that spread from the Americas to the rest of the world. Some, including tobacco and chocolate, were promoted variously as food, drinks, or drugs (tobacco was said to cure scrofula, rheumatism, and any number of other ailments), and sometimes ran into regulatory opposition as a result. Significantly, as a sign of slipping hierarchy control over the network-hierarchy intersection, regulation

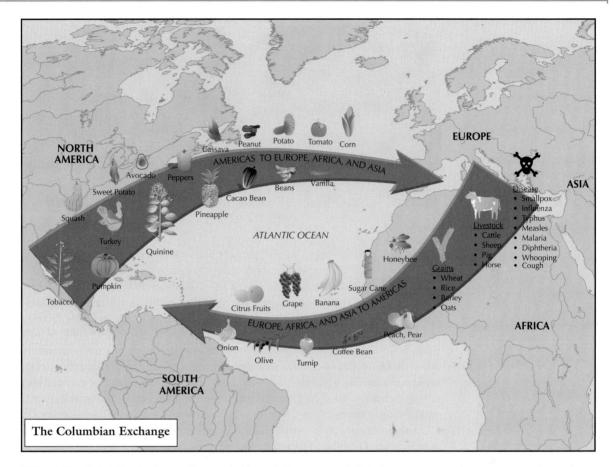

FIGURE 15.2 Columbian Exchange. Plants, animals, and diseases went global when Europeans connected the Americas to the Afro-Eurasian network.

mostly failed. Other crops, such as tomatoes, spread despite an initial reputation for being poisonous. But the most important American crops were food: maize, various squashes and peppers, and above all potatoes, which fueled significant population growth in southern China from the seventeenth century and also became a staple crop in the cool, wet regions of northern Europe. In addition to growing more easily and providing better nutrition than wheat, potatoes also proved less susceptible to damage by passing armies, since the tubers grew underground.

But cultural preferences played at least as big a role as nutrition in the spread of crops. Thus, wheat came with Europeans to the Americas, along with the large domesticated animals lacking there before: pigs, cattle, and (for military and transport purposes more than food) horses. In all cases, the spread of new crops and domesticates entailed significant reshaping of local landscapes. Nowhere was this more true than on many Caribbean islands, where many indigenous animals went extinct along with the people native to the islands, replaced by pigs, rats, sugarcane, coffee, and slave populations imported to grow the latter two crops. In the end, many of the world's best-known "local" cuisines are in fact products of the Columbian exchange:

FIGURE 15.3 Brazilian Sugar Plantation. Source of vast profits and demand for slave labor.

hamburgers with ketchup; the chili peppers heating up many Indian curries; pasta and tomato sauce; and the coffee-chocolate-sugar combination of a mochaccino.

The more immediate consequences of the Columbian exchange during the Late Agrarian age were huge in themselves. We have noted briefly already the demographic effects of the exchange of microbes and crops. Populations in the Americas dropped precipitously, first in Central America and the Andes and then spreading outward from there. But indigenous populations also began to stabilize and recover within a century and a half of initial contact, remaining a majority in the increasingly mixed populations of much of Central and South America. The recovery took longer or came not at all only in areas such as the North American and the Argentine plains, where significant European immigration in the nineteenth century combined with intentional policies of genocide. Meanwhile, diversification of diet and the potato miracle led, as we have seen, to the most significant population growth in Eurasia since the great plagues of the 1300s.

The range and value of the commodities involved in the Columbian exchange stimulated global commerce, adding wealth and influence to the flows of the world-wide network. Here the most significant crops were not necessarily the most widely grown—potatoes spread to many places, but made few people much money because they were easy to grow in many soils and climates. Crops that required unique microclimates in which to thrive, however, such as many of the spices of the islands of Southeast Asia including cinnamon, nutmeg, mace, coriander, and others, could not easily be grown in new places and so became part of a growing pattern of regional specialization of production. The most valuable crop of the age commercially, sugar-cane, grew best in subtropical conditions that Caribbean islands supplied perfectly but that lacked labor. Thus, the Columbian exchange also stimulated the Atlantic slave trade, to which we will return later in this chapter.

The Silver Circuit

One important aspect of the exchange of commodities that emerged on the newly global network was a significant global flow of silver. This followed the discovery and exploitation by the Spanish in Peru of a literal mountain of silver at Potosí in the 1540s (we will discuss the labor aspect of mining this mountain later in the chapter). To understand this flow, the first thing we need to recognize is the central place of China in the global network. China was the biggest and richest unified economy in the world in the Late Agrarian Era. (This was nothing new: it has been estimated that Asia—mostly China and India—produced more than half of world GDP in 18 of the last 20 centuries.) As it was a heavily monetized and commercialized economy, it demanded huge amounts of currency. This need had been met with the world's first paper currency under the Song, but the Mongol crisis undermined the feasibility of paper, and under the Ming silver assumed the role of basic currency. Japanese silver mines supplied some of the demand this created (to the advantage of Japanese merchants), but demand still exceeded supply—a reminder that gold and silver were themselves commodities, not "money," which is an abstraction of exchange value that can be instantiated in any number of materials.

Thus, when Potosí began supplying vast quantities of silver to the Spanish crown, the metal tended to take two routes around the world. The first took it by ship up to the Isthmus of Panama, where it was transported over to Spanish galleons that took it to Spain. The crown used it to pay its armies, which were being used to fight Spain's wars in Europe, especially against a revolt in the Netherlands. The troops used their pay to buy food and clothes from merchants along their routes of march through Italy, Germany, and in the Netherlands. Some of that was used by merchant companies to pay for Chinese goods, and so ended up in China. The second route took it by Spanish galleons directly across the Pacific to the Spanish-held Philippines, where it financed Spanish trade for Chinese goods and so ended up in China. (See Figure 15.4.)

Plenty of silver traveling the first route stayed in Europe, where the increase in the money supply in a smaller economy than China's caused inflation, which was worst in Spain. This had several effects. By making the real cost of borrowing money lower, it encouraged borrowing to invest in trade and manufacturing—except in Spain, whose even higher prices made Spanish goods less competitive. Higher European prices also drew Ottoman merchants who, prohibited by the Ottoman government from trading abroad, traded instead on the black market—another sign of the increasingly difficult task hierarchies faced in managing their network connections. Finally, when returns from the Potosí mine began to decline in the 1650s, not only did the power of the Spanish monarchy decline, but the decreased flow of silver into China caused deflation. Since taxes and rents were fixed, lower market prices for their goods meant that farmers faced harder times.

Distant Luxuries

The silver circuit is actually a specific example of a more general class of commodities traded on the network: high-value luxury goods. Such goods, which included spices, cloth, dyes such as cochineal, weapons, and precious metals and gems, were in high demand by elites everywhere as status symbols in a world where conspicuous consumption advertised social standing. Distant origins for such goods made them even more valuable because of their scarcity and the higher cost of transport. And because they carried high value per unit weight, a single shipload of such goods could reap fabulous profits for merchants dealing in them. The long-distance luxury trade thus formed the glittering pinnacle of network activity during the Late Agrarian Era, as it already had for millennia.

One of the social patterns driving the shifting demand for various luxury goods arose where commercial market relations were prevalent and where formal and informal political restrictions on consumption—sumptuary laws, established customs, or

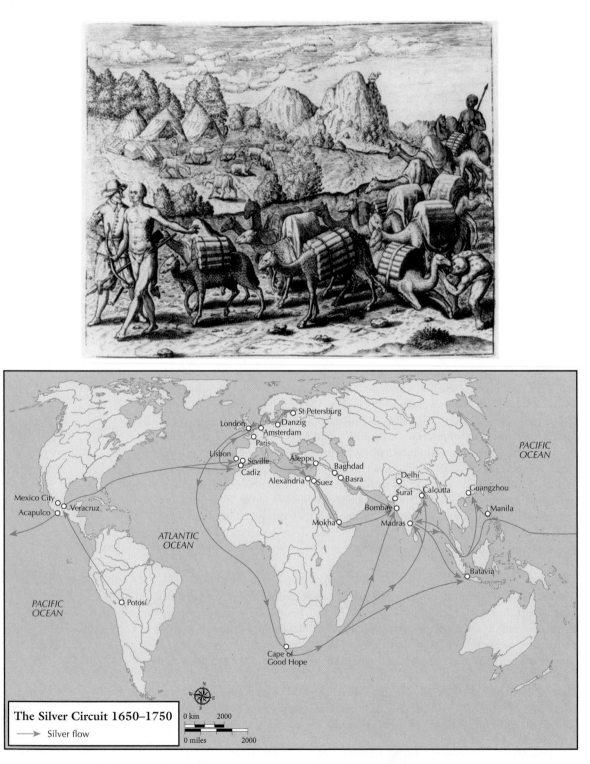

FIGURE 15.4 The Silver Circuit. (Top) Silver being transported from Potosí, the Peruvian mountain of silver, on the backs of llamas. (Bottom) The routes of the global silver trade.

both—were weak. In such places, elites used luxury consumption to set themselves apart from those beneath them, as elites had always done. But the commercial market allowed those in the next social layer—often including rich merchants, to the horror of traditional priestly, warrior, and scribal elites—to aspire at least to the *appearance* of elite status by buying similar goods if they could afford them. If they succeeded to any significant degree, this in turn drove the elites to shift to more exotic and expensive versions of the commodity. Thus, for example, elites in Europe before 1500 could show off by serving Indian black pepper in their meals. But as trade with India expanded after Vasco da Gama's voyages (see Chapter 14), the pepper supply increased and prices dropped enough for its use to spread. It then declined in use among the upper elite in favor of spices such as cinnamon, cloves, and nutmeg. The prevalence of the imitation-distinction pattern tended to spread as the Late Agrarian Era proceeded, indicating again the problems for maintaining a stable traditional social structure in the face of increasing network flows. Such flows threatened to undermine not just formal legal regulation by states, but informal cultural structuring led by traditional elites. We shall see reactions to this problem at both the formal state level in Chapter 16 and at the level of culture and construction of personal and communal identity in Chapter 17. We may also count ideas among the high-value goods that traversed the network, whether implicitly attached to goods or explicitly as inventions and scientific or religious knowledge. We shall turn to this, too, in Chapter 17.

Local and Bulk Goods

The vast majority of both the bulk and the value of network trade, however, consisted not of long-distance luxury goods but of more staple items traded in bulk over shorter subcircuits of the network, creating the dense local networks so valuable to the hierarchies that usually arose over them. Even more than for the luxury trade, for which cities provided concentrations of rich elites, cities were the driving force for local commodity trading. Cities concentrated people on a sometimes vast scale (though still far less than in the Industrial Era: cities of over a million people were almost nonexistent outside China before 1750) and these people had to be fed. The vast majority of urban merchants therefore made their living supplying their own cities. Because of the bulk and sheer quantity of goods for local consumption, cities of any size had to have water-borne transport available, whether a seaport, a navigable river, or, as for some of the great Chinese cities, a canal. A city's immediate hinterland might supply some of its needs, but beyond a certain distance, cartage overland was neither economically feasible nor, ultimately, even possible.

Two different items that fit the description of local bulk goods deserve special mention, however, for their strategic importance and the distances over which they traveled. One was cod. Probably the first Europeans to systematically exploit the resources of the Americas were not the Spanish conquistadors who followed Columbus's path, but fifteenth-century Welsh fishermen who

De Piscatura periculosa in Noruegiano Oceano.

FIGURE 15.5 Cod Fleets. Sixteenth-century cod fishing ships. The cod industry was important enough that wars stopped when the cod fleets returned from the Newfoundland Banks.

had most likely begun making regular voyages across the North Atlantic to the cod banks off Newfoundland. (Columbus almost certainly spent some time with such fleets before undertaking his own voyages.) They did not "discover" North America because they were interested neither in land nor in advertising and sharing their lucrative find. But as the Atlantic opened up, a huge cod-fishing industry emerged that supplied so much fish to northern Europe that wars were at times suspended to allow the return of the cod fleets after their months-long fishing season. The trade was made possible by the development of onboard techniques for preserving the fish by drying, smoking, or salting.

The other commodity, perhaps even more basic to the operations of the network itself, was timber for shipbuilding. Wood is bulky and heavy, and most of the trade in wood conformed to the pattern of local growth, short-range transport, and consumption. But most of that involved wood for heating and cooking in households of peasants on up to elites. Timbers for seagoing ships had to be made from especially large trees of certain types. One reason for the decline of Chinese long-distance trade after the Ming stopped sending out the Treasure Fleets (see Chapter 14) was that the government felt no need to regulate the price or supply of timber, and big ship timber became prohibitively expensive. European states, more dependent on both aggressively maintaining their overseas connections and protecting them with oceangoing navies, regulated prices, protected domestic supplies as they could, and contracted for timber from distant suppliers. One advantage of wood is that it floats and so could be transported on rivers and canals and even across restricted sea passages—the British navy drew timber supplies from parts of Scandinavia and the Baltic. Still, Venetian shipyards periodically shut down for lack of timber, and in many of the most populous areas of Eurasia the demands of heating, cooking, and shipbuilding combined to create a growing problem of deforestation in the Late Agrarian Era.

Human Commodities: The Slave Trade

A final category of commodity traded on the global network was humans themselves. Slavery was as old as complex hierarchical societies—slaves appear in the Mesopotamian Code of Hammurabi—and indeed was a product of a combination of hierarchy, warfare (itself a product of complex hierarchy), and the subordination of economics to politics that underlay Agrarian hierarchies. Slavery was, in other words, simply the most extreme version of the various forms of coerced labor common to much of the Agrarian world. But slavery was usually inefficient economically and culturally, as overt coercion cost more and produced less than labor ideologically convinced to work within the system. The universal characterization of slaves as lazy reflected slaves' lack of incentives under coercion. Slavery therefore tended to appear where demographic or cultural factors made other forms of labor scarce. It is therefore the extreme case of our general rule that labor shortages in traditional Agrarian hierarchies led to declines in labor freedom.

PRINCIPLES AND PATTERNS

In Agrarian hierarchies, labor shortages led to declines in labor freedom.

This rule meant that in the High Agrarian Era, the most common form of slavery was small scale and domestic: slaves served as household servants. Domestic slavery, often of young women, reduced the problem of coercion compared to mass agricultural labor and allowed the substitution of "family ideology," ties of personal relationship and (pseudo)adoption, for the cultural and religious ideologies of social control necessary for replacing coercion among mass labor.

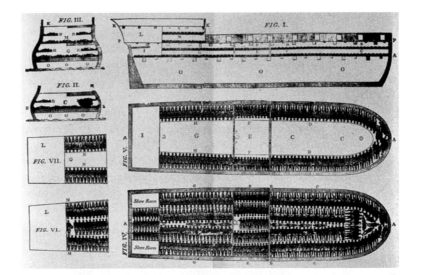

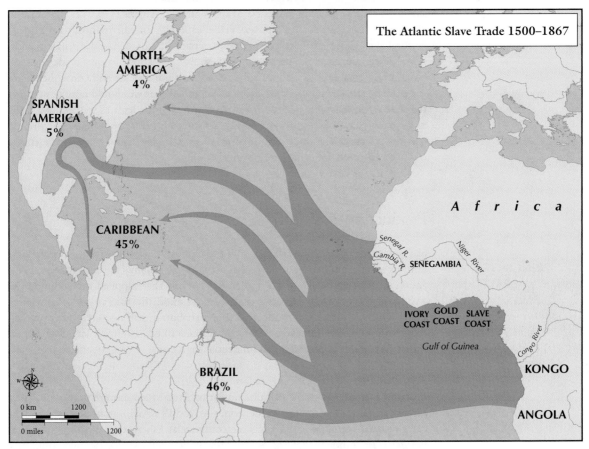

FIGURE 15.6 Human Commodities. (Top) Depiction of slaves packed on a slave ship as commodified cargo, clearly not as human beings. (Bottom) The flow of slaves to the Americas.

Many West African societies practiced this form of domestic slavery, which was connected to a culture of war that encouraged the taking of captives to bolster the prestige of warrior kings. This produced more slaves than African societies themselves needed, and for centuries Africans had entered the Islamic world as domestic slaves. The first slaves brought to Portugal by Henry the Navigator's ship captains were employed as domestic slaves (see Chapter 14). But Henry's settlement of the Azores and Madeira and their development as sugarcane-growing economies pointed to a new source of demand. When the islands of the Caribbean fell into European hands, their suitability for growing sugarcane became obvious. But equally obvious was that the indigenous population was dying out rapidly from disease and harsh exploitation, and for cultural reasons did not work well in a totally new form of agriculture. The European labor market, predicated on a contractual culture and a monetized, market economy, failed to provide much labor at all: sugar plantations were unattractive to wage labor (at least at affordable rates for plantation owners) and indentured servitude provided only small numbers for limited terms. Labor shortage opened the door to slavery.

The result was the emergence of a growing trade in African people who were shipped to the Caribbean and parts of the mainland Americas to work agricultural plantations. Little or no attempt was made, especially on the islands, to substitute cultural mechanisms of control for raw coercion, perhaps because small islands, brutal discipline, and high rates of mortality and thus labor turnover made coercion economically viable. We shall return to other cultural aspects and consequences of the Atlantic slave system in the next two chapters. What we should note now is that the slave trade was truly trade: African slave sellers did at least as well economically as European slave buyers. It was also, at least through 1700, on a small enough scale that the effects of the trade within Africa were relatively minor, though the effects on those captured and sold were obviously tragic.

Production Systems

PRINCIPLES AND PATTERNS

Low productivity and slow communications shaped the Agrarian world in every way.

Slaves were, of course, not just commodities but, as we have just seen, laborers. This leads us to an examination of the global network of exchange in terms of the organization of labor and capital into production systems that supplied the commodities traded on the network. Here we must bear in mind the fundamental constraints under which Agrarian Era production *and* distribution still operated. Low productivity and slow communications still constrained all economic activity, even if that activity was more widespread and influential than ever.

Agriculture

Probably around 90% of the world's population lived by agriculture in this era. Their meager surpluses fed the rest (aside from the world's remaining hunter-gatherers, a category that could be said to include commercial fishermen). Where agricultural villages existed independent of complex hierarchies, subsistence farming could be a source of prestige for those engaged in it. But in the more common situation where farmers had been subjected to the macroparasite of a chiefdom or state, with its landed elites exercising class power over primary producers, prestige was replaced with the burden of taxes, rents, and coerced labor services. It was through such political mechanisms that most peasant surplus was extracted. The accumulated wealth of peasant surpluses then turned into elite consumption: either the products were stored and eaten directly, or the landowner sold them to pay for luxury goods.

Subsistence and Markets

But market mechanisms were becoming more common in the developed network of the Late Agrarian than they had been in the Early or High Agrarian eras. The Ming abolished subject labor services by imperial decree in favor of markets, and the post-plague labor shortages of western Europe, set in the context of a legal-contractual cultural frame, were steadily undermining serfdom there (see Chapter 14), for example.

Converting labor services and rents-in-kind to cash payments, however, required a surrounding economy that was sufficiently monetized and commercialized. This required the presence of merchants and cities. For it was from cities, with their voracious appetites for food and other goods noted above, that the tentacles of commerce reached out into rural communities of peasants in many places, altering traditional patterns of peasant subjugation and forced labor to landed elites, as well as introducing market incentives for the growing of cash crops instead of food staples—the very substitution that so worried the *cabildo* of Tlaxcala concerning cochineal. Not that elites necessarily suffered. Where traditional subjugation held, landowners reaped the profits of cash cropping, and where peasants sold directly, it was often to pay taxes or rents in cash. Commercialization of agriculture did, however, affect peasant society. It tended to introduce greater divisions of wealth and status into rural communities, as some peasant families proved more adept than others at taking advantage of market opportunities. Thus, commercialization and the greater freedom it brought sometimes met resistance among peasants themselves, as it meant change and less stability. Even at the level of peasant farmers, the network intersection with hierarchies was tense, conflicted, and potentially subversive of traditional social structures.

Traditional Labor in Colonial Contexts

Still, even with variations in commercialization, peasant labor systems shared the same basic dynamics in almost all Agrarian Era hierarchies. The interchangeability of systems of subject labor is illustrated by the Spanish imposition of labor services on the indigenous populations of their empire in the Americas. These drew on pre-conquest traditions of labor services to native chiefs or states and were exploited by Spanish landholders to draw a profit from their new possessions—at first with little or no oversight or authorization from the Spanish Crown. The *encomienda* system, as the first of two different systems was called, assigned groups of Indians to an *encomiendero*, often a former soldier granted an American estate for his services, who could demand tribute and labor services from "his" Indians, theoretically in exchange for protecting them and teaching them Christianity.

The requirement for protection and conversion can be interpreted as an attempt by the Crown to bring native labor within the same cultural frame as their Spanish

activity—not surprisingly, given the foundational nature of family ties to social structure everywhere. But the scale of long-distance trade, both geographically and in terms of the amount of capital invested in merchandise at any one time, meant that much more often than in urban manufacturing, merchants entered into cooperative arrangements that transcended familial ties. Merchants necessarily and readily entered into partnerships with each other, for example, and entrusted shipments to associates in faraway ports to dispose of in the most profitable way possible. We saw some of the workings of such systems in Chapter 8; by 1500 the scale and reach of such operations had grown even further. Cooperation was necessitated by slow communications and the need for local knowledge and connections for merchants, the wise practitioners of the global network, to trade successfully.

FIGURE 15.11 **Medieval Financial Capitalism.** Italian merchant bankers: "bank" comes from the Italian *banco*, or bench, where money-changing transactions took place.

Two further factors also pushed mercantile business organization to more complex levels than manufacturing required. The first was the problems of conducting economic exchanges across vast distances and numerous hierarchies. The second was the high risk associated with transporting valuable goods.

The economic exchange problem in a world without formal mechanisms for setting monetary exchange rates (and indeed a world with a plethora of monetary systems, not all of which were even based on precious metals, as with the cacao beans that served as small-scale currency in Mexico) stimulated the development, across the network, of credit arrangements and bookkeeping in various forms—fifteenth-century Italians invented the double entry method of bookkeeping to track their various investments. These proved useful not just for managing trade but for managing purely monetary transactions, such as money changing and making loans at interest. (Again in Italy, these two functions were combined to get around church restrictions on charging interest on loans: money was lent in one currency and paid back in another, with the exchange rate set favorably to build profit into a nominally interest-free loan.) It was thus from mercantile activity and the profits it generated that banking emerged in various places.

The risks of transport encouraged the invention of different mechanisms that facilitated trade. Primary among these was splitting up one's shipments onto different ships or other means of transport so that if the ship went down the merchant would not suffer a total loss. But this left the ship to be filled with portions of other merchants' shipments. This led to ships themselves being owned (or hired) in shares, ships being the largest, most expensive piece of capital necessary for long-distance trade. Obviously, since the investing merchant could not sail on several ships at once, this also created separation between the investors in a shipping enterprise and the labor that actually sailed the ships. In smaller scale, shorter distance trade, ship crews had often become partners in the enterprise, sharing in the profits of the trade. But as distances and absentee investors multiplied, so too did wage labor. To see the significance of this, we must pause to define an important term.

Capitalism

"Capitalism" dominates both the practicalities and the theoretical analyses of the modern world economy. The origin of capitalism—often mistakenly placed in Late Agrarian Europe as part of the "European modernization" story discussed in the Issues box earlier in this chapter—is therefore an apparently important issue in world history. But, in truth, capitalism has ancient and multiple roots: small-scale capitalism was not uncommon across the world's networks at least by the Age of Empires. The better question is how and where the influence of capitalism spread, a question that this book ties into the general failure of western Europe to contain its merchants, a story we will pursue in later chapters. But for now, we need to define what we mean by capitalism.

This book adopts a simple definition of *capitalism*. Capitalism is an economic system that involves three elements. The first element is *the private ownership of capital*. "Private" here means both non-state and non-communal. (Agricultural land was usually conceptualized in the Agrarian Era as "owned" by either the state, in the person of the king, or collectively by the local communities that farmed it, or both. Capitalist agriculture was therefore rare, though Roman private estates worked by slave labor, for example, qualify.) "Capital" is defined as the means of doing business, including but not limited to cash. As we have just seen, ships were vital pieces of capital for many merchants. An oven is capital for a baker. The second element is *the division of capital and labor*. This means that an enterprise in which the labor is performed by the owners of capital—the baker who bakes in his own oven—is not capitalist. (Nor is a baker with an apprentice, who constitutes in effect a junior profit-sharing partner, his share being room, board, and training.) Nor are partnerships such as ships' crews that take a share of the profits. Wage labor is capitalist. Slave labor, in which the slaves are, technically, both capital and labor, is a potential complication for this distinction, but distinguishing slaves as capital from slaves as people performing labor seems morally as well as analytically justifiable. Third, *the benefits of doing business (profits) accrue to the owners of capital*. This, too, eliminates partnerships, while further qualifying slave labor.

Modern economists' definitions of capitalism often incorporate notions of free markets and "private enterprise" into definitions of capitalism, but for purposes of historical analysis, these should be treated as separate concepts that are not only unnecessary to the core definition of capitalism but whose inclusion elides important historical developments. As we shall see shortly, capitalist businesses can operate quite happily in unfree markets. We shall explore the operations and consequences of capitalism as a mode of economic organization further in Chapter 19. For now, we can use the definition to examine some aspects of the Late Agrarian network.

Merchant Capitalism

To emphasize a key point again, transport constituted the most expensive aspect of the operations of all pre-Industrial networks. Thus, those who controlled means of transport, especially ships, were in a position of central importance. This can be illustrated by tracing the role of merchant capitalists in systems of production. It was merchants who bought raw materials, brought them to manufacturers, and then brought the finished products to buyers. An examination of the common organization of the western European wool cloth industry, often referred to as the "Putting Out" system, illustrates the dynamics of this sort of organization, though it was simply a variant on an age-old practice. (As we saw in Chapter 8, Abraham bin Yiju, a twelfth-century Jewish merchant, organized the shipping of broken metal household objects such as lamps from Spain and Morocco to India for remaking by the local metalsmiths before shipping them back to their place of origin, "putting out" the actual handicraft work to where labor was both skilled and cheap.)

In the twelfth and thirteenth centuries, wool merchants usually brought the raw wool they bought (the best sources were in England and Spain) to their home cities (concentrated in the Netherlands and northern Italy), where those who dyed the wool, spun it into thread, wove it into cloth, and finished it (each a separate specialized process) were concentrated, before transporting the finished cloth to market. This was efficient, but it also put the skilled workers in a potentially powerful position. Guilds of weavers, especially, since they owned their own looms but not the vital capital of the raw wool, began acting more like modern trade unions than craft guilds. The merchant capitalist response after 1400 or so was to decentralize production by "putting out" the raw wool and work to numerous small household spinners and weavers in the countryside, who had no chance of organizing collectively, given the limits of communication and the pressures of competition among them. As with Abraham bin Yiju's Indian smiths, "cheap" (as well as cooperative) was as important as "skilled" in the merchant capitalist search for productive labor and, ultimately, profits.

After 1500, in a process common to many Agrarian societies, really rich merchants in Europe attempted to buy their way out of the non-noble status automatically associated with manual labor (in which category merchant activity definitely counted). Some families did this over a period of generations, buying land, assuming the trappings of a noble lifestyle, and abandoning the merchant business in favor of lending money to the state. The more direct approach was to buy noble titles and state offices, really another way of lending money to the state at interest paid back in guaranteed salaries. But unlike in China, for instance, where the merchant and gentry classes gradually assimilated to each other around Confucian values, the "new nobility" in Europe had no cultural pathway to assimilation with the old warrior elite, and conflict between the two groups remained a sometimes violent screen issue in many European societies. The exceptions were northern Italy and the Netherlands, where ennobled merchant interests dominated, and England, where nobility was not a closed caste but had been dependent on (landed) wealth (and royal favor) for centuries. We shall return to the structural and cultural consequences of this process in Chapter 18. But one economic and political consequence may be dealt with immediately.

Joint-Stock Companies

The development of merchant capitalism and its mechanisms of credit, joint ownership distanced from labor, and risk mitigation, set in the legal-contractual cultural frame of western European society and given political voice in the merchant-influenced states of the Netherlands and England, gave birth around 1600 to an institution known as the *joint-stock company*, the ancestor of the limited liability corporation and in particular of the multinational corporation. Joint-stock companies, starting with the British East India Company (BEIC), founded in 1600, and its competitor the Dutch East India Company (VOC, from its name in Dutch), founded in 1602, took the principle of risk sharing by multiple owners of ship cargo to a new level of abstraction. The companies, chartered (given legal status) by their respective governments, sold stock, or shares of joint ownership, to anyone willing to invest in the new enterprise. The companies, run by professional boards of merchant directors who also tended to be stockholders, used the capital they raised from selling shares of ownership to buy both ships and trade goods. Any profits they made after expenses (including salaries for the board and labor such as ship captains and crews) were then returned to investors as dividends in proportion to their shares of ownership. In order to make an attractive level of profit more likely, in the context of risks and costs that were still very high, each company was

FIGURE 15.12 Company Man. Sir James Lancaster commanded the first British East India Company fleet in 1601.

granted a monopoly within its home state on trade with its designated part of the world. (Though the VOC and the BEIC competed with each other in the "East Indies," in practice they effectively divided the territory, with the Dutch operating in the Malaysian spice islands and the BEIC concentrating on trade with India.)

Thus, as Figure 15.13 illustrates, joint-stock companies represent a significant new mechanism for hierarchy management of the potential tension at the intersection of networks and hierarchies. Regulation by hierarchies (whether through formal state regulations or via the dominance of hierarchy-based cultural frames that limited merchant influence) had been the norm. Exceptions were mostly small, network-centered city-states such as classical Athens, medieval Venice, and the trade-kleptocracy of Srivijaya in the Straits of Melaka, whose network operations were effectively hierarchy-dominated. Joint-stock companies were, instead, true partnerships between private, network-oriented merchant activity and significant traditional hierarchies. As formal legal institutions, they linked their hierarchies to network activity in ways that benefited both but that were possible only because of the weakness of the BEIC's and VOC's states' traditional elites—a weakness mostly of elite ideology of a traditional, anti-mercantile sort. As institutions, they also gave institutional memory to their individual members, a crucial step in professionalizing, bureaucratizing, and *combining* the functions of network-based wise practitioners and hierarchy-based

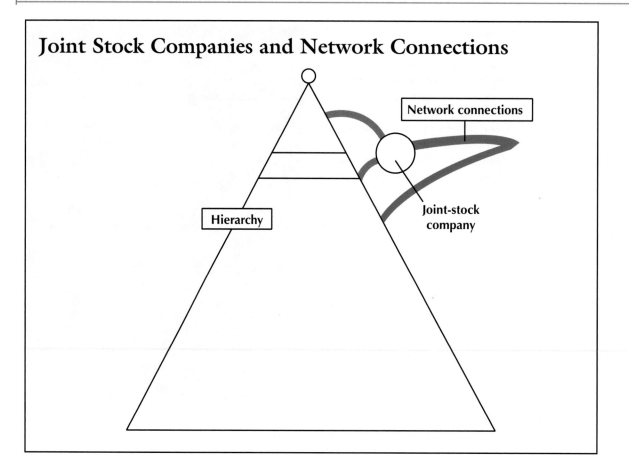

FIGURE 15.13 New Way to Connect. Joint-stock companies as a new structural element linking the company's hierarchy to the network (though not as the only such link).

informed officials. This professionalization and bureaucratization, within the framework of a legal charter laying out the rules that determined how governance of the company was to operate, can be interpreted as an experiment in constitutional government, an experiment made possible by its restricted scope and separation from the governance of the hierarchies that chartered them. In terms of our model, they can be represented abstractly as a new sphere linking the global network to an individual hierarchy, as Figure 15.13 shows. They are a crucial development, and we shall return to their expanding influence in Chapter 18.

Cores, Peripheries, Colonies

The invention of joint-stock companies directs our attention more generally back to the tense and conflicted intersection between networks and hierarchies that has been one of the central themes of this book's analysis of world history. Joint-stock companies were, of course, only one method for managing that intersection, and numerous other methods had long since been in place around the world, each more or less successful in its own society and each creating its own systems of interaction. In the context of a global network, however—whose influence was reaching farther and farther into the internal workings of individual hierarchies, as the example of our cochineal producers illustrates—the differences between how hierarchies regulated networks began to matter more. Furthermore, the richest areas of the world, cores of economic activity, exerted significant influence over network flows and peripheral economies in their regions. The following two sections survey the global network from the perspectives of core-periphery relations and systems of network-hierarchy interactions.

Cores and Peripheries

Four regions stand out in the Late Agrarian networked world as particularly rich. We should note two things about these core areas. First, by the standards of the modern industrial world, disparities in the wealth of regions were small. In the seventeenth century, the richest regions of the world were not that much richer than the average— perhaps twice as rich on a per capita basis of production and consumption as the average region. (Today's disparity is a factor of many thousands.) This reflects the still universal constraint of low productivity. Because the "productivity multiplier" of even these rich regions was still very low, the weight of these regions derived mostly from their relatively high and dense populations, which was in fact the main result of their richness. But each also acted as a center of high quality manufacturing, and their influence over their peripheries included a pattern of the exchange of manufactured goods for food and raw materials that was advantageous to the core areas. Second, measuring wealth on a per capita basis, as in today's world, gives an acceptable rough measure, but disguises the huge and systemic difference between elites and commoners within regions. We are still in a world of tiny elites extracting a small surplus from a vast mass of peasant farmers.

The first of the four cores was southeastern China, centered on the Yangzi River valley and adjacent coastal areas, a region built on highly productive wet-field rice agriculture, abundant local manufacturing, and a dense set of internal and external network connections. Its main peripheries were other regions of the Chinese Empire itself, which under the Qing Dynasty reached its greatest extent yet. (We shall examine the major hierarchies of the Late Agrarian world in the next chapter.) These peripheral areas included the political center of China in the north, around the capital at Beijing, and even more the western frontier regions connected to the southeast by the Yangzi. This was the core, in other words, of a huge dense local network whose internal connections far outweighed even China's significant volume of external trade.

The second core was the Kanto plain in eastern Japan, centered on Edo (modern Tokyo), the capital of Japan under the Tokugawa Shogunate. This, too, was the core of a dense local network covering all of Japan, which grew increasingly rich during the two hundred years of internal peace that followed the establishment of the shogunate in 1603. The shape of this network mirrored (and influenced) the political shape of Tokugawa Japan. Remarkably, this dense local network expanded despite being almost totally cut off from the global network by an act of

FIGURE 15.14 Network Regulation. Japanese print showing the kind of Dutch ship that sailed into Nagasaki once a year.

political will on the part of the shogunate: starting in 1640, the Shoguns prohibited Japanese leaving or foreigners entering Japan, save for a single Dutch trading ship a year. While this solved the shogunate's problem of external network management quite neatly, the intersection of Japan's own internal network and its hierarchy structure nevertheless proved as subversive as any external flows, as we shall see in Chapters 16 and 22.

The third core was the central Ganges Plain in northern India, home to the political center of the Mughal Empire that united most of India for most of this period. Its peripheries extended throughout India, again reflecting the political organization of the empire. Both the network and political connections of this core area to its peripheries, however, were more segmentary and contingent than in China and Japan, and proved more open to disruption and reorientation, contributing to and affected by the decline of Mughal power after 1700.

Finally, there was the dual core surrounding the English Channel: southeast England, centered on the capital at London, and the Netherlands. The rest of Great Britain and Ireland provided some limited periphery to the British part of this core, while the Dutch Republic, independent from Spanish rule after 1648, had no immediate politically controlled periphery, though much of northwestern Europe was economically peripheral to the Dutch. But both developed far-flung peripheries. The British peripheries were in the Americas, both in its North American colonies and its increasingly extensive hold over the sugar islands of the Caribbean. The Dutch, by contrast, held only a few limited possessions in the Americas. Instead, they in effect colonized large parts of the network itself, especially the Indian Ocean circuits of it, leading to Dutch control of a network of port cities and later parts of Indonesia and Malaysia.

Colonies

As this brief survey of Late Agrarian core economic areas already indicates, their relationships with their economic peripheries formed part of a larger set of interactions between the global network and the hierarchies with which it intersected. These interactions can only be fully understood, however, by examining the role played by cultural frames, the third part of our model, in those interactions.

In both China and Japan, the close congruence of dense local network and political boundaries meant that cores and peripheries operated, for the most part, within the same cultural frame. Mughal India, by contrast, had to deal with a disjunction of cultural frames between its Muslim ruling elites and its largely Hindu subject population, which included its own elites, and which reflected the cultural and linguistic diversity of the subcontinent. As a result, Mughal political control of its extended provinces was relatively loose and insecure, even at the height of the empire.

In this disjunction between the cultural frames of rulers and ruled, the Mughal Empire bears comparison with the Spanish Empire in the Americas. We noted above the *encomienda* and *mita* labor systems there. In those cases, the disjunction of cultural frames between colonizing authority and colonized labor allowed greater exploitation of colonial labor. This can be compared, in its early phases, to what happened when steppe nomads conquered sedentary societies—essentially what happened with the Mughal conquest of India. The difference emerged over time, as steppe nomads such as the Mughals, lacking strong administrative structures of their own, either adopted local forms and the cultural frames that went with them or went back to the steppes. Despite significant Persian cultural influence, assimilation was essentially the fate of the Mughals politically. But the European colonizers of the Americas came not from the steppes but from their own deeply rooted sedentary hierarchies. Their colonial rule therefore proved more transformational (though not necessarily more permanent politically) of labor patterns and cultural frames. Still, the Spanish faced the strong survival of indigenous peoples and cultural frames.

British colonization of the Americas, by contrast, followed two paths. In the Caribbean, the elimination of the natives and their replacement by a polyglot set of rapidly turned over fragments of various African societies meant that the colonizer's cultural frame was both separate from and only weakly challenged by the slowly constructed culture of Caribbean slave labor. This allowed a brutal and lucrative exploitation. In their North American colonies, the colonists carried a British cultural frame with them and assumed they shared it with the mother country. This assumption was true in some ways, but proved not to be completely shared by the London ruling elite when British and colonial interests diverged. We shall explore further some of the consequences of these different relationships of cores, peripheries, and cultural frames in Chapters 17 and 18.

Conclusion

When Columbus's voyages connected the Americas to the Afro-Eurasian network, the subsequent flow of goods, from the plants, animals, and diseases of the Columbian exchange to the silver of Potosí and the cochineal of central Mexico, significantly increased the impact of the network on the world's hierarchies and their various cultural frames. The network reached farther, moved more wealth, and affected labor systems and patterns of production more pervasively than ever before—still constrained by the low productivity and slow communications that shaped the Agrarian world, but beginning to press at those limits. This put new pressure on the tense intersection of the network with the world's hierarchies. The network also carried ideas, bringing cultures into contact with each other and challenging their established cultural frames. The next two chapters survey the Late Agrarian world from these political and cultural perspectives.

FRAME IT YOURSELF

Extending the Frame

This chapter talks about a number of global commodities exchanged on the Late Agrarian network, but traced only one, silver, in any detail. The operations of the network and its global and political ramifications are often visible in fascinating detail when you follow the travels of a single commodity. Pick one of the commodities mentioned here (or another one)—sugar, coffee, tobacco, cotton cloth, potatoes, muskets—and map the network of its travels. What new information does your map reveal about the workings of the global network?

Further Reading

Crosby, Alfred. 2003. *The Columbian Exchange: Biological and Cultural Consequences of 1492*. 30th anv. ed. New York: Praeger.

Gunder Frank, Andre. 1998. *ReORIENT: The Global Economy in the Asian Age*. Berkeley: University of California Press.

Hawthorne, Walter. 2010. *From Africa to Brazil: Culture, Identity, and an Atlantic Slave Trade, 1600–1830*. Cambridge: Cambridge University Press.

Mintz, Sidney W. 1985. *Sweetness and Power: The Place of Sugar in Modern History*. New York: Viking.

Pomeranz, Kenneth, and Steven Topik. 2005. *The World That Trade Created: Society, Culture, and the World Economy, 1400 to the Present*. New York: M. E. Sharpe.

Rediker, Marcus. 2007. *The Slave Ship: A Human History*. New York: Viking.

For additional learning and instructional resources related to this chapter, please go to www.oup.com/us/morillo

CHAPTER SIXTEEN

The Late Agrarian World II: Hierarchies in a Global System, 1500 to 1800

Jahangir's dream of embracing Shah Abbas.

Introduction

According to the memoir of Jahangir, the emperor of the Mughal Empire from 1605 to 1627, the very first ordinance he issued in his reign established a "chain of justice." This was a literal chain,

> . . . one end of which I caused to be fastened to the battlements of the royal tower of the castle of Agra, and the other to a stone near the bed of the river Jumnah; to the end that whenever those charged with administering the courts were slack in dispensing justice to the downtrodden, he who had suffered injustice by applying his hand to the chain would find himself in the way of obtaining speedy redress.

The redress would come directly from the emperor himself, alerted to injustice by the chain of justice.

Jahangir ruled an empire that covered nearly the entire Indian subcontinent and contained perhaps 60 million people, almost none of whom lived within walking distance of the stone post on the banks of the Jumnah. This does not, however, mean that Jahangir's chain of justice was worthless. Its practical use was, of course, limited. Those of the downtrodden who might have pulled the chain when the emperor was not in residence, being engaged instead in one of the ceremonial tours of the Mughal army to the provinces that helped hold the empire together, could have gone unnoticed. Even if he were home, the emperor might ignore a claimant. But those lucky few who did get a hearing from "the safeguard of the world; the sovereign splendor of the faith, Jahangir, son of the imperial Akbar," as he called himself in his memoirs, might well see their case addressed and some unlucky official executed for malfeasance.

But such a verdict, along with the mere existence of the chain and Jahangir's advertisement of it in his memoirs, served an important symbolic purpose, confirming Jahangir's role as a defender of cosmic and social order and thus legitimizing his rule. In a Late Agrarian world that was more highly networked than ever before, such symbolic claims assumed greater importance, not just in terms of internal politics (justifying the emperor's rule to the elites who supported him and the common subjects who bore the burden of a coercive hierarchy), but also in a cultural context that increasingly transcended individual hierarchies: Jahangir was in competition with other rulers, not just politically and militarily, but symbolically. In a world where the limitations of low productivity and slow communications still constrained the actual abilities of hierarchies to do such things as administer justice fairly and thoroughly, such symbolism was vital.

Jahangir's chain of justice, as local as it seems, therefore introduces us to the themes of this chapter. Linked together by the increasingly pervasive network connections explored in the last chapter, hierarchies faced a more complex world in which they had to manage their internal tensions

Framing the Argument

- The challenges hierarchies faced in managing their own societies, their intersections with the network, and their competition with other hierarchies

- The three major patterns of hierarchy relations: the closing of the central Asian steppes, regions of warring states, and maritime empires

- The maturity of the Late Agrarian system of hierarchies

FRAMING   The Late Agrarian World II: Hierarchies in a Global System, 1500 to 1800

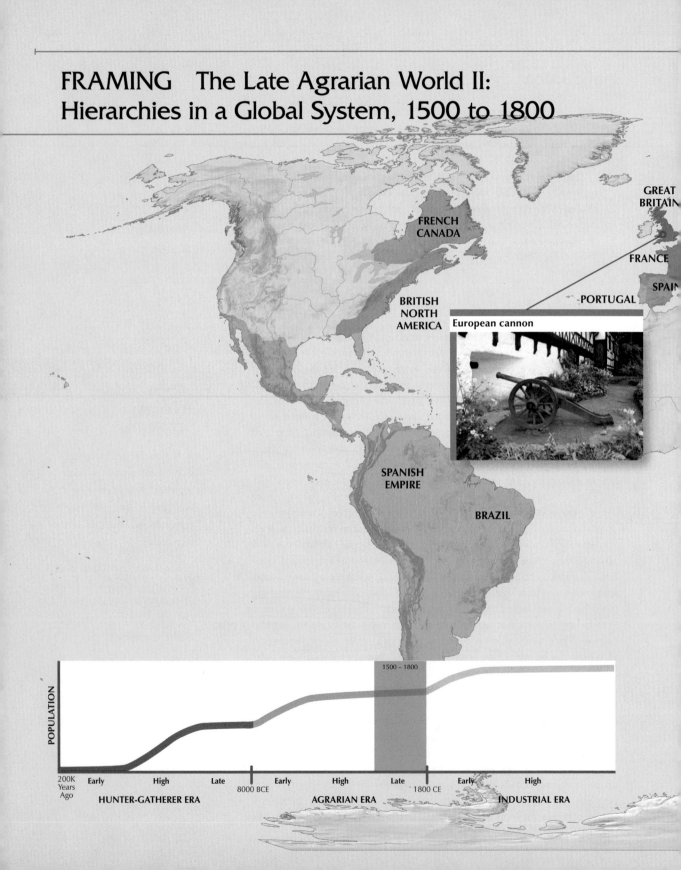

GREAT
BRITAIN

FRENCH
CANADA

FRANCE

SPAIN

PORTUGAL

BRITISH
NORTH
AMERICA

European cannon

SPANISH
EMPIRE

BRAZIL

1500 – 1800

POPULATION

200K
Years
Ago

Early   High   Late   Early   High   Late   Early   High

8000 BCE   1800 CE

HUNTER-GATHERER ERA   AGRARIAN ERA   INDUSTRIAL ERA

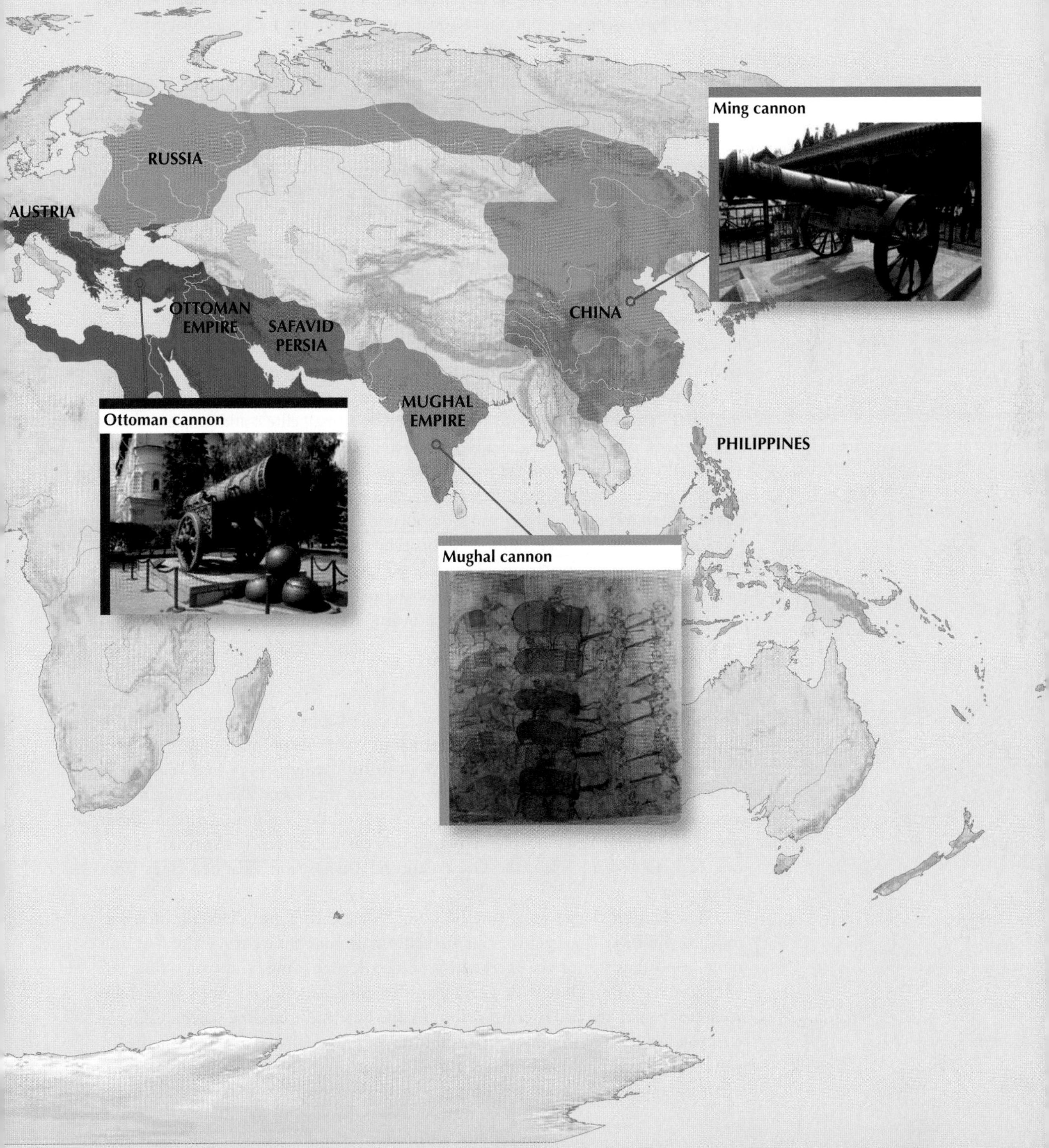

Ming cannon

Ottoman cannon

Mughal cannon

AUSTRIA

RUSSIA

OTTOMAN
EMPIRE   SAFAVID
PERSIA

CHINA

MUGHAL
EMPIRE

PHILIPPINES

while they interacted with the network and with each other. We shall examine these issues in two ways: first by examining some of the more universal themes visible in the global system created by the intersection of hierarchies and the global network; and then by looking at important regional patterns of trans-hierarchy relations.

———— ✳ ————

Global Systems

We should remember that Late Agrarian hierarchies, like their predecessors throughout the Agrarian Era and like the global network examined in the last chapter, were shaped by the fundamental constraints of low productivity and slow communications. It was these two constraints that virtually forced hierarchies into the pyramidal shape illustrated by our model. Except in unusual circumstances (mostly involving small hierarchies with unusually strong network connections), only a sociopolitical structure that was hierarchical, coercive, and managed by a single decision maker supported by a small elite could keep a complex Agrarian society functioning as a single coherent entity. Hierarchies had to manage potential tensions between the formal state and its society, between the hierarchy and the network, and among different hierarchies. Mostly, communications were far too slow and most people were far too poor for anything like a mass democracy to work under Agrarian Era conditions. Monarchy thus predominated to such a degree that it was taken as the "natural" form of political organization throughout most of the world. But the very success of monarchy in appearing natural points to the central role of cultural mechanisms in allowing hierarchies to meet the challenges they faced.

States and Societies

The norm among Agrarian hierarchies was a close congruence between the formal mechanisms of state power and the informal mechanisms of social power, whether exercised top-down as class power or front-to-back as gender power. Inadequate state resources, a result of low productivity, meant that social elites usually had to assume de facto administrative functions in their local communities, often without pay. This general situation posed two consistent challenges to Agrarian rulers, one each above and below the Great Cultural Divide that separated elites from the masses.

The first challenge was "elite building," or creating a unified elite that was loyal to the ruler. In practice, this turned out almost always to be the first and most important job of the hierarchy's unitary leader (king, emperor, sultan, or whatever the title). Only with a loyal, unified elite could a ruler hope to exercise whatever control he had over his realm. By the Late Agrarian Era, mechanisms for creating loyalty were sophisticated and often of great cultural age and usually involved some combination of divine right and heredity. The rules and abstractness of this combination varied. In China, a sitting emperor was the Son of Heaven, but the concept of the Mandate of Heaven allowed for overthrowing bad rulers, as when the Manchus conquered the Ming, founding the Qing Dynasty. This located legitimacy in the imperial system more than in a particular bloodline. In Japan, on the other hand, the sanctity of the imperial family remained unquestioned, but the potential for incompetence was buffered by making the emperor a figurehead whose presence legitimized the government of the Tokugawa shoguns. The Ottomans also confined hereditary right to a single family, but had no rules within that constraint, which led to periodic fratricidal competition among the sultan's sons. By contrast, primogeniture dominated European dynasties because of the legalistic attention to rights in a way that was typical of the western European cultural frame in general.

Mechanisms for creating and maintaining elite unity were always less effective, given the small size of the upper elite class, the personal nature of politics, and the scale of the rewards at stake. Factionalism therefore remained the chief political problem rulers faced, whether the factions were personal or more abstractly based. The Ming emperor Wanli (r. 1572–1620) grew so tired of mediating squabbles among his scholar-bureaucrats that in the last two decades of his reign he virtually withdrew from governance, preferring the private pleasures of the palace, thus contributing to the decline of the dynasty.

The second challenge for states in ruling their societies was to tie the state and its elites firmly to the mass of society across the Great Cultural Divide. Technologies of social control in the form of ideologies—essentially cultural screen images, which with luck and persistence might become cultural frame values—were essential in bridging this divide. Religion and royal imagery remained the chief tools that rulers deployed for this task. Jahangir's chain of justice and his role as "the safeguard of the world; the sovereign splendor of the faith, [and] son of the imperial Akbar" sum up these tools neatly. The chief threat to this top-bottom tie was the pervasive and deeply rooted localism of the Agrarian world, which directed people's loyalties first to family, village, guild, or region rather than to the monarch. Internal geographic frontiers that led to major differences in subsistence, as between farmers and herders or between villagers and forest hunters in India, could exacerbate this threat. Finally, given the central role that religion continued to play in constructing peoples' cultural frames around the world, religious pluralism could be a significant threat. Late Agrarian societies faced this problem across religious frontiers, as the Muslim Mughals discovered in ruling Hindu India. They also faced it within the salvation religions that by now were well-rooted, whether in Sunni-Shi 'a conflict within Islamic polities or Catholic-Protestant divisions in post-Reformation European states (see Chapter 17).

FIGURE 16.1 Screen Image of Legitimacy. The Qianlong Emperor (r. 1735–1795), fourth emperor of the Manchu Qing Dynasty in China.

The widespread Late Agrarian creation of vast empires, especially maritime empires whose component parts were non-contiguous, made such challenges even more complex, as we noted in the last chapter. The larger an empire, the less likely were elites and common people to share a common cultural frame that could replace coercion in maintaining imperial unity. And such replacement was necessary, because no state had the resources to rely on coercion alone.

The State-Society Connection: Examples

China, in addition to being the center of gravity of the global network in the Late Agrarian Era, as we saw in the previous chapter, was also successful in creating a stable sociopolitical structure. The legitimacy of the imperial state as a whole went unquestioned, even if particular rulers or dynasties proved unworthy of the Mandate of Heaven. The pervasiveness of Confucianism as a frame value both in the official state bureaucracy and in society at large provided common ideological ground between state and society, despite the factional disputes among different schools of Confucianism, which grew increasingly disruptive under the later Ming. The formal mechanism for this link was use of the civil service exam system based on the Confucian canon to staff the imperial bureaucracy. Shared Confucian values and access to state service through education allowed the gentry, or important local land-owning class, and the richer merchant class to converge, defusing China's potential merchant dilemma such that rich network connections tended simply to reinforce the extant power structure. (See Figure 16.2.)

The strength of China's state-society connection is demonstrated by the fact that it survived essentially intact, despite takeover by the non-Han Manchus from 1644. There was, to be sure, "anti-foreign" resistance—the new Qing Dynasty was not really secure, especially in the south, for several decades after 1644. But the early Manchu rulers deliberately stressed continuity, including adopting the Ming capital at Beijing as their own (new dynasties had traditionally founded new capitals) and by reappointing most Ming officials. Indeed, the success of the Manchu "conquest" of China was due less to the military efficiency of the Manchu army and its Mongol allies than to the defection of large parts of the Ming army to the Manchu cause. The Ming fell, in effect, because of economic crises brought about by the slowing of silver imports and vast war expenses, made worse by severe factionalism at the Ming court. The Qing picked up the pieces, defeating not only Ming forces but the forces of a serious domestic rebellion based in the south that had sacked Beijing before the Manchus occupied the capital and restored order. Chinese notions of legitimacy allowed the Qing to create a system that combined a Manchu army, the Eight Banners, with a native Chinese army. This Confucian cultural frame also allowed the Manchus to adopt Chinese culture and to set themselves apart in terms of ethnic identity (enforced through mandated clothing and hairstyle differences and through setting aside state positions exclusively for Manchus). The synthesis proved powerful, as Qing China was the world's biggest, richest power through the eighteenth century.

By contrast, the Late Agrarian Islamic world inherited from its predecessors a disjunction between state and society (see Figure 16.3). For a variety of practical and ideological reasons, Islamic states had difficulty establishing their legitimacy

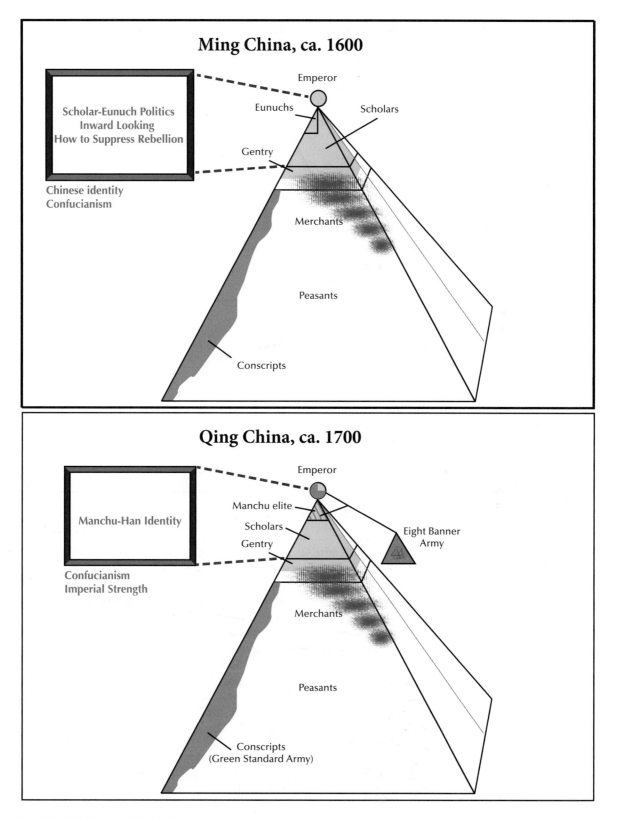

FIGURE 16.2 Ming and Qing China.

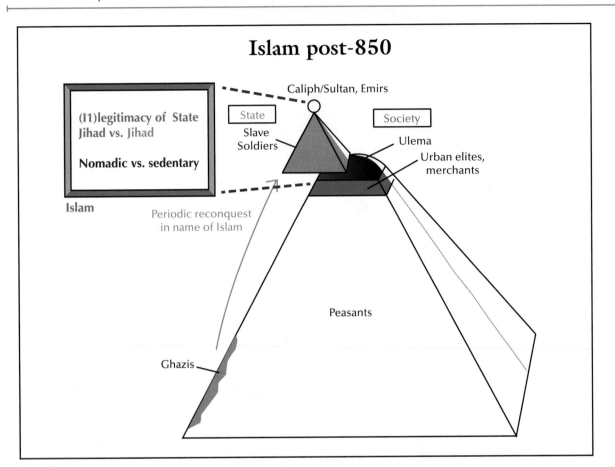

FIGURE 16.3 State-Society Disjunction. The structure of High Agrarian Islamic societies.

in ways that could create active links with society, especially social elites. A passive acceptance of the state by society instead remained the norm. Even when nomadic tribes from the state's own frontiers periodically reconquered the state and its urban heartlands in the name of Islamic purity, state and society remained disconnected.

The result was that Islamic hierarchies tended to resemble conquest societies, with the state defended against its own society by the institution of slave soldiers. The major Islamic powers of the Late Agrarian Era, the Ottoman Empire, Safavid Persia, and the Mughal Empire in India, all developed mechanisms designed to overcome this disjunction, but succeeded only in part and to varying degrees. The Ottomans could claim to be defenders of the (Sunni) faith after their conquest of Mamluk Egypt in 1517 gave them possession of the Holy Cities of Mecca and Medina. The Safavid rulers of Persia, in direct competition with the Ottomans, appealed to Shi 'a ideology to legitimize their rule and set off their realm's identity. The Mughals, minority Islamic rulers of a Hindu country, had the hardest task: policies of religious toleration and limited syncretism bought cooperation but not

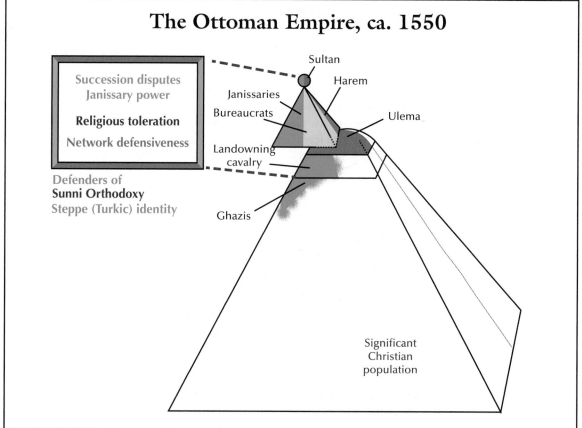

The Ottoman Empire, ca. 1550

Succession disputes
Janissary power

Religious toleration

Network defensiveness

Defenders of
Sunni Orthodoxy
Steppe (Turkic) identity

Sultan

Harem

Janissaries

Bureaucrats

Ulema

Landowning
cavalry

Ghazis

Significant
Christian
population

FIGURE 16.4 Image and Reality. (Top) Screen Image of Legitimacy: Hagia Sophia, Constantinople's greatest Christian church, converted to the central mosque of the Ottoman Empire. (Bottom) The Ottoman hierarchy at the peak of its power and efficiency.

deep loyalty and threatened to alienate their Islamic military forces. All three also managed to link service in their provincial cavalry to landholding and some local administration, creating in limited form something like a service aristocracy. But only for the Ottomans did this develop into a strongly centralized system. (See Figure 16.4.)

Ottoman efforts worked best among those parts of the empire's population whose identity could be constructed as "Turkish"—meaning not just an ethnic-linguistic identity but also one that looked back to the steppes. But by excluding both Arabs and the subject Balkan-Christian population of the empire, this strategy also emphasized the conquest side of Ottoman rule. Such issues arose even more acutely in the colonial empires of the age, where the Spanish ruled indigenous Americans, the Dutch took possession of Indonesian islands, and the British and French established colonies both in North America and on Caribbean sugar islands. As we noted in the previous chapter, such true conquest societies were characterized by serious disjunctions between the cultural frames of the colonizers and those they ruled, exacerbated by the sheer geographic distances separating state (or at least the ultimate central state) from society.

State-society connections were, of course, never static, having to be constantly maintained and revised as states, social structures, and cultural frames all evolved in connection with each other. The growing influence of the global network was central to this evolution, heightening the merchant dilemma. (Remember, merchants were inherently subversive of traditional elite-dominated hierarchies.) The diverging paths of various western European hierarchies are instructive in this respect. Spain, a deeply traditional European hierarchy despite its vast colonial possessions, had a small military and religious elite and a large subject peasantry. Ironically, the American wealth that flowed through Spain created inflation that hurt Spanish manufacturing and trade, as we saw in the previous chapter; this in turn weakened a Spanish merchant class that had never been very strong, muting Spain's potential merchant dilemma and allowing the monarchy to continue to run the empire in traditional state-centered ways.

By contrast, in the less traditional and more merchant-friendly English and Dutch societies (the inventors of the joint-stock companies introduced in Chapter 15), tensions grew between traditional structures of rule and the changing shapes of their societies. In England, under a more traditional monarchy, this produced a military interregnum and then a constitutional reorganization in the mid-seventeenth century, which we will discuss further in Chapter 18. At the opposite extreme from Spain was the small merchant-ruled Republic of Venice. France, between the extremes of Spain and Venice, had both a growing merchant class and a strong traditional elite, the combination that produced the "merchant capitalist tumor" that we have seen as a growing part of western European hierarchies since the 1100s. (See Figure 16.5.)

Still, the global network did not threaten all traditional societies. The Tokugawa Shogunate, established in 1603 at the end of a century of internal division and war, dealt with many of the same military, economic, and social pressures that appeared in northwestern Europe in this period by cutting off its contact with the global network and creating a carefully balanced sociopolitical structure. The shogunate froze

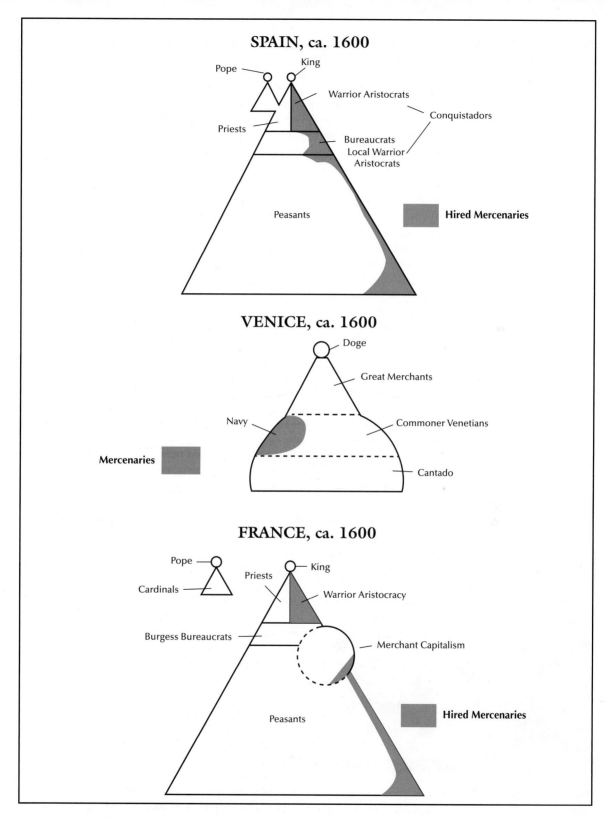

FIGURE 16.5 Varieties of European Hierarchies. (Top) The Spanish hierarchy at the height of its power. (Middle) The Republic of Venice, dominated by merchants. (Bottom) The traditional kingdom of France. The latter shows much more of the "merchant capitalist tumor" in its structure than the Spanish kingdom does at the same time, but far less than Venice.

class divisions and tied social status closely to formal state position, though its internal merchant class continued to develop. The option of cutting off global network connections was neither possible nor even desirable in the competitive multistate environment of Europe, of course. But that's the point: context matters for the sorts of change similar pressures brought to the world's societies, in the Late Agrarian as at any other time.

Hierarchies and the Network

We surveyed the global network in the previous chapter. The various flows of goods, labor, and ideas outlined there provided both resources and challenges to the hierarchies the network connected. Different societies reacted in different ways to their intersection with the network, depending on the cultural frame through which they viewed it.

To begin with, the greater reach and volume of traffic on the global network connected hierarchies, even relatively distant ones, more closely than ever before. Where state-level complex societies met simpler societies, as in much of the Americas or when Russia began to expand into Siberia, the resulting encounters and frontiers tended to be constructed as a meeting of "civilization" and "barbarism" (see discussion later in this chapter and in Chapter 17 for more on the cultural aspect of Late Agrarian encounters of this sort). But contacts between societies at similar state-based levels of organization tended to result in much more equal exchanges of goods, ideas, and formal connections. Again, we shall return to the cultural aspect of such meetings in the next chapter. Here we can note, as an aspect of the maturity and multicentered nature of the Late Agrarian world, that such encounters tended to be perceived as between relative equals. Indeed, even interactions between state-level societies and chiefdoms or less complex societies usually involved more cooperation than lopsided conflict. Against the image created by the initial Spanish conquest of the Americas and isolated episodes of British and Dutch military success in South Asia and Southeast Asia (often exaggerated) may be set the reality of, for example, French cooperation with the Iroquois Confederation, the role of local producers in the Dutch spice trade in the East Indies, and the major role of conflict between various Indian powers and of European-trained Indian soldiers in the expansion of British power in India.

Even more representative at the state-to-state level are the respectful views different states had of each other's political and military arrangements. Ogier de Busbecq, a Belgian diplomat sent by the Austrian Hapsburg court from Vienna to the Ottoman capital at Istanbul, wrote back extolling the meritocracy of the Ottoman administration, although this had as much to do with his own ambitions, frustrated by his semi-outsider status as a Belgian at the Austrian court, as it did with an objective view of Ottoman practice. More concretely, network connections allowed the formation

FIGURE 16.6 Cross-Cultural Networks. Iroquois people with goods obtained from French traders.

of some far-flung alliances. The French monarchy, threatened by Hapsburg lands that surrounded them from both Spain and Austria, periodically allied with the Ottomans against the Austrians, who in turn made alliances with Safavid Persia to occupy the Ottomans. More economically, various Europeans made concerted efforts to learn and bring back (that is, steal) the blue-and-white porcelain manufacturing techniques developed by Ming Chinese craftsmen, whose products dominated the global market from the Islamic world to the British colonies in North America, reproducing the direction of industrial espionage that had earlier spread silk manufacturing from China.

More generally, as we saw in Chapter 15, states reacted to network flows with various regulatory regimes that attempted to limit or harness the most threatening aspects of foreign goods and ideas. The usual response by the great Asian empires was to limit their own merchants' mobility and to let trade come to them through restricted foreign enclaves in specified ports. The extreme version of this was the Closed Country Edict issued by the Tokugawa shogun in 1640 that limited foreign trade to one Dutch ship a year in Nagasaki. Smaller, poorer countries were more likely to have fewer regulations, with the extreme at that end being the state-private partnerships to promote overseas trade developed in northwestern Europe. These efforts resulted in some colonization not of other hierarchies but, effectively, of portions of the network itself. Both the Portuguese and Dutch trade empires in the Indian Ocean and Russian expansion into the fur-producing regions of Siberia exemplify this trend.

States, Other States, and Screen Images

The encounters between different state-level societies resulted in the emergence of elements of an informal set of international standards or understandings that came to characterize Late Agrarian international relations. The mutual intelligibility of these understandings and their similar enactments across much of the world is another sign of the maturity of the Late Agrarian world in political terms. The signs of this international system were linguistic, symbolic, and practical, all constituting a sort of code of screen images that states increasingly projected not just to their own populations but to each other.

Titles and Status

One element of this was a recognized "hierarchy of hierarchies" encoded in the terminology for rulers and diplomatic protocol. Recognizing linguistic differences, it is still possible to see that in the Late Agrarian Era, "emperors" outranked mere "kings." Among emperors, the Chinese and Mughal rulers held pride of place; the Ottoman sultans, Persian shahs, and, by 1700, the Russian czars operated on similar planes.

More ambiguously, the Hapsburg Holy Roman Emperors held a prestigious title, though the office itself was divorced from their real base of power in Austria, while the Hapsburg kings of Spain ruled an actual empire. Though Japan had emperors, they were figureheads, and the status of the shoguns is probably best indicated by the Ashikaga shogun Yoshimitsu, who seems to have contemplated deposing the emperor and seeking recognition from Ming China as king of Japan.

It is perhaps an indication of the disruptive diplomatic dynamics of sixteenth-century Warring States Japan (see discussion later in this chapter), as well as his own search for prestige, that Hideyoshi, the warlord who united the country in the 1580s, invaded Korea in 1592 with the ultimate goal of conquering Ming China. Below kings there existed various princes, chiefs, and other semi-independent rulers of state-level societies. Beyond that was the still-extensive world of village agriculturalists and hunter-gatherers who fell, as always but now more systematically, into the realm of "barbarism."

Mapping and Status

Conquest, colonization, and rulership also came to be symbolically projected through mapping projects that shared remarkable similarities across many of the world's great powers. The great impetus for new mapping projects at the European end of Eurasia was of course the discovery that two entire continents existed that previous maps did not show at all. Inevitably, the efforts to map the "new world" became tied up in different powers' claims to parts of it, a link represented most powerfully in the treaties of Tordesillas (1494) and Zaragoza (1529) that theoretically divided the entire world between Spain and Portugal, though its most important applications were in the Atlantic and the Americas. Global mapping also had roots in the development of navigational charts in the Indian Ocean world since the mid-700s. By the 1500s, even without Portuguese intervention in the Indian Ocean system but reinforced by their arrival, mapping there had taken on aspects of territorial claim-making. By the 1700s, competing Chinese and Russian interests in the Amur River region were staked and demarcated by map as well as treaty.

For imperial powers, geographic mapping was often accompanied by ethnographic mapping of the frontier peoples who came under imperial rule, whether native Americans, Siberians, or peoples in southwestern China. Descriptions and drawings of "exotic" indigenous appearance, both physical and cultural in terms of dress, constructed barbarian inferiority as a step to regulating behavior and imposing political control. A common result was an inversion of the traditional imperial pattern in which the core population was ruled more closely than distant frontier provinces. Now, regulation became tighter on the frontiers than at the core, reflecting the increasingly competitive nature of imperial projects in a more tightly connected world.

Enacting Status

Rulers backed these various symbolic claims to status—the screen images of an international system of competitive relations—with practical moves to bolster their prestige and power. Rising network resources, as well as some population increase made possible by the Columbian exchange, gave rulers some potential to strengthen their position. There were limits. Local political and cultural structures, especially religious divisions, could limit rulers' options. Central governments that overreached their resources, especially if they became engaged in expensive wars, could regress or collapse—a pattern visible from the Ming war against Japan in Korea in the 1590s to the Spanish wars of 1570–1650 to the expansionist wars of the last effective

Mapping Authority

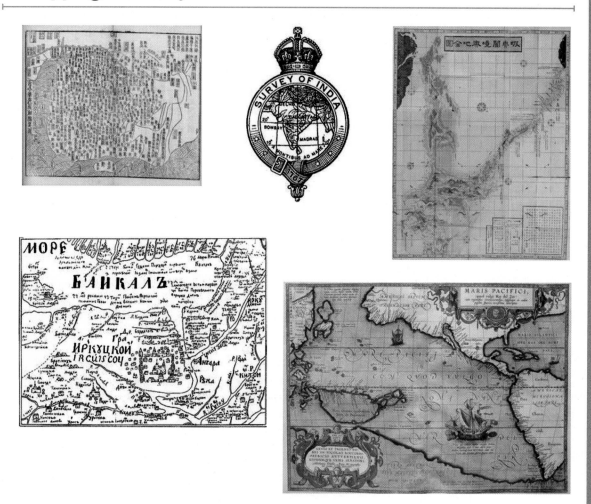

Maps acted as claims of authority over people and places: projected knowledge equals power. (Top row, left to right) A Ming Era map of China carefully labels provinces and places. The British Survey of India, whose seal symbolically wraps India within the ties of the British crown, mapped colonial authority. Tokugawa cartographers surveyed the northern island of Hokkaido, extending the Shogun's claims. (Bottom row, left to right) A Czarist map establishes Russian expansion in Siberia. And Spanish claims to Pacific lands, including the Philippines, are laid out in this section of a 1587 world map.

Mughal emperor, Aurangzeb, in the 1690s. Still, greater centralization of states at the expense of local or regional power was a broad if uneven trend across the Late Agrarian world. Conscious promotion of royal power, as in the seventeenth-century elaboration of the theory of Divine Right of Kings in Europe, legitimized royal moves to exercise greater control over their bureaucracies and to tie the top elites, always vital to the functioning of Agrarian era hierarchies, into state service. Maintenance of expensive and (sometimes) effective artillery trains had both symbolic and practical value in reinforcing royal power. Still, the ultimate effectiveness of such developments should not be exaggerated: the congruence of social and political power created serious limits on centralization and bureaucratization, and the entire process was still constrained, as always, by low productivity and slow communications.

Regional Patterns

In addition to the global trends in hierarchy development just outlined, we may discern several regional patterns of political and military development in the relationships of hierarchies with each other and the network. The three "regions" into which we can divide this survey were the topics, roughly, of Chapters 9 through 11: inner circuit Eurasia, the lands surrounding the central Asian steppes; outer circuit Afro-Eurasia; and the formerly more isolated worlds now linked to the Eurasian core and each other by the increased reach of the global network's maritime connections.

Cavalry, Cannon, and the Closing of the Steppes

Inner circuit Eurasia witnessed perhaps the most significant development of this period, especially viewed from the deep perspective of pre-1500 world history. The long cycle of nomad-sedentary relations that we first outlined in Chapter 3, which dated back to the domestication of horses before 3500 BCE, finally came to a close. Between 1500 and 1750, the nomadic steppe powers of central Asia moved from continued vitality to being effectively contained and subordinated to the sedentary societies that surrounded the steppes. (See Figure 16.7.)

Several long-term factors contributed to the closing of the steppes. Most fundamentally, sedentary societies had steadily increasing advantages in demography and economic productivity that, eventually, the military advantages of the steppe nomadic lifestyle could no longer overcome. Farming societies simply supported more people, as well as gradually learning to use more varied sorts of land, even bringing versions of pastoralism, or the herding of animals that formed the basis of nomadic societies, within the confines of settled towns and fixed markets. The Columbian exchange only increased this advantage. Sedentary economies could also produce more specialized goods and technologies in greater quantities.

One sort of technology in particular proved important in this period. Gunpowder weapons, both cannon and individual firearms, helped offset the advantage in firepower that the compound recurved bow had given steppe armies for several millennia,

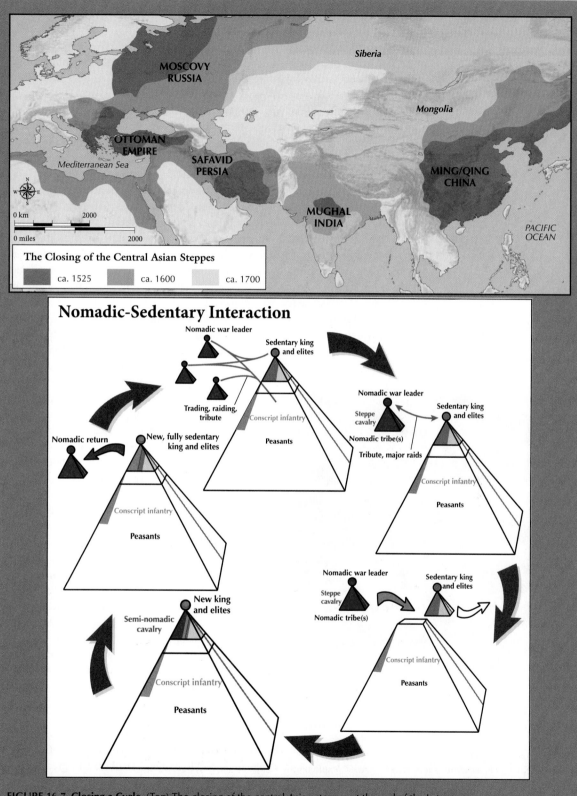

FIGURE 16.7 Closing a Cycle. (Top) The closing of the central Asian steppes at the end of the Late Agrarian Era. (Bottom) The cycle of nomadic-sedentary interaction that ended when the steppes closed.

especially when placed within the fortifications that increasingly surrounded sedentary settlements encroaching into the steppes. Such fortifications also hindered the mobility that was the nomads' other great military advantage.

Although cultural exchange was a central feature of the nomad-sedentary cycle, sedentary societies also developed some advantage in terms of the rootedness and durability of their cultural traditions, reflected in the fact that nomadic political groupings, including the nomadic empires of this period, shifted more and disappeared more quickly than sedentary states did.

But the advantages of sedentary societies and the one-sidedness of the end result should not be exaggerated. Each of the major sedentary states that contributed to the closing of the steppes was in fact a product, especially militarily but also culturally, of a synthesis of steppe and sedentary elements. In particular, each combined the mobility and firepower of steppe-style horse archers with the cannon, fortifications, and often the solid infantry of a sedentary state, creating the age's most powerful and dynamic military systems, which were responsible for taming the steppes. Nor was this always a case of sedentary appropriation of nomadic strength: while Safavid Persia and Muscovite Russia used nomadic-style allies, the rulers of the Ottoman Empire, Mughal India, and Qing China identified themselves as children of the steppes. Thus, from this perspective, the closing of the steppes was not defeat, but suicide by synthesis.

FIGURE 16.8 Screen Image of Ottoman Identity. This gold and jewel-encrusted water container, made in the shape of a traditional steppe canteen, symbolizes perfectly the Ottoman attempt to maintain a steppe nomadic identity while exploiting the resources available to the rulers of a sedentary empire.

The impact of the end of the steppe threat is debatable. It certainly removed a long-standing threat and made sedentary frontiers more secure. It is possible that the closing also shut down an engine of change and innovation for surrounding societies. What effect that had is virtually impossible to measure without reading too much of the future into this period. But the closing of the steppes can be read as another sign of the Late Agrarian era as an age of culminations rather than beginnings (see discussion later in this chapter and in the Issues in Doing World History box in Chapter 15).

The Islamic Big Three: Ottomans, Safavids, and Mughals

On the southern frontier of the steppes lay the Islamic world. The sixteenth century saw that world divided among three major powers: from west to east, the Ottoman Empire, Safavid Persia, and the Mughal Empire. Though they shared structural similarities, they formed a far from unified frontier, as military competition and cultural divides marked their frontiers with each other.

The Ottoman rise to great power status was marked by their conquest of the Byzantine capital at Constantinople in 1453. Renamed Istanbul, the great city resumed its role as the center of an equally great hierarchy.

Ottoman armies gathered there each spring to pursue nearly annual campaigns of conquest and expansion both farther into southeastern Europe—Ottoman armies besieged the Austrian Hapsburg capital Vienna in 1529 and again in 1689—and against both the Safavids and Mamluk Egypt, the latter of which fell to the Ottomans in 1517.

The rural landowning elite who made up the bulk of Ottoman cavalry, still trained in the traditional steppe-archer style of warfare, worked with gunpowder artillery, controlled by the central government, and with the Janissary Corps, slave soldiers taken as boys from the Christian population of the Balkans, who were perhaps the best musket-bearing infantry of the sixteenth century, to create a formidable military machine that synthesized the complementary strengths of steppe cavalry and gunpowder-armed sedentary infantry. Although the Ottomans ended the traditional Turkish practice of dividing the ruler's inheritance among his sons, this led to fratricidal competition among brothers and gave a significant political role to the harem, the wives and concubines of the sultan, who produced his heirs. Finally, the Ottomans inherited from their Byzantine predecessors a significant naval role in the Mediterranean Sea and a corresponding defensive attitude about network connections, expressed in close control of Ottoman merchants and prohibitions on their leaving the empire. This forced foreign trade to come to Istanbul and Turkish merchants into the black market.

Ottoman claims to be defenders of Sunni orthodoxy were deployed especially against their rivals the Safavid Dynasty in Persia, who were aggressively Shi'a. Founded by Shah Ismail I in 1501, the Safavid Dynasty reached its peak under Shah Abbas (r. 1587–1629) and disintegrated in the early 1700s. The Safavids employed cannon and a core of slave infantry alongside provincial cavalry. But unlike the Ottomans, who allied with steppe tribes north of the Black Sea, the Safavids faced a direct steppe threat from the Uzbeks and did not identify themselves as steppe descendants. The Safavid hierarchy was also increasingly less well networked than the Ottomans as global maritime trade grew, which was both reflected in and caused by a much lower level of urbanization in the Safavid heartland. The small Safavid merchant community thus hardly needed the level of regulation the Ottomans devoted to their merchants.

The Mughal Empire in India began in 1526 under Babur, a Persianized descendant of Timur (see Chapter 14) and thus distantly of Chingiz Khan—"Mughal" derives from "Mongol." But its rapid expansion and strong centralized rule date from the reign of Akbar the Great (r. 1556–1605), father of Jahangir. During its height it was huge, well-networked, and prosperous for its elites and merchants, producing the world's finest cotton cloth, among other products. Mughal culture featured a magnificent synthesis of Persian and Indian artistic,

FIGURE 16.9 Screen Image of Mughal Identity. The Taj Mahal, epitome of the Persian-influenced architectural style of the Mughal court.

literary, and even linguistic styles. It could deploy both an effective core army of steppe-style horse archers supported by artillery and slave infantry, as well as a vast ceremonial army useful in maintaining the allegiance of distant provinces. But the empire and its religious divisions overlay a vast and varied subcontinental geography that had historically made political unity difficult to maintain. The Empire began to disintegrate after the death of Jahangir's grandson Aurangzeb in 1707.

China and the Steppes

By 1500 the strategic and cultural outlook of the Ming Dynasty in China had turned defensive, especially against the Mongols, who had captured a Ming emperor in 1449. This cemented the end of China's active role on the maritime network, and the state turned to regulation of trade in designated ports. Ming rule, in serious decline after 1600 for reasons noted earlier, ended when regional revolts turned into civil war that invited intervention by the rising Manchu power to the north.

The new Qing Dynasty was thus born with a synthetic military system that combined steppe nomadic cavalry forces with the vast Chinese army of gunpowder-armed infantry and artillery. The combination of this flexible military force and skillful diplomacy effectively ended the Mongol threat to China once and for all, contributing directly to the closing of the steppes. As a result, Chinese power and prestige, as well as the territorial extent of the empire, were at their historical height throughout the eighteenth century.

The Expansion of Russia

Chinese expansion north and west into former steppe territory met an equally impressive Russian expansion eastward across Siberia, as the imperial czarist state occupied the source of a lucrative fur trade as well as timber and other forest products. This expansion encountered mostly tribal peoples without horses, but from the mid-1400s, when Ivan III ("the Great") and his son Ivan IV ("the Terrible") defeated the declining Golden Horde and freed Russia from Mongol rule, Russia had also expanded southeastward toward Ottoman territory, defeating and annexing several nomadic Kazar khanates and effectively sealing off the western end of the steppes. Again, as with the great Islamic powers and Qing China, Russian success on the steppes owed a good deal to a combination of centrally raised gunpowder infantry and artillery, based in fortifications, with steppe-style cavalry, in this case the Cossacks.

The Russian achievement in building what became territorially the largest state in Asia is even more impressive given that it was involved in nearly constant warfare with European powers, especially Poland-Lithuania and later Sweden, at the same time. War with the latter in 1700 prompted the czar, Peter the Great, to reform the Russian army along western European lines. Though, like Safavid Persia, Russia's network connections, cities, and merchant class were underdeveloped, in an age of slow technological change in the military sphere, Peter's reforms laid the foundation for a century and a half of Russian status as perhaps the great continental power in Europe. Russia's reach regularly extended into Germany, Sweden, and Austria and, in 1814–1815, as far as Paris, while at the same time projecting power into the Ottoman Balkans and maintaining a stable frontier with China along the Amur

River. Politically and militarily, if perhaps not economically, Russia was one of the top three or four powers of the Late Agrarian Era.

Warring States

Peter's reforms and Russian involvement in European wars connect it to one of the three regions that can be characterized as "warring states" in the Late Agrarian. In all three—Europe (especially western Europe), Japan (for a time), and the African Sahel—intense military and political competition was both caused by and stimulated significant social changes. The results were quite different in each region, but similar processes were at work.

Europe

Europe had been divided into numerous small polities, often at war with each other, since the breakup of the Carolingian Empire in the 800s (see Chapter 10), but at some level had maintained a vague ideal of imperial unity inspired by memories of the Roman past. It was this abstract ideal that made the Holy Roman Emperor the most prestigious (though not always the most effective) ruler in Europe. But when a set of marriage alliances made one man heir to all of Spain and its burgeoning American empire in 1516, the Burgundian realm that included the Low Countries since 1506, and Hapsburg Austria and the title of Holy Roman Emperor in 1519, suddenly the ideal came far closer to reality than it had since Charlemagne in the combined inheritances of Emperor Charles V (Charles I of Spain). And this proved a threat rather than an ideal for the other well-established independent states of Europe. At the same time, in 1517, Martin Luther initiated what would become the Protestant Reformation (see more in Chapter 17), dividing Europe religiously both between and within countries. The threat of Hapsburg hegemony plus competing religious ideologies brought subcultural viciousness and the intensity of fights for survival to European warfare, especially in the century 1550–1650. Though the religious element then cooled off somewhat after 1650, as both Catholics and Protestants realized that neither could eliminate the other, the threat of hegemony remained, now in the shape of Louis XIV's France, and large-scale wars continued into the eighteenth century. (See Figure 16.10.)

Unending military competition took place within and reacted with the structural variety and the legal-contractual-military cultural frame of European societies to stimulate social changes already under way. We have noted earlier in this chapter and in Chapter 14 the subversive effect of merchant capitalism on the internal workings of European hierarchies, as network and merchant values increasingly competed with the hierarchy-centered values of traditional warrior and priestly elites. We will return to these themes in detail in Chapter 18. Here, we may note that life-or-death military competition gave more room for and stimulated the spread of merchant capitalist values and practices. Competition for colonies increased because of the resources that overseas holdings could provide to warring states. States raised armies by contracting with private entrepreneurs for mercenary units. They bought weapons, especially cannon and handguns, from private manufacturers who competed in terms of quality, leading to steady incremental improvements in military technology. All of this steadily shifted battlefield dominance from

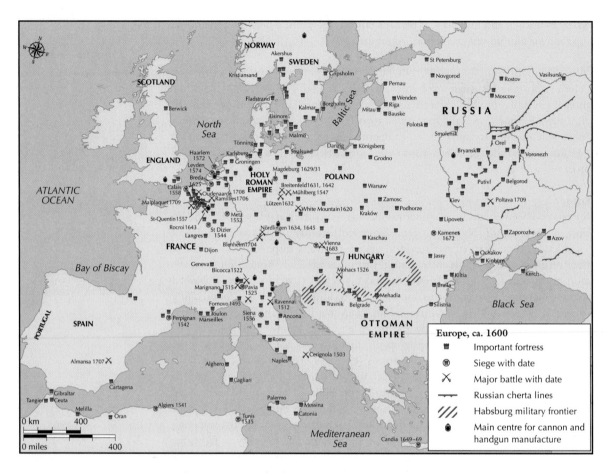

FIGURE 16.10 Warring States Europe, ca. 1600.

noble horsemen toward lower-class infantry forces, with aristocrats assuming the role of officers—part of a larger trend toward social mobility (at least for men; see Chapter 18).

War, however, was very expensive, and rulers sometimes resorted to ad hoc means of financing their wars that could undermine long-term central authority. It was the states that took advantage of periods of peace to reform and centralize their bureaucracies and develop better means of raising money that gained an advantage in the next round of wars—the consolidation of French royal power in the 1660s being the leading and in many ways trend-setting example. But the impact of increasing state power and the military efficiency of European armies should not be exaggerated: in many ways, "warring states" Europe was simply catching up with the great Asian powers (see the Issues in Doing World History box in this chapter), and indeed many of the military-political changes in Europe between 1500 and 1700 resemble the transformations in Warring States China between 450 BCE and 220 BCE (see Chapter 5). What is centrally important is that previously established social structures and cultural frames not only allowed these developments, but guided political and military development along paths that increasingly emphasized the network connections of European hierarchies and the cultural influence those connections exercised.

Japan

As in Europe, Japan's "warring states" period—the *sengoku jidai,* literally "age of the country at war"—began with the dissolution of a previous unity. But whereas European unity had been a distant ideal that turned threatening when it came closer to reality, the Ashikaga Shogunate that had ruled Japan nominally since 1333 and effectively since the reunification of the imperial line in 1392 really did disintegrate. In the Onin War (1467–1477), the leading military governors, who all lived in the capital at Kyoto where the shoguns also resided, fell into civil war and virtually destroyed each other and the shogunate, though figurehead shoguns would hold the office until 1573. In place of a single

FIGURE 16.11 Infantry Rising. Dutch pikemen shown in a drill book of the sort used to train masses of lower class infantry.

government over the whole of Japan, the many local warlords, or *daimyo,* who had been subordinate to the military governors began to create their own daimyo domains—effectively small, independent states. These then went to war with each

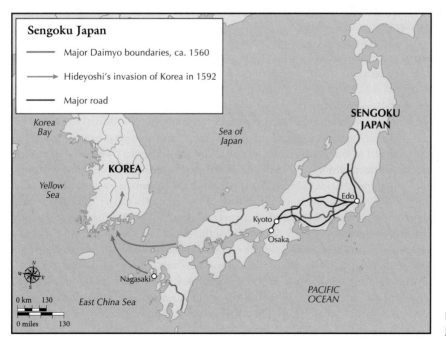

FIGURE 16.12 Warring States Japan, ca. 1590.

FIGURE 16.13 More Infantry Rising. Japanese *ashigaru* (lower class soldiers) wielding muskets. Social mobility facilitated by military service marked the "warring states" hierarchies of both Europe and Japan at this time.

other, and although the wars of sixteenth-century Japan lacked the religious-ideological fervor of Europe's contemporary wars, they were no less intense in being fought for the survival of each domain and its ruling family. (See Figure 16.12.)

The results of this warfare bear striking resemblances to European developments. Japan's network connections had expanded considerably under the control of the Ashikaga shoguns before the Onin War. Now, many daimyo sought to establish market towns at the centers of their domains as a way of fostering trade and so collecting network-based resources to support their wars. They centralized their administrations and took censuses to better exploit their fiscal and human resources. They then used their resources and administrative powers to create armies of massed infantry armed with bows and spears, shifting battlefield usefulness away from the horse-riding elites who had dominated it before—part of a larger social trend toward social mobility, at least for men. As a result, when Portuguese ships opened trade with Japan in 1542, some daimyo could adopt muskets into their infantry forces readily. Indeed, Japanese smiths quickly mastered the art of manufacturing their own muskets, often of higher quality than European imports. By the 1590s, Japanese armies were effective enough to fight the Koreans and their Ming allies in Korea.

As those unified Japanese armies indicate, however, the outcome of Japan's "warring states" era was ultimately quite different from Europe's. Japan was much smaller than all of Europe, and maintained an ideal of political unity throughout the warring states era—a unity possible to envision because of the lack of sectarian ideology that infused Europe's wars and because the emperor still existed as a symbol of unity. From about 1570, a series of three leaders progressively united all the daimyo domains into a centrally dominated federation. The second, Toyotomi Hideyoshi, was the one who invaded Korea, but it was the third, Tokugawa Ieyasu, who ultimately succeeded in creating a new shogunate based at Edo (modern Tokyo) in 1614.

With each stage of unification, the stimulus of war on social change, state development, and military innovation lessened, and Japan's leaders were able to reassert traditional hierarchy values. Hideyoshi initiated "sword hunts" designed to disarm the civilian population. Under Tokugawa rule, social mobility was frozen as peasants, merchants, and warriors (samurai) became hereditary classes, and the political structure was arranged to maintain a finely balanced stasis. In order to prevent outside ideas, goods, or people from disrupting this delicate balance, the third Tokugawa shogun outlawed Christianity, which had accompanied Western trade into Japan in the 1500s, and in 1640 issued the Closed Country Edict, which shut off all of Japan's external network connections, except for one Dutch ship a year allowed into Nagasaki harbor—no foreigners could enter, no Japanese could leave. And he shut down Japan's domestic gun industry. A newly invented Cult of the Sword came to be the screen image of samurai status, while in practice most samurai became administrators.

Stasis was of course impossible to achieve. The continued development of Japan's internal network worked slow changes within the constraints of the Tokugawa structure until Japan had to face industrially based European imperialism in 1853. We shall pick up that story in Chapter 22.

West Africa

The third "warring states" region of the Late Agrarian Era was in West Africa. Here, too, the collapse of imperial unity triggered fragmentation and military competition. The dominant power in the region since the mid-1400s had been the Songhai Empire, which had succeeded the Empire of Mali when the latter declined. Through the 1500s Songhai flourished, as its predecessors had done, by controlling the southern end of the trans-Saharan trade routes. But a succession crisis and civil war starting in 1582 led to an invasion by the Islamic rulers of Morocco in 1591.

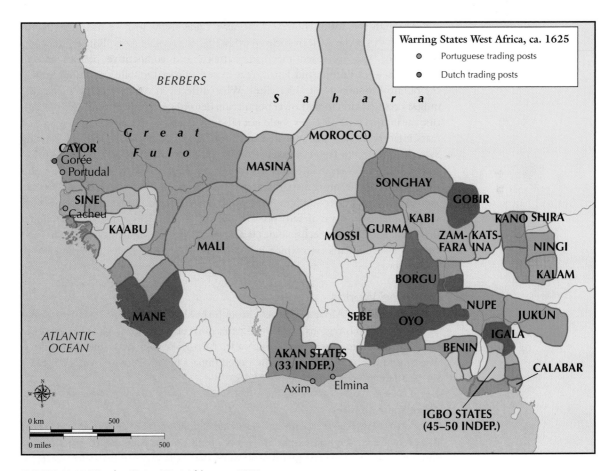

FIGURE 16.14 Warring States West Africa, ca. 1625.

The Moroccans routed the Songhai army, sacked many of the major cities of the empire, including Timbuktu, one of the great trade and university cities in the world at the time, but were unable to impose their own rule. The region fragmented and warfare among the numerous successor states intensified. (See Figure 16.14.)

The Portuguese opening of maritime trade routes along the West African coast undermined the prosperity of the trans-Saharan caravan trade, removing one of the tools for state-building in the region. In addition, maritime trade with Europe gradually developed a focus on the slave trade that began to supply agricultural labor for European colonies in the Caribbean and the Americas. This worked to stimulate further warfare, as, in a pattern that extended well back in African history, one of the outcomes of African warfare was the taking of slaves. West African agriculture supported a less dense population than in some of the most populous Eurasian centers. In our usual pattern, chronic labor shortages led to lower labor freedom, here in the form of widespread slavery. But it is important to note that slavery within Africa was usually both domestically (or household) oriented, and that slaves became incorporated into the society that captured them. The new slave trade instead removed people from functioning societies.

Through the 1600s, however, the slave trade seems to have had little demographic effect on the African societies whose labor was sold away. Rather, the combination of war, increased merchant activity, and competitive politics created conditions, as in Europe and Japan, that increased social mobility and undermined the political monopoly of older elites. What differed in Africa was the shape that military competition took. Lower population densities and less concentrated agriculture meant that African states could not raise and maintain the sort of densely packed mass infantry armies that appeared in Europe and Japan (and, indeed, in Warring States China). As in Japan, muskets from Europe became incorporated into African ways of war—muskets in fact constituted one of the main items traded for slaves. But instead of being fit into a mass-infantry system, as in Europe and Japan, muskets in West Africa and farther south in Angola and Kongo were adapted to the open-order skirmishing style of war already prevalent in the region. This is a striking reminder that the impact of new technologies is always crucially dependent on the social and cultural environments into which it is introduced (see the Issues in Doing World History box).

Maritime Worlds

The connection of African societies through the slave trade to the Americas brings us to the last of our regions, the formerly marginal or isolated worlds of the Agrarian Era, now linked to inner Eurasia and outer Afro-Eurasia by maritime connections. The central theme here is simply the varied impact of new network connections on these different worlds. (See Figure 16.15.)

Asian Trade Empires

The Portuguese, whose captain Vasco da Gama pioneered the route around Africa to Asia, established the first empire of this era built not on conquest of other hierarchies, but on maritime connections between Portuguese-controlled ports scattered around the edges of the Indian Ocean. Usually though not always established with

---

ISSUES IN DOING WORLD HISTORY

The "Military Revolution"

One of the most significant historiographical concepts of the last twenty years in Late Agrarian ("early modern") history has been the idea that there was a "military revolution" in western Europe that laid the foundations for modern European states and European imperial dominance in the world. While the debate about the so-called military revolution has been very productive in scholarly terms, the view of this book is that the military revolution thesis itself is fundamentally wrong in a number of ways.

Briefly, the thesis states that the introduction of handguns (or, in a variant version, cannon) into European warfare led inexorably to the need for larger armies, either because of the linear tactics that handguns demanded or the larger sieges that cannon created. Larger armies necessitated better run states to create and support them (the foundations of the "modern state"), and the new, improved gunpowder armies Europe created in this period gave Europe a significant military advantage and allowed European powers to begin building massive colonial empires.

The comparative context provided by our other "warring states" regions exposes some of the problems with this thesis. As African warfare shows, nothing about muskets demands either linear tactics or larger armies. Even when mass armies appeared, as in Japan, mass preceded the adoption of firearms, indicating that social and administrative changes preceded new technology, calling the direction of causation in the thesis into question. Japan, where cannon and sieges played relatively little role in military transformation, also calls the role of cannon into question.

Finally, the supposed results of the "revolution" are open to question. As we noted above, European states, especially up to 1700, were basically playing catch-up with states in many other parts of the world, and there is no evidence that European armies before 1700 had any advantage over armies elsewhere in Afro-Eurasia, at least, while the Spanish conquest of the Americas depended much on swords and horses, used across Eurasia, and little on firearms. Even the better trained and more reliable European armies of the eighteenth century had few decisive advantages over their non-European foes, and had very limited reach in the world. There was, arguably, an eighteenth-century military revolution in naval warfare (see Chapter 18), but European imperial dominance in the nineteenth century was the result not of an "early modern military revolution," but of a far more fundamental revolution in humans' relationship to their environment, the emergence of industrialization.

---

the cooperation of the major local hierarchy, ports such as Goa on the west coast of India were protected by fortifications, cannon, and careful diplomacy. Portuguese holdings stretched from the east coast of Africa to India and into the spice islands of the Malaysian archipelago, and Portuguese trade connections stretched from these bases to China and Japan. In effect, as we have noted already, the Portuguese colonized the network itself.

The problem Portugal faced in maintaining this far-flung web of outposts was that Portugal itself was relatively poor and under-populated. Finding the resources, especially the manpower, to protect all its vital ports was therefore a constant problem, even with the employment of local troops under Portuguese command. The problem became critical when the kingdom's ruling line died out in 1580. Philip II, Hapsburg king of Spain, claimed the throne and until 1640 (when a revolt secured

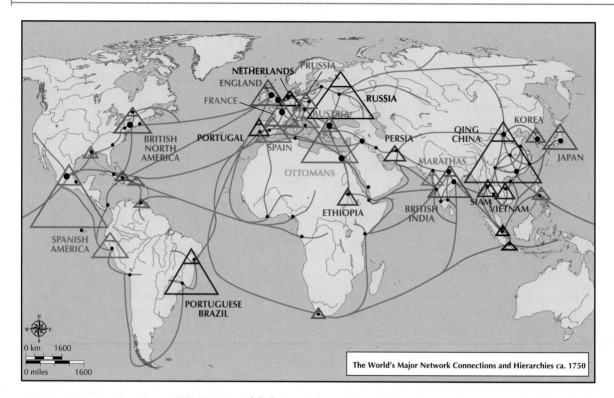

FIGURE 16.15 **Global Intersections.** The world's major network connections and hierarchies, ca. 1750. Note the significant development since 1500.

renewed independence) the two kingdoms were united. But all this brought Portugal was second-rate status in the union and the hostility of the Netherlands, who were fighting for their own independence from the Spanish.

As a result, the Dutch built their own empire of trade ports in part by taking Portuguese outposts in a war that lasted from 1595 to 1663. The Netherlands, with a much larger population and far greater naval resources than Portugal, added possessions in North and South America to their Indian Ocean holdings, which were run by the VOC, the Dutch East India Company, one of the leading joint-stock companies of the age.

The Dutch already dominated the coastal carrying trade of much of northwestern Europe, so when they established themselves in the Indian Ocean, they not only took over the Portuguese fortified port system, they aggressively worked for a substantial share of the coastal carrying trade in Asia. This helped fund their imports of Asian goods, since like all European trading powers their trade in goods with Asia was in the red with the deficit paid in silver and gold (themselves also

FIGURE 16.16 **Maritime Outpost.** Dutch coffee plantation in Indonesia. Dutch colonization of the network led to attempts to control sources of supply.

commodities, of course). The Dutch also made much greater use of local allies and ended up conquering and ruling substantial centers of spice production in Indonesia and the Malaysian islands so as to guarantee access to supplies at favorable prices.

American Worlds

It was not so much Columbus's discoveries that made the Americas the New World—the continents and their societies had been there all along, after all—as it was the various patterns of European settlement on the continents. For here, new social worlds really did emerge.

Spanish (and Portuguese) America made a remarkably rapid (though incomplete) transition from being a conquest society to becoming a naturalized hierarchy. This attests in part to Spanish success at assuming the mantle of legitimacy from their Aztec and Inca predecessors and at using native mechanisms of rule, for instance the *mita* labor system discussed in Chapter 15, to exercise authority. It also signifies the level of syncretism that emerged between Spanish Catholicism and indigenous beliefs, though this too remained incomplete (see more in Chapter 17). But it also arose of necessity: Spanish administrators were so thin on the ground in the vast American Empire that formal rule by the state could not possibly have succeeded. Spanish settlement and rule depended, therefore, on the exercise of informal social power by elites, both European and, at a lower level, indigenous. Thus, as in pre-Columbian hierarchies and in Agrarian Era hierarchies everywhere, the sociopolitical pyramid was constructed from a tight congruence between social structure and what passed for state authority. The Spanish crown cultivated the allegiance of American elites, under a thin layer of direct Spanish administration, by projecting the presence of the distant king artistically (especially by displaying portraits) and architecturally in the major cities of the empire, a process completely analogous to Jahangir's chain of justice.

The characteristic difference between Latin American hierarchies and those in most other places was that the transition from elite to commoner went through a fine gradation of ranks tightly tied to skin color and whose boundaries were very fuzzy, despite ethnographic attempts to define and depict in paintings the various racial mixes that emerged. This racial gradation, or system of *castas*, ran from European-born whites, mostly temporary administrators, to the creoles, or American-born Europeans who came to dominate colonial society because they owned most of the land, and then down through native populations (with their former elite-commoner divisions carrying over into the new dispensation) to Africans, both free and slave. Because there was a serious shortage of European women at the top—both temporary administrators and emigrants tended to be predominantly male—mixing occurred mostly as European males married noble native women and native men married African women, leaving African males, especially slaves, at the bottom. The other remarkable aspect of Latin American hierarchies was the severe shortage, by global standards, of formal military power they contained. (See Figure 16.17.)

By contrast with Latin America, European colonies before 1700 in North America were small and poor. Dutch holdings were tiny and fragmented, and French territory was vast on paper but had a serious paucity of settlers. The set of British colonies along the Atlantic seaboard were growing faster than either, but were as yet

PRINCIPLES AND PATTERNS

The traditional Agrarian pyramid usually shows the congruence of formal state power and informal social power (see Islamic hierarchies for an exception).

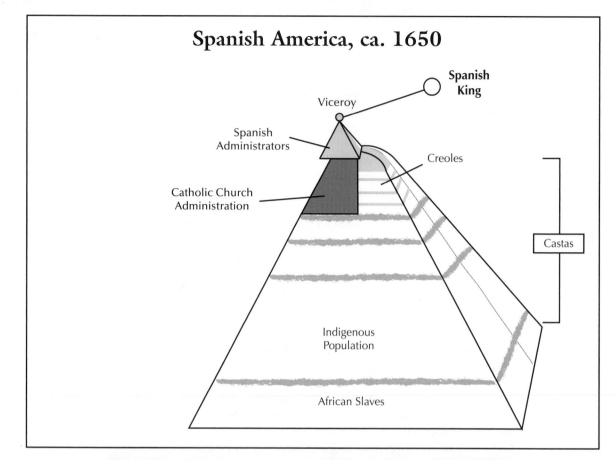

Spanish America, ca. 1650

Spanish King

Viceroy

Spanish Administrators

Catholic Church Administration

Creoles

Castas

Indigenous Population

African Slaves

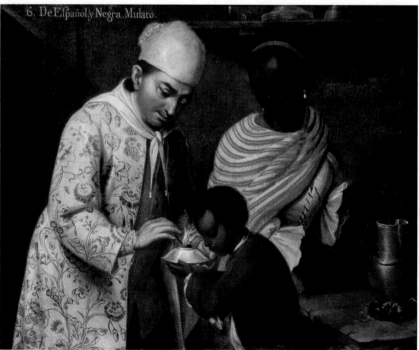

6. De Eſpañol y Negra. Mulato.

FIGURE 16.17 Racial Hierarchy. (Top) Spanish American hierarchies. (Bottom) A *casta* painting showing that a Spanish male and an African female produce a mulatto, one of the many mixes from which Latin American social hierarchies were constructed.

themselves fragmented and somewhat peripheral to British interests. We may note three things about them that we will return to in more detail in the next two chapters.

First, the colonies divided between those north of Virginia and those from Virginia south in terms of social structure. The plantation-based agricultural economies of the South began to create something like a traditional pyramid, with elite landowners on top and incompletely free labor, both European indentured workers and African slaves, beneath. The more northern colonies, peopled more by the migration of entire communities, often for religious reasons, can mostly be characterized as fragment societies, which we have seen before possibly in ancient Crete and certainly in medieval Iceland (see Chapters 3 and 11). This produced more egalitarian societies with some suspicion of strong centralized leadership.

In both North and South, the British colonies differed sharply from Latin American ones in creating sharply constructed racial divides, with almost no intermarriage. Mixed race offspring of coercive relationships with African slaves were viewed by Europeans as being of full African descent, and the divides applied equally to the indigenous populations. We shall return to the cultural aspects of this system in the next chapter.

Finally, whereas Spanish and Portuguese colonies emerged within a cultural frame that had come to emphasize royal power, British colonies were born within the legal-contractual framework of northwestern European (and specifically British) culture and the partnership between state and private interests that this had created. This was reflected in the founding documents of the colonies, which varied from private contracts among the settlers, such as the Mayflower Compact, to royal charters, to colonies run by joint-stock companies. This, as well as British parliamentary tradition, resulted in representative assemblies becoming a standard part of colonial governance. It also created a more formalized, legalistic, and somewhat distanced connection between state and society than was the global norm, with results we shall pursue further in Chapter 18.

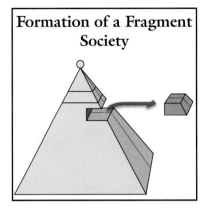

Formation of a Fragment Society

FIGURE 16.18 **Formation of a Fragment Society.**

Systemic Maturity

Our surveys of common trends and regional patterns allow us to reconsider the shape of the Late Agrarian world from the perspective of networked hierarchies. This perspective reinforces the argument that this was a period of systemic maturity—a culmination of the Agrarian Era—more than an "early modern" age (see Issues in Doing World History box in Chapter 15), in several ways.

For starters, the universal constraints of low productivity and slow communications still held everywhere. Manufacturing and transport were undoubtedly more efficient than they had been in the Age of Empires (200 BCE to 200 CE), but still depended on power generated by wind, water, and muscle. As a result, no hierarchy or region dominated politically: this was a polycentric system with low gradients of differential power and wealth. The wealthiest regions of the world were no more than about twice as rich per capita, roughly, as the global average, and differences in political effectiveness were likewise limited. A comparison to the vast differentials visible in the Age of Empires or in the nineteenth century—both near the beginning of a new era before new ways had diffused widely—is instructive.

States themselves looked mature. They were mostly monarchies, as they had been throughout the Agrarian, but had reached new levels of bureaucratization and effectiveness of their technologies of social control. And they treated each other, for the most part, roughly as equals, and understood each other. This was clearly a mature world, not an early one.

Conclusion

Our surveys of the Late Agrarian Era from the perspectives of networks and hierarchies have referred frequently to the vital role of cultural frames and screens in mediating the relationship of network to hierarchies, hierarchies to each other, and states to societies within hierarchies. In the next chapter, we look at the Late Agrarian Era explicitly from the perspective of this third aspect of our basic model, cultural frames and screens.

FRAME IT YOURSELF

Frame Your World

This chapter (like Chapter 15) argues that the period 1500 to 1800 was Late Agrarian rather than "early modern." This chapter is also about states and their relationships to societies. Think about the political structures and issues you've read about in this chapter: Who ruled? What rights did people have? How was power distributed? List the differences and the similarities between the hierarchies described in this chapter and the society you live in today. Are the similarities or the differences more striking?

Further Reading

Jackson, Peter, and Lawrence Lockhart, eds. 1986. *The Cambridge History of Iran.* Volume 6, *The Timurid and Safavid Periods.* Cambridge: Cambridge University Press.

Le Donne, John P. 2003. *The Grand Strategy of the Russian Empire, 1650–1831.* New York: Oxford University Press.

Murphy, Rhoads. 1999. *Ottoman Warfare, 1500–1700.* New Brunswick, NJ: Rutgers University Press.

Parker, Geoffrey. 1988. *The Military Revolution: Military Innovation and the Rise of the West.* Cambridge: Cambridge University Press.

Parrott, David. 2012. *The Business of War: Military Enterprise and the Military Revolution in Early Modern Europe.* Cambridge: Cambridge University Press.

Ricklefs, Merle. 1993. *A History of Modern Indonesia since 1300.* Palo Alto, CA: Stanford University Press.

Rowe, William T. 2009. *China's Last Empire: The Great Qing.* Cambridge, MA: Harvard University Press.

Russell-Wood, A. J. R. 1998. *The Portuguese Empire, 1415–1808.* Baltimore: Johns Hopkins University Press.

Totman, Conrad. 2000. *A History of Japan.* Oxford: Blackwell.

For additional learning and instructional resources related to this chapter, please go to www.oup.com/us/morillo

CHAPTER SEVENTEEN

The Late Agrarian World III: Cultural Frames, Cultural Encounters, 1500 to 1800

Hans Staden among the Tupi.

Introduction

Hans Staden was a Hessian, born sometime in the 1520s near Marburg. Like many in central Europe at that time, he supported himself as a mercenary soldier. In the late 1540s, he found himself in Portugal, seeking work as a ship's gunner. This led him to Pernambuco in Portuguese Brazil, where he stayed from January to October 1548, learning the language of the local Tupi peoples. Returning in 1549, he stayed in the colony but was captured by the Tupinambá tribe of the Tupi. Staden lived for six years among the Tupinambá, taking a Tupi wife and participating in their rituals. Since the Tupi were enemies of the Portuguese, Staden had to convince them he was French—the only other Europeans the Tupi knew of—a task complicated by the presence of another Frenchman among them who for some time refused to confirm Staden's claim.

Eventually, in 1555, he returned to Europe in a French ship. In 1557, he published his *True History and Description of a Country of Wild, Naked, Grim, Man-eating People in the New World, America* about his experiences in South America. Printed first in German and subsequently widely translated, the book told Staden's story in three different ways. The first was a narrative of his experiences, modeled on Christian saints' lives, with Staden in the role of God's servant among the heathens. The second part of the book was an ethnography of the Tupi—an objectively presented description of their customs and practices. Both parts seem to have been dictated by Staden without much further editing. And both were illustrated by woodblock prints, executed either by Staden or under his close direction; these constitute the third, pictorial version of his story. All three depict the Tupi as cannibals, as the title advertises. Staden went to great lengths to present his story as true. In addition to the title, the book received a foreword from a prominent professor of math and medicine, a friend of Staden's father, attesting to the reliability of the author and the veracity of the story itself.

Hans Staden and his *True History* introduce all the key themes for our third look at the Late Agrarian Era, an examination through the lens of the Cognitive-Linguistic Revolution with which human history started and through the third part of our model, the cultural frames and cultural screens that revolution created. Through language and art—through storytelling in different forms—Staden constructed (and periodically reconstructed) identities, both his own (and more broadly of his own culture) and of the Tupi for a European audience. These constructions arose out of a cultural encounter typical of the globalizing world of the Late Agrarian, and contributed to the accumulation of knowledge and expertise that marks the Late Agrarian culturally as a mature age, a maturity we have already explored in the network and hierarchy relations of the period. Knowledge, stories, and identities in turn helped the people of the Late Agrarian make their world meaningful. These processes are the topic of this chapter.

*

Framing the Argument

• The impact of globalized encounters and spreading technologies, especially printing, on how different peoples and societies constructed their identities and made their worlds meaningful

• How such cultural encounters, including religious conflicts and the development of scientific views of the cosmos, contributed to the growing complexity and maturity of the Late Agrarian Era

• How specific cultural encounters involving slavery led to important developments in notions of race that continue to affect our world

FRAMING   The Late Agrarian World III: Cultural Frames, Cultural Encounters, 1500 to 1800

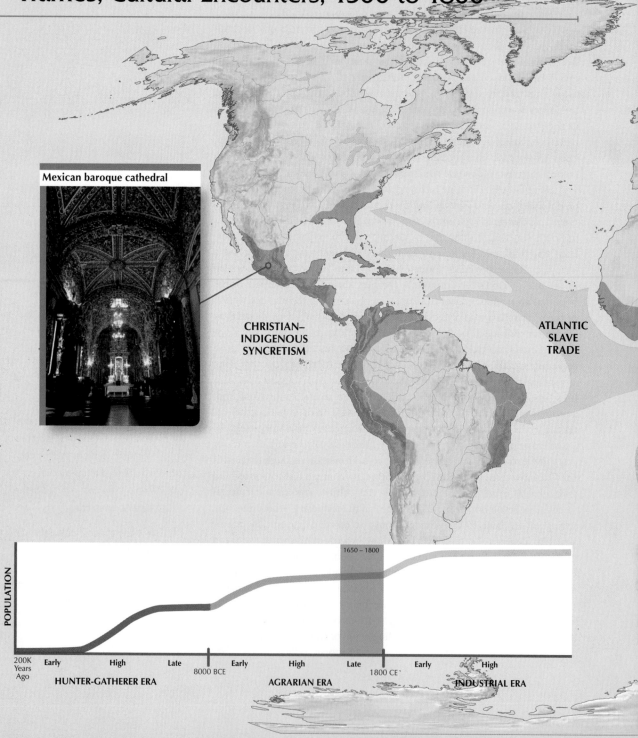

Mexican baroque cathedral

CHRISTIAN–
INDIGENOUS
SYNCRETISM

ATLANTIC
SLAVE
TRADE

POPULATION

1650 – 1800

200K
Years
Ago

Early   High   Late   Early   High   Late   Early   High

8000 BCE   1800 CE

HUNTER-GATHERER ERA   **AGRARIAN ERA**   **INDUSTRIAL ERA**

Mughal mosque

PROTESTANT–
CATHOLIC

SUNNI–SHIA

JESUITS IN
EAST ASIA

MUSLIM–
HINDU

Tokugawa shrine

Ottoman mosque

Cultural Frames and Screens: Themes and Patterns

Cultural frames and screens are our model's metaphorical way of capturing such cultural themes as identity formation. They represent the way in which all humans experience the world through a cognitive filter—not that there is no external "reality," but that all such realities, especially including interactions with other people, must be experienced from a particular perspective. Frames represent the almost unconscious sets of assumptions people in different cultures use to understand the world, while screens represent the public representation of issues ranging from personal identity to political issues.

Constructing Self-Identity

One of the central functions represented by cultural screens is the construction of identity, as Staden's *True History* shows. While each individual could be said to project his or her own screen, the screens of our model, projected by entire cultures, represent the composite identity created by the combination of many individual

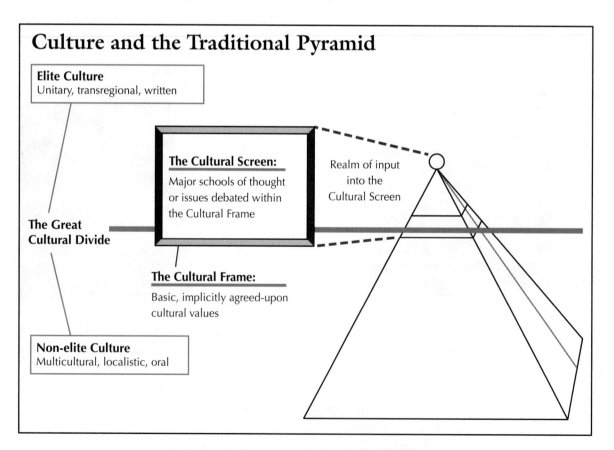

FIGURE 17.1 The Structure of Culture in the Agrarian Era.

screens. This highlights several issues crucial to the historical analysis of identity formation.

Most important, we must ask "which self?" of a society's self-identity. In other words, we must remember that a composite identity does not represent any one person accurately, and that some individuals and groups contribute disproportionately to the composite image of a society. Our model shows this by showing the projection of the screen coming mostly from the elite levels of the social pyramid. Those above the Great Cultural Divide had much larger input than non-elites because their (usually) written mode of cultural production could fix images on the cultural screen more permanently, though not necessarily more pervasively, than oral culture below the Divide, though the spread of the printing press in the era began to affect this dynamic somewhat (see further discussion later in this chapter). This disproportionate impact is undoubtedly even greater in historiography than it was during the life of the society—that is, it is disproportionately elite sources from which we write our histories. In addition to class, the same dynamics apply to gender (the back half of the pyramid, being private, contributed only indirectly to public discourse and thus little to the historical record) and to many of the subcultures often subsumed in a dominant cultural construct (Christian religious minorities in the Ottoman Empire, for example). Such dynamics may be partly represented by competing screen images, but the "right" of a group to project screen images—to speak or otherwise represent themselves publicly—was not automatic.

Thus, only the most pervasive, deeply agreed-upon values move from the screen out to the virtually unspoken, nearly universally agreed-upon realm of a society's cultural frame (and can, when social or cultural conditions change, reemerge as disputed screen issues). Such values often show up, as we have seen throughout this book, in the ways that societies mediated the most basic level of social interactions—Confucianism in Ming China, caste in the Hindu world of Mughal India (though not for the minority of Muslim rulers, marking their regime as a variant of a conquest society), legal-contractual relationships in western Europe.

Encounters

Cultural encounters that resulted from the increasingly pervasive linking of Late Agrarian societies through network connections were one of the main ways in which frame values could be called into question over the long run. In more immediate terms, the cultural encounters of the Late Agrarian Era highlight some patterns common to many such meetings through history.

One is that interpretations of newly encountered societies reflected more about the interpreters than those they interpreted. In other words, Others often acted as mirrors in which those they encountered saw their own hopes and fears rather than real people. The accuracy of

FIGURE 17.2 Scary Screen Images. One of Hans Staden's woodcuts, depicting a cannibalistic feast. Staden himself is at the right, bearded and covered strategically with a fig leaf, with his initials above his head.

Hans Staden's characterization of the Tupi as cannibals is hotly disputed by scholars to this day for just this reason, since cannibalism is one of the more common charges leveled against "savages" but has proven to be true very rarely. Adding to the controversy (and proving the mirror effect), Staden was a Protestant, and many of his Protestant audience read commentary about the Catholic Eucharist into his account of Tupi man-eating. (Another common charge, perhaps reflecting male-explorer fantasy as much as moral condemnation, was that a society held all their women in common.) In another mirror example, we noted in the previous chapter Ogier de Busbecq's portrayal of Ottoman meritocracy as a comment on his own Austrian court. We shall explore European views of the Americas in this light further in this chapter.

It was, of course, possible for observers to see through the mirror and perceive aspects of foreign cultures somewhat accurately. Some perceived differences reflected deep frame differences and real threats, and thus led to condemnation, as in religious differences between Sunni Ottomans and Shi'a Safavids or the Protestant-Catholic split that came to divide Europe after 1519—a case of subcultural encounter and conflict. But some mutual frame perceptions were both accurate and friendly at surprising levels, as in the encounter between Confucian scholars and Jesuit missionaries discussed later in this chapter. More common, however, were reasonably accurate but superficial observations of foreign screen images that could be commodified in travel writing as "curiosities," and genuine borrowings of foreign ideas and technology, although as we saw in the last chapter, items of technology such as guns were usually adopted and interpreted in terms of the recipients' own cultural frame. Much rarer was the response that in some way rose above cultural frames and "meta-framed" an encounter. Michel de Montaigne, a French essayist who commented on Staden's story of the Tupi in his essay "On Cannibals" (1580), reached the conclusion that "one calls 'barbarism' whatever he is not accustomed to."

Emphasis only on "encounters" between peoples with different frames risks underplaying the role of political-military power in such meetings (and indeed of unseen power in the form of disease). Power differentials were important. Cultural diffusion, especially of militarily useful technologies and politically useful cultural technologies of social control, often flowed from the more powerful to the less, as illustrated by the widespread adoption by native Americans of European horses, guns, and steel weapons. Conquest that crossed cultural boundaries, whether overseas by Europeans in the Americas or more traditionally by steppe nomads of adjacent sedentary states, usually produced, at least for a time, "conquest societies." Conquest societies and colonialism in general are marked by a disjunction between the cultural frame of the rulers of a society and the cultural frame(s) of those they ruled. While the usual result of steppe nomadic conquests had been the absorption and acculturation of the conquerors (or their eventual expulsion), resolving the frame disjunction, some elements also blended in a process of syncretism. Syncretism became a dominant feature of the meeting of cultural frames in Spanish America (see discussion later in this chapter).

Making Meaning

Ultimately, cultural frames and screens arose out of the universal human need to make the world meaningful. From this perspective, we can characterize the *content* of Late Agrarian Era processes of encounter, mutual interpretation, and syncretism as attempts to answer the same fundamental questions that had engaged the great thinkers of the Axial Age (Chapter 4): What is the nature of the cosmos? How best to create and maintain social order? How does the individual fit into the cosmos and society, especially in terms of ethical decision making? Indeed, the more pervasive network connections of the Late Agrarian Era echo the rising connectedness and complexity of the Axial Age that stimulated its philosophical and religious speculations. Late Agrarian philosophy and religion were dominated by sophisticated, mature reworkings and elaborations of the traditions established by the synthesis of Axial Age thought and the salvation religions. But it also saw the birth of a new method for attempting to answer these fundamental questions: science, a topic to which we will return at the end of the chapter.

The vast and global encounters of the Late Agrarian also brought to the fore a perhaps even more fundamental question underlying the issues of cosmic and social order and individual ethics: To whom do these questions apply? That is, who counts as human? We touched on an aspect of this question earlier in relation to composite constructions of societal identity. But we may consider it here in its more fundamental form. In almost every Agrarian Era philosophical and religious tradition, the answer, more or less explicit, was that free adult males embodied full humanity. Thus, women did not count as fully human, a view represented by Aristotle's

FIGURE 17.3 Three Strikes? Women, children, and slaves did not count as fully human.

view of embryonic development in which females resulted from the failure of naturally male fetuses to develop properly. Nor did children count. Nor did slaves—and here the Late Agrarian saw significant developments in the theorizing of slavery to which we will return later in the chapter. Whether "barbarians" or "savages," that is, people whose ways "one is not accustomed to," were (or were capable of) becoming fully human led to some serious debates. The most famous and formal was the debate between Bartolomé de Las Casas, a Dominican friar who argued before the Spanish royal court that native Americans were full humans who merely needed exposure to the Gospels and therefore should not be subjugated, and Juan Ginés de Sepúlveda, who argued back that the Americans were "natural slaves" for whom subjugation to the Spanish would be a benefit.

Technologies of Culture: Printing

The sophistication and maturity of Late Agrarian thought were given a boost by the spread of the technology of printing, which allowed much faster and wider reproduction of texts than scribal technology (i.e., hand-copying). Like many Agrarian Era technologies, printing was a Chinese invention, where it had originated during the Song Dynasty as block printing, first of whole pages, then using movable blocks for individual characters. The technology spread from there in a pattern remarkably similar to that of gunpowder, traveling across Eurasia to be taken up most forcefully in western Europe, where an alphabetic writing system allowed movable type for individual letters. Like gunpowder, the European adoption and improvement of printing depended on the fairly advanced state of European metallurgy, as well as the prior spread, also from China starting as far back as under the Han, of papermaking, which provided a cheaper and more abundant material for printing on than parchment, and a more flexible one than bamboo strips or papyrus. It was the spread of papermaking in the High and Late Agrarian, even more than the later spread of printing, that fostered the greater levels of bureaucratization among Late Agrarian hierarchies we noted in the previous chapter.

The European adoption of printing also depended on the contractual frame of European society and the spread of merchant capitalism. A private inventor, Johannes Gutenberg, backed by private investors (one of whom sued Gutenberg before his invention started turning a profit and took control of Gutenberg's assets) put together the pieces, and the new technology spread as a business model allied to a technology.

The fundamental effect of printing where it was introduced was to loosen the limits on information recording and dissemination imposed by the handwriting of documents. Because more books could be produced, making books cheaper and more accessible, more areas of knowledge could be explored simultaneously within a culture by more people. And even though paper does not last as well as parchment, the texts printed on paper were more likely to survive simply because there were so many more of them and they could be reprinted more easily. But like gunpowder, print technology had different impacts depending on the cultural context into which it was introduced, since what texts got printed, by whom, was still a matter of cultural preferences and their relationship to power structures. A brief comparison of the impact of printing in China and Europe will illustrate this.

In China, the cultural weight of the civil service exam system by which people could enter state service—always the most prestigious career path—meant that what got printed most was the Confucian canon of classics upon which the exams were based. This democratized access to education and thus to civil service jobs to some extent, though the cost of an education limited this effect significantly. But the effect is most visible in the merging of the gentry, the substantial local landowners who before the spread of printing had provided most of the candidates for the exams, with the rising merchant class who now had not only the money but access to the tools for converting their merchant fortunes into the currency of social respectability. Thus, printing in China helped to diffuse the society's potential merchant dilemma by creating a pathway for merchants to buy into the cultural norms of the power structure. This in turn further reinforced those very norms.

It is not clear if the reinforcement and spread of cultural norms arbitrated by the imperial court and based on classical models had some effect in slowing scientific and technological innovation in China from the Ming onward. The Black Death of the 1330s seems to have hit China's urban intellectuals hard, which is the commonly cited reason for this slowdown. The Ming, however, did generally react conservatively to the century of Mongol rule (as did many areas, as we saw in Chapter 13),

PRINCIPLES AND PATTERNS

The impact of new technologies and ideas depends on the cultural frame through which they are seen by those adopting the new technology or idea.

and a print culture dominated by the court may have spread that reaction further through society.

In Europe, print had many of the same effects in democratizing culture to a certain extent. But in the context of a society divided religiously by the Reformation, intellectually by the claims of Renaissance Italian humanists against the learning of church schools, culturally by languages whose alphabetic written or printed forms differed from each other (whereas Chinese writing could represent different spoken tongues with the same characters), and politically, the democratization of culture emphasized divisions and competition. This was true even when Europeans printed their version of the Confucian canon. The Bible was the first and most frequently printed book, but it was printed not just in the Catholic Church–approved Latin version, but by Martin Luther in German and soon in other vernacular languages. This made practical the Protestant belief that one should read the Bible for oneself, bypassing and undermining the authority of priests over interpretations of scripture. The papacy's index of banned books proved mostly ineffective at stemming the flow of subversive ideas through print.

Furthermore, literacy, at least to a certain level, was easier to obtain with an alphabetic writing system (though this is not a hard and fast rule: by 1700 Tokugawa Japan probably had the highest literacy levels in the world). Spreading literacy created a market for books (and the spread of print in turn encouraged spreading literacy), which in a context lacking a norm-setting center such as the Chinese imperial court meant that competition for readers led to publishing of interesting new material such as Hans Staden's sensationally titled *True History*. We can see here the first signs of erosion of the Great Cultural Divide. Printing certainly abetted the spread of new scientific and technological knowledge, including (naturally) publications on infantry drill and artillery ballistics that served Europe's warring states, as we saw in the last chapter. Europe's surge of technological innovation, visible from the 1300s even if much of it consisted of borrowing and improvements, therefore received a further boost. In general, print everywhere began to act something like an amplifier, magnifying the impact of cultural encounters and developments across the globe.

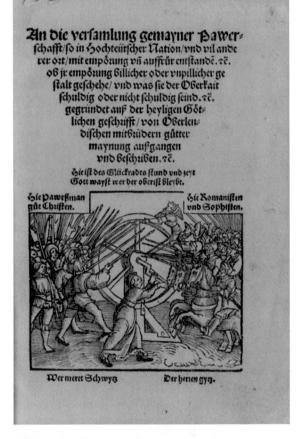

FIGURE 17.4 Subversive Printing. Printed report of an armed peasant uprising.

Encounters

As we have noted in earlier chapters, no textbook can be exhaustive in its coverage, and this book in particular makes no claim to cover everything. Rather, our model provides a framework for analyzing whatever specific evidence and cases you might wish to examine. In this section, therefore, we will give somewhat closer attention only to a representative set of cultural encounters and their associated screen images and frame values that characterized the networked societies of the Late Agrarian Era.

Subcultural Encounters

One set of encounters occurred within societies, across subcultural boundaries. These encounters tended to focus on the intersections between the three fundamental questions outlined earlier, that is, on the relationship of individual ethics to social order, and of social order to cosmic order.

Individual and Society

The flow of ideas generated by the Late Agrarian Era's global network, amplified by print technology, met the maturity of the era's philosophical and religious traditions, especially in terms of their ability to act as technologies of social control, and raised questions about the rigidity of social order. Two examples stand out. First, Italian scholars of the 1400s had looked back to classical models of the education of individuals to propose an educational philosophy less focused on serving social order than the courses in law and theology that dominated European universities at the time. In the process, they constructed themselves as heroic revivers of that classical learning, much of it Roman but a significant part of it newly available Greek texts brought west from the collapsing remains of the Byzantine Empire as the Ottomans advanced. Their humanism—meaning a focus on the humanities and their role in developing the potential of the individual—was at the core of the "Renaissance" they advertised themselves as starting, as we explained in Chapter 14.

As we saw there, "newness," justified or not by reality, began to pervade European screen images. Applying this to themselves, Italian humanists promoted the idea of the heroic individual—not just great warrior-kings or saints, the usual "great men" of history (see Issues in Doing World History box in Chapter 19), but inventors, artists, and scholars. Italian humanism spread to the rest of Europe in more religious form than in Italy (Italian humanists were not anti-religious, but their focus was usually elsewhere, leading to a somewhat misleading characterization of them as secularists), contributing to aspects of the Protestant Reformation (see discussion later in this chapter). It is debatable how accurately the screen image of "heroic individuals" describes any changed reality in European society, but the image itself and the theoretical potential of anyone to improve themselves through education paradoxically both contributed to the self-image of Europe's more assertive monarchs after 1500 and raised questions about the socially (and gender) stratified societies they ruled.

Meanwhile, in China, the Neo-Confucian scholar-official Wang Yangming (1472–1529) established an influential school of thought that, like Italian humanism, stressed the potential in all individuals, through education, to become sages. Building on the strand of Confucianism that followed Mencius, Wang located ethical knowledge as innate in every human. Wang's philosophy in particular united knowledge and action, suggesting that an observant peasant could learn as much from what he did as a farmer as a scholar could from reading. The anti-hierarchical, socially egalitarian implications of such ideas were much more explicit in the writings of Wang and especially some of his followers than in most Italian humanism—some

Projecting Individualism

Cultural encounters brought questions of identity to the fore in the Late Agrarian Era, and artists responded with projections of their own cultures as well as images of Others. Rogier van der Weyden's late fifteenth-century *Portrait of a Lady* (top left) and a sixteenth-century portrait of the Neo-Confucian scholar Wang Yangming (top right) show Dutch and Chinese versions of creating self-identity. Rembrandt van Rijn's seventeenth-century *Portrait of a Turk* (bottom left) and Annibale Carracci's sixteenth-century *Portrait of an African Slave Woman* (bottom right) exemplify how Others could be projected.

advocated for female education, teaching that there was no intellectual difference between men and women.

Wang and his followers ran into trouble with the Censorate, a conservative state department far more effective, in the context of Chinese political unity, at shaping public discourse (that is, regulating projection of screen images) than the papacy's index. Furthermore, the concentration of intellectual life at the imperial court caused the philosophical disagreements between Wang and his more orthodox opponents to become the basis for the vicious factional infighting that contributed to the fall of the Ming Dynasty.

Religious Schisms

One of the accusations against Wang's Confucianism, possibly true, was that it had been tainted by Chan Buddhism (Zen in Japan), a peculiar form of Mahayana Buddhism that stressed reaching a state of this-world enlightenment—or "direct apprehension of reality"—through meditation. Orthodox Confucian suspicion of religious "superstition" and of Chan's potentially subversive effect on hierarchical social order brings us to the relationship of social order to cosmic order. Questions of cosmic order, tightly tied to many societies' frame values, inevitably expressed themselves in religious terms, and subcultural encounters across religious divides are visible in a number of regions of the Late Agrarian world.

The Sunni-Shi'a division of the Muslim world was well-established and thus, aside from justifying diplomatic rivalry between the Ottomans and the Safavids, caused no new problems in this era. Similarly, Muslim rule in Hindu India was not new, and for the most part Mughal attempts to connect and include Hindu elites in their administration worked well enough to keep the state running smoothly. In "warring states" regions, however, religious divides could at times raise the cosmic stakes of political power struggles. Japan witnessed two different examples. The first, much less cosmically fraught, involved the showdown between secular power, embodied in Oda Nobunaga's growing power in central Japan in the 1570s (the first stage of the unification of Warring States Japan, as we saw in the previous chapter) and the entrenched regional power of the great Buddhist monasteries near Kyoto, which Oda won. The second really did involve a clash of frame values. The growth of a substantial Japanese Christian community with (at least perceived) loyalties to the pope in Rome posed a serious threat in the eyes of the Tokugawa shoguns to their delicate political settlement, which required that all loyalties point to the shoguns in Edo. The seriousness of the perceived threat is indicated by the scale of the response: persecutions, mass executions (in the tens of thousands), and the banning of Christianity and all missionary activity as part of the closing of the country to the outside world in 1640.

FIGURE 17.5 Clash of Frames. Seventeenth-century Japanese portrait of St. Francis Xavier. The potential allegiance of Japanese Christians to the pope became a serious problem for the Tokugawa shoguns.

The Protestant Reformation in Europe, stemming from Martin Luther's theological challenge to the papacy in 1517, gradually escalated by 1550 into a full-scale century of subcultural warfare as the Catholic Counter-Reformation, led by the Hapsburg Holy Roman Emperors and kings of Spain, attempted to eliminate the Protestant heresy. This divide, however, was seriously complicated by sectarian rivalries within Protestantism and by non-religious political rivalries, especially between Catholic France and the Catholic Hapsburgs, and dragged on inconclusively until the mid-1600s. At that point, the major political leaders of Europe seem to have agreed, more or less explicitly, that religion was too disruptive and intractable an issue to keep fighting over, and uneasy coexistence replaced open war. Within countries, though many major European states continued to have significant religious minorities within their borders, the dominant screen image everyone agreed to project was that the religion of the ruler was the religion of the people.

Meeting the Americas

The most important cross-cultural encounter of the Late Agrarian was between Afro-Eurasia and the Americas—from the perspective of the former, Old World and the New World. These names alone give some hint of the impact of the linking of previously separate circuits into one global network. This impact was not confined to the vast Columbian exchange of diseases, crops, and people or the rise of new colonial hierarchies on both continents, topics we explored in the previous two chapters. The impact was also and at least as importantly cultural, and it operated in both directions.

Noble Savages in a Barbaric Paradise

Reactions to the existence and character of the Americas were, unsurprisingly, sparse in Asia, as news of them traveled slowly and had much less direct relevance than to Europeans. We have almost no evidence for African perceptions of the Americas aside from some later slave narratives whose writers unsurprisingly view what little they knew of their destination (if anything) with terror. It was therefore in Europe that multiple images of the Americas were projected by a range of interested parties. There was little agreement among them, in part because of the range of environments and social structures among the native Americans whom the Europeans encountered—from the state-level, urban-based hierarchies of the Aztecs and Incas to tribal hunter-gatherers such as the Tupi with whom Hans Staden stayed—and in part because of the very mixed motives with which Europeans approached this New World.

Still, three general categories of reaction may be discerned. All three show up about as early as possible: in a letter written by Christopher Columbus to an advisor of King Ferdinand of Aragón during his return trip in 1493 from his first voyage of exploration. Columbus did not know that he had discovered islands off a continent unknown to Eurasians—he thought (and continued to think until his death) that he'd found a way to East Asia. But he did know what he could tell his patrons that he'd found. First, resources, both natural and human, and this sort of utilitarian assessment (much exaggerated in Columbus's case) became a constant theme. Columbus promises his monarchs gold, spice, cotton, aloe, and slaves. And as the last named "resource" shows, he also found people. The ones he met "all go naked," have "no iron or steel weapons," and are in fact "marvelously timorous . . . guileless and . . . generous with all they possess." They "do not know any creed" and are

FIGURE 17.6 Noble Savage. European depiction of a Native American "great Lorde of Virginia," published in 1590.

"very intelligent." On the other hand, he has heard of an island where the inhabitants are very fierce and eat human flesh.

Thus, aside from calculations of commercial value, Europeans tended to see the Americas and their people either as a Paradise filled with innocents in a "state of nature"—an Eden untouched by original sin—or as an untamed wilderness filled with barbaric savages. Or, indeed, both at once: the image of the "noble savage," a kind of human both uncorrupted and unrefined by "civilization," became a strong theme in European images of the Americas. All these images corresponded with and justified different treatments of native peoples. Those treatments themselves became the subject of image making. Particularly lasting was the "Black Legend" of Spanish ill-treatment of natives spread by English and Dutch propagandists. This legend says much more about English-Spanish hostility than it does about either Spanish or English relations with indigenous peoples. Like-wise, both positive and negative images of native peoples said more about European attempts to make the New World meaningful for themselves than they did about the realities of native American societies.

Disruption, Adaptation, Syncretism

Those realities on the ground proved difficult enough for the native Americans to interpret. What proved most disruptive was the spread of infectious diseases before the Americans were even aware of European contact, as happened through much of North America. Mass deaths for no apparent reason caused villages to be abandoned, societal structures to collapse, and cultural frames to evaporate. The latter is more serious than it might sound, as studies have shown that in condi-tions of societal chaos, it is the loss of meaning in people's lives that leads to de-spair, despondency, and even death. Visible conquerors such as the Spanish were in some ways easier to deal with, as they could be understood (at the least as having been sent by the gods as a punishment) and tended to maintain significant elements of the old order in place so that they could enjoy the benefits of ruling their new lands.

The conquerors brought their own cultural frames with them, however, so even where the Spanish took over previous structures, cultural change was inevitable. Although, as we noted in Chapter 15, Spanish landlords preferred that the indigenous peoples on their lands not convert to Christianity so as not to limit the landowners' ability to exploit native labor, Spanish missionaries worked hard to spread the faith and so gain souls for the church. Over the long run, this effort was successful. Incen-tives to convert came from the power differential created by the conquest and by the same rule that tended to apply in Europe in terms of the Protestant-Catholic split— that the religion of the ruler was the religion of the people, a rule that gained force from the continuing hierarchical nature of Spanish-American societies.

But conversion must not be seen in the simplistic terms of giving up an old religion to take up a new one. The Christianity that emerged throughout Spanish

America was in many ways a new syncretic version of the faith. Certainly the most famous example of this is the Virgin of Guadalupe, a painted image of the Virgin Mary housed in a church built on the site of a temple to the Aztec goddess Tontanzin just outside Mexico City. Like Hans Staden's story, the Virgin illustrates almost every aspect of cultural frames and screens at work. She conforms to Catholic imagery perfectly, yet the rays of the sun behind her can also be read as spines of the maguey cactus, source of the sacred drink pulque. Her robe is the color symbolic of the divine Aztec couple Ometecuhtli and Omecihuatl, and her skin is brown. The image was painted before 1556 by an indigenous artist under the direction of a Spanish Dominican archbishop. The (possibly invented) story attributing the origin of the image to a vision that appeared in 1531 to an indigenous peasant was published (more than a century later) in both Spanish and Nahuatl versions. It is impossible to say whether the image and its setting is a native appropriation of Christian images, a clever Spanish construction to draw new converts, or both. Whatever the impulse, it worked: the Virgin rapidly became the symbol of a new *mestizo* or mixed Spanish-native Mexican identity that gave meaning to the events of the conquest.

Confucians and Jesuits

Conflict and accommodation of a different sort characterize our third example of Late Agrarian cultural encounters. The Jesuit religious order had established missions in southern China in the mid-1500s. In 1582, a thirty-year-old Italian Jesuit who had been stationed for four years in Goa, a Portuguese port in India, arrived in the Chinese port of Macau. From then until his death in 1610, Matteo Ricci spearheaded a cultural meeting between European and Chinese learning.

FIGURE 17.7 Syncretism on the Screen. The Virgin of Guadalupe, a classic image of the blending of Catholic and pre-Christian religious imagery.

Ricci set to work to learn not just to speak Chinese, but to read and write classical Chinese characters, the medium for scholarly communication in China—he and a colleague produced two different Chinese-Portuguese dictionaries that featured the first consistent transliteration into the Roman alphabet of the Chinese language. His skill and his sensitivity to Chinese cultural norms allowed him to expand Jesuit missionary activity from Macau to other major cities. In 1598 Ricci himself reached the capital at Beijing, and from 1601 until his death was an advisor to the imperial court of the Wanli emperor. Ricci gained this honor because of his scientific knowledge, chiefly in astronomy (and therefore for Chinese astrology), especially his ability to predict eclipses, vital events in Chinese cosmology. But he also worked with Chinese cartographers to produce the first Chinese European-style map of the world in 1602.

FIGURE 17.8 Network Knowledge. A 1604(?) color edition of Matteo Ricci's 1602 world map, produced for the Ming court in China.

FIGURE 17.9 Elite Connection. Matteo Ricci dressed in the traditional robes of a Chinese scholar. Jesuit priests and Confucian scholars could sometimes understand each other very well.

The map placed China at the center of the world; more important, it introduced China (and later Japan) to the existence of the Americas. Other Jesuit scholars contributed to Chinese scientific knowledge in mechanics and, above all, became cannon founders and ballistics experts for the imperial army.

Ricci produced the first translations into Latin of the writings of Confucius and his followers, and indeed "Confucius" and "Mencius" are Latinized forms of Kung Fuzi and Mengzi that date to Ricci's translations. Ricci's knowledge of Chinese culture, especially of the Confucian classics that were at the heart of Chinese intellectual life, allowed him to "translate" Catholicism into Chinese terms. His basic approach was to claim that the Chinese had been practicing Christianity all along, but not in its most perfected form. But this approach had limits. It did gain some converts, but angered many other missionaries, who thought Ricci had taken accommodation too far—the same problem Mughal emperors ran into with their Muslim supporters in appealing to Hindus, and indeed the same problem the image of the Virgin of Guadalupe ran into with Franciscans, who protested against encouraging indigenous idolatry, before she won papal approval with Dominican backing (remember, composite cultures never speak with one voice). His approach was outlawed and Christian missions faltered when identified too closely with European culture. Still, Ricci's success at making connections at the level of elite culture showed that some cultural groupings (for instance of well-educated, misogynist men in robes) could transcend common cultural borders. The Jesuit-Confucian connection is also perhaps the best example of the sorts of intellectual, cultural, and even diplomatic connections that a mature, polycentric Late Agrarian world was capable of.

PRINCIPLES AND PATTERNS
The Great Cultural Divide meant that elites from one hierarchy often had more in common with elites from another hierarchy than with their own commoners.

Slavery and Race

At the opposite end of the cultural and geographic spectrum from the intellectual meeting of Jesuit and Chinese cultures in the Late Agrarian Era was a cultural development focused on slavery and racial identity that began to emerge in the Atlantic world, and that had long-term implications well beyond the Atlantic.

Images of slave identity had been projected by both slaveholders and slaves themselves since slavery had appeared as a regular part of complex hierarchies. These had varied widely depending on the type of slavery (domestic or agricultural, for example), the source of slaves (debt bondage within a society or foreign war captives, for example), and on other factors such as gender and the social role or status of slaves (educated

Greek slaves who tutored elite Roman children and Islamic slave soldiers had better images than common laborers). It was relatively common for agricultural slaves to be thought of by their masters as lazy and stupid. The structure of agricultural slavery usually held no incentives for slave initiative and often rewarded "stupidity" of the sort that could reduce workload: "Oops, I plowed into a rock and broke the plow!" It was also not unheard of for certain ethnic characteristics to become associated with slavery in some societies: Roman stereotypes of slaves at some point included red hair when Celts made up a large proportion of agricultural slaves; Islamic stereotypes after 900 associated black skin and slavery because most domestic slaves were of African origin. But such associations tended to be ephemeral due to the variety of sources of slaves. Furthermore, the suitability of some peoples for slavery had almost always been explained in terms of cultural characteristics such as military weakness or, more generally, barbarism. Sepúlveda, who argued against Las Casas for the enslavement of native Americans by the Spanish, said that their cowardice and lack of "civilization" (including having no written laws) justified their enslavement, *just as the ancient Spanish peoples had been enslaved by the Romans.* This implied that a people could transcend the conditions that made them suitable for slavery by learning from some more civilized masters. This conclusion was common in images of slavery before 1500.

The conditions of slavery, the slave trade, and slave societies that developed in the Atlantic world after 1500 gradually encouraged a new construction of the image of slavery. Several factors contributed. First, the gradually rising scale of the slave trade created more substantial slave populations than had existed in most places and times previously. This was especially true of slaves as a percentage of the total population. True slaves had never been a majority of a society's people. Subject peasants might be considered partly or mostly unfree, but religious and philosophical framing of social order disguised or mitigated their degree of unfreedom. On most of the Caribbean islands and in parts of the southern British colonies in North America, and also in parts of Portuguese Brazil, slaves came to make up a substantial percentage—and in the Caribbean often a huge majority—of the population. All these places saw slavery as a key to plantation agriculture. But second, unlike subject peasant populations elsewhere, Atlantic world plantation slaves (as we noted in Chapter 15) were intentionally excluded from the cultural frame of their rulers, as this justified harsher exploitation of their labor. That this led to high death rates and the need to constantly import more slaves into a workforce that did not reproduce itself sexually was acceptable to the plantation owners because their profits, particularly on sugar, remained so high. All this meant that American slave populations tended to be viewed in even more dehumanized ways than had been the norm for global slavery.

The final ingredient to be added to this mix was the racial composition of Atlantic slavery—that is, the coincidence that most slaves were African (just as in Islamic domestic slavery). In most of Latin America, this fact was subsumed into larger forces. The initial enslavement of some native Americans weakened the association of slavery with Africans alone. Racial blending through intermarriage, discussed in Chapter 16, mitigated somewhat the formation of sharp racial boundaries between peoples. And the traditional hierarchical structure of Latin American societies, carried over from both the European conquerors and the empires they conquered, meant that theorizing about social status focused on traditional cultural qualities in addition to skin color. Widespread conversion among natives and Africans put Sepúlveda's "civilizing" vision of slavery at least partially into action.

Meanwhile, in the Caribbean the very vastness of slave populations—up to 90% on some islands, with a small European elite over them—meant that brute force and near-total dehumanization rather than theorizing about social structure were the rulers' tools of choice for controlling a potentially explosive labor force. The racial divide here remained (at first) a social fact rather than a cultural image.

It was in the southern British colonies of North America that race was invented as a crucial theoretical factor for image projection as a tool of social control. In Georgia, parts of the Carolinas, and above all in Virginia, plantation economies created a European elite of landowners. Their workforce was mixed: substantial numbers of African slaves, but also considerable numbers of poor Europeans, many of them at least initially indentured servants—a form of unfreedom. But the origin of most of these workers from within the British cultural frame of legal rights and contractual relationships had the potential to limit or challenge the power of elite landowners—with a different model of small-farmer independence as a reminder of this potential becoming common in the British colonies just to the north.

Thus, viewed through an economic-contractual frame of reference (that is, in terms of material "reality"), early Southern colonial society looked something like the top diagram in Figure 17.10. Any alliance on legal-contractual cultural grounds between European and African workers could quite clearly threaten the social and economic power of the elite. The response of the landowning elite was to project a very different image of the society that was based not in economic conditions but in racial ones, a projection illustrated in the bottom diagram in Figure 17.10. In other words, Southern colonial elites spread the idea that the crucial divide was racial, which involved inventing a new notion of "whiteness." This made alliances based on economic conditions impossible and substituted, for poor Europeans, racial superiority and cultural alliance with the elites for economic advancement.

In order to make this image work, the *idea* of "race" as an essential difference between human beings had to be substituted for the idea that culture (as Sepúlveda had argued) was what divided people. This idea of race, defined by skin color, was paired with the idea that some races were *inherently,* because of their race, *inferior* to others—in particular, that African races were inferior to European ones, or in the new language, blacks were inferior to whites. This had profound consequences for views of slavery, as racial inferiority and the subjection to enslavement that inferiority justified were no longer conditions that a people could escape by acculturation to their owners. Blacks could learn the language, convert to the religion, adopt the culture of their masters, but nevertheless remained, in this view, inferior, less than human. The idea worked powerfully against racial mixing and elided the considerable mixing that did happen, relegating anyone not "purely" white (the moral norm) not just to non-whiteness but to blackness.

This Southern construction not only worked, it rapidly became a dominant screen image (and arguably a frame value) throughout the British colonies. It did not conflict with the de facto structure of the Northern colonies. There, a dominant mutual suspicion between European colonists and the native tribes of the area affected relationships between the European settlers and a much smaller population of African slaves and free people, all of which could be interpreted in terms of "racial" differences. The idea also seemed to both explain and justify conditions in the Caribbean. And the less clear racial boundaries in Latin America could be viewed (from the north, not in Latin America itself) as an impurity in a clearly natural racial hierarchy.

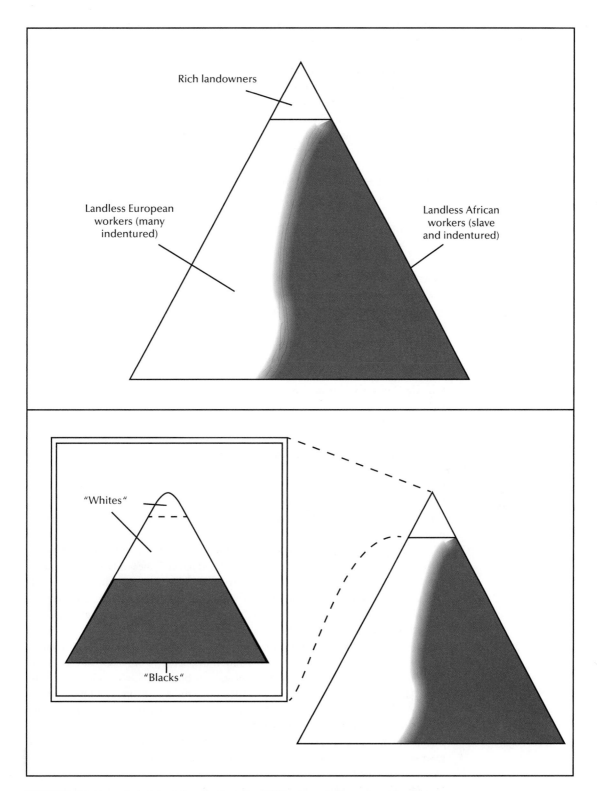

FIGURE 17.10 Control via Screen Image. (Top) Simplified schematic hierarchy of Southern colonial society. (Bottom) Projection of a racial hierarchy from a socioeconomic one.

Both the idea of race itself and the idea of racial hierarchy spread as significant screen images over the following centuries, reaching their height in the nineteenth and much of the twentieth centuries. The idea of racial hierarchy almost always met open opposition and so almost never became a true frame value outside the American South, though it was clearly a very large screen image. The idea of "race," however, as an essential division of the human species encountered much less opposition—opponents focused, in other words, on the *equality* of races, not on the *existence* of races. By the time biological arguments against "race" as a category gained traction in the late twentieth century (after a long and inglorious history of scientific support for the idea), race as a cultural reality was entrenched as a legacy of the Late Agrarian world's cultural encounters.

The Scientific Revolution

"Scientific" support for the idea of race as an essential, biological division of the human species was only possible, meanwhile, as a result of another Late Agrarian cultural development, the Scientific Revolution that gave birth to science as we know it. Although it is easy to label the result "modern science" and so view the revolution itself as a sign of "early" modernity, the contexts, processes, and even results at the time clearly fit into our picture of a mature, networked Late Agrarian world. Also, science itself is a process, not a fixed body of knowledge. So while the process was born in the Late Agrarian and even contributed to the shift to the Industrial world, "modern science" is perhaps better seen as what modern scientists do. (See also the Issues in Doing World History box in this chapter).

Contexts and Origins

"Scientific Revolution" is the name given to a set of intellectual developments in Europe, mostly in the 1700s, that led to new understandings of the physical world, primarily about physics and biology. The name denotes the conscious development of a different method for finding out about the universe. It is one of the key developments that fits our explanatory structure outlined in the Issues in Doing World History box in Chapter 14 on "European Exceptionalism," in that it was the unpredictable product of global inputs interacting with aspects of European culture that were not necessarily advantageous in themselves, but that in the context of those global inputs produced results significant from our own perspective today.

Global network flows of information were in fact a key context for the emergence of science in Europe. Prior importation into Europe of Arabic numerals and mathematics, as well as recovery of a substantial body of classical Greek learning from Arab and Byzantine sources, provided both tools and topics of investigation. The printing press, discussed earlier, made spreading and building up knowledge faster and thus more productive. The discovery of continents previously unknown to Europeans, filled with peoples, animals, and plants unaccounted for by received wisdom—and indeed that sometimes did not fit into inherited understandings of the world—demanded explanation.

These external factors came together within a European cultural frame whose values guided the investigation of new knowledge in particular ways. Four seem especially important. First, the revival of Greek learning, above all of Aristotle, brought to the fore the emphasis in Axial Age Greek philosophy on method rather than fixed Truth (see Chapter 4). Although Aristotle's own conclusions (along with those of other Greek authorities, including Ptolemy) about the natural world had achieved the status of dogma, the potential of a logical method of investigation to overturn its own findings remained. Second, the legal-contractual view of society that had framed European social relations for centuries allowed for and perhaps even encouraged the possibility of understanding the Creator's universe in terms of laws of nature, in a parallel to understanding moral aspects of that universe in terms of Natural Law. Third, the spread (along legal-contractual channels, as we have seen) of network-based merchant values contributed to framing laws of nature in specific ways. Merchant activity requires measurement and quantification of the world (or at least some of its valuable parts); calculation and decision making, including prediction of future conditions, of essentially material realities, arguably with less reference to authority than in a hierarchy-based set of values; and a basically optimistic outlook about the future. All of these can be seen as aspects of a scientific frame on the world as well. Fourth, an emphasis on newness and innovation had entered European culture in the wake of the Black Death (see Chapter 14).

These frame values made it possible for some (certainly not all, in a composite culture) European thinkers to contemplate new methods of investigation and conclusions that might differ from received wisdom. They also made the potential practical value of new understandings of the physical world visible to a wider audience. It was the "warring states" condition of European international politics that made scientific advances in metallurgy, ballistics, and fortress design attractive to rulers, but underlying that political competition was economic competition. We have seen already how the western European legal-contractual frame value led to rising wages in times of labor shortage, contrary to the usual rule (and contrary to European use of slave labor in the Americas, where that frame value did not automatically apply); this also meant that labor-saving mechanical devices promised higher profit rather than loss of control over people. From this perspective, full-rigged ships, cannon, the printing press, and the windmills and watermills that had spread across Europe from the 1200s, among other inventions, were all labor-saving devices. In short, scientific advance promised better weapons, bigger profits, and in general greater control over nature itself.

Models, Data, and Meaning

Such promises were made explicit by writers such as René Descartes and Francis Bacon, who promoted new scientific methods. And ironically, since they proposed rival methods, a combination of their approaches came to describe the new scientific methods quite well. Descartes stressed quantification and mathematical description, a sort of deductive approach to explaining natural phenomena. Bacon promoted systematic observation by experimentation from which inductive generalizations could be drawn. How the two worked together can be seen in the sequence of advances that revolutionized human understanding of the heavens.

The accepted and religiously approved description since classical times had been Aristotle and Ptolemy's earth-centered model. This explained terrestrial physics in terms of four elements (earth, air, fire, and water) and celestial physics in terms of orbits that were perfect circles and perfectly spherical planets and stars set in perfect

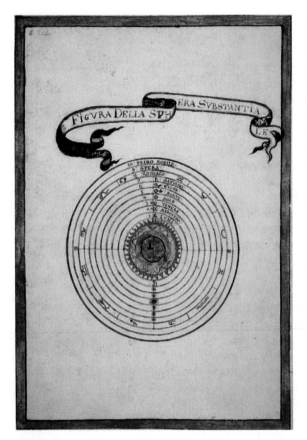

FIGURE 17.11 Ptolomaic Dogma. The geocentric Aristotelian-Ptolomaic universe: descriptive and meaningful.

celestial spheres. The perfection of the celestial realm was part of the *meaning* of the system, as the heavenly bodies were, literally, heavenly, being part of the divine setting for the earth, and the circle and sphere were thought of as the most perfect shape. But as description of observed reality, the system had by the 1500s become complicated with epicycles—circles on circles—to explain observations such as the periodic retrograde motion of the planets. The system, in other words, retained its meaning at the expense of a somewhat inelegant description.

Enter math: the Polish mathematician and astronomer Nicholas Copernicus, in a work published just before his death in 1543, proposed (as a mathematical hypothesis, not necessarily as a claim about reality) a heliocentric (or solar) system in which the planets circled the sun in perfect circles. This instantly made the mathematics of describing planetary motion much simpler—more elegant—but threatened the cosmic meaning of the system, despite the still perfectly circular orbits. Enter new observations: before he died in 1601, the Danish astronomer Tycho Brahe made the most complete and careful observations of planetary motions and celestial events yet. These posed serious new problems for the Ptolemaic system (he observed the birth of a new star, or *nova*!), but also showed that the planetary paths predicted by Copernicus were not quite accurate, either. Back to math: Brahe's assistant Johannes Kepler calculated elliptical orbits that predicted the observed data. Finally, observation again: using his newly invented telescope, Galileo Galilei saw that the phases of the (now visibly spherical, earth-like) planets Venus and Mars conformed to the predictions of the heliocentric, not the geocentric, model.

So why did Galileo, who died under house arrest in 1642, run into such trouble with the Catholic Church? Because while observation and mathematics had provided a better *description* of the universe, that description appeared meaningless. Why did planets travel in ellipses, of all things? Where was heavenly perfection? Where was God?

It turns out a bit more math was needed. Isaac Newton, born the year Galileo died, supplied it. It was complicated math—he had to invent calculus to do the calculations. But it turned out that three simple and universal laws of motion and one force that acts across distances in a mathematically describable way (gravity) *predict* elliptical orbits. That gravity acted across empty space was crucial to Newton: that, for him, was where God worked, for Newton opposed Descartes' theory that all forces that were transmitted across apparently empty space really operated through a chain of invisible particles. For Newton, this left no room for God and implied atheism. Gravity was proof of a mathematical Creator whose clockwork creation ran according to (obviously divine) laws of nature. Thus, Newton both *described* and restored *meaning* to the system. Newton published his *Principia Mathematica* in 1687. (The Catholic

Church still didn't buy it, but Newton lived in England, where disagreeing with the pope was a virtue.)

Science in the World

Newton's achievement created a sensation in European intellectual circles, and Newton himself became the first scientist to achieve cultural stardom. As the English Catholic poet Alexander Pope put it in his epitaph for the scientist at Newton's death in 1727:

> Nature and Nature's Laws were hid in night.
> God said, Let Newton be, and all was light.

Confidence in the ability of science to unlock all the secrets of the universe soared—not just in physics and astronomy but in biology, psychology, politics, the study of human society, and so forth. It was this confidence that led people to turn not just to "scientific" theories of racial hierarchy, but to seventeenth-century "scientific" defenses of male superiority and privilege. We will return in more detail to these and related topics in the next chapter.

Yet actually making scientific progress proved to be far harder and slower. Few aspects of nature proved as easy to measure and describe mathematically, in ways that generated testable predictions, as astronomy and physics, for one thing. There had been other breakthroughs in the course of the Scientific Revolution of the seventeenth century, building on developments that preceded it. Mathematics generally, as well as human anatomy and biology, saw significant breakthroughs. But the screen image of Revolutionary Science ran well ahead of the reality. Newton himself symbolizes the ambiguities and traditionalism of seventeenth-century science quite well. In addition to his God-centered physics, Newton was a dedicated and lifelong alchemist. Even his physics can be interpreted as an adjustment, following Aristotle's method, of Aristotle's conclusions. This was Late Agrarian science as much, if not more, than it was "early modern" science. This was certainly true of the views of Newton and his fellow scientists, who (necessarily) looked back to previous work rather than forward to results of their discoveries, scientific and cultural, that they could not anticipate.

But, since this is a chapter on culture, it has to be acknowledged that the screen image mattered and to some extent created its own reality, just as the screen image of race as an essential feature of the human species did. Scientific societies, both professional organizations such as the British Royal Society, of which Newton was a founding member, and popular groups dedicated to spreading the word about the new science, sprang up across northwest

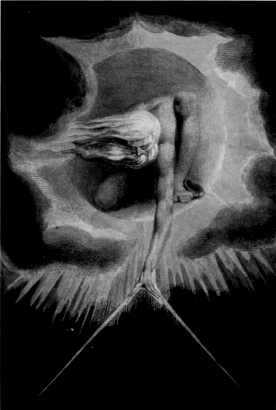

FIGURE 17.12 **Divine Watchmaker.** William Blake's *Ancient of Days*, depicting a Newtonian God creating a universe designed according to natural laws.

ISSUES IN DOING WORLD HISTORY

Science and Religion

Newton's religious interests and motivations are a strong reminder about a central problem in history: the tension between understanding the past on its own terms, on the one hand, and using the past to help us understand our own world today. The (perhaps somewhat surprising) image of the Anglican alchemist Newton is surprising, I suspect, mostly because of our modern expectations about conflicts between science and religion. This is not how the natural philosophers (as they called themselves) of the Late Agrarian Scientific Revolution saw things.

As the phrase "natural philosophy" implies, seventeenth-century "scientists" (a term only coined, significantly, in the nineteenth century) saw themselves, just as theologians and other philosophers did, as engaged in trying to explain the workings *and the meaning* of the universe. In other words, they were trying to figure out not just *how* things worked, but *why* they worked that way, with "why" interpreted in moral-cosmological terms, not just in terms of mechanistic cause-and-effect (that's the "how" question).

What complicates our efforts to understand the world of the Scientific Revolution is the subsequent development of science in the nineteenth and twentieth centuries. The better science got at explaining the "how" questions, the more it focused on those questions to the exclusion of "why" questions that, from

the perspective of the developing scientific method, were essentially unanswerable. It left those "why" questions to philosophy and religion. By now, it is hard to remember that natural philosophers worked on both at once, inseparably.

Further complicating our efforts have been the reactions of some religious people to some of the findings of science. The dispute between Galileo and the church is often seen this way, though from a seventeenth-century perspective, that episode is better interpreted as a dispute about what Christianity said, rather than between science and religion—and both the official church and almost all believers have since happily reconciled faith and heliocentrism. The real crisis came with Charles Darwin's theory of evolution in 1859 (see Chapters 20 and 24). Then—and to this day—the findings of science about "how" seemed, to many believers, too threatening to their received "why" answers to accept. This reaction is unnecessary—in 2009, for example, the Dalai Lama began sending Tibetan monks to Emory University to study science in order to teach it in Tibet, saying, "Even the Buddha himself said 'All my followers shouldn't accept my teachings out of faith, but out of constant investigation.'" It also further clouds our reading of the seventeenth century by projecting modern hostility back to a setting in which it did not exist.

Europe and especially in England. The outlines of "the scientific method"—hypothesis (carefully if not always mathematically stated) that makes testable predictions; observation (ideally through controlled experimentation) to test the predictions; adjustment of the hypothesis based on the results of observation, leading to new predictions, and so on, with advances made not by "proving" new Truths, but by disproving old ones, with no answer accepted as final—were increasingly accepted as the way to generate new knowledge. (The model around which this book is based is the historian's version of this method, as I explained in the Introduction.) And, most significant, where the science really was worked out, as it was with the Newtonian mechanics of movement and force, it worked. That is, it could be put to practical uses just as Descartes and Bacon had promised, and as Thomas Newcomen and James Watt were to prove as they tinkered with an ancient idea (the steam engine), made it work, and so powered a global transition out of the Agrarian Era. We will take up that story in the next two chapters.

Conclusion

We have now surveyed the Late Agrarian world from the perspectives of networks, hierarchies, and cultural frames and screens—the three principal components of our model of world history. My argument has been that this was a mature, sophisticated, and networked but polycentric world whose key characteristics from all three perspectives are best seen as culminations of the long-term trends of the Agrarian Era. Thus, although the revolutionary transition from the Agrarian to the Industrial Era happened to begin in one specific part of the Late Agrarian world, it was a product of that entire connected world, and indeed its connections, which continued, guaranteed that the processes and effects of industrialization spread to the whole world. We will turn to those global processes and effects in Chapter 19. First, in the next chapter, we examine why the revolution started where it did.

FRAME IT YOURSELF

Extending the Frame

The Late Agrarian world was full of cultural encounters that we have no room to explore in detail here. Russians encountering Siberians, Chinese emigrating to Malaysia, Portuguese trading and fighting with East African peoples—the list is vast. Pick such an encounter, one of these or another that you discover with a bit of research, and analyze it in terms of the general categories and trends laid out in this chapter. Does your encounter fit the categories? Are there trends this book's discussion has missed?

Further Reading

Burkholder, Mark A., and Lyman L. Johnson. 2008. *Colonial Latin America.* 6th ed. Oxford: Oxford University Press.

Duffy, Eve M., and Alida C. Metcalf. 2012. *The Return of Hans Staden: A Go-between in the Atlantic World.* Baltimore: Johns Hopkins University Press.

Eisenstein, Elizabeth L. 2012. *The Printing Revolution in Early Modern Europe.* 2nd ed. Cambridge: Cambridge University Press.

Goetz, Rebecca Anne. 2012. *The Baptism of Early Virginia: How Christianity Created Race.* Baltimore: Johns Hopkins University Press.

Margolis, Howard. 2002. *It Started with Copernicus: How Turning the World Inside Out Led to the Scientific Revolution.* New York: McGraw-Hill.

Spence, Jonathan. 1984. *The Memory Palace of Matteo Ricci.* New York: Viking.

For additional learning and instructional resources related to this chapter, please go to www.oup.com/us/morillo

CHAPTER EIGHTEEN

Late Agrarian Transitions: North Atlantic Revolutions, 1650 to 1800

Sir Robert Walpole (left) in Parliament.

Introduction

Robert Walpole was born in Norfolk, in eastern England, on August 26, 1676, in Houghton Hall, his family's residence for four hundred years. The Walpoles were well-off landowners, important wielders of local power. Robert's father, also named Robert, held the rank of colonel in the local militia; the younger Robert studied at Cambridge and intended to become a clergyman before his elder brother died, at which point he left school to help manage the family estates. When his father died in 1700, Robert assumed his duties in local and national government. He proved competent and capable of making connections, and rose to become a minister in the king's government—indeed, between 1721 and 1742, the leading minister, based on his close relationship with the two kings under whom he served during that time and his alliances with other great aristocrats. He was given the noble title Earl of Orford in 1742; until his death in 1745, he remained a close, if informal, advisor to the king.

Told in this (admittedly somewhat undetailed) way, Robert Walpole's life and career may be made to look typical of countless Agrarian Era elites across the globe. Landed wealth and connections to the state: here is the close congruence between social and political power typical of Agrarian pyramid-shaped hierarchies. Typical elite roles—warriors, priests, scribes—characterize the family's ambitions within a monarchical government. And indeed, Walpole was, in exactly these ways and in much of his self-image, a typical Agrarian elite. But if we look more closely at the details within this outline, especially at his role within the government of England, the picture starts looking decidedly odd.

For starters, his service in the government started with, and remained based in, his serving as a Member of Parliament for the borough of King's Lynn. Parliament was an elected body that represented diverse interests within the kingdom. Parliament, not the king, controlled taxation and the state's military forces. In fact, the government Walpole ran between 1721 and 1742, though nominally "the king's," was more accurately Walpole's: he and his "cabinet" of chief ministers set policy, and they adhered to a philosophical position that aimed at limiting the influence of the king over official decisions. He is now seen as England's first prime minister, though that title was not formalized until almost 40 years after Walpole left office. War, that staple of glorifying royal prestige, was absent from British international relations for most of Walpole's tenure because it was bad for business, especially the lucrative overseas trade of England's great merchants and their joint-stock companies that supported Walpole's government. Finally, despite his power, Walpole had to put up with vocal opposition in Parliament that both law and public opinion prevented him from suppressing.

Though precedents for pieces of this package of oddities can be found in the Agrarian Era, the package as a whole was both very odd and,

Framing the Argument

• The nature of northwest European hierarchies as a group, especially their problematic failure to effectively contain their merchant dilemma

• The oddity of the English hierarchy in particular, an oddity that allowed a new model of hierarchy to emerge there in the early eighteenth century

• The spreading impact of the new English political model and the screen images that supported it, instantiated in American, French, and Haitian revolutions

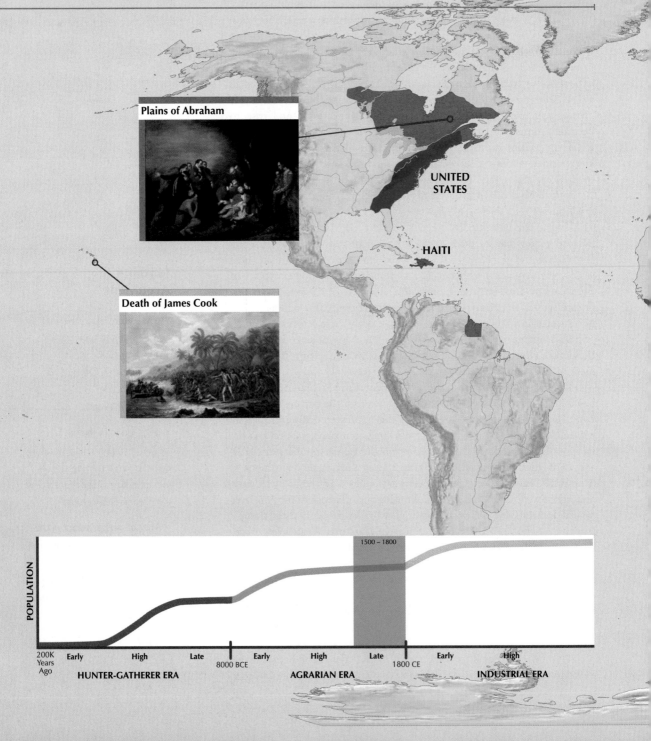

FRAMING Late Agrarian Transitions: North Atlantic Transitions, 1650 to 1800

Plains of Abraham

Death of James Cook

UNITED STATES

HAITI

1500 – 1800

POPULATION

200K Years Ago

Early   High   Late

8000 BCE

Early   High   Late

1800 CE

Early   High

HUNTER-GATHERER ERA   AGRARIAN ERA   INDUSTRIAL ERA

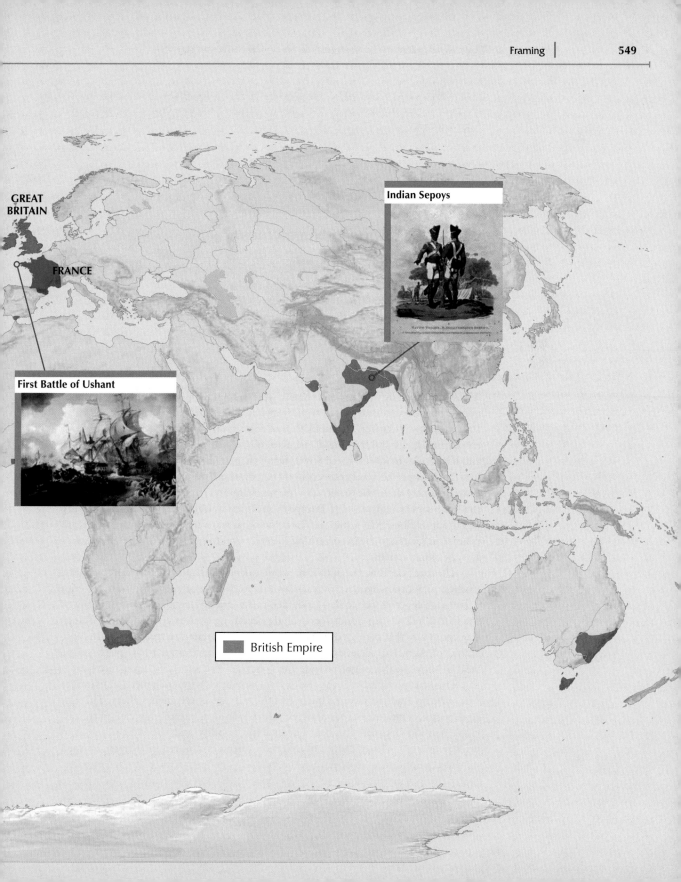

GREAT
BRITAIN

FRANCE

Indian Sepoys

First Battle of Ushant

British Empire

in retrospect, very important. This chapter explores the context, details, and impact of a place whose strangeness birthed the industrialization that brought an end to the Agrarian Era.

———— ✶ ————

Changing European Hierarchies

England was one of a connected set of European states that were in turn part of the globally networked world of the Late Agrarian Era. (These included Scotland, which voluntarily united with England to form Great Britain in 1707.) Under the impact of network flows, those European states had developed along their own Late Agrarian trajectory, forming a crucial set of contexts for English transformations.

Networks and Social Change

As we have seen in the previous three chapters, increasing global network flows of goods, people, and ideas placed strains on traditional hierarchies around the globe. In most places, however, a combination of coercion (as in the closing of Japan) and, more usually, cultural framing of the place of merchants in society allowed societies and hierarchies to absorb these flows within their traditional structures. In much of western Europe, however, especially in northwestern Atlantic Europe, hierarchies proved vulnerable to the penetration of merchant and network influence because of the legal-contractual values of European societies' cultural frames and the disunity of European elites. As a result, network flows that were materially similar to those in other places came to mean something different and to put stress on the structure of European hierarchies.

The key was that the influx of wealth generally, and of new foods, drinks, clothes, and other markers of social status and identity specifically, in societies where such symbols were only weakly tied to any underlying ideological ordering of the world, led to such goods increasingly becoming "status commodities": things one could buy that conveyed social status. This threatened to reverse the usual dynamic of Agrarian societies, in which authority (advertised by display) led to wealth—now wealth might provide the appearance of authority, upsetting hierarchy. This was most visible in the rise of "new nobilities" from rich merchant families who gave up trade in favor of buying both land and government offices. This not only became a new avenue for network values to infiltrate states, but caused considerable tension between the new bureaucratic nobility and the old military and priestly nobility. The dynamics of imitation-distinction noted in Chapter 17 sped up this commodification of status. At Louis XIV's French royal court at Versailles, yearly changes in the fashion of clothes replaced the previous tendency for styles to last up to a century. Lower in the social structure, the same dynamics spread the habits of a consumer society.

FIGURE 18.1 Status Commodities. The family's possessions, as depicted in and including this portrait, *Jean Le Juge and His Family* painted by Hyacinthe Rigaud in 1699, proclaimed their social standing.

Framing (and Screening) Social Change

The influx of foreign commodities, as well as the influx of new knowledge about the world (including both the New World and increasing knowledge about the achievements of Old World civilizations such as China) also had greater potential for disruption, in part because the legal-contractual framework of social relations in Europe was fundamentally methodological rather than cosmological: it mediated social relationships in terms of practicalities rather than the underlying meaning of the universe. This is evident in the changing screen images about meaning generated in Europe during this time. We can highlight attempts to think about the state and about the world more broadly.

Theorizing the State

Medieval European political philosophy had taken the sacred nature of kingship for granted, and had been dominated by the church versus state arguments about whether royal power came directly from God or came from God via the pope. On the other hand, taking sacred kingship for granted had not prevented debate about limits on the power of kings (could they make law or merely interpret it, were they over or subject to the law, did they need the advice and consent of the aristocracy or not). Note that these disputes assumed a legal framework for the state—the particular application of law was the issue.

Two transformations affected mainstream European thinking about monarchy. First, in the 1500s and 1600s, kings felt it necessary to assert in increasingly explicit terms the Divine Right of Kings to rule absolutely, that is, without hindrance. This was both a response to challenges to royal authority by nobles and others, often in the context of religious conflict, and an ideological tool in royal efforts to build more effective administrations to support their incessant warfare. Interestingly, however, just as absolutism based in Divine Right reached its pinnacle in the reign of the French king Louis XIV around 1700, it went out of favor. Under the influence of Enlightenment thinking in general (see discussion later in this chapter) and theories arising from English political developments that we will discuss later, absolutism came in the eighteenth century to be defended in terms of rationalist efficiency, a theory known as Enlightened Despotism. That is, kings should rule unfettered not because God put them there, but because that was the best way to run society smoothly. What these debates really reveal is that social changes were making it less clear to Europeans that kings should rule absolutely.

At the same time, the importance of network wealth and merchant interests showed up in the emergence of a new sort of thought about state power: economic theory. Mercantilism was a theory about, in our terms, the intersection between hierarchies and the network. It assumed that there was a fixed value of world trade. It also assumed that a country wanted to export more than it imported, because then the surplus would come to it in gold and silver, which could be used to pay for armies (note the political motivation for economic theory). It therefore encouraged promoting exports (and thus legitimized the founding of joint-stock companies) and limiting imports by establishing domestic manufacturing. Although mercantilist theory was wrong about the value of world trade and misunderstood money and trade balances (as Adam Smith would show—see Chapter 19), it probably did lead to policies that were beneficial, on balance, to economic growth, and it certainly illustrates the impact of social change on thinking about the role and meaning of states.

Thinking Society and the World

Social theory and intellectual trends in the eighteenth century show even more clearly European societies searching for meaning in a world of social change. The most important changes in European worldview are encapsulated in the movement called the Enlightenment. Newtonian science (see Chapter 17) and the political philosophy of John Locke (which we will return to in more detail later) formed the twin founts of Enlightenment thinking. Both emphasized universal laws of nature arrived at through rational analysis; Locke derived from this outlook the existence of universal human rights and located the origins of society and government in the protection of these rights. Enlightenment thought aimed at discovering, in all areas of human knowledge, universal truths. Like Confucianism, it did not seek these in religious tenets—the Newtonian notion of a divine clockmaker who, having created the universe, sat back, watched, and did not intervene in his creation (as this would violate the laws by which it ran) dominated Enlightenment thinking. Finally, taking its cue from Newton's achievements, Enlightenment thinkers were optimistic about uncovering all the laws for everything and using them to make the world better: it was in the Enlightenment that the idea of "progress" fully displaced in the European worldview the traditional Golden-Ageism that was common to most Agrarian Era societies. Progress would come to frame European attitudes toward further scientific discovery and toward history. In sum, the Enlightenment produced a worldview that was rational, secular, and optimistic.

FIGURE 18.2 Founts of Enlightenment. John Locke (left) and Isaac Newton (right). Their ideas informed Enlightenment views of politics and science.

Enlightenment principles had significant effects on European politics. They undermined Divine Right in favor of Enlightened Despotism (and later, in a few places, in favor of democracy). They encouraged European rulers to abandon torture as a legal tool. And they led to attempts to abolish serfdom and other class privileges that conflicted with the notion of equality before the law that universal human rights implied, as well as contributing to the rise of movements to abolish slavery and the slave trade. But these last attempts also demonstrate the limits of the impact of Enlightenment principles. Entrenched interests made reform difficult. We will return to the slave trade in the next chapter; in terms of serfdom and what Enlightenment thinkers began to call "feudalism"—the economic privileges of the aristocracy—well, kings might free their own serfs, but could not compel their aristocrats to do the same, nor could they easily overturn the tax exemptions that most European aristocrats outside England enjoyed. Finally, while some Enlightenment thinkers (especially female ones) extended the idea of universal human rights to women, the general trend was more toward increased naturalization of gender differences. The authority of science, especially the new biology, backed up growing restrictions on female opportunities in the economy. This forms another case, like classical Athens and Heian Japan (see Volume 1) where a society whose class power was in flux or allowed greater social mobility hardened its gender power to compensate.

PRINCIPLES AND PATTERNS

Reductions in class power tended to be balanced by more strictly enforced gender power in Agrarian hierarchies.

It is easy to point out, especially in terms of race and gender, the contradictions between the stated principles of Enlightenment thinkers and the actual practices of their societies—the Declaration of Independence and the Constitution of the new United States provide ready examples. But the conclusion that some draw today, that Enlightenment principles themselves were flawed, is wrong. Not only are Enlightenment principles ideals against which an imperfect reality may still fruitfully be compared, but—like the Axial Age Greek frame from which the Enlightenment evolved—the Enlightenment proposed a method, not a set of fixed Truths. Thus, the conclusions reached by eighteenth-century Enlightenment thinkers were later subjected to criticism, using the same rational analysis that had led Enlightenment thinkers to question the established religious and political principles of the seventeenth century. In this way, the Enlightenment really was a cultural frame (or at least a powerful set of screen images) based in the principles of the new science that encouraged continued inquiry about the world.

Stretching the Pyramid: Social-Political Disjunction

One of the effects of the spread of the Enlightenment worldview was to highlight for many Europeans at the time the structural effect of the expanding merchant-capitalist tumor on many European societies (see Figure 18.3). (Not that they put it in those terms, of course.)

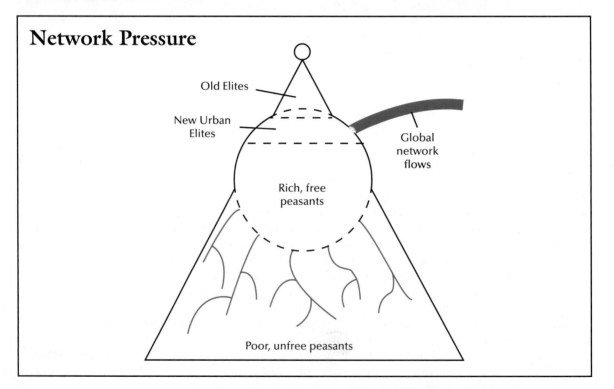

Network Pressure

Old Elites

New Urban Elites

Global network flows

Rich, free peasants

Poor, unfree peasants

FIGURE 18.3 **Network Pressure.** The growing merchant-capitalist tumor in western European societies, creating potential new elites and reaching ever further into rural communities.

As we noted above, the influx of wealth and subversive goods and ideas from the global network into western European hierarchies challenged the hierarchical structure of those societies, in part because there were no cultural frame values that could interpret those flows successfully in terms of the old structure. Thus, capitalist modes of business and merchant values began to permeate those societies. This created several sorts of stresses. Among peasants, the increased stratification that came with greater market-based relationships, as some succeeded and some failed in a more open, competitive economy, caused problems. Merchants (and the increasingly well-off urban consumer markets they served) found themselves with increasing wealth but with little direct voice in the state whose taxes and commercial policies could affect their businesses. Some, as we noted, bought offices and noble pedigrees, but, especially under theories of royal absolutism, even this did not buy them the policy influence they thought appropriate to their financial status. Finally, old warrior and priestly elites found themselves squeezed from two directions. The wealthy new urban merchant elites challenged their social dominance, while absolutist kings tried actively to exclude them from policy making (partly on the basis that they paid no taxes).

In short, with Enlightenment ideas implicitly challenging the very value of hierarchy, a serious disjunction was developing in the structure of western European hierarchies. The more the merchant capitalist tumor grew, the more trouble the rigid, politically defined pyramidal social structure had containing it. This meant in turn that the close congruence between informal social power and formal state power that characterized Agrarian hierarchies (and without which they could not operate, given the limited resources imposed by low productivity and slow communications) was threatening to break apart. That break happened differently and with different results in the major political revolutions of the eighteenth century. It happened first in England.

The Oddity of England

Structurally and culturally, England was an outlier even from continental Europe. Before explaining how, though, let us stress a vital historiographical point one more time. "Different" does not mean "better." All places had their peculiarities. It's just that, unlike the Agricultural Revolution, the Industrial Revolution started once, in one place. That it started was a contingent event—an accident, if you will, that nobody was aiming at. But accidents (as opposed to random events, if there are such things) are explicable after the fact. Given the importance of the Industrial Revolution—one of the three great transformations in the history of the modern human species—it is worth examining in some detail the context, including global network connections, that gave birth to industrialization.

State and Society

England's oddity starts with its central government. The Norman Conquest of England in 1066 had combined precociously centralized Anglo-Saxon institutions with vigorous Norman rule under a new aristocracy. Thus, England combined a strong central state and formal authority with strong social divisions and informal authority. In the 1100s, in the context of a legal-contractual cultural frame, this combination produced a legal system, the Common Law, which among other things made the state the guarantor of private property rights, which were the basis of social power. The importance this gave the state meant that politics became a matter of factional struggles for control of the mechanisms of central government. The first real oddity here was that the king became merely one of those factions, along with the landed aristocracy. This resulted in 1215 in the Magna Carta, an (uncomfortable) agreement between the monarchy and the aristocracy that the law was the ultimate arbiter of their political disagreements—that is, the royal office was made, in principle, subordinate to the law of the land, and the rule of the king was to be formally subject to the advice and consent of the barons of the realm, who were taken as the natural representatives of the people.

FIGURE 18.4 Queen in Parliament. Elizabeth I (r. 1558–1603) presiding over Parliament. The combination of monarch and Parliament constituted the legitimate English state. (The Granger Collection, New York)

Efforts to implement this principle in practice during the 1200s, however, proved difficult, causing two so-called Baron's Wars (1215–1217 and 1264–1267) between the monarchy and supporters of collective government by barons. What emerged from the second, under King Edward I, was the calling of Parliaments as the mechanism by which strong kings could obtain the advice and consent of the political classes of the kingdom. Parliament included not just the great barons and church leaders, but the untitled warrior aristocracy of local knights, who surprisingly met in the House of Commons with representatives of the towns (and thus merchants) of the realm. The key power obtained by Parliament was that any new taxes had to be introduced in and approved by the House of Commons. Given the limited private resources of the crown, this meant that royal war-making was subject to parliamentary approval at some level (as during the Hundred Years War, 1337–1453). Thus, the mechanisms of the English state developed between 1265 and 1600 as a series of legally negotiated bargains between king and Parliament—a process afforded to the English state in part because of its security as an island kingdom.

The other result of the centrality of the state to politics in a society with still-strong social power and an increasingly strong legal-contractual cultural frame was that English society never developed firm hereditary class divisions. The power of the state to enrich and ennoble its supporters and to legally define military and tax obligations in terms of income, not birth, meant that the English aristocracy was always open to newcomers. Lower down the social pyramid, serfdom disappeared especially early in England because of the financial advantages of free renters and wage labor to landlords whose status depended on actual income, not just birthright. Of course, this backfired on landlords in the wake of the Black Death in 1348. As we discussed in detail in Chapter 14, the labor shortages the plague created were met, not with the traditional hierarchy-oriented response of clamping down on labor freedom, but with rising wages and falling rents. Thus, by the mid-1300s at least, this was already a society of unusual social mobility whose social relationships were heavily influenced by market mechanisms that were interpreted in terms of traditional political-cultural codes of status. In other words, English society was even more vulnerable to the metastasizing merchant capitalist tumor and its network values than other societies in western Europe.

The gradually increasing influx of wealth from overseas trade that began for England in the 1500s simply exaggerated these already extant trends in English socioeconomic structure. English approaches to the New World were conditioned in part by a long history of overseas commerce necessary for an island kingdom. Commerce had involved private merchants, increasingly organized in associations, along with state management and taxation. It is not surprising in this context that, when overseas trade expanded, the British East India Company was invented as the first joint-stock company.

What emerged socially in the 1500s and 1600s was an increasingly large "middle class" of gentry landowners (given a windfall of wealth by Henry VIII's confiscation

FIGURE 18.5 **Emerging Consumer Society.** *The Levee,* the second painting in William Hogarth's series *The Rake's Progress.* Tom Rakewell's new riches attract musicians, artists, and other purveyors of commodified culture.

and cheap sale of extensive monastic lands during the Reformation) and urban craftsmen and professionals of various sorts (including, given the frame, lawyers) who formed a growing consumer society—the extreme mass case even in Europe of the link between consumption and status. These trends went into overdrive with booming eighteenth-century trade in Asian goods and above all the wealth generated by slave-produced sugar. By 1800, Napoleon—in many ways a very traditional Agrarian Era ruler—could contemptuously refer to England as "a nation of shopkeepers." China and Japan had similar concentrations of shopkeepers, but English shopkeepers and their gentry cousins had representation in Parliament and thus an increasingly loud political voice. This was an odd society, by Agrarian Era standards, ruled by a similarly odd state.

Culture and Identity

The structural evolution of the English state and society went hand in hand with the development of the English cultural frame. The course of structural development was shaped by the particularly strong legal-contractual value embedded in the English cultural frame. This value in turn fit with and fostered other central elements: the legitimacy of the state was strong and was taken as a separate issue from the legitimacy of a particular king or set of policies; and individual rights (implied by contractual social relations enforced by law) had unusual force. Two rights stand out: the set of rights associated with owning private property; and the right of political speech.

It is probably both anachronistic and teleological to refer to the latter as a full-fledged and individual "right," especially before 1500. But it captures a central aspect of English political culture. Parliamentary debate and the right of Parliament as a collective to question and challenge royal policy was the most salient instantiation of this cultural frame value, but it was also embedded in the English legal system in its widespread use from the 1100s of juries of free men to investigate crimes, settle lawsuits, and (later) decide criminal cases. Free Englishmen (this was still definitely a gendered society) were obligated, at times, to give their opinions, across class lines and with (at least theoretical) legal protection—leading to a modern characterization of the medieval English state as "self-government at the king's command." By the 1600s, this frame value influenced the surprising extension of the right of political speech to the new print technology. The poet John Milton defended the concept of freedom of the press in the mid-1600s; by the 1690s, England's private printing presses had remarkable legal freedom to print what they wanted.

The right to free political speech inevitably generated massive numbers of vigorously argued screen issues, not all of which were settled peacefully within the framework of the legal system. Thus, religious dissent and dispute became widespread with the Reformation, England's (and Scotland's) Presbyterians, Quakers, Puritans, and Catholic population all vying with the established Church of England for followers. But the plethora of screen issues also included scientific ideas, and the legitimacy of political speech generally allowed scientists, engineers, and entrepreneurs to talk to each other (and form contractual legal partnerships) quite readily, erasing that part of the Great Cultural Divide common to almost every Agrarian Era society that separated manual workers (such as engineers and merchants) from thinkers (scientists).

It was in part this emphasis on political speech that also fostered a growing conscious sense of English identity. Other factors mattered: island isolation (with the Welsh, Scots, and Irish to provide reminders of cultural difference); the Hundred Years War that increasingly pitted English (and Welsh) speakers against French speakers; and the continuity and centrality of the English state. But widespread political speech helped create a sense of Englishness that applied (in theory) to all the people. This would prove one root of the eighteenth-century invention of the idea of "nationalism," to which we will return in a major way in Chapter 20.

Political Transformations

By 1603, when Queen Elizabeth I died, the sociopolitical structure of England looked like the model shown in Figure 18.6. The state was seen as exercising its most legitimate authority when the king acted through (or in) Parliament, with decisions made there and enforced through the courts of the legal system. Over the course of the 1500s, Parliament had assumed a larger role in this "King-in-Parliament" conception of the state. This was because Henry VII, the ultimate winner of the civil war known as War of the Roses (1460–1485), who founded the Tudor Dynasty in 1485, had a somewhat shaky hereditary claim to the throne. He, his son Henry VIII, and the latter's son Edward VI and daughters Mary I and Elizabeth I, therefore took special care to work through Parliament in order to legitimize their position.

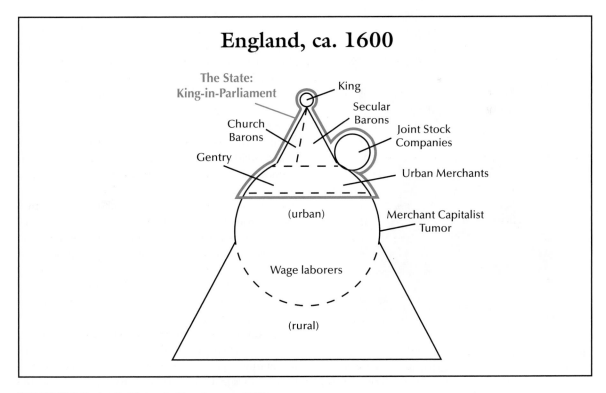

FIGURE 18.6 England's Hierarchy Structure, ca. 1600.

This worked very well, fostered the growing maturity of Parliament as an institution, and disguised the hidden question within this system: Where did sovereignty (or ultimate authority) reside?

As long as monarch and Parliament agreed with each other, the question could be answered by a vague "both." But when Elizabeth died without a direct heir, her cousin James VI of Scotland took the throne as James I of England. He was not only unused to dealing with a parliament, he was a proponent of the new theory of Divine Right of Kings and therefore found the constraints of Parliament and the English legal tradition philosophically objectionable. In this context, the question of sovereignty became a visible screen issue in English politics. Still, James was diplomatic enough to manage the relationship with Parliament throughout his reign. His son Charles I was not.

FIGURE 18.7 Agrarian Radicals. The "Declaration and Standard" of the Levellers, a radical group with followers in Cromwell's army. They wished to abolish all social distinctions and guarantee land to everyone.

Sovereignty: A Fight without a Resolution

Taking the throne in 1625, Charles quarreled with Parliament over taxation and royal prerogative in an atmosphere made more tense by religious factionalism and economic problems. Charles attempted to rule without Parliament after 1629, living on traditional royal income that did not go through Parliament. This outraged the political classes represented in Parliament, but he managed until he was forced to go to war to suppress what he saw as a religious rebellion in Scotland in 1639. Fiscal crisis forced him to call Parliament in 1640, and all the structural and cultural conflicts that had built up over eleven years boiled over. By 1642, civil war between Royalists and Parliamentarians broke out.

The Parliamentarians, led by the Puritan Oliver Cromwell and his New Model Army, won, capturing Charles. In 1649 they tried and executed the king and established the Commonwealth, a republic, with Cromwell acting as chief executive, backed by Parliament. But a funny thing happened. Cromwell couldn't get along with Parliament any better than Charles had, because the war had not answered the theoretical questions of what happens when executive and Parliament disagree. Cromwell disbanded Parliament in 1651 and proclaimed the Protectorate, with himself as Lord Protector. Backed by the army, Cromwell's rule was essentially a military dictatorship, lacking historical lineage or legitimacy.

Sovereignty: A Resolution without a Fight (Almost)

Cromwell died in 1658; two years later, his son Richard voluntarily stepped down in favor of the restoration of Charles I's son Charles II, who had grown up at the French court of Louis XIV. Charles, having no wish to, as he put it, "go on his travels again," worked hard to keep peace with Parliament, which tried hard to pretend that the whole period between 1629 and 1660 never happened. Still, tensions remained. These stemmed especially from Charles's friendship with the French king, which associated him both with Divine Right and with Catholicism, which for most Protestant English represented tyranny, as well as putting England on what many saw as the wrong side of European diplomacy.

These tensions heightened when Charles died in 1685 and was succeeded by his younger brother James. James was more belligerent about royal prerogatives and Divine Right. James was also Catholic, and opposition to his accession was calmed only by the fact that his two daughters were Protestant. But when a male heir was born in 1688, the prospect of an unending line of pro-French Catholic monarchs united opposition. Leading nobles and parliamentary leaders invited James's sister Mary and her husband William, prince of Orange and ruler of the Netherlands, to take the throne. William landed with an army, James fled to France, and William and Mary became co-monarchs. But, in a move shaped by the English cultural frame and the century's struggles, they did so on the basis of a legal contract with Parliament known as the Bill of Rights of 1689.

Constitutional Monarchy

The Glorious Revolution of 1688 and the Bill of Rights that codified it settled the fundamental structural question underlying the century's struggles. It said that no army could be maintained without parliamentary consent and that no taxes could be levied without parliamentary consent; it guaranteed regular meetings of Parliament, freedom of speech within Parliament, and the right to petition the king without retribution; and it prohibited royal interference in the law (among other provisions). In short, it established Parliament—and more specifically the House of Commons— as the sovereign power within the English state, limiting the powers of the king to those specified by the law—or as it was coming to be seen, by the (unwritten) Constitution of the kingdom. It was joined by the Act of Exclusion of 1701 that prohibited a Catholic from taking the throne and the Act of Union of 1703 that united the thrones of England and Scotland into that of Great Britain.

William of Orange was happy to agree to these limitations. He was not an absolute monarch in the Dutch Republic, but held the office of Stadholder, nor was he deeply interested in English domestic affairs. Involved in a struggle for survival in wars against Louis XIV's France, he wanted to bring England into the struggle on the Dutch side. During the many periods when he was on the continent fighting, his wife Mary and a council of ministers governed in his place. The bargain worked for both sides.

Forging a New Hierarchy Model

William proved a transitional figure in the transformation of the English/British state. He was an active executive and formed alliances with supportive factions in Parliament—first the Tories who had been supporters of James II's accession and were more open to royal prerogative, then with the Whigs who were anti-Catholic, anti-French, and thus more pro-war regarding Louis. Regular elections validated these shifts. But when William died in 1702, with a new war against Louis having

FIGURE 18.8 Images on the Thames. The first performance of Handel's *Water Music* by musicians on a barge on the Thames River, playing for King George I, seated on another barge.

opened the year before, the question of who actually ran a Parliament-dominated government became more pressing.

A New Executive

William was succeeded first by his sister-in-law Anne, an unfortunate woman whose seventeen children all died before the age of ten. When she died in 1714, the throne passed by law to George, Elector of Hanover, a minor German prince descended from James I's eldest daughter, who spoke no English (but had great taste in music, bringing Georg Friedrich Händel with him as his court composer). George I, like Anne, was incapable of running the government himself, and so councils of ministers, known as the cabinet, became increasingly important. Even before 1721, with Robert Walpole, these cabinets were identified as being headed by a chief minister who set policy. Walpole also established that the chief ministers and their cabinet were most effective when they themselves held seats in the House of Commons and commanded majority support within the body. Thus, a sovereign Parliament spawned its own executive body.

Parties, Elections, Politics

Failed plots to restore James and later his son had discredited the Tories, so British politics between 1714 and the late 1700s consisted of factional fights among groups of Whigs. (The later Tories were a Whig faction that reclaimed the old name within a new context.) Because the factions might disagree about policies but shared many fundamental frame values about the principles of British government (and because parliamentary speech was legally protected), they could contest policies and elections without the losers being seen as treasonous. This gave birth to the idea of a "loyal opposition" without which elected government is impossible, as it allows governments to succeed each other peacefully and without bringing legal punishment down on their predecessors. Ultimately, this led to formal political parties; it also meant that British policy makers benefited from open debate about policy options, as politics became a public rather than a private matter, unlike in traditional Agrarian hierarchies. Politics openly entered the cultural screen and as a result became more professional.

It should be stressed that Britain was far from a democracy in the eighteenth century. Voting was limited to owners of a fairly substantial amount of property (more restricted than it had been in the mid-1600s, in fact). Parliament had not been redistricted since the 1400s, meaning that some growing cities such as Manchester had no Members of Parliament (MPs) at all, while many "pocket boroughs" or "rotten boroughs" had an MP for no or almost no population, giving the landowner himself an automatic seat. This was a monarchical oligarchy masquerading in the clothing of democratic mechanisms. The voices and interests of the working class and of women went mostly unheard. But Parliament nevertheless managed to be representative of many interests in the realm, including not just those of landowners but also merchant and urban interests and, in a general sense, the interests of "the people," especially over levels of taxation. And the screen image of "representative government" grew increasingly powerful and affected what the state could accomplish.

The Benefits of Cooperation over Coercion: Taxes and Professional Bureacucracies

Traditional Agrarian hierarchies were almost always built on coercion. Ideological grease might ease the friction of governance, but the nature of the structure was coercive, extracting surplus from the bottom and feeding it upward. The new British state certainly didn't reverse that flow, but it broadened it and made it more cooperative. Eighteenth-century Britain is often said to have been lightly governed by comparison with continental absolute monarchies. This is true in some ways, but measured by per capita tax levels, the burden of the state lay heavy on the British people. But they put up with this because they agreed voluntarily, through their MPs, to taxes they were convinced were necessary. This started, importantly, at the top of the social scale: rich Britons ran the state, and so rich Britons agreed to pay for the running of the state through taxation on themselves and their land. This contrasts sharply with continental absolute monarchies, whose aristocrats, excluded from policy making, resisted any attempt to eliminate their traditional tax-exempt status.

Rich merchants, too, with a voice in policy through Parliament, agreed to import-export taxes, though these were harder to enforce. As a result, probably the most important taxes were excise taxes, those paid on goods such as beer and soap sold within Britain itself. These were often the least popular, and in order to win enough support had to be administered fairly and impartially. This led to the professionalization and de-politicization of the excise bureaucracy, perhaps the most extensively bureaucratized part of the English state at the time. The excise then set a standard for the professionalization of other departments of state.

Leveraging Wealth: Professional Money Management

Cooperation-based taxation allowed Britain, far smaller than France economically and demographically, to at least equal its rival fiscally. It further leveraged its wealth by inventing professional money management for state finances. This started with the chartering in 1694 of the Bank of England as a private company to act as the state's banker. Prompted by a naval crisis in the war against France, the Bank's initial investors lent a huge sum of money to the state (half of which went to rebuilding the navy). Their loans, on which the state paid interest, became shares in the company, which gained the right to issue bank notes as the official currency of the state. In other words, the state set up a joint-stock company to connect itself to network wealth directly. To maintain lender confidence, Robert Walpole created the "Sinking Fund," a reserve of state surpluses dedicated to paying off the principal of government loans and so reducing the national debt. When the Bank issued bonds that paid interest backed by the Sinking Fund, the state itself had become something of a joint-stock company. Britain's hierarchy had become thoroughly network-ized.

All of this meant that whenever the state needed more money than it could collect immediately in taxes, it could borrow whatever it needed because, between the

FIGURE 18.9 Joint-Stock State. The original Bank of England building in London.

Bank of England and the Sinking Fund, it had made itself bankruptcy-proof. By contrast, France defaulted on its debts three times in the course of the eighteenth century, had to borrow at much higher rates, and eventually faced a fiscal crisis with revolutionary consequences in 1789.

Defense Policy: Your New Hierarchy at Work

War was the contingency that forced states to borrow beyond immediate income. England's considerable network wealth, accessed through bureaucratically professional taxation and leveraged through professional financial management, allowed it to maximize its weight in international affairs. As Walpole's long maintenance of peace shows, war remained a tool resorted to only when absolutely necessary, as it was both expensive and risky—all the resources in the world couldn't guarantee victory unless they were skillfully deployed. But Britain could resort to it whenever it needed to. Not only did Britain maintain its own armies in overseas wars (only a small part of the regular standing army was maintained in Britain itself, the old fear of military tyranny guiding policy here), it subsidized allied armies regularly.

Above all, Britain's political leaders decided on a strategic outlook that emphasized protecting and building the country's overseas holdings and guarding the

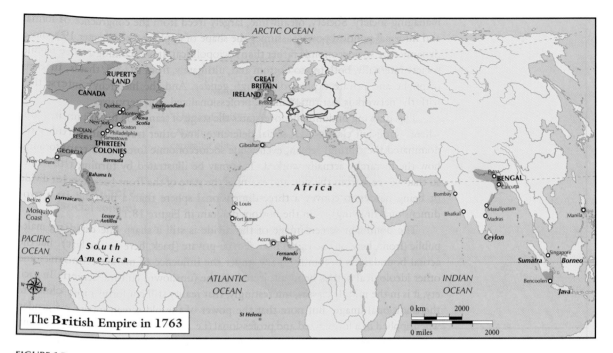

FIGURE 18.10 The British Empire in 1763.

home island with the world's most powerful navy. The naval crisis of 1692 that had pushed much of the new structure into place was not repeated. Given the expense and complexity of eighteenth-century warships, state orders through privately owned shipyards had a significant impact on the development of the eighteenth-century British economy. Indeed, the modernity (to use a dangerous word) of Britain's political structure is signaled by the emergence of fears that the economic influence of the whole set of naval industries would lead Britain to war more than necessity dictated, benefiting those industries but hurting the economy generally—in other words, some Britons perceived the threat that what would later be called a "military-industrial complex" would distort policy. The bottom line, however, is that Britain's more professional state mechanisms magnified its capabilities such that the country became a Great Power on the global stage. (See Figure 18.10.)

Summarizing the New Hierachy Model

The new structure of the British hierarchy requires a new picture of our model, as the traditional Agrarian pyramid, with its close congruence between formal (state) power and informal (social) authority and its values antithetical to network practices no longer applies in Britain's case. By 1780, the British model looks something like the top diagram in Figure 18.11.

What has happened is that the state and its formal mechanisms of authority have "popped off" the top of the pyramid to become a professional apparatus for

Revolution. Locke's trinity of rights to life, liberty, and property have spread as screen images and even frame values ever since.

(Two quick comparisons: Thomas Hobbes had come up with almost the same theory thirty years earlier, but started from a more pessimistic assumption about human nature—rational but too selfish to be entirely reasonable. His State of Nature was therefore one of war, not inconvenience, and justified a more one-sided and irrevocable contract with an absolute state to keep peace. The Swiss thinker Jean-Jacques Rousseau, a century later, saw the contract as forming society itself, which subsumed individual rights to the good of the social collective.)

The spreading of Locke's theory of government began with the French writer Montesquieu, whose popularization of Locke formed a central stream of Enlightenment thought. The interesting point here is that Montesquieu got Locke wrong: Montesquieu saw the key to the Lockean-British system as *separation of powers* between executive, legislative, and judicial functions of government. As the American Revolution would show, his mistake would be a productive one.

English Infections: Political Revolutions

The political transformation that began in seventeenth-century England set practical examples and provided ideological fuel to a further set of political upheavals.

The American Revolution

The American Revolution might well be called the Second English Civil War. It was caused by an interesting mixture of very specific issues framed in the universalist terms of Enlightenment thought. The specific issues focused on the economic relationship between Britain as imperial power and the colonies as subordinate pieces of the empire. Britain had added to its debt in the Seven Years War (in North America, the French and Indian War) and wished to tax its colonies to help pay for the protection it had given the colonies during the war; it also exercised some control over American markets and trading opportunities. Since the French threat had been eliminated in the war, the colonies could safely object to the taxes (in what became something of a consistent theme in American history); colonial business elites also wished to exercise greater control over trade. (See Figure 18.12.)

American revolutionary leaders cleverly framed these disputes in terms of their rights as Englishmen as universalized by Lockean theory, focusing their rhetoric against the royal tyranny of George III rather than against the parliamentary government (save for the slogan "no taxation without representation," which simultaneously highlighted and ignored the problem with Parliament's centuries-out-of-date electoral districts and how interests were represented in Parliament, while also framing anti-tax orneriness in terms of rights). They were successful enough to mobilize just enough support at home and to find vocal supporters within British political factions.

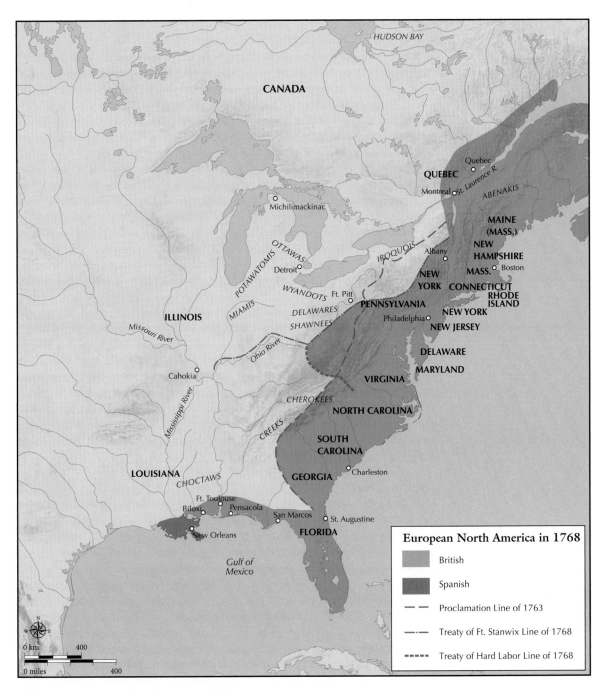

FIGURE 18.12 **European North America, 1768.**

Britain struggled to formulate a successful strategy for suppressing the rebellion. It faced immense logistical problems fighting a trans-Atlantic war against a popular insurgency rather than the state-controlled armies and navies of European warfare. But the colonial forces, hamstrung in part by their people's anti-tax sentiments and by the autonomy of each colony, struggled to field an effective resistance. The inspired and improvisational leadership of George Washington allowed the new United States to survive long enough that the French entered the war (to avenge their loss of Canada in the Seven Years War). This forced the British government to concede that winning was too expensive to keep pursuing.

The new country then launched into a process of state-making that was conservative and radical at the same time, reflecting the original causes of the war. When the Articles of Confederation failed to create a coherent state, colonial leaders drafted a new Constitution that went into effect in 1789. Despite Jefferson's substitution in the Declaration of Independence of a right to "the pursuit of happiness" in place of "property" in Locke's trinity of rights, the Constitution carefully protected the business and property interests of colonial elites, including Southern slaveholders such as Jefferson himself, and insulated the electoral process from "too much" democracy. In many ways, one oligarchic government simply replaced another.

And yet, revolutionary leaders had deployed the rhetoric of universal rights and democracy so effectively—and embedded those ideals so eloquently in the country's founding documents—that they were accepted as frame values by the new society even when they obviously conflicted with actual conditions. Much of US history would then play out as a dynamic (and often violent) process of the United States trying, on its own continental island of self-perceived exceptionalism, to hold itself to its own ideals. Meanwhile, that same eloquence projected the United States as an enlightened experiment onto the cultural screen of Europe (and later the world), superseding Britain as the new political ideal for many Enlightenment thinkers. The impact of this experiment hit first in France.

The French Revolution

The French Revolution was far more complicated than the effort of a distant British fragment society to achieve political independence. Examining the causes of the French Revolution bring us back to the continental European social-political disjunction caused by the growing merchant capitalist tumor. This disjunction formed part of the long-term, structural causes of the revolution.

The social stresses between new and old elites over tax exemptions and legal privileges were the visible manifestations of this disjunction, as the economic importance and the political influence of different groups grew increasingly distant. The contradictions of royal absolutism itself, which (in theory) placed all political decision making in the king's hands alone but expected all classes to contribute (via taxation) to the support of the state, exacerbated this structural problem. These long-term causes were brought to an explosive edge by a set of medium-term cultural issues, most prominently a loss of cultural legitimacy on the part of the French monarchy because of the scandalous sexual affairs of Louis XV. The general climate of Enlightenment thought shaped the growing discontent. The sparks that set off this explosive mixture were a combination of short-term causes. Bad harvests and a flood of cheap British cotton cloth, which undercut French peasant sales of homemade cloth—marking the first disruptive intrusion of industrial production—heightened peasant misery. A fiscal crisis brought on by the costs of supporting the American Revolution forced Louis XVI to call the Estates General (État général), the long-dormant French version of Parliament. The Third Estate, which represented commoners, declared itself the National Assembly, issued the Declaration of the Rights of Man, and the French Revolution exploded.

The details of the Revolution need not concern us in detail here. A series of revolutionary governments abolished the monarchy in 1792 (executing Louis in 1793) and instituted a series of measures that remade weights and measures (inventing the metric system), the calendar, and the legal order of society. They abolished "feudalism"—the legal and fiscal privileges of the aristocracy, as well as serfdom—and made everyone equal before the law as citizens of a French Republic. When the other monarchies of Europe attempted to intervene to restore "proper order," the revolutionary state called out every able-bodied male to defend the Revolution. This *levée en masse* brought a huge revolutionary army into being that taught the values of the Revolution to every recruit. "Liberty, equality, and fraternity" and the idea that all men were French citizens transcended regional identities and created the foundations of French nationalism almost instantly. In short, by contrast with England, which simply had to remake the state to fit a society that had already evolved in significantly non-traditional directions, the French Revolution had to remake society, a much more difficult and violent process.

While the Revolution did succeed in deconstructing the old class structure and placing those most transformed by the merchant capitalist tumor (the "middle class," or *bourgeoisie*, to use the French term) in a dominant social position, the limits of social reconstruction are indicated by the fate of the French state as the Revolution progressed and France faced repeated wars. The state first became more coercive: over 40,000 Frenchmen died in the Terror in 1795, most of them peasants resistant to rapid social change. It then fell into the hands of a unitary political leader—the successful general Napoleon Bonaparte, who became First Consul in 1799. By 1804, Napoleon recreated a hereditary monarchy with himself as emperor, and in 1810 even married the daughter of the Austrian emperor.

Napoleon's France was thus an odd mixture of traditional and transformational elements. In traditional terms, it still had a massive peasantry, who loved Napoleon for restoring the Catholic Church when he became emperor (the pope attended his coronation). This reflected an economy that was still basically agrarian. But Napoleon's legal and administrative reforms confirmed some of the most important social transformations wrought by the Revolution and went a long way toward professionalizing the French state along British lines. The contradictions extended to his restoration of monarchical rule, which was confirmed by a popular plebiscite

FIGURE 18.13 New Old Tradition. *The Coronation of Napoleon* by Jacques Louis David. Napoleon's self-crowning completed his transformation from revolutionary to traditional Agrarian monarch.

Images of Revolution

The original text of the Bill of Rights of 1689, the contract between Parliament and the monarchs William IV and Mary II that forms the foundation of modern representative government, sits behind images of increasingly radical revolutions. William and Mary (top left), brought to the throne by the Glorious Revolution of 1688 that produced the Bill of Rights, were constitutionally limited monarchs portrayed here in traditional fashion. The gentlemanly, conservative revolutionaries who formed the debate at the US Constitutional Convention of 1787 are idealized in Junius Stearns's 1856 painting (top right). The Parisian mob—mostly women!—demand that the French royal family return with them to Paris (bottom left). And the last image depicts the bloody violence of the Haitian Revolution (bottom right).

(the yes vote was 94%), giving his personal absolutism a veneer of Rousseau-ian legitimacy. Even Napoleon's army showed this mix. It was a mass, national army—in this sense it looked forward to the armies of the nineteenth century. But it lived (barely) on a well-developed but still Agrarian logistical system and in 1812 died in Russia as a result of the system's limitations. Its weaponry, tactics, and strategy are best seen as culminations of Agrarian Era military trends, rather than as new directions.

Napoleon and his army were extremely successful, especially at first, and carried the impact of the Revolution beyond France to much of Europe. (See Figure 18.14.) Bourgeois-oriented social and legal reforms challenged old social structures. Even more powerfully, the French army unintentionally exported the emerging idea of nationalism (which we will return to in detail in Chapter 20), which turned the conquered against French rule in a pattern destined to be repeated many times over the next two centuries. The French impact was important but indirect and not immediate. Its most important (and again unintentional) effect may be described

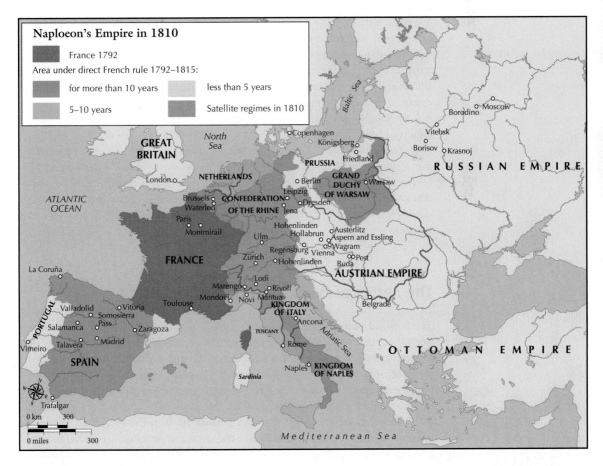

FIGURE 18.14 Napoleon's Empire in 1810.

metaphorically in computer terms: Napoleon's spreading of Revolutionary ideals re-configured western European social hardware so that it was more compatible with the new "Industrial Operating System" that Britain was in the process of developing.

The limits of Napoleon's achievement are indicated not just by the fact that in the end he lost the wars he fought, but that the big winners of the Napoleonic Wars that lasted until 1815 were Britain and Russia. Both were powers with vast network interests beyond Europe itself. Britain's naval power was crucial. Admiral Nelson's victory at Trafalgar in 1805 was the most decisive battle of the wars, as it guaranteed the safety of Britain from invasion and allowed Britain to dominate the war period economically. Napoleon may have sneered at the "nation of shopkeepers"—a signifi-cant sign of his still-traditional attitudes—but those shopkeepers, and the distances and manpower of Russia, defeated him.

Haiti

When the National Assembly of the French Revolution declared all men free and equal, this had a profound impact in Saint-Domingue, the largest and richest of the French Caribbean sugar islands. The impact was not, at first, on the island's nearly one million slaves, but on its mulattos or "free people of color," almost all offspring of European plantation-owning fathers and slave mothers, who demanded equality with the island's whites, whose culture they shared. Then, in 1791, a massive slave revolt broke out. More than ten years of bloody, confused fighting that included British and Spanish interventions eventually resulted in the French colony gaining its independence as the nation of Haiti.

Although the Saint-Domingue slave revolt was the only successful one of hundreds before and after in the New World, Haiti and the revolt's most successful black general Toussaint L'Ouverture became symbols for anti-slavery and indepen-dence movements among millions of New World slaves. As an independent state, however, Haiti faced serious problems. A small elite of mulattos continued to domi-nate the politics, economy, and society of the island while the vast majority lived as subsistence farmers. Haiti was independent, but continued as a traditional Agrarian hierarchy.

The Limits of Politically Led Restructuring

The political outcomes of the French and Haitian Revolutions point to the limits of political-led restructuring to truly transform societies. The Haitian case is clear: an Agrarian socioeconomic structure consisting of a small landowning elite and a mass of subsistence farmers—effectively peasants even if no longer slaves—produced states that followed the traditional Agrarian Era model. The same is true of France, even if the state reached a much higher degree of professionalism and male social mobility was higher than usual in Agrarian societies. After the Revolution, in a further confirmation of the inverse relationship between class power and gender power, women generally found their roles even more restricted, as bour-geois norms based in the male-public/female-private split dominated the cultural screen. More androgynous aristocratic images of gender were erased with the old regime.

Indeed, even the British and American political revolutions, which caught up with social change more than they led it, faced potential limits. The British state in 1780 was more "modern" in its structural organization and relationship to society, but it was still an oligarchy run by a small elite. The US experiment was more radical (especially in the North, where much lower levels of slaveholding and more equitable distribution of land supported a more democratic culture), but the vote was still limited to white male landowners. And in both places, experimentation with collective government at a scale unprecedented in Agrarian Era history was made possible, in part, by their insulation from any foreign threat to their basic existence. The British navy protected the British experiment and allowed rules against domestically based standing armies to be possible. The United States had it even easier, sitting on its own continent that lacked almost any other state-level complex society, outside tiny and British-protected Canada. Absent any further socioeconomic development, it is not difficult to conceive of both experiments coming to grief in a later era of more intense military competition, one of the constant drivers of traditional hierarchy dynamics, much as the French Revolution produced both Napoleon and then a restoration of the old monarchy that lasted into the 1830s.

This is because the basic constraints that shaped Agrarian Era societies and states, low productivity and slow communications, still held. It was these constraints

ISSUES IN DOING WORLD HISTORY

The Meaning of the Word "Revolution"

The word "revolution" is applied to all sorts of historical phenomena, and has been equally often criticized as inappropriate. Was the European "Military Revolution" of the seventeenth century really a revolution? The Glorious Revolution, which changed one king for another? How about the fairly conservative American Revolution? Should the term just apply to politics? Does a revolution have to occur in a fairly limited time frame to avoid being mere evolution? Does it have to entail a large change in who rules whom—a "revolving" of the order of things to make the high low and vice versa?

Many of these historical arguments come down to semantic quibbles, matters of definition, and don't ultimately seem that important. If the arguments force more careful research about and description of the historical phenomena under dispute, so much the better. But it seems unlikely that a consensus can be reached over a precise definition of what "revolution" means. One person's revolutionary change is another's case of, as The Who sang, "Meet the new boss, same as the old boss."

From this book's perspective, there are three great and truly revolutionary changes in human history: the Cognitive-Linguistic Revolution that produced modern human minds, culture, and historical development; the Agricultural Revolution that produced complex state-level societies, writing, and "history"; and the Industrial Revolution that produced (and continues to produce) our modern world. The rest is detail. While some events have been called "revolutions" long enough that trying to call them anything different would just be confusing—the Glorious, American, French, and Haitian Revolutions certainly qualify here—in general we as historians should be more concerned with understanding than naming.

that brought Napoleon's Grande Armée to grief in Russia. It was these constraints that continued to make true mass democracy difficult, if not impossible, and allowed limited experiments in representative government only in isolated safety and/or on a very small scale. It would take a truly revolutionary change in human relations to the natural world to break those constraints and allow the new hierarchy model pioneered by the British to reach its full potential—and indeed to become the new necessity. Industrialization would accomplish that revolution. What is significant about the British transformation is that it created the context within which industrialization could be born.

Conclusion

A large part of this chapter has been devoted to a more microscopic examination (at least for this book) than we have engaged in elsewhere of a particular society in a particular time and place. This is justified by that time and place being the context for the birth of industrialization, which we will turn to in the next chapter. But when we do, we will not remain confined at this microscopic level for long: the Industrial Revolution may have started in Britain, but it rapidly became a global phenomenon. We will see it that way.

FRAME IT YOURSELF

Changing the Frame

At the Battle of Beachy Head in 1690, Admiral Tourville's French fleet heavily defeated a combined Anglo-Dutch fleet in the English Channel. Control of the Channel fell temporarily to Louis XIV's France. But the Sun King failed to seize the opportunity to invade England, and the chance never reappeared. England remained safely odd and gave birth to the Industrial Revolution within a century.

What if Louis had invaded successfully and put a Catholic absolute monarch on the throne, backed by a French army of occupation? Would parliamentary government been strangled in its crib? Would John Locke be a footnote in history? Would all of North America have come under French rule? Write a brief alternate history of the 100 years after 1690, assuming a successful French invasion. What key concepts and patterns of history guide your ideas about this possible path of events?

Further Reading

Brewer, John. 1989. *The Sinews of Power: War, Money and the English State, 1688–1783*. New York: Routledge.

Black, Jeremy. 2008. *Crisis of Empire: Britain and America in the Eighteenth Century*. London: Continuum.

Doyle, William. 2001. *The French Revolution: A Very Short Introduction*. Oxford: Oxford University Press.

Dubois, Laurent. 2005. *Avengers of the New World: The Story of the Haitian Revolution*. Cambridge, MA: Harvard University Press.

Pincus, Steve. 2011. *1688: The First Modern Revolution*. New Haven: Yale University Press.

Purkiss, Diane. 2007. *The English Civil War: Papists, Gentlewomen, Soldiers, and Witchfinders in the Birth of Modern Britain*. New York: Basic Books.

For additional learning and instructional resources related to this chapter, please go to www.oup.com/us/morillo

Lord Kitchener.

PART VI

Convulsions

1750 to 1914

The activities in the odd room we explored in Chapter 18 were the beginnings of the Industrial Revolution, which birthed the Industrial Era. Part VI takes us into the Early Industrial Era, a period characterized, like the Early Agrarian though at a much faster pace, by intense innovation and the exploration of new architectural styles across the mansion.

Chapter 19 gives us an aerial view of how the mansion changed from 1750 to today under the influence of industrialization. It introduces us to the new tools industrial architects used to change the architectural style of the mansion's rooms and to the vast power surge that industry sent through the mansion's network. Chapter 20 shows that this power surge caused more rooms to change to the new industrial shape as the mansion's new wiring and plumbing gained vastly in capacity. The problem was that industrialization at first affected only a limited set of rooms. The inhabitants of those rooms decided to go marching through the mansion, claiming ownership of other rooms and trying to paint the walls everywhere the color of their own rooms. Chapter 21 examines these actions from the perspective of the people marching around the mansion, Chapter 22 from the perspective of those whose rooms were invaded.

English Origins

Much of this chapter will view the Industrial Revolution from a global and long-term perspective. But since industrialization was an invention that, like the alphabet, happened only once, we shall start by tracing its origins to the British context sketched in the last chapter.

Context

That context, again, was made up of the intersection of a mature and developed world network of trade and cultural connections with the specific features of the British hierarchy—local and global creating a mix that neither on its own would have generated.

Britain was highly networked. It dominated the world trade in sugar, produced on slave plantations on Caribbean islands. The total value of British trade in sugar in the mid-1700s exceeded the total value of all its other overseas trade—which, with the British East India Company importing Indian cotton cloth and spices and Chinese luxury goods, was not inconsiderable. And even after the successful rebellion of its American colonies, Britain retained Canada and a substantial trade with the new United States. The British navy, the biggest and most powerful in the world by a wide margin by 1780, protected the sea lanes along which foreign trade flowed.

The influx of wealth from this network position fed into an internal economy organized according to the peculiar structures and cultural frame of the British hierarchy—structures allowed to develop in part because the navy's wooden walls protected Britain's island security. Political struggles within frame values centered on law and property rights had produced a professionalized state that, because it could project a (not entirely inaccurate) screen image of representative government, could tax society relatively heavily and yet otherwise maintain an image (again, not altogether inaccurate) of governing lightly and letting people go about their business. And business was important, because the British class structure was based much more than anywhere else (except the new United States) on wealth rather than birth, so pursuit of wealth through entrepreneurial enterprises assumed significant weight. The lines between landed aristocrats and merchant capitalists were blurred, if still visible. Since all wealthy groups had a voice in Parliament, this accounted for the business-friendly, lightly regulated British internal market. The workings of that internal market were further enhanced by good communications. The state added to navigable rivers and a long coastline by building canals and, by the late 1700s, Europe's first paved roads, on which ran stagecoach services that could move mail and people rapidly, if only to a limited number of destinations.

Social mobility based in large part on wealth, an influx of network-generated wealth, and an open internal market with few divisions stimulated the growth of a consumer-oriented social culture—served by that

FIGURE 19.1 Less Slow, Less Low. Early nineteenth-century British stagecoach, a step toward faster communications.

"nation of shopkeepers" Napoleon sneered at—that could absorb and indeed began to demand more goods than traditional manufacturing processes could easily supply.

Economic Resources

Britain happened to have two sorts of resources in relative abundance that allowed it to create a new way of meeting that demand for goods: human resources and natural resources.

The first was a product in part of social mobility and the dominance of wage labor, meaning that workers were potentially available for work other than farming. But like any Agrarian Era society, the low productivity of agriculture in the 1600s meant that most people had to work in farming anyway as wage laborers. But in the late 1600s and early 1700s, a series of developments increased the efficiency of British farming. Earlier developments in British landowning patterns had created a number of unusually large farms with almost nobody living on them—largely as a result of "enclosures" whereby landowners fenced in fields on which to graze sheep, evicting small renters in the process. Owners of large tracts unencumbered by peasant farmers felt free to experiment on parts of their private property with new crops and crop rotations, knowing that failure would not lead them to starve, while success could increase their profits. Migrant wage labor could be had seasonally when necessary. Gradually, British farms began to produce more food with fewer workers, while supporting a population that grew rapidly in the 1700s.

In addition to improvements in domestic agriculture, British overseas colonies and trade, especially with the land-rich American settlements in Canada and the United States, helped meet the growing demand for food without dependence on domestic farming. (Political attitudes and policy lagged behind economic trends, slowing this particular trend somewhat. Farming was so ingrained in people's worldviews as the foundation of a country's prosperity that Corn Laws placed tariffs on imported grain, protecting British farmers, well into the 1800s.) These developments in domestic agriculture and favorable overseas trade in food and other raw materials freed a greater proportion of the population for non-agricultural work, though until new jobs appeared many would have called the result "underemployment" rather than freedom.

While Britain's abundance of available human resources was arguably a result of its developing political and social structure, its wealth in very specifically useful natural resources was a matter of sheer geographic luck. Britain in the 1600s, like a number of areas of the Late Agrarian world, was beginning to face shortages of that most basic of resources, wood. Necessary for cooking and for heating homes, as well as building (including, in Britain, building warships, which led to the importing of timber from the Baltic region), wood was becoming both more expensive, despite state attempts at price controls, and scarcer. Thus, deforestation was becoming an environmental problem. Britain, however, turned out to have large deposits of coal in the Midlands, the southwest, and in Wales that were accessible because they started near the surface. The problem was that when the pits got deeper, they tended to fill with groundwater. It was therefore the exploitation of such coalfields for heating and cooking that led Thomas Newcomen to invent his steam engine, which could pump the water out of mines.

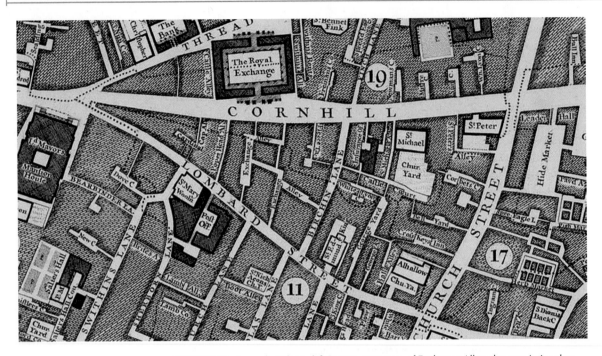

FIGURE 19.2 Emerging Financial Center. 1747 map of Exchange Alley, the area in London where the Stock Exchange and insurance companies arose from coffeehouses.

Britain also turned out to have abundant deposits of iron ore. These had been exploited since the mid-1500s, when it turned out that southern English iron ore was naturally alloyed in such a way that it produced strong yet flexible cast iron that did not shatter when made into naval cannon. (Cannon founding also, as we saw in James Watt's story, had brought into being precision methods of drilling out the bore of a gun, which transferred readily to drilling out the bore of a piston.) The further piece of luck was that even in a relatively small country with good internal communications, as Britain was, its coal and iron deposits often lay right next to each other. Combining them in processes of iron and steel making and the production of machinery was therefore made easier and less expensive because of very low transport costs. By contrast, Song China, whose iron industry had been by far the world's largest in the late 1000s, had been burdened by the great separation of southern iron and northern coal, the latter of which actually fell out of Song control in 1127 when northern China fell to invaders from the steppes.

In addition to human and natural resources, Britain also had, in the large naval shipyards that built Britain's warships, models of large-scale industrial organization that resulted from the spending power and strategic outlook of its professionalized state. Finally, in joint-stock companies it had a model of corporate organization that allowed individual firms to tap into the accumulating wealth of the British population. Increasingly formal stock exchanges existed in Britain beginning in 1688, along with insider trading, stock bubbles and crashes, and consequently increasing state regulation. In 1801, the state chartered the London Stock Exchange. Such organizational models formed a part of the cultural resources that shaped British responses to the country's developing demands.

Early Industries

One of the key products for which demand was soaring and outrunning supply was for cotton cloth. Cotton was not only far more comfortable for undergarments than wool cloth, but imports of Indian cotton cloth printed with colorful designs had become popular. But the vested interests of the English wool weavers of the south and southeast part of the country convinced Parliament to pass restrictions not only on imported Indian cloth, but on the sorts of cotton cloth that northern English weavers could produce. It was only when loopholes and exemptions from these protectionist measures were found that cotton cloth production began increasing in the mid-1700s.

FIGURE 19.3 Arkwright's Water Frame, ca. 1775. A labor-saving device, something that no traditional elite would really want.

It was at this point, with demand exceeding supply, that various inventors began introducing improvements to existing technologies for carding (cleaning and combing) cotton wool, spinning it into thread, and weaving the thread into cloth. Any one invention increased demand elsewhere in the chain of production—for instance, a more efficient loom created greater demand for thread, which led to the spinning jenny, which allowed one worker to spin several times more thread. Richard Arkwright's water frame, so called because it ran on power generated by a water mill, though later versions could be powered by steam engines, combined a number of such innovations in spinning and weaving. In 1771, Arkwright installed his machinery in a purpose-built factory. He hired workers as employees rather than contracting with them for piecework output as had been traditional, and he established work shifts determined, for the first time, by mechanical clocks.

Not that these developments happened without opposition. On top of protectionist legislation sponsored by established industries, the new machines sometimes met resistance from workers themselves. The common fear was that the new technology would take away jobs. And indeed, it did, though in the slightly longer term it created more new jobs (because it generated more wealth) than it destroyed. But the mercantilist assumption that the total value of trade was constant made such an effect difficult to see before the Scottish philosopher Adam Smith exploded that assumption in his *Wealth of Nations,* published in 1776. Even so, the real difficulties caused by technological transitions still follow this pattern, as current disputes over robotics and the impact of free trade demonstrate. Early industrial workers also resisted the new clock-driven work discipline, as it represented a loss of control over their own working conditions. And at least British workers had some voice, if only through outbreaks of machine breaking. When industrially produced British cotton cloth still proved uncompetitive in India with Indian handwoven cloth, the British rulers of India effectively shut down Indian weaving, forcing uncounted weavers back to villages unable

ISSUES IN DOING WORLD HISTORY

"Great Men"

Newcomen, Watt, Wedgwood, Arkwright—the story of the Industrial Revolution has often been told in terms of the "Great Inventors" whose inventions changed the world. We have mentioned some of these men in this chapter. But we have tried to place them in their social, political, and economic contexts, and to emphasize the impact of those contexts. For every society has clever, inventive people. The question is, does the society's structure and culture give room for that inventiveness to thrive and make a difference? For most of history before the Industrial Revolution, the answer is no: Agrarian hierarchical societies were built to resist change and to keep people rigidly in their social place doing their assigned job, no matter what their "true" talents. Even hyper-inventive early Industrial Britain seriously suppressed the talents of the female half of its adult population. Furthermore, the very contexts that allowed individual inventors to flourish meant that if they hadn't, someone else almost certainly would have—witness the explosion of improvements to and applications of the steam engine after Watt's key patents expired and anyone could modify his basic design.

This de-emphasis on the heroic achievements of the great inventors is the result of outlooks on the writing of history that emphasize the dynamics of whole societies and their cultural frames, as well as the history of

unremarkable people who are representative more than exceptional. Such approaches have largely displaced a traditional style of historical writing that applied not just to the history of the Industrial Revolution, but even more to political, military, and even religious history generally—that is, many of the great traditions of historical writing of the Agrarian world—a style (or outlook) known as "Great Man" history. Great Man history, which remained prominent in the nineteenth century and in popular history well into the twentieth, attributes historical change to the genius and decisions of great leaders, not to broad social, economic, and cultural forces. It arose in part from the hierarchical structure of Agrarian societies with their culturally prominent kings and elites, but it fit well with the creation of "national" histories in the nineteenth century (see the Issues in Doing World History box in Chapter 20, where the reasons for the scare quotes around "national" will become clear), as it provided a pantheon of heroes around which new group identities could be constructed.

Interest in past individuals is compelling and is expressed today in biographies (which need not be of "great men"). But doing world history virtually compels a broad, systemic approach to historical change in preference to a narrow focus on so-called great men.

to support them, and exported raw Indian cotton to Britain instead. Politics and global connections were part of industrialization from the start. The difficulties of the transition from Agrarian to Industrial cultures of production, even in a British hierarchy structured in ways favorable to the transition, remind us of the contingent nature of the Industrial Revolution: it didn't have to happen.

Industrialization: A Global Overview

The British Industrial Revolution did happen, of course, and with increasing speed after 1800, as industrial production of cotton cloth, porcelain pottery at Josiah Wedgwood's factory, and steam engines themselves, among other products, took off. Furthermore, the British Industrial Revolution would prove to be simply the first step in a global process that spread, by the standards of previous history, with remarkable rapidity and transformative power. In this section, we will overview the spreading global impact of industrialization over the two centuries since it took off in Britain, outlining topics that we will return to in detail in later chapters.

Chronology

We can divide the history of the Industrial Revolution (or the spread of industrialization) into four phases. In each phase, we can identify the countries that were industrializing during that phase, the character of industrialization in those countries (that is, how industrialization got started), and the key industries.

Phase One: 1770 to 1870

Industrial countries: Britain; from the 1830s, in limited ways, Belgium and New England in the United States.

Character: the first (and only) spontaneous, largely private industrialization. Like the alphabet, industrialization is one of those rare instances in world history of an idea invented only once, and spread subsequently by direct borrowing, or at least knowledge of the idea.

Industries: a limited number of "heavy" industries, primarily textiles, steam engines themselves (for production), as well as steam engines used in transport (railroads and steamships), and steel. In addition, the application of industrial production to weaponry came rapidly and preceded full industrialization in many places: this was part of the new and newly threatening intersection of the global economic network with hierarchies. Thus, the number and scope of industries may have been limited in Phase One (and continued to be in Phase Two), but these industries had a huge global impact both within Britain, which became the world's Great Power of the mid-nineteenth century, and beyond.

Phase Two: 1870 to 1914

Industrial countries added: the United States, Germany, Japan, France. Limited industrial development in parts of Spain, Italy, Austria, Russia, and Argentina. As this list makes clear (with the notable exception of Japan), industrialization spread first to countries with strong network connections to Britain, both cooperative (economic) and competitive (military), with compatible social structures and cultures (a result, in continental Europe, partly of Napoleon's spreading the ideals of the French Revolution, as we noted in the previous chapter), and—in very nineteenth-century terms—with racially white population (again with the notable exception of Japan). Thus Egypt, grower of quality cotton wool, began to industrialize in the 1840s but found its efforts stifled by the British at the same time as British investment was jump-starting the industrialization of textile manufacturing in New England.

Character: the spread, via investment, of privately owned industrialization, but in many of these cases stimulated by conscious state policies

FIGURE 19.4 Industrial Countries: Phase One.

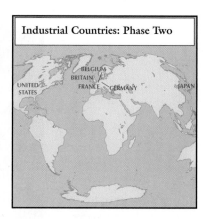

FIGURE 19.5 Industrial Countries: Phase Two.

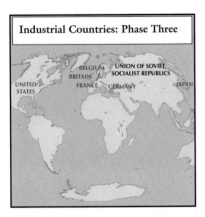

FIGURE 19.6 **Industrial Countries: Phase Three.**

designed to foster the growth of an industrial base. Industrial competition became a major aspect of geo-political competition among the Industrial powers, further spreading the impact of industrialization beyond the Industrial powers, especially in the form of imperialism.

Industries: pretty much the same set as in Phase One, but with an increasing pace of scientific innovation, especially in industrial chemistry.

Phase Three: 1914 to 1970

Industrial countries added: before World War II, the Soviet Union industrialized heavily and virtually without outside investment. After the war, this sphere of industrialization spread to much of Soviet-controlled eastern Europe. Germany and Japan, their industrial infrastructure virtually demolished during the war, were rapidly re-industrialized with a massive infusion of US investment.

Character: This phase was dominated by the Communist-run sphere of industrialization, which was state controlled, forced, and brutal, with little outside investment. At least in its early stages in the 1930s, however, it appeared very effective, if limited to the usual set of heavy (and especially military) industries. Russia's industrial output grew rapidly while the already industrialized countries of western Europe, the United States, and Japan suffered through the Great Depression. Beyond the communist sphere, the spread of industrialization was seriously impacted by the period of the World Wars and the Depression between them. The United States dominated the period after World War II industrially, almost as much as Britain had a hundred years earlier.

FIGURE 19.7 **Old Meets New.** Inuit tribesmen out for a spin in an early automobile. (The Granger Collection, New York)

Industries: outside the new communist Industrial countries, which concentrated on traditional heavy industries, especially military production, this phase saw in the already Industrial countries what is sometimes called the "Second Industrial Revolution," which featured an explosion of light industry and the mass production of consumer goods. The automobile industry, a consumer-oriented light industry with heavy industry infrastructure, rose to prominence. The "light industries" of this phase may also be said to include the first mass-market entertainment industries (movies, a few sports, radio).

Phase Four: Since 1970

Industrial countries added: a rapidly expanding list extending by the 2000s to most of the major regions of the world, especially East Asia and South Asia, including the Pacific Rim, major parts of Latin America, and in a more limited way, parts of the Islamic world and sub-Saharan Africa.

FIGURE 19.8 Industrial Countries: Phase Four.

Character: as in Phase Two, a mix of private investment and state sponsorship, with the mix tending more toward state investment and protectionism early in the period, but shifting toward more private (corporate) investment by the 1990s, for both economic and political-ideological reasons, most prominently the collapse of the communist model of industrial development in 1989.

Industries: a vast proliferation of consumer-oriented industries, including what are called service industries, or businesses that offer services and expertise instead of goods, and an explosion of entertainment industries. The world's largest industry by the 2000s, tourism, embodied both of these trends. Finally, the most characteristic and important new field of manufacturing and service involved the rise of electronic and especially digital media: television and all its offshoots and the computer-Internet age, sometimes called yet another (third? fourth? the namers don't agree) Industrial Revolution. In our longer term, less hype-filled view, this is just another phase of an ongoing transformation into an Industrial Era that, unlike the Agrarian Era, is built to generate and absorb rapid change, which becomes its own sort of stasis. We shall return to these issues in the rest of this book, as well as to others outlined in the following overview of the impact of industrialization.

Impacts: Mass and the End of the Agrarian World

The shift from an agrarian to an industrial mode of production affected every aspect of life, with its effects extending well beyond the Industrial countries because of the effects of the global network.

In the most basic demographic terms, industrialization is the third of the three great revolutions in world history, as our fundamental graph of total world population, the top diagram in Figure 19.9, reminds us. In terms of absolute numbers, moreover, this logarithmic chart understates the numbers of people alive in the Industrial Era (the cost of letting us see comparable rates of change in different eras). An arithmetic graph of total human population looks like the bottom diagram in Figure 19.9.

Mass population was accompanied by and made possible by industrialization's basic economic effect: mass production and consumption in mass markets. The number of things in the world went way up, their price went way down, material standards of living increased—in short, the basic scarcity that characterized the

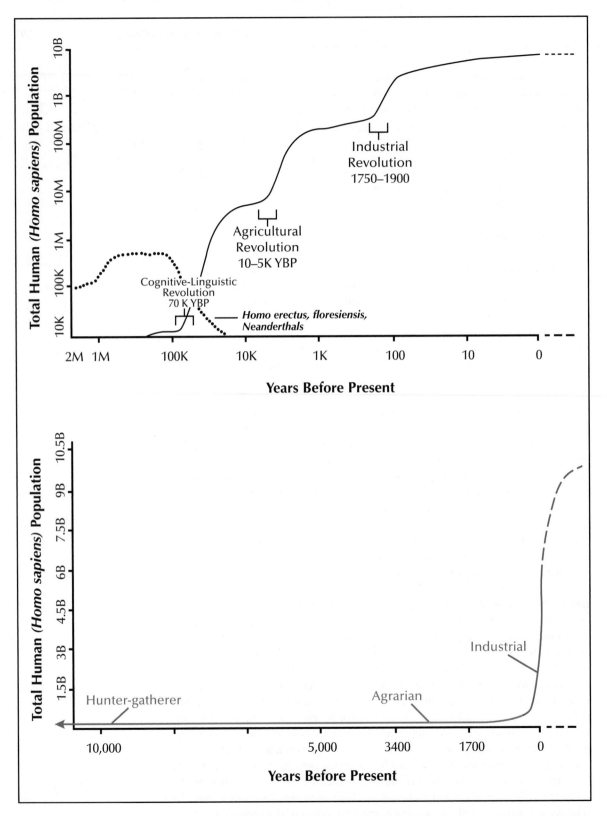

FIGURE 19.9 Demographic History Revisited. (Top) The three great revolutions in world history. (Bottom) The population explosion of the Industrial Era.

Agrarian Era came to an end, and an Age of Profligacy began. This impact vastly increased the power of the global network, which carried these effects around the world. We will explore these effects in more detail later in this chapter, as well as in later chapters.

This network power surge added substantially to the transformative effects of merchant capitalism on the structure of hierarchies globally. The effect on societies was, sooner or later, to blow up traditional pyramids and create mass societies that moved toward being socioeconomic spheres. Class structures changed, urbanization accelerated greatly. Wealthier societies made individualism far more affordable. Social transformation was accompanied by and necessitated changes in states and politics within hierarchies. The bases of power and authority changed, and mass politics, in one form or another, became a necessity. New resources and the new challenges posed by Industrial economics and society added greatly to the power of the state. We shall explore these effects initially in Chapter 20. The impact of the power differentials created by uneven industrialization is a central topic of Chapters 21 through 25.

Finally, the cultural impact of industrialization became pervasive. Mass societies and politics expressed themselves through mass culture, as access to the cultural screen widened and new frame values emerged to meet new conditions of life. The visible impacts of industrialization generated reactions both favorable and hostile, as well as numerous attempts to shape those impacts in various ways. Furthermore, the mechanisms of industrial production themselves transformed cultural expression in new ways. Industrial-scale printing and later electronic forms of mass media met the communications needs of mass society and erased the Great Cultural Divide. Capitalist frame and screen values affected not only material production, but worked recursively on the production of culture, making cultural output a commodity. We shall explore early features of this topic in Chapter 20, and we will return to these themes frequently in later chapters.

Implications

This brief overview highlights two central implications about the Industrial Revolution and the world it created. First, the revolution spread unevenly and affected different areas in different ways, an effect that continues to be visible today in differences between developed and developing countries, and even between regions within countries (Shanghai versus rural southwestern China, for example). The global network meant that an area did not itself have to be industrial to feel the effects of industrialization elsewhere, but the most transformative effects—what we might call "modernization"—were felt where industry took hold locally.

This in turn emphasizes that industrialization was (and continues to be) a global process, not a discrete event. The "Industrial Revolution" did not happen just in Britain between 1780 and 1830, but was a global process even then, thanks to the network connections and flows that were vital both to launching it and to spreading its effects. In demographic terms, our logarithmic chart in Figure 19.9 suggests that the most explosive growth (and therefore the approximate extent of the Early Industrial Era) lasted until the early 1900s, though there may be arguments for pushing that into the mid-1900s. That only a small number of the world's countries were at all industrialized by that time parallels the model of the Agricultural

PRINCIPLES AND PATTERNS

Industrialization accelerated the long-term trend that saw networks increase in importance relative to hierarchies.

Images of Industry

Industrialization elicited reactions from artists, who projected varying images of the new Industrial world. Some, such as J. M. W. Turner in his painting *Steam and Speed* (top left), emphasized the excitement of steam power, its ability to break the limits of "low and slow." Others, represented here by Camille Pissarro's painting *Factory Near Pontoise* (top right), incorporated industry into a nostalgic, neo-pastoral image of the world. Finally, a darker image (bottom) of "dark satanic mills" (to use the poet William Blake's evocative phrase) emerged as the impact of industrialization spread.

Revolution: by 200 CE (where we have set our approximate endpoint of the Early Agrarian Era), only certain core areas of the world were fully based on farming—indeed, substantial regions were still occupied by hunter-gatherers in 200 CE—but those areas dominated the global political landscape. That the Industrial Revolution spread far faster and more pervasively than the Agricultural Revolution demonstrates the increased power of the global network, with Industrial Era communications technologies further multiplying that power by many factors.

Finally, the process of industrialization created what we think of as the "modern" world. As we shall see, Industrial hierarchies tend to become variations on a common model, just as Agrarian pyramid-shaped hierarchies were variations on a common model. But the single point of origin of industrialization has made it easy to conflate "modernization" with "Westernization," so that the process of transition from Agrarian to Industrial was much more consciously contested on various cultural screens (see the Issues in Doing World History box in Chapter 22) than the slow spread of agriculture.

Industrial Economics: Good-bye Low and Slow

Industrialization's transformative impact began at the economic level, or more accurately as a revolution in the relationship between humans and the earth and its natural resources. Low productivity and slow communications evaporated as constraints on the worlds of human social, political, and cultural organization.

Mechanisms of Transformation

The primary mechanisms that brought about this transformation were new sources of energy, put to use through new technologies, and organized in new ways in physical space.

Energy

The low productivity and slow communications that characterized the Agrarian world (and the Hunter-Gatherer world before it, even more) resulted from the relatively weak sources of power through which humans could get work done. These were almost exclusively wind power, water power, and muscle power, the last overwhelmingly human but supplemented in important ways by animal power. Muscle power was by far the most important of the three. Muscle power is limited, even when multiplied by pulleys, levers, ramps, and the other basic mechanical force multipliers, and is furthermore expensive (inefficient) in terms of the fuel needed to generate it. (Human muscle is actually relatively efficient compared to much animal power: an individual horse is more powerful than an individual human, but consumes proportionately more food. This is one effect of human evolution for endurance, efficient body cooling, and above all a short gut built to digest processed foods. It's the human brain, site of the cognitive-linguistic power that jump-started human history, that is metabolically expensive.) Wind power mostly drove ships, which had proved increasingly important across the Agrarian Era, and water power

FIGURE 19.10 Making Oil. The ferns and feathered dinosaurs that became fossil fuels. They lived in a much warmer world than we do. So far.

was the least exploited, running mills (and Arkwright's water frame) in a few regions.

The Newcomen-Watt steam engine opened the path to converting heat from fires into work, which was economically viable because fossil fuels—first coal and later oil and natural gas—concentrated combustible carbon at levels far beyond wood and peat. Further technological developments followed, opening alternatives to fossil fuels, including hydroelectric, geothermal, nuclear, and solar, as well as generating power in the form of electricity rather than heat-driven machinery. But fossil fuels remain (as of the writing of this book) the primary food for the Industrial Era's insatiable hunger for energy, including for generating electricity. The carbon in fossil fuels was captured by the vast fern and coniferous forests from the age of dinosaurs and before, when the earth's climate was significantly warmer than it is today. The energy demands of the Industrial Era, by releasing increasingly large amounts of this trapped carbon into the atmosphere, naturally threatens to return the global climate to something closer to its previous levels. But in the meantime, the energy generated by burning fossil fuels powered the machinery and industrial processes that supported massive population growth, filled the world with cheap commodities, and allowed those goods and their attached ideas to be moved around at previously unimaginable rates.

Technology

The new sources of energy were applied through new technologies. Industrial machinery from the spinning jenny on, by allowing the substitution of new energy sources for human muscle, acted as labor-saving devices. This might seem like one of those "well, of course" paths of development; indeed, in hindsight, the tremendous multiplication of labor power that industrial machinery allowed did support increased standards of living for many more people. But the move is counterintuitive at the local level, as resistance to new labor-saving devices from the time of Arkwright to today demonstrates. The broad effect of increased labor productivity does come at the immediate cost of some people's traditional jobs. Furthermore, the new wealth and jobs that technology creates don't always go to those displaced from old jobs. Thus, technological transition entails real suffering for some.

Even more important historically, however, the use of labor-saving devices required a complete shift in the economic bases of social power. Elite status in the Agrarian Era depended on authority over human beings, the source of almost all work and wealth. A member of an Agrarian elite who deployed labor-saving devices therefore threatened to reduce the number of people who depended on him for a living and so reduce his own social power. Thus, innovations in modes of production were just as (or even more) likely to be resisted by elites as by laborers in a securely hierarchical society. This highlights the prior changes in British society and its bases of status and authority that had already taken place by the early 1700s—with status based largely on wealth, and wage-labor and overseas trade having already abstracted, to some extent, the connection between labor and wealth creation—that made the first industrialization possible. In short, the shift from Agrarian to Industrial society entails a shift from labor-intensive to capital-intensive socioeconomic organization and cultural outlook.

Once industrialization was under way, however, steady technological innovation became an integral part of the ongoing process. This was not just because new labor-saving technologies could give particular producers an edge, in labor costs and profits accumulated, over their competitors in making things such as cotton cloth or washing machines. It was also because new technologies were themselves potential commodities, as Watt's own experience selling steam engines shows. This meant that technological innovation was driven not just by perceived needs that a new invention could meet, but by new inventions that met needs people didn't even know they had—needs that were, in effect, called into being by a new product. In this way, industrialization is characterized by the wedding of economics and science: it made science itself an industry.

Organization

The third mechanism of transformation in industrialization was the social reorganization of work around technology. Especially with production centered on large steam-driven engines, work could no longer be "put out" by a merchant capitalist to a decentralized, even rural workforce. The workers had to come to the machinery, and the factory system of production was the result. This involved, as we noted above, some serious changes in the culture of work from Agrarian Era patterns of manufacturing. Workers came to factories as employees. They were paid an hourly wage rather than by the piece produced, as the machines established the pace of work. This moved work from a culture of organic time to one of mechanical time: shifts of workers organized by the clock instead of the sun.

Some aspects of Agrarian work habits survived at least for a time under the factory regime. Often, entire families, used to working together in agriculture or domestic manufacturing, entered factory employment together in the early decades of British industrialization—it was not child labor itself, but child labor beyond parental oversight that proved upsetting. But factories also introduced new cultures in their workforces. Drawn together daily from their separate farmhouses or new urban dwellings, factory workers developed a stronger consciousness of their common problems and concerns, as well as a greater ability to organize and give common voice to those concerns. Such organizing was not surprisingly slowed by the much louder voices of employers in the government—voices fewer in number but amplified by money—that long kept unions or other working associations illegal. But workers' voices slowly gained in force and political influence.

Finally, factories tended to aggregate together in cities because of the economics of attracting workers from a common pool of labor. Factory production therefore stimulated the growth of cities by encouraging immigration from the countryside, with a vast range of social and cultural consequences that we will explore in the next chapter. Urbanization proved one of the most significant and irresistible trends of the Industrial Era. Well over 90% of the world's population in the Agrarian Era lived

PRINCIPLES AND PATTERNS

In the Agrarian Era, power led to wealth. In the Industrial Era, wealth leads to power.

FIGURE 19.11 **Men and Machines.** Interior of an eighteenth-century textile mill.

in the countryside, growing or gathering food. In 2008, barely 200 years after industrialization began, for the first time more than 50% of the world's population was
living in cities. Industrialization has been a powerful and pervasive transformative
process indeed.

Mass: Production, Consumption, Markets

The key word for the Industrial economics that emerged from the transformations
of energy, technology, and organization is "mass." "Low and slow" no longer kept
economics small.

Mass Production

As we have noted, the industrial mode of production made it possible to make many
more things far more cheaply than was possible under conditions of hand
manufacturing. While in the early decades of British industrialization it was (and remains today) easy to decry a loss of quality and craftsmanship in the shift away from
handicrafts, the actual evidence for such decline is impressionistic at best. Certainly
at the very highest levels, as for example with the Ottoman jewel-encrusted canteen

shown in Chapter 16, Agrarian Era specialists were capable of astonishing crafts-manship. But they could also make shoddy products, while industrial concerns such as Josiah Wedgwood's porcelain factory could maintain very high standards of production. And since for many items, including ones such as weaponry whose operation had life-or-death consequences, mass production depended on interchangeable parts, industrialization encouraged greater and greater precision in standards of engineering. This started with steam engines themselves, as Watt's experience trying to create a tight-fitting piston reminds us.

Mass production thus made better products available more cheaply. Counterintuitively, despite increasing demand for such products (and thus rising demand for the raw materials they are made from), mass production has also, over the course of the last 200 years, brought down the price of such basic commodities. Whether it's iron, copper, or aluminum, or wheat, cotton cloth, or corn oil, the long-term trend of prices for basic commodities has been steadily downward, as the chart in Figure 19.12 of the real price (adjusted for monetary inflation, as opposed to the nominal price) of basic commodities shows. More efficient production, competition to meet growing demand, and cheaper transport costs accounts for this trend. Whether the trend will hold as industrial levels of demand penetrate more deeply into the huge developing economies of China and India remains to be seen. The question is complicated by

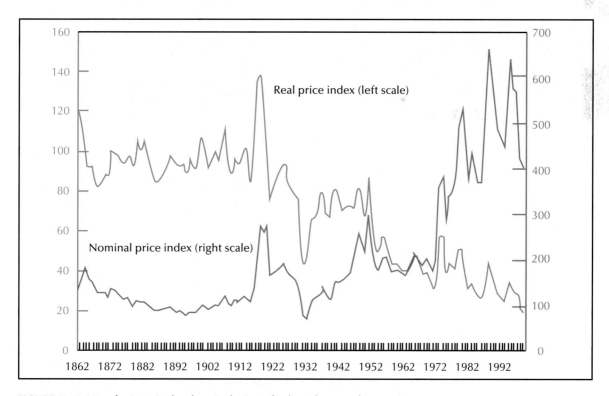

FIGURE 19.12 More for Less. Real and nominal prices of industrial commodities, 1862–1999, according to the International Monetary Fund (IMF). Vastly more demanded, but sold for steadily less as production rises.

technological development allowing substitution of specific goods—the real price of oil seems certain to rise in the next century as economically accessible reserves dry up, but the overall price of energy may well continue to fall as something like more efficient solar power generation spreads.

Networks and Markets

The industrial mode of production was both called into being by and served to expand mass consumer markets. This is another way of saying that industrialization depended on network flows in order to get started, and then served to greatly increase the volume and power of network flows. Some of this was driven by inexpensive goods: Karl Marx famously said in *The Communist Manifesto* that "the cheap prices of its commodities are the heavy artillery with which [Industrial Capitalism] batters down all Chinese walls." The Opium Wars (see Chapter 21), however, as well as the fate of Indian handweavers of cotton cloth under British rule, reminds us that real guns and political coercion also played a role in spreading the effects of industrialization. Moreover, the best mass markets are in industrialized countries with higher levels of wealth. Thus, for most of the past 200 years, the industrialized countries have sucked in raw materials *and* consumed most of their own industrial output.

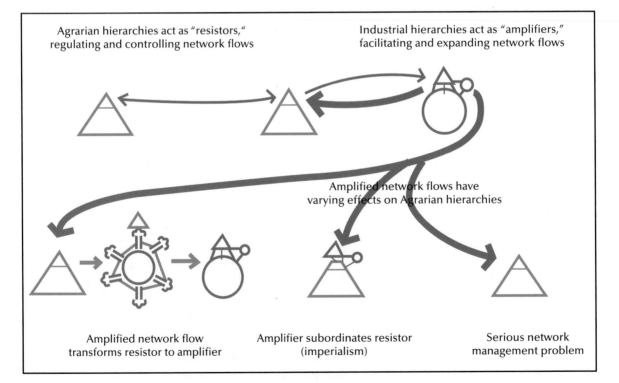

FIGURE 19.13 **Industry: Network Power Surge.** Industrial hierarchies amplified network flows. Agrarian hierarchies resisted them. Amplified flows started blowing up resisters, some of which turned into amplifiers themselves.

Industrially based trade created complex problems for hierarchies, industrial and not, in managing their network intersection. (See Figure 19.13.) Free trade (which theoretically benefits everyone and certainly in practice benefits established Industrial powers) became viable as a screen image competing with protectionism. The latter nevertheless remained the dominant practice in countries attempting to foster their own industrialization. In an ironic twist, however, Britain, the leading advocate of free trade in the nineteenth century, led the way in the early 1800s in shutting down, partly through coercion, the slave trade it had supported for three centuries. Abolitionists drew on Enlightenment notions of human rights, religious ideals, and the economic notion that a free market in labor on the Industrial model was the proper form of trade in labor to shift the British stance.

Impacts

To repeat the main theme of this chapter, the key economic impacts of the Industrial Revolution were to allow mass population growth and to bring an end to low productivity and slow communications, the major constraints that had shaped the structures of Agrarian Era hierarchies. This opened the way to new forms of social and political organization and the cultural frames and screens that accompanied them. All this combined to increase the human impact on the global environment.

Demographics

The demographic effect of industrialization is partly a simple matter of Industrial economics increasing the earth's "carrying capacity," at least for humans. Over the last 200 years, industrial agriculture—with machine power, the economies of scale that were opened up by machines (large farms are generally more efficient), the scientific application of chemistry in fertilizers and of biology in genetic engineering, and the organizational and financial resources of corporate business organization— produces far more food per acre and per person than Agrarian farming did. Thus, farmers made up less than 6% of the population of the United States in 2000. Modern transport can deliver what is produced almost anywhere. Although there are questions about the sustainability of some of the practices of modern agriculture, hunger, at least at the moment, is more a result of political and economic problems with distribution rather than of total production.

The mechanism of Industrial population expansion, however, is a bit more complex than people simply reproducing more in a richer environment. It turns out that beyond a certain level, more wealth tends to cause people to have fewer children, not more. In fact, one of the most interesting pieces of evidence for the relative poverty of the Agrarian world, even among elites, compared to the Industrial world, is that the richest families (or, more specifically, men) in the Agrarian world had the most children—think of Chingiz Khan's millions of descendants (see Issues in Doing World History box, Chapter 13) or (for a female example) Queen Anne's seventeen children. Admittedly, cultural restraints as much as economics limit the ability of today's richest men from following Chingiz Khan's hyper-fatherly path, but the trend is nevertheless clear: richer people in the Industrial world have fewer children.

The reasons for this are complicated, though economics plays a strong role: under Agrarian conditions, children were usually an economic (and for elites a political) asset. Under Industrial conditions, they are more likely to be an economic liability. They are also, under Industrial conditions, far more likely to survive: remember that all of Queen Anne's children died before age 10. It is in this latter fact that we find the key to population growth during industrialization. Increasing standards of living, as well as scientific and medical advances, meant that with industrialization, life expectancy increased—or put another way, death rates per year per 1,000 people dropped, with lower infant mortality contributing to this significantly. Birth rates per year per 1,000 also dropped, but much more slowly (and when Industrial medicine was exported to non-Industrial regions, much more slowly). The graph in Figure 19.14 shows the result. Birth and death rates tended to be roughly in balance at high levels in the Agrarian Era, though with sometimes catastrophically wide variations in the death rate. And they tend to balance out at low levels in fully Industrial countries, with the birth rate sometimes dropping below the death rate (i.e., below replacement level). This is why demographers expect world population to level out by the middle of the twenty-first century.

The differential transition during industrialization is where growth happened. That different regions industrialized at different times gives this graph major significance. In 1800, roughly 1 in 5 of the world's population was of European origin. By 1900, that figure was 1 in 3. In 2000, it was back down to 1 in 5. Hello, nineteenth-century exceptionalism.

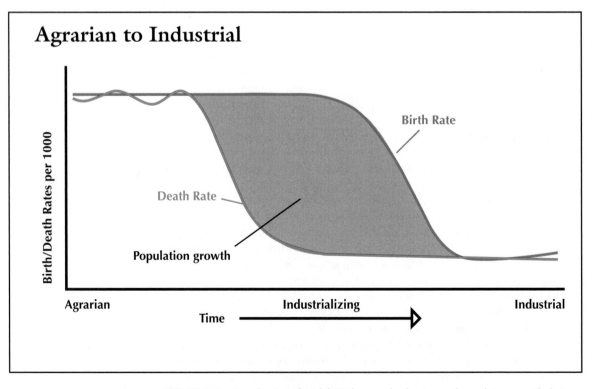

FIGURE 19.14 Agrarian to Industrial. Birth rates, death rates, and population growth during industrialization.

Industry and the Environment

Coal burning, carbon emissions, vast urban areas piling up trash—industrialization was bad for the environment, right? Yes, but we must be careful to qualify that statement in a number of ways. Humans have been transforming their environments since before agriculture. The Cognitive-Linguistic Revolution and the more effective hunting techniques it made possible were enough to contribute to some species going extinct as humans spread over the earth. Farming made such transformations more intentional and pervasive. Deforestation became a periodic problem from perhaps as early as with the Harappan civilization of the Indus Valley around 2000 BCE down through the English wood shortage that led to greater use of coal.

Industrialization multiplied the environmental impact of humanity in several ways. Simply increasing the number of people in the world so vastly makes the human footprint bigger, of course. In that context alone, the ability of many non-human species to survive in a world so full of humans (and their domesticated animals, whose numbers have also increased greatly) is obviously in question. And in the same way that new sources of energy running labor-saving devices multiplied the productivity of human labor, it also multiplied its environmental impact. Finally, aspects of the cultures of production, both capitalist and state-planned, contributed to worsening environmental problems, a topic we will return to in more detail in Chapter 26.

On the other hand, the deep involvement of science in industrial development has also led to new understandings of environmental issues and to new ways of mitigating environmental problems, an option not available to Agrarian Era populations. In assessing the environmental impact of industrialization, as in many other issues, the continuity between 200 years ago and today—and so the ongoing nature of issues whose eventual outcome we do not yet know—complicates the problem of historical analysis.

Economic Culture: Capitalism

The trajectory of industrialization was shaped not just by the material realities of energy, technology, and physical organization, but also by the cultural frames within which industrialization took place and the screen issues raised by the industrial transformation. We will return to the main screen issues in the next chapter. Here we analyze capitalism, which was both a system of economic organization and an *idea* that, if not quite a frame value itself (especially after socialist thinkers increasingly challenged it from the 1830s on), was a dominant screen image because it drew on certain deep frame values of British and then western European societies. Capitalism has therefore shaped industrialization in important ways over the last 200 years.

Capitalism as an Economic System

To repeat what we said in Chapter 15, this book adopts a simple definition of *capitalism*. Capitalism is an economic system that involves three elements. The first element is *the private ownership of capital*. "Private" here means both non-state and non-communal. "Capital" is the means of doing business, including but not limited to cash. Machinery became a key form of capital with industrialization. The second element is *the division of capital and labor.* This means that an enterprise in which the labor is performed by the owners of capital—the baker who bakes in his own oven—is not capitalist. Nor are partnerships where every worker takes a share of the profits. Wage labor is capitalist. Third, *the benefits of doing business (profits) accrue to the owners of capital.* Joint-stock companies and their direct descendants, corporations whose stock is publicly traded, are capitalist: it is the owners of stock who receive proportionate shares of the corporation's profits. (Top managers can be very well compensated, of course, but that compensation counts as an expense against the corporation's profits. Compensation in stock options is a potential complication to this definition, but has also raised enough practical and legal complications to validate the principle of the definition.)

As an economic system, capitalism comes in three main variants historically: merchant capitalism, in which the capitalist owns the means of transportation; industrial capitalism, in which the capitalist owns the means of production—the type that became newly prominent with industrialization, obviously; and financial capitalism, in which the capitalist uses capital in its most liquid form (money) to make more money.

Capitalism as a Screen Image

Capitalism existed not just as a system of economic organization, but increasingly from the early nineteenth century as a screen image, or in more conventional terms, as an ideology, an idea self-consciously promoted (and opposed) rather than simply practiced.

It is with capitalism as an idea that we must distinguish it from other ideas with which it is often wrapped up in a package of ideas presented as one. To begin with, capitalism is not market economics, free or otherwise. Free markets can exist without capitalism, and capitalist enterprises operate in unfree markets all the time, for example utility companies granted legal monopolies by the state. The distinction between capitalism and free markets is also recognized in anti-trust regulations. Capitalist enterprises may often operate most efficiently in a free market setting, but they are not the same thing. There is as much coincidence as organic connection between the rise of capitalism as a screen image and the rise of free market economics as a screen image. Adam Smith's *Wealth of Nations* created the science (and screen image) of market economics, but he had little to say about capitalist organization in itself (and nothing to say of industrialization, as it had not really started when he wrote).

Nor is capitalism the same as democracy, which should be obvious, as democracy is a political system and idea, while capitalism is an economic system and idea. Capitalist corporations have existed quite happily in non-democratic states such as Nazi Germany, and democratic states have existed without capitalist enterprises. Capitalism, market economics, and democratic politics do have a history that has become increasingly entangled since the beginning of the Industrial Revolution. They have often gone together, but are not necessarily mutually supportive.

The power of capitalism as a screen image and its conflation with free markets and democracy rest on its foundation in key frame values of the British culture in which capitalism went industrial, values which have spread with the spread

FIGURE 19.15 Soviet Soda.
Drink sold in the Soviet Union, c. 1990. Capitalism does not require democracy to flourish.

of industrialization. Probably the most important of these is the legal structure of private property rights, which are important to the operation of markets and, through John Locke's interpretation of the Glorious Revolution in terms of "natural rights," to much modern democratic theory. The complex relationships between capitalism, markets, and democracy will be a recurring subject of analysis through the rest of this book.

Consequences of Capitalism

Capitalism and industrial modes of production amplified each other. Capitalism gave to industry a flexible, socially dynamic organization within hierarchies, while industrial production multiplied the power of capitalist firms to spread through the global network to other hierarchies (a process already under way under merchant capitalism, as we have seen).

Commodification and Economic Culture

One of the key consequences of the capitalist culture of much industrialization was in fact to increase the tendency of economic activity to be expansionist. The centrality of the profit motive in capitalism, especially when sharpened by competition in an open market, drives a constant search for new markets, new products to offer to those markets, and new processes through which to offer the products more cheaply and efficiently. This may seem so obvious as be "natural" today, but this perception is evidence of the power of the capitalist screen image. Many forms of Agrarian economic activity did not put profit first and so were not expansionist. Indeed, the norm for the coercive, hierarchical societies of the Agrarian world was to put politics before economics, privileging stability and security over the perils (and opportunities) of economic freedom. Thus, sumptuary laws restricted certain kinds of clothing, food, and other goods to certain classes of people. Guilds limited entrance into crafts and trades in order to guarantee quality and protect the livings of approved masters. Both state-imposed restrictions (kings were often conceived as owners of all land, and its distribution was a matter of vital political import) and social restrictions (land was often conceived of as communally or at least family-owned and thus not subject to sale by an individual) constrained sales of land, a literally foundational commodity even in Industrial economies. Industrial capitalism reversed these priorities, privileging individual private ownership over communal forms of property and setting economic growth as a primary political objective for Industrial Era hierarchies, with stability and security often relegated to secondary status.

The expansionist (we could call it "predatory") nature of capitalist economics accounts for its culturally subversive character. The profit motive drives expansion of the sorts of things that can be offered on the market—the process of *commodification,* or turning things into commodities that can be bought and sold—as well as expansion of the market itself. The chief victim of this tendency over the last 200 years has been traditional values of various sorts. Sumptuary laws gave way to mass marketing, niche marketing, and imitative fashion. Traditional restrictions on women's activities gave way (slowly) before the logic of replaceable labor. Not that capitalist forms of wage labor are above taking advantage of traditional

FIGURE 19.16 Cheap and Nimble. Child textile-mill laborers in Macon, Georgia, early twentieth century.

attitudes. Women—and children, for that matter—made attractive employees for early industries, especially in textile mills, not just for their manual dexterity but because traditional gender structures made it possible to justify lower wages than men could be paid. Women and children, after all, were not expected to support a family themselves, only to supplement male earnings, whatever the reality. Ironically, the social and cultural effects of industrialization that we will return to in the next chapter have tended to remove children from the formal economy in advanced Industrial economies, converting them instead to a niche market of consumers and an economic burden on parents that leads rich people to have fewer children. Religious restrictions on mercantile activity, including such things as Sunday "blue laws," are commodified and marketized away. Here the spirits of traditional Agrarian elites nod knowingly: you see, merchants really are subversive of social order and traditional values.

Nor are the impact of commodification and the logic of private property rights restricted to material goods, as James Watt's patents demonstrate. Patents had existed sporadically for centuries in Europe, and were understood as exceptional privileges, temporary monopolies granted by the state to an individual, usually (though not always) for a new product. In the legal-cultural context of eighteenth-century

Britain, with its frame values of law, private property, and Lockean rights, patents came to be reconceived in terms of "intellectual property" from which their creators had a right to benefit—a right the state was obliged to protect through granting of patents. This reconception was advanced enough by 1775 that Edmund Burke's arguments against granting unnecessary monopolies could not prevail against vested interests deploying the idea of intellectual property. An occasional privilege had become a legal right connected to property, a shift embedded in the name of the newer associated concept of copyright. Nor was there free market logic to the new position, despite arguments (enshrined in the US Constitution) about encouraging innovation— remember that steam engine improvements and manufacturing took off *after* Watt's key patents expired, and

FIGURE 19.17 Selling Love. If you can't market the thing, market the image.

that Adam Smith argued consistently against monopolies. Instead, "intellectual property" is a capitalist concept implying ownership and profit, not market competition. Rather, it is safe to say that in imposing monopolies, intellectual property rights replaced guilds as "protectors of the craft" and guarantors of the livelihood of existing "masters," at the cost of economic expansion.

In a less ideological way, commodification can operate by selling the image of a thing if the thing itself is not readily commodified. The Beatles might claim that "money can't buy me love," but the greeting card industry will happily sell you an image of love (while the beer industry sells the image of sex, the actual commodification of which is also common if legally risky in some forms).

Capitalism and Patterns of Economic Activity

The profit motive and expansionism built into the capitalist culture of economic activity have had two other historically significant effects in shaping regional and global patterns of economic activity since industrialization.

The first is that profit-driven competition in market economies leads to periods of intense expansion during which workers are added to payrolls and output rises. Eventually, expansion becomes overexpansion as the market is saturated. Firms then contract, laying off workers, with some companies going out of business. With competition thereby reduced, new opportunities arise and a new period of expansion begins, restarting the cycle. This pattern of business cycles, of expansion and recession (or depression, depending on the severity, breadth, and depth of the contraction), of boom and bust, is visible from early in the history of industrial Britain, and spread with industrialization. The pattern is reflected in Figure 19.12: commodity prices have fallen over the long term, but show a spiky pattern of sharp rises during periods of expansion, when many firms are competing for the same raw materials, and equally sharp falls during contractions, as firms close or sell off already extant inventory, leading to large declines in demand for raw materials.

Such cycles proved problematic because the periodic contractions caused serious hardship among the growing masses of urban laborers. And because factories and urbanization concentrated the misery more visibly than in dispersed rural settlements, as well as concentrating those in misery where they could recognize their common plight, contractions threatened to destabilize the politics of industrial hierarchies. Business cycles therefore became one of the major factors leading to the growth of state power via intervention in the operations of the economy. This has taken two major forms. First, states have stepped in to provide some form of social safety net—unemployment insurance, welfare schemes, and so forth—to ameliorate the misery during downturns. Second, states have attempted to intervene in the economy proactively, adjusting the money supply and other factors in order at least to reduce the severity of contractions, since eliminating them has proven nearly impossible (at least without also eliminating expansions).

The second effect of a capitalist culture of industrial economic activity is that the profit motive leads inevitably to the concentration of wealth and thus to significant disparities between rich and poor, despite industrialization generally raising standards of living for entire societies. This effect is visible both between societies and within individual societies. In terms of the former, the best estimates (based on admittedly sketchy evidence) for the late eighteenth century are that the richest regions of the world—southeast England, southeast China, the Edo region of Japan— were perhaps twice as rich as the global average. By 1850, Britain was 50 times as rich as the global average. While the spread of industrialization has reduced that factor—in 2010 the richest countries were about six to eight times richer than the global average—the disparity between the richest and the poorest is up to a factor of between 800 and 1,400, depending on the source. While the wealth disparities between rich and poor in the Agrarian world were also vast on a relative scale (which is what the politically coercive, hierarchical complex societies of the Agrarian Era were designed to create and perpetuate), in absolute terms they were small because of everyone's poverty compared to Industrial Era economies.

In addition, wealth disparities within Industrial societies exist, despite the fact that their political structures are not necessarily designed to create such gaps. But the capitalist tendency is to concentrate wealth: in the United States in 2010, approximately 10% of the population controlled 80% of the country's financial assets. This effect of a capitalist culture of economic activity has also been a central political issue for Industrial countries since industrialization began to spread, inspiring the projection of screen images (ideologies) by numerous interested parties. As with the impact of business cycles, over the last 200 years wealth concentration has, because of its potential to destabilize the politics of Industrial hierarchies, prompted various forms of state intervention in economic activity or attempts to deal with this outcome of economic activity, mostly focused on mechanisms such as progressive income taxes designed to redistribute wealth.

Conclusion

The Industrial Revolution was truly revolutionary in changing the material relationship of humans to their environment, with massive demographic and economic consequences that brought an end to the Agrarian world and ushered in the new

Industrial world. The global network was crucial to both the initiation and the spread of this revolution, and we have seen the impact of capitalist industrialization on network activity. In the next chapter, we will examine more closely the Agrarian-to-Industrial transition in terms of the shape of hierarchies, including both states and the societies they governed, and in terms of the third component of our model, the cultural frames and screens of Industrial societies.

FRAME IT YOURSELF

Frame Your World

Commodification, the process of turning something into a salable good, is a central mechanism of capitalist industrialization, as we have seen in this chapter. By now, that process has advanced unimaginably compared to the world of 1800. Is there anything that is not for sale in your world today? Be careful about your answers. Two answers that might suggest themselves show the scope of commodification. First, are humans for sale? Setting aside illegal sexual slavery in parts of the world, there is still a legal trade in human organs for transplants. Second, how about what the Beatles claimed: "money can't buy me love"? Is selling the image of a thing (Valentine cards, for example) the same as selling the thing? If so, what's not for sale? Best essay wins a new car. Heh.

Further Reading

Allen, Robert C. 2009. *The British Industrial Revolution in Global Perspective.* Cambridge: Cambridge University Press.

Jacob, Margaret C. 1997. *Scientific Culture and the Making of the Industrial West.* Oxford: Oxford University Press.

More, Charles. 2000. *Understanding the Industrial Revolution.* London: Routledge.

Nef, John U. 2009. *Cultural Foundations of Industrial Civilization.* Cambridge: Cambridge University Press.

Pomeranz, Kenneth. 2001. *The Great Divergence: China, Europe, and the Making of the Modern World Economy.* Princeton, NJ: Princeton University Press.

Stearns, Peter N. 1993. *The Industrial Revolution in World History.* Boulder: University of Colorado Press.

For additional learning and instructional resources related to this chapter, please go to www.oup.com/us/morillo

CHAPTER TWENTY

Industrial Hierarchies:
Society, State, Culture

Samuel Smiles.

Introduction

Samuel Smiles was born in Haddington, Scotland, in 1812, one of eleven surviving children of Samuel Smiles, Sr., and Janet Wilson. Apprenticed to a doctor at age 14, he entered medical school at the University of Edinburgh three years later. His father died when the younger Samuel was only 20, but through hard work and faith his mother kept the family general store going, enabling Samuel to finish his schooling. He graduated in 1832 and founded a successful medical practice in Haddington.

At university, however, he had become involved in the movement for parliamentary reform, supporting the Chartist six-point program: universal suffrage for all men 21 and over; redistricting into equal-sized constituencies; secret ballots; abolishing qualification for Parliament by property holding; pay for elected members; and annual Parliaments. His writings for reform in the newspaper *The Leeds Times* led to an offer to edit the paper, and Smiles abandoned his medical career in 1838 to work full-time for reform. But in the mid-1840s he lost faith in parliamentary reform as the key to improving society, breaking with the Chartists over some of their leaders' advocacy of violence to force the pace of reform. He turned instead to the idea of individual self-improvement, and in 1859 published *Self-Help*, the book that made both his fortune and his reputation.

Self-Help and Smiles's later books, such as *Thrift*, advocate self-improvement through hard work, providing numerous biographical examples of "self-made men" drawn from history, mostly relatively recent British history. Institutions, the focus of his earlier reform efforts, he dismissed as capable only of providing the freedom for individual effort: "Even the best institutions can give a man no active help. Perhaps the most they can do is, to leave him free to develop himself and improve his individual condition." Most men's poverty was, he claimed, the result of laziness and lack of planning and saving. Thus, he approved of the New Poor Law of 1834 that established workhouses that were little more than prisons for the poor. Yet Smiles was not an advocate of merely accumulating riches: for him, the ultimate goal of self-improvement was humanistic, focused on gaining an appreciation for literature and the life of the mind. Nor was he an advocate of pure *laissez-faire*, writing in *Thrift*, "When typhus or cholera breaks out, they tell us that Nobody is to blame. . . . Nobody adulterates our food. Nobody poisons us with bad drink. Nobody supplies us with foul water. Nobody spreads fever in blind alleys and unswept lanes. Nobody leaves towns undrained. Nobody fills gaols, penitentiaries, and convict stations. . . . Nobody has a theory too—a dreadful theory. It is embodied in two words—*Laissez faire*—Let alone." Finally, Smiles placed self-improvement within a larger frame: "The spirit of self-help is the root of all genuine growth in the individual; and, exhibited in the lives of many, it constitutes the true source of national vigour and strength." Thus, especially for the English, in whom self-help "has in all times been a marked feature in the English character," self-improvement was virtually a nationalistic duty.

Framing the Argument

- The ways in which industrialization and the rise of mass society shaped hierarchies, including the formation of a corporate sphere and the growing power of professionalized states

- The impact of mass society on forms of cultural expression, resulting in the disappearance of the Great Cultural Divide

- The patterns of screen images and frame values that emerged in the Industrial world, especially the rise of nationalism and other self-conscious expressions of ideology

FIGURE 20.1 **The Agrarian Pyramid.**

Samuel Smiles's attempts to make sense of and bring improvement to his world introduce us to the key themes of this chapter: rapid social change; the role of the state; and the cultural frames and cultural screens through which people viewed these issues. While this chapter focuses mostly on nineteenth-century Industrial societies, these themes continue to dominate the Industrial world, and so this chapter also continues the broad overview of the transition to an Industrial world begun in the last chapter, especially in terms of Industrial Era hierarchies.

⊢ * ⊢

The Shape of Industrial Hierarchies

To contextualize these topics, we need to view the transition from Agrarian to Industrial in terms of our model of hierarchies. We have represented Agrarian hierarchies throughout this book as sociopolitical structures shaped like pyramids (see Figure 20.1).

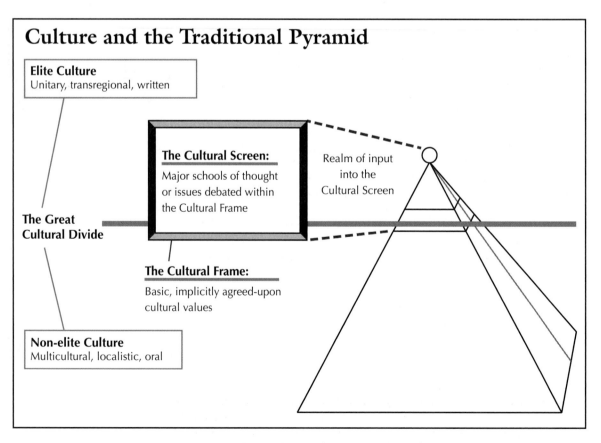

FIGURE 20.2 **Culture and the Traditional Pyramid.**

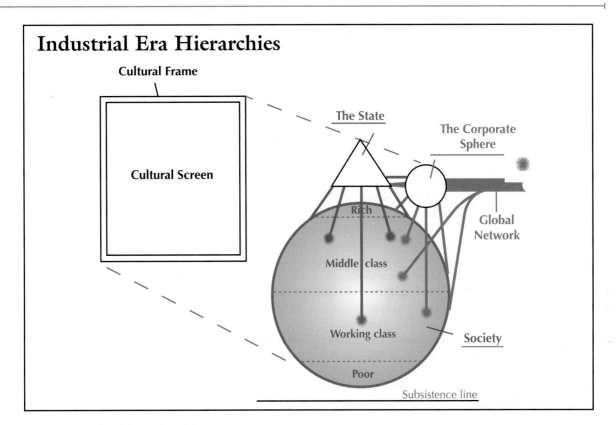

FIGURE 20.3 Industrial Era Hierarchies.

The pyramid shape of this model represents not just the unequal distribution of wealth, but the rigid structures of formal and informal power that kept people in their place both in class and gender terms. In other words, the pyramid was a shape necessitated by low productivity and slow communications and constrained by the pervasive exercise of power. The restrictions of power are reflected in limited, elite-dominated access to the cultural screen and in the Great Cultural Divide. (See Figure 20.2.)

The new model of Industrial hierarchies emerged first in Britain, as we saw in Chapter 18. It created conditions in which industrialization could get started, and the spread of industrialization then necessitated the spread of the new model of hierarchies, shown in Figure 20.3.

This is a structure whose component parts are more separate, though still tied together, than in the unified pyramid. Society, represented by the main sphere, is now a socioeconomic structure. It is no longer constrained by low productivity and slow communications, and is less constrained by political power than managed by it. The state has become a professional managerial organization, perhaps pyramid-shaped but without the informal social aspects of a pyramid structure. Connected to both the state and society, and acting as a more formalized intersection between hierarchies and the global network than had existed in Agrarian pyramids (which had aimed at an ideal of self-sufficient isolation), is the corporate sphere. Finally, mass society and mass media have opened up access to the cultural frame and screen, with society, state, and corporate sphere all able to project images and shape values to a significant degree.

Clearly, the Agrarian and Industrial models of hierarchy are significantly different, and the transition from one to the other has been, repeatedly over the last 200 years, a disruptive and highly contested one, even in the original British case. We shall examine the transition and the new forms that emerged in the rest of this chapter.

The Social Sphere

We noted in the previous chapter, especially with respect to the tendency of a capitalist economic culture to create wealth disparities, that a sphere does not exactly represent the distribution of wealth in Industrial societies. Why then a sphere in the model? Several reasons. Absent gravity or other constraints, a drop of water assumes a spherical shape. Thus, a sphere represents the reduction of "economic gravity" that allows Industrial societies to rise above the subsistence line—the line on which the base of Agrarian pyramids sat—and the removal of the constraints of low productivity, slow communications, and consequently rigid social order. And the "middle" of the social order in Industrial societies is far larger and more important than in the "elites and commons" Agrarian model; a sphere represents the growth of a middle class society well. If we bear in mind that the narrow slice of "rich" at the top of the sphere stands for wealth disparities that can be much greater than the shape of the model implies (something that is also true of the pyramid), then a sphere serves our purposes quite well.

The fluid, unbounded nature of the sphere also represents the long-term tendency toward social mobility within Industrial societies, unlike the rigidity of Agrarian ones. Both the impact of open labor markets and the influence of egalitarian political philosophies (including Enlightenment notions of universal human rights) tend to move social structure toward an internally fluid sphere (something like a three-dimensional bell curve) in which both up-down (class) mobility and front-back (gender) mobility are much more in evidence. This is not to say that such tendencies move quickly, evenly, or only in one direction. Each generation of the very rich has an incentive, which can be implemented through influence on state policy, to reduce social mobility in order to ensure their continued place at the top. Furthermore, "echoes of the pyramid," or the inherited structural and cultural legacy of the hierarchical Agrarian past, continue to shape the transition from Agrarian to Industrial structures and the perceptions of Industrial society. This is clear in terms of the gender divide, as the pay gap between male and female workers still shows in many advanced industrial societies, including the United States, and in the representation of early twentieth-century US social structure by the International Workers of the World (IWW).

Looked at in another way, however, cultural constraints such as racism, ethnic and religious discrimination, and so forth, do not re-create the pyramid (and note that gender distinctions do not appear in the workers' or capitalists' layers of the

FIGURE 20.4 Capitalist Pyramid? Cartoon critique of the "Pyramid of Capitalist System," published in an International Workers of the World (IWW) newspaper in 1911. From the top: Capitalism; We Rule You; We Fool You; We Shoot at You; We Eat for You; We Work for All, We Feed All.

IWW pyramid—only the state structures remain gendered male). They tend to create semi-isolated (and only semi-coherent) social groups, something like bubbles in the fluid sphere, that can appear at just about any economic level within the sphere. These can, of course, be problematic, unjust, and enduring, but in themselves do not re-create Agrarian hierarchy. We will return to these issues in Chapters 27 and 28.

Mass Society

The dynamics of industrial society were predominantly shaped by mass production, rising wealth, and demographic growth, as we saw in the previous chapter. Mass society transformed the social groupings people lived in and identified with. At the most basic level of the family, however, it is hard to generalize because family structure has proven so flexible and culturally malleable. It used to be thought that industrialization, especially in nineteenth-century Europe, created the "modern" nuclear urban family from the extended rural families of the Agrarian past. But more recent research shows that nuclear families long preceded industrialization in much of Europe, while the extended life spans of many people in Industrial societies actually makes extended families more possible (if also, at times, more extended geographically) than before. Family structure generally is subject to romanticizing of the past and to politically motivated "analyses," making the topic even more complex.

It is safer to say that mass society fostered new class structures and new class consciousness, particularly among the working classes. The main shift, noted above, was from an essentially two-way sociopolitical split between elites and commoners to a more fluid socioeconomic classification based on wealth.

Much social change was driven by industrial factory production and urbanization. Massive urbanization concentrated laborers—men, women, and children—in ways that not only fostered awareness of their shared interests, but also created new problems. Housing often proved the first issue, as floods of rural immigrants sought places to stay and squeezed into rapidly and shoddily built tenements and row houses. Closely related was the problem of sanitation in suddenly huge cities such as Manchester that had no systems of running water. Cholera epidemics broke out regularly: Samuel Smiles's father died in one of these, as did Queen Victoria's consort Prince Albert. By the mid-1800s, the Thames River was so fouled with human waste that Parliament had to adjourn a number of times because of the stench outside its windows. It was research into cholera that then led to advances in understanding microbes and germs. Massive urbanization also intensified issues of poor relief during economic downturns and of crime.

Meanwhile, factory discipline and coordinating mass workforces spread the culture of mechanical time, of life lived by the patterns of the factory whistle instead of the sun and seasons. A crucial further factor here was the spread of railway networks connecting the growing urban agglomerations and contributing to their growth by bringing people in (Smiles worked as secretary to several rail companies). Railway schedules not only ran according to mechanical times, but the speed with which they could move people forced coordination of local mechanical times into nationwide common time—and ultimately, with air travel added, into a global system of time zones.

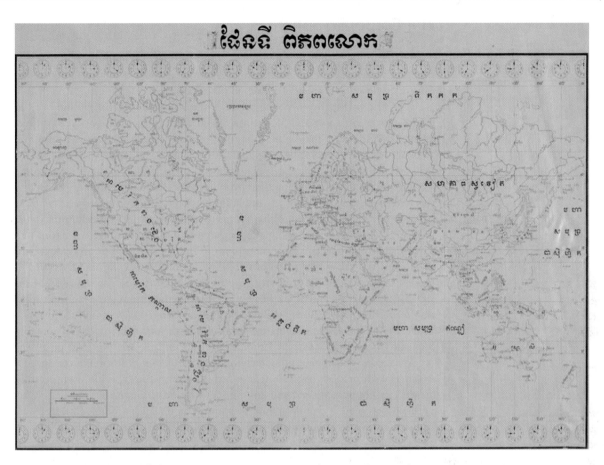

FIGURE 20.5 Thai Time. Global time zone map in Siamese, created in 1885, the year after the International Prime Meridian Conference standardized time zones.

A final social transformation wrought by industrialization and mass society was, paradoxically, the growth of notions of individualism. Greater wealth and mobility meant a wider range of opportunities for people to break out of the narrowly defined roles Agrarian society usually created. Individualism became more affordable. It was no longer necessary to follow the trade of one's father (or mother) or master. This was a trend that grew with the spread of state-sponsored social safety nets and rising wealth. But the luxury of individualism, of "finding oneself" (a concept largely foreign to an Agrarian world in which you were what your social position said you were: you didn't have to find your identity, it was given to you), was already visible in industrializing countries in the nineteenth century. The result was the emergence of screen images designed to guide people in their search for themselves, of which Smiles's *Self-Help* is a prime example. Smiles himself, the son of a shopkeeper (Napoleon takes another turn in his grave), became in turn a doctor, an editor, a railway secretary, and a mass-market author. Such advice might also take the form of how to escape mass society, as for example in Henry David Thoreau's *Walden,* which detailed his experiment in self-sufficiency (well, except for his mother doing his laundry).

The Corporate Sphere

We will return to the development of the corporate sphere as an integral part of our model of Industrial Era hierarchies (and networks) in more detail in later chapters. But we may outline a few key features and connections here.

The first is that the corporate sphere is the institutionalized expression of the intersection of networks and hierarchies, an intersection that had proved tense and conflicted for much of the Agrarian Era due to the differences between network and hierarchy values. Corporations, especially those operating across state boundaries (commonly known as multinational corporations, or MNCs), occupied that intersection comfortably, drawing on their hybrid origins as state-chartered organizations that nevertheless operated privately and in the network. Their own internal hierarchical structures were therefore compatible with network values and with capitalism in both its forms, as a principle of economic organization and as a cultural screen image.

What proved particularly advantageous for the growth of the corporate sphere in this role was the combination of frame values under which corporations spread: legally sanctioned private property rights and Enlightenment notions of human rights. The legal fiction that allowed corporations to operate so successfully was that they were effectively persons, whose workers and managers were simply the component parts of the single corporate person. When various court decisions (notably Supreme Court decisions in the US in the 1880s) conflated human rights principles (as expressed in the Fourteenth Amendment to the US Constitution in our specific example) with property rights in these fictive persons, corporations' own separate "social" sphere was ensured and continued to spread through the network. What needs to be noted is that corporate persons are not subject to biological death as real persons are. As the players of any fantasy role playing game will attest, if you pit a class of immortals against a class of mortals, someone's got a serious advantage in the game.

We shall return to the connections between the corporate sphere and the state in the context of nineteenth-century imperialism in the next two chapters.

The State

First, however, we must examine the transformations of the state in the shift from Agrarian to Industrial. This transformation shows up in a huge growth in state power, in mass politics, and in the professionalization of state functions.

Industrialization and the Growth of State Power

Much of the growth of state power over the last 200 years has been the result of industrialization, which has both created new demands for state action and provided the resources with which those demands could be at least partially met.

Demands came from heightened problems of managing the emergent social sphere and the network-hierarchy intersection. On the social side, we noted some of the issues raised by urbanization above. Shoddy, dangerous housing called for safety regulations and building standards (or led people such as Samuel Smiles to call for them, against the voice of *laissez-faire*). Sanitation proved an even bigger challenge: at least private companies built housing in order to have a handy labor force. No such incentive existed for the creation of water and sewer systems, and the state therefore had to intervene, or Smiles's "Nobody" would. Thus, either the state built and ran sewer systems itself or chartered corporations and granted them a monopoly to guarantee the business a profit. Systems of poor relief were created and elaborated to ameliorate (or at least control) the periodic misery of recessions. Above all, municipal police forces came into being, separate from the military, for dealing with everyday urban crime, starting with the London police force of "peelers" or "bobbies," named for the Home Secretary, Robert Peel, who created the force in 1829. Further social management was necessitated whenever universal male suffrage

FIGURE 20.6 Professional Policing. "Peelers," the London force created by Sir Robert Peel in 1829; the professional state deploys professional enforcers.

gained ground in an industrializing country. The educated classes already voting and in power saw that, to lessen the chance of the working classes voting in a revolution, systems of universal public education had to be established to indoctrinate the masses in safe citizenship.

Network management problems arose as well. We saw in the previous chapter that broad issues of concentration of wealth and business cycles led to calls not just for poor relief but for economic management and, in time, policies aimed at redistributing wealth via progressive taxation and the like. Furthermore, states found themselves over time promoting economic development and industrialization, for instance either facilitating the growth of railway networks through favorable land pricing and tax breaks (as in the US), or actively planning a rail net around the needs of military planning (as in Germany). Protective tariffs (taxes on imports) remained a staple tool of network management. Before long, the power of corporations that states had helped to create could be reined in and regulated only by the collective power of the state; indeed, in the longer term, MNCs threaten to escape state power in significant ways altogether.

On the other hand, industrialization provided new resources to states that helped them meet these new demands. States readily tapped the new levels of wealth created by industrial economies through taxation, enabling the professionalization of government, a topic that we will return to later in this chapter. New communications technologies made it possible for states to collect and store vastly more data about their societies than ever before, and new scientific approaches to the analysis of statistics made such mountains of data at least somewhat accessible as guides to policy decisions. The amount of census data and other official records available to bureaucrats—and historians—rises significantly following the industrialization of a country, such that the problem becomes sorting through too much information rather than trying to find enough. (Historians and bureaucrats can always complain about their data.)

The State and Warfare

Industrialization also contributed indirectly to the growth of state power through the changes it brought to warfare. Weaponry underwent steady and at times revolutionary developments from the 1830s, when rifled muskets first appeared in significant numbers, driving cavalry from any significant offensive role on battlefields, though the application of railroads and steamships to warfare probably had the most significant technological impact. Furthermore, greater resources, professionalized bureaucracies, and demographic growth made possible, though did not dictate, the raising and supporting of far larger armies than before. State power therefore grew both because it could be backed domestically by more effective military force ("We Shoot You") and because heightened threats from other industrializing states necessitated and justified state growth to create and maintain adequate defensive forces.

The great dilemma faced by industrializing powers, first in Europe in the nineteenth century, then in various ways by non-European societies when faced with European military challenges in the age of imperialism from 1870 on, was how to take best advantage of new military capabilities without adding to the potential for social revolution. This dilemma was a strong expression of the problem of transition from Agrarian to Industrial state and social structures. Raising a mass army of conscripts was not an obvious policy in this transitional stage, because doing so threatened to arm the very classes that, under Agrarian conditions, had to be coerced. Thus, many mid-nineteenth-century European powers followed the French

FIGURE 20.7 Loyal Conscripts. Prussian conscript infantry, whose state-directed training allowed them to defeat France's long-term professional soldiers in 1870.

lead in maintaining small(ish) armies of long-term professionals, whose training and separation from the bulk of society made them not only more effective soldiers individually (at least in theory), but went a long way toward guaranteeing their loyalty to the elite-run state that employed them.

It was Prussia that pioneered an alternate model, which was to conscript all eligible males each year for a couple of years of active service and training, followed by a long period of reserve duty with occasional refresher training. This provided a far larger pool of trained soldiers than the French model, and as the Franco-Prussian War of 1870–1871 was to show, the conscripts fought just as well as the professionals. But the key to the Prussian system was that military training was also made into nationalist-motivated citizenship training, a militarized extension of systems of universal public education that were emerging at the time. Mass conscripts thus did not become revolutionaries because they were acculturated to loyalty, obedience, and nationalist passion—effectively, the image of foreign enemies projected by the state overshadowed images of internal class oppression projected by reformist or revolutionary social groups. Much of Europe was antagonistically militarized by the end of the nineteenth century.

Mass Politics

Conflicted conceptions of how to create armies was an issue because industrialization brought not just mass production, consumption, and society, but mass politics as well. Part of the increase of mass politics was a straightforward effect of increasing state power. A state with greater ability to interfere in the lives of its subjects fostered greater levels of resistance, while the very pervasiveness of its power channeled that resistance into political channels. At the same time, a more powerful state became a much more attractive political "commodity," something more individuals and groups wanted to "buy into" in order to use or benefit from that power. Thus, more powerful states attracted more political action. But industrialization also directly affected both the fact and the forms of mass politics.

Industrialization, Capitalism, and Mass Politics

The economic roots of mass politics, as we have already seen from different angles, lay in urbanization and the concentration of workers that flowed from factory-based production. This concentration gave the masses a political weight that states had to account for in one way or another, with the French Revolution operating as a historical reminder of the power of mass uprising for European states of the early nineteenth century. The old form of monarchical government had been reaffirmed by the peace settlement of 1815 after Napoleon's final defeat. Another political uprising in France in 1830, however, followed in 1848 by a whole series of revolutionary movements across Europe—which combined middle class unhappiness with elite dominance of politics with working class unrest at changing economic conditions—showed that mass movements were a force to be reckoned with, even by strong monarchies. Ironically, the violence of 1848 moved the middle classes toward alliance with aristocratic elites against the working class—Samuel Smiles's political beliefs reflect this split—making for gradual and limited reform rather than revolution in most places. (See Figure 20.8.)

FIGURE 20.8 The Revolutions of 1848.

The increasingly capitalist culture of European economics, as well as the continued development of Enlightenment political ideals, gave ideological shape to middle and working class demands. Enlightenment abstractions about equality and rights gained force from the economic logic of commodification, especially in labor markets but also in the market culture of consumerism. Economic growth and faster internal communications fostered unified domestic markets that in turn helped nurture political consciousness at a broader, "national" level of politics; more pervasive modes of mass communication, especially mass-produced newspapers and political pamphlets, brought more and more people into political dialogues.

But the conservative outcome of the 1848 revolts also highlights emerging tensions between capitalism and proposals for democratic forms of government as the right way to express mass political movements. Enlightenment statements of human rights, which implied (and sometimes expressly asserted) the right of the majority to alter social and economic conditions, ran up against the Lockean property rights at the heart of capitalist economic culture. This clash was especially evident in the course of the Latin American independence movements of 1808–1830, in which Enlightenment political rhetoric threatened the privileged interests of great landowners in what was still, effectively, an Agrarian pyramid-shaped set of societies. But industrializing Europe also saw states siding with propertied interests not just against mass violence, but in everyday ways such as making trade unions illegal, using police to break up strikes or defend against machine breaking, and so forth.

Working class voices, given further ideological shape by the emergence of socialism and communism as important political philosophies, remained loud and insistent enough to keep pushing the pace of gradual economic reforms, and rising wealth also eased some of the worst problems of early industrial economic and social misery and unrest. Mass movements also aimed at political reform—as in the Chartist demands for more democratic, representative ways of electing Parliament that Samuel Smiles initially supported—and social reform. The latter is represented not just by Smiles's later championing of self-improvement, but also by demands from clergymen and other moralists, horrified by the conditions of child labor, for systems of public education, by growing movements in (or aimed at) the United States for the abolition of slavery, and the slow growth across the nineteenth century of temperance (anti-alcohol) movements. These moves for social reform saw the first mass expressions of female political voices, as women, assigned by middle class conventions to moral guardianship of the domestic sphere (an echo of the Agrarian pyramid's gender divide), asserted their moral superiority while claiming "domestic" status for many social issues.

The Slow Spread of Democracy

Mass politics does not necessarily mean democratic politics. Mass movements have expressed themselves through protests both violent and non-violent, strikes, clandestine organizing, and so forth. But variations on representative democracy have proven, over the last 200 years, to be the most effective and stable way to organize mass politics and to harmonize politics with market-based and capitalist forms of economic organization. Not that democracies are always effective or stable. Winston Churchill's comment that democracy is the worst possible form of government

FIGURE 20.9 Beyond "Universal." Female suffrage was a major extension of democracy.

except for any of the alternatives often seems far too appropriate. Furthermore, democratic forms of government—parliaments or legislatures, elections, even opposing political parties—have often served as fronts for rule by one person, one faction or party, or one social group in democratic-looking non-democracies. But real democracy's practical and moral advantages are, arguably, the reason that democratic mass politics have spread, in form and reality, albeit slowly and fitfully, over the last 200 years and are more prevalent in the early 2000s than ever before.

That spread in terms of countries has generally followed two paths. The first path includes areas affected directly by British rule and models of politics, including its offspring and co-model of nineteenth-century democracy, the United States. Perhaps the most significant of these in the long run, beyond direct British colonies populated by British emigrants, is modern India. The second path includes areas that industrialized, though democracy usually lagged well behind industrialization, with the length of the lag determined by various cultural and social factors. Even for countries on the second path, the forms of British and US politics proved important as models, with the prestige of British industrial might adding to its political reputation.

Democracy has also spread, again slowly and fitfully, within countries. Secret ballots and principles such as "one man, one vote" have made democracy more democratic. Even more, the formulation of the latter principle points out that democracy has slowly been extended beyond property-owning white males. "Universal" (white male) suffrage has been followed by "universal" (male) suffrage (a more contested extension in the US than in some other countries), then by female suffrage (which had to be called female suffrage, or votes for women, because "universal" had already been used up—the notion that women are not really people has been an echo of the Agrarian Era that has proven especially difficult to shed). The "self-evident" Enlightenment truth that all people are created equal has had to be constantly reasserted; it has gained force as industrialization spreads the material prosperity, mass society and communications, and market economics that fertilize the soil in which democracy grows.

Professionalization

Mass politics was a driving factor behind the professionalization of the state—the process represented in our model by the state "popping off" the top of society to become its own part of the model, connected to but distinct from the social sphere and the corporate sphere. Professionalization in turn enabled much of the growth of state power necessitated by the challenges of managing industrial societies and network connections.

Depersonalized Structures

The difference between Agrarian and Industrial states can be seen most clearly in the relationship between individuals and institutions within the state. In the Agrarian

Era, a man holding a government position (and officeholders were all men) gained not just official power but social status and informal power and prestige, as well. Conversely, since most posts were filled by men who were already of elite social status (whether local, regional, or statewide), in taking a government post they lent their own prestige to the state, reinforcing its authority and legitimacy. (The oddity of many medieval Islamic states, as we saw in Volume I, is that their most important state functionaries, the soldiers who formed the core of state armies, were slaves with no inherent status in society. This is why this book refers to them as soldiers rather than warriors, as "warrior" denotes elite social status.) Thus, the foundation of state authority and legitimacy in the Agrarian Era lay in types of elite people: scribes, warriors, and priests. Their status was often marked by official styles of dress whose use was restricted by law, as in the yellow robes of Confucian scholar-bureaucrats. If a commoner met such a person in public, he owed him social deference as well as formal obedience.

In the transition to the professionalized states of the Industrial Era, the same categories of authority continued to apply—organizational, coercive, and moral, respectively—but came to rest in abstract, depersonalized institutions or ideas instead of in individual people. Similarly, legitimacy came to apply to the state as an abstraction. It did not depend on the status of the mass of individuals who filled state posts. Nor did state service, for the most part, convey to individual officials social status outside the official functions of their office. We can see this more clearly by examining the transition of each sort of authority.

The change from Agrarian scribes to Industrial bureaucracy was not dramatic in terms of form. Agrarian states had bureaucracies made up of scribes, or scholar officials. But again, if you met a Ming Confucian scholar in his office, you'd bow and quake, and if you met him in a public restaurant, you'd owe him a certain deference that would show up in forms of address and probably more bowing and perhaps quaking. You didn't have to like him, but you had to respect him, personally. On the other hand, if you meet a modern tax official in his office, you may still shake hands politely and quake (depending on why you're there), but if you met him (or her) in a restaurant, you might find his or her job interesting, repulsive, or plain boring, but the thought of social deference would probably not enter your mind. Elite status has been replaced by the status of a cog—a specialized, professionalized cog at that—in a (powerful and sometimes intimidating) machine.

Furthermore, the power and intimidation now comes not from the social status of the bureaucrats, but from the fact that modern bureaucracies, because of their far greater resources and information technology, can know and affect so much more of your life than previously. Commoners' best strategy for dealing with the state in the Agrarian world was to avoid it. If you did not come into personal contact with its representatives, you rarely had to worry about it—this is the limitation of authority built on personal status. But paper or electronic records and the vast expansion of tasks that states have taken on with industrialization means the state is

FIGURE 20.10 The Depersonalized State. Locus of state authority but not of social prestige: a local BMV office.

CHAPTER TWENTY-ONE

Imperialism: Structures and Patterns

The *Nemesis* destroying Chinese war junks in Anson's Bay, 1841.

Introduction

Lin Zexu took up his appointment as imperial commissioner of Guangdong province in southeast China in 1838. A skilled administrator and an official known for his firm moral principles and incorruptibility, he had risen through the ranks of the Chinese bureaucracy ever since he passed the imperial examinations, based on the Confucian canon, in 1811 at age 26. The Daoguang Emperor of the Qing Dynasty chose Lin as commissioner in order to deal with a set of problems that threatened to spiral out of control, problems that called for an incorruptible governor who cared for the welfare of his people.

Guangdong province was home to the port city of Canton, through which all trade with the "maritime barbarians" (Europeans) was supposed to be channeled. The Portuguese and British were the main trading powers in Canton, and British merchants were importing opium into China by the ton. This had begun in 1781 as a response to the flow of silver from Britain to China as payment for Chinese goods, especially tea. To reduce the flow of precious metals, the British government coordinated incentives and monopolies so that formerly cotton-growing land in British-controlled India was devoted to growing opium poppies. British merchants had exclusive rights to export the resulting opium to China, despite imperial bans on non-medical use of the drug.

By the 1830s, perhaps 2 million Chinese were addicted and British trade accounts were healthy. But Commissioner Lin did not approve. On his arrival in 1838, he arrested over 1000 Chinese opium dealers, confiscated tens of thousands of opium pipes, closed the Canton channel to trade (trapping many British merchants in the city), and banned all trade in opium on pain of death, asking all foreign merchants to sign a "no opium" agreement. Finally, he seized about two and a half million pounds of opium from the warehouses of those same foreign merchants, destroying the entire inventory. He then published an open letter to the British monarch (which Queen Victoria never received), calling on him to join in eradicating the immoral trade.

Charles Elliott, the superintendent captain of the British settlement in Canton, had convinced the British merchants to surrender their opium by promising that the British government would compensate them for their loss—a promise that must have sounded plausible to the merchants, as they agreed. But compensating drug dealers proved politically impossible. Instead, mistreatment of British merchants and restrictions on "free trade" became pretexts for a war to force the Chinese to pay compensation. Though Commissioner Lin had made preparations for war, the mobility and firepower of the British naval forces, including steamships that could sail up rivers, allowed them to strike at unprepared provinces. China lost, was forced to pay compensation, to open more ports to British trade, and to lease Hong Kong to the British government. Lin was reassigned to an obscure western province.

Framing the Argument

- The causes of the rise of European imperialism in the second half of the nineteenth century, including the network impacts of uneven industrialization, the internal politics of Industrial countries, and the cultural frames through which Industrial societies viewed the world

- The technological, organizational, and cultural tools that allowed these causes to be converted into empires

- The patterns of economic and political exploitation that characterized imperial relations

FRAMING Imperialism: Structures and Patterns

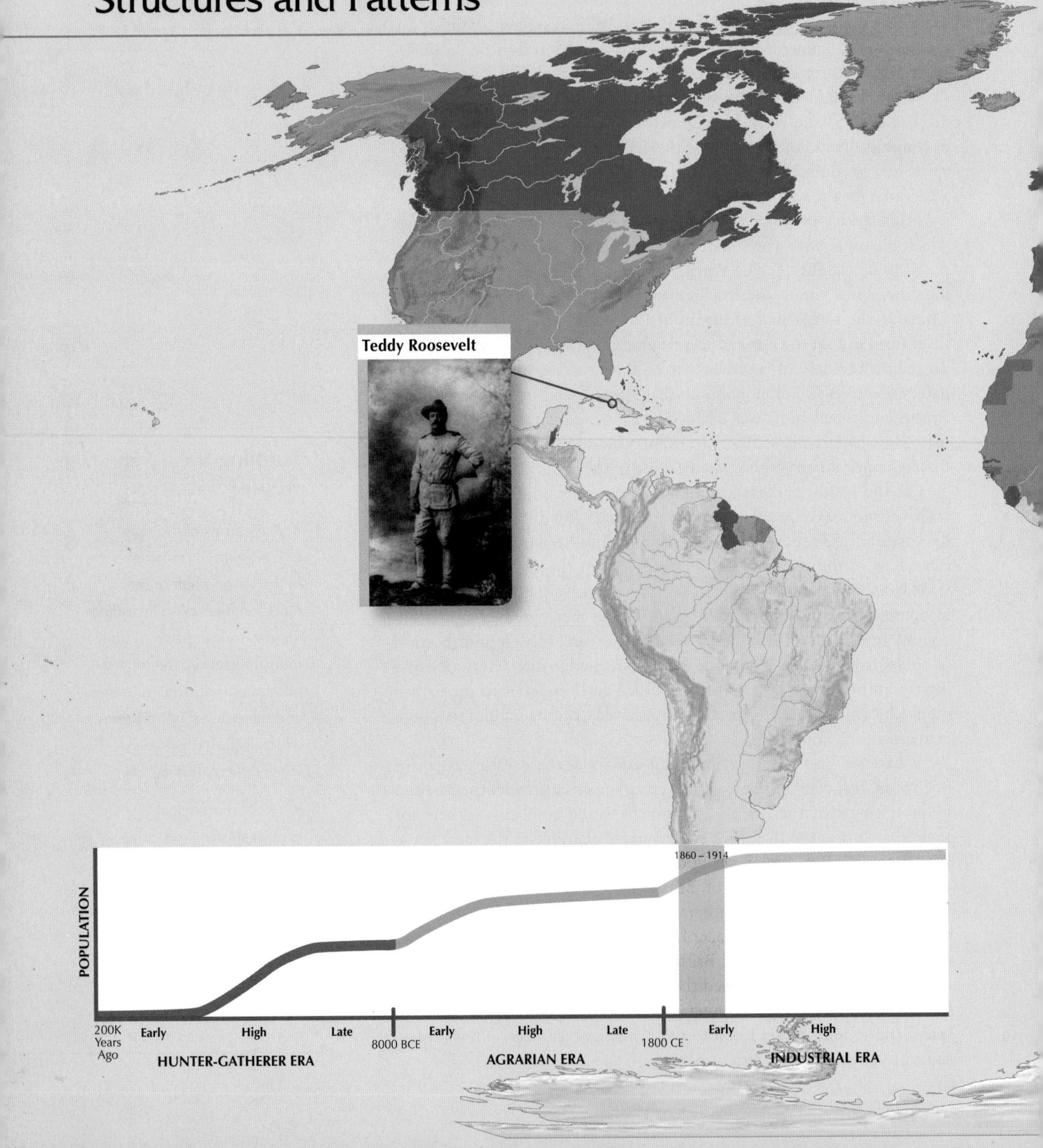

Teddy Roosevelt

POPULATION

1860 – 1914

200K Years Ago	Early	High	Late		Early	High	Late		Early	High
		HUNTER-GATHERER ERA		8000 BCE		AGRARIAN ERA		1800 CE		INDUSTRIAL ERA

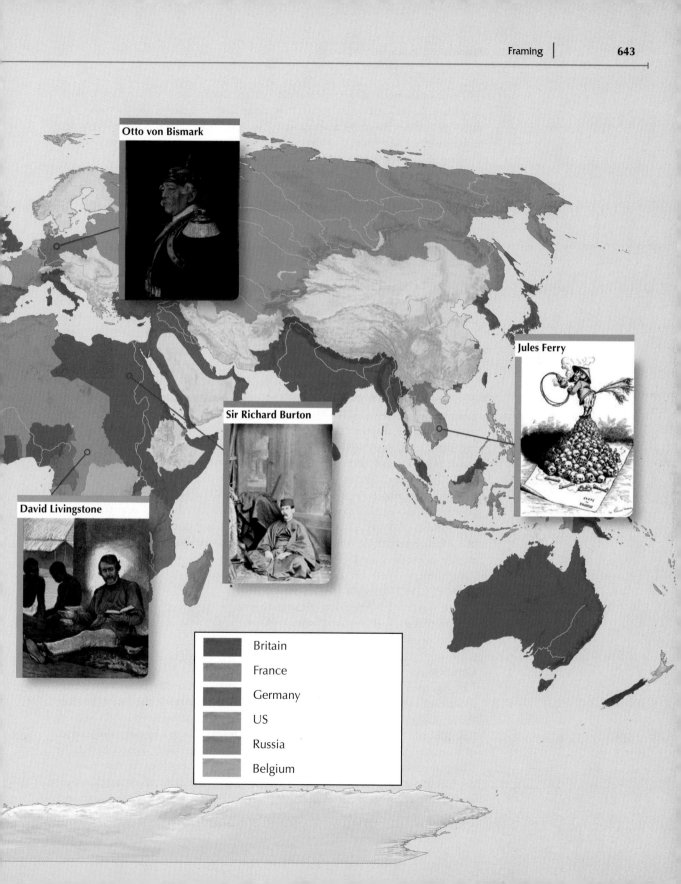

Otto von Bismark

Jules Ferry

Sir Richard Burton

David Livingstone

Britain
France
Germany
US
Russia
Belgium

Commissioner Lin, Superintendent Elliott, and the start of the First Opium War illustrate the key themes of this chapter: the clash of Agrarian and Industrial Era styles of network-hierarchy management; the sudden and unexpected military advantages of the new Industrial hierarchies; and the resulting growth of a new age of empires. It is to these themes that we now turn.

———| ＊ |———

The Imperialist Moment

Industrialization created all of the economic, social, political, and cultural effects we have outlined in the last two chapters. The British origin of industrialization and the limited spread of industrialization to (mostly) European powers and the United States during the nineteenth century created the conditions in which the imperialism of the Early Industrial Era could arise. Those conditions, it is important to emphasize, were anomalous, contingent, and temporary. "Western dominance" lasted from the mid-1800s to a bit beyond the mid-1900s (and Japan made that dominance less than fully "Western"). This trajectory is even clearer when we distinguish between "Western" and "Industrial" (or "modern"), and we will return to this topic later in the chapter.

Thus, Early Industrial imperialism arose not just from the various advantages industrialization gave to European powers that allowed them to expand so dramatically. The Europeans' new ability to do so was further a complete surprise to all involved, including Europeans themselves. They had no real idea how to use their power, and the non-European world had even less idea how to deal with these new wielders of power. The mutual understandings and mature network exchanges of the Late Agrarian Era simply disappeared, replaced seemingly overnight by a less mature style of relationship, which we will discuss further later in this chapter.

A Brief Overview of Imperialism

First, however, a brief overview of the chronology and geography of Early Industrial Era imperialism will provide a framework for the thematic analysis in this chapter and the further themes and case studies of Chapter 22.

Chronology

Late Agrarian European colonialism had come to a close, effectively, by the early nineteenth century. The French empire had fallen to the British, the British had lost the biggest, richest piece of its North American empire, and between 1808 and 1830 Spanish Latin America gained its independence from Spain in a bloody, confused set of wars. Only British India, under the control of the privately owned East India Company, transitioned from the old mercantilist style of empire to the new industrially based style, with Indian manufacturing suppressed in favor of raw material production for British factories in the process. After a major mutiny of the Company's Indian troops in 1857, the "crown jewel of the British Empire" came under direct

British rule. Defending India guided other British overseas decisions. First, the British kept the route to India through the Red Sea free from potential industrial rivalry in Egypt as well as Russian interference, the latter entailing support for the weakening Ottoman Empire in the Crimean War (1854–1856). Second, the British established naval coaling stations in South Africa; finally, they carefully monitored the Afghan and Southeast Asian neighbors of the subcontinent. Indian cotton also meant that Britain had no need to enter the American Civil War (1861–1865).

Through the 1850s, Britain was alone as an Industrial and imperial power. After that, it faced increasing competition from its old rival France (in Southeast Asia and Africa) and from Belgium (in the Congo). By the early 1880s, other (mostly European) nations were beginning to enter the competition. The years between 1885 and 1914 saw the height of imperialist expansion. At the Berlin Conference of 1885, the major European powers took a virtually blank map of Africa and divided it up for imperial partition, with some vaguely defined rules about the meaning of "effective occupation" guiding the subsequent "scramble for Africa." By 1914, the empires of the Early Industrial Era had reached their greatest extent, dominating large parts of the world in one way or another.

The imperialist powers largely managed to hang on to their empires through the two World Wars, from 1914 to 1945. Germany's was divided among the victorious imperialists after World War I, and Japan's empire evaporated with Japanese defeat in World War II. Despite the costs of war and increasing nationalist resistance in the colonies, the rest of the imperial colonies survived as such, with British India, for example, even assisting in their imperial rulers' war efforts. British control in Southwest Asia actually expanded after World War I with the division of Ottoman holdings outside the area that became Turkey. The material and moral underpinnings of imperialism had been destroyed, however, and between 1945 and 1975 the world saw the end of these Industrial empires in a process of decolonization that we will return to in Chapter 25. The longer term impact of Industrial imperialism has since echoed in post-colonial politics and in academic arguments (see the Issues in Doing World history box below).

Geography

The scope of nineteenth-century imperialism is difficult to convey on conventional maps. In terms of direct colonial control, the world looked like Figure 21.1 before World War I. This map fails to convey, however, the extensive areas of indirect control and influence that rendered the "independence" of much of the gray area of this map less than full. Thus, direct imperial rule is visible in South Asia; in all of Africa except Ethiopia and Liberia (which gained New World political immunity from European takeover); in Southeast Asia except for Thailand; in Malaysia; in the Pacific; and in Japanese control in Korea. Invisible in this mapping are significant pieces of China that had slipped from the emperor's full grasp with the granting of legal privileges and immunities to foreign merchants in various enclaves. Afghanistan was ruled (more or less—it is not an area that has ever been "ruled" firmly) by British clients. Persia suffered rival zones of British influence in its southern region and Russian influence in the north, and Mongolia operated in the shadow of Russia. Finally, much of Latin America, although immunized from political reconquest by

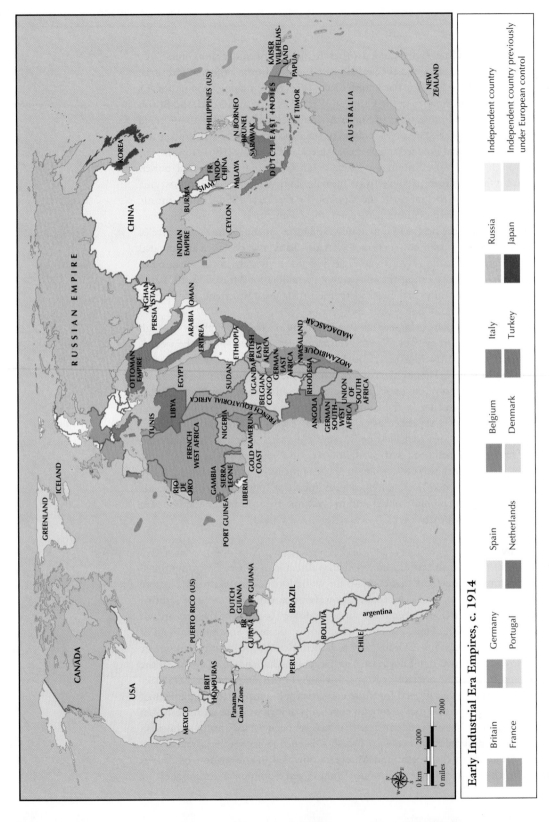

Early Industrial Era Empires, c. 1914

Britain   Spain   Germany   Belgium   Italy   Russia   Independent country

France   Netherlands   Portugal   Denmark   Turkey   Japan   Independent country previously under European control

FIGURE 21.1 Early Industrial Era Empires, ca. 1900.

the Monroe Doctrine, had governments more or less in debt to and therefore heavily influenced in policy terms by European and US corporations and governments. From 1901, Panama (whose independence was engineered by the United States to facilitate greater influence) effectively ceded a strip of itself to the United States (to which the Monroe Doctrine did not apply) so the Panama Canal could be built, partly on the model of British control in Egypt that allowed the construction of the Suez Canal, which shortened the trip to India considerably. In other words, not much of the world really escaped imperial influence, except a glacial Antarctica that nobody wanted. And even that got explored, just to make sure it wasn't worth grabbing.

What caused this great rush to claim and control regions of the world remote from the imperial powers? (This geographic disjunction distinguishes nineteenth-century imperialism from most of its Agrarian precursors but connects it to Late Agrarian colonial enterprises.) How was such dominance achieved and exercised? What did the imperial powers gain? We turn to these topics in the rest of this chapter, after which we examine the era from the perspective of the colonized in the next chapter.

Causes of Imperialism

The causes of nineteenth-century imperialism can be examined in terms of the three major parts of our model: the global network, hierarchies, and cultural frames and screens.

Network Dynamics

The key to the network dynamics of imperialism is the recognition that imperialism did not create many new connections, but rather built upon the preexisting connectivity of the global network. Some parts of central Africa and Latin America became more firmly networked, but even there, imperialism was more a matter of reorienting connections than forging new ones.

What did change was the dynamics of the intersections between networks and hierarchies. Most of the world still operated in Agrarian style. This meant, as Commissioner Lin demonstrated, close regulation of network connections based in fundamental distrust by hierarchy leaders of the influence of network values. The Industrial powers, however, following the lead of Britain, integrated network and hierarchy policy, partly through the emerging capitalist corporate sphere, as Superintendent Elliott showed. The expansion of hierarchies via the network was therefore one expression of the expansionist, predatory tendencies of capitalism, and network interests drove hierarchy policy—witness the First Opium War. Industrialization, meanwhile, vastly multiplied the power of the network and thus of the hierarchies operating this way. When the clash of frame values and material interests inherent in the meeting of Agrarian and Industrial management styles came to the fore, the Industrial powers had the ability to force their position on reluctant network "partners" far more effectively than their Late Agrarian mercantilist predecessors had—witness the result of the First Opium War.

FIGURE 21.2 Networks Coerce Hierarchies. After losing the First Opium War, the Chinese had to pay a huge indemnity to Britain. To do so, they taxed peasants—especially from ethnic minorities such as the Hmong—heavily. In this painting by Cy Thao, a Chinese official oversees Hmong families digging up their buried valuables to pay the taxes. (*The Taxing of the Poor,* from the series "The Hmong Migration," 1993–2001 (oil on canvas), Thao, Cy (b.1972) / Minneapolis Institute of Arts, MN, USA / The Bridgeman Art Library © Cy Thao)

It was this fundamental difference in how hierarchies managed their intersections with networks that shaped the dynamics of the more particular economic needs and incentives of the industrializing imperial powers. Two perceived needs dominated the motives of the imperialists: for raw materials and for markets.

Growing industry demanded raw materials of a number of sorts. The obvious ones are those used directly in manufacturing. Though the Early Industrial powers all had their own deposits of coal and iron—both too basic to be imported in bulk—metals such as copper, zinc, and nickel, useful for telegraphic wires and in alloying with iron to produce increasingly specialized types and grades of steel for machinery and military uses, could come from all over the world. Other industrial inputs—rubber, cotton, indigo and other dyes for textiles (both agriculturally grown like indigo and chemically synthesized from various minerals), bird and bat guano for fertilizers, palm oil as a machinery lubricant, later petrochemical oil, and so forth—often came from tropical agriculture or from unpredictable and scattered sources. The less obvious resources went not into industrial manufacturing directly but into the growing urban workforces who labored in industrial factories. Food was one such resource, as the proportion of farmers in industrializing countries fell steadily. Thus, sugar remained a valuable import whose quick calories nourished—if badly— industrial workers. It was often mixed into drinks, mainly coffee and tea, whose caffeine helped workers negotiate the jarring shift from biological to mechanical time. Imperialism, especially from a capitalist perspective that viewed the rest of the world as potential private property, could thus be justified as a way to ensure supplies of vital raw materials. Imperial powers furthermore saw a need to ensure themselves markets to which they could sell the products of their industry. Imperialism could thus be justified as guaranteeing access to overseas markets.

As justifications for imperial conquests, however, both perceptions proved somewhat illusory. Access to markets, in particular, rarely panned out. Even mass-produced industrial goods were usually too expensive for all but the few elites of the Agrarian societies controlled by imperial rule, and the elites sometimes rejected such goods for cultural reasons (as we will see further in the next chapter). And in fact, almost all industrial output in the nineteenth century was consumed by domestic markets and by the populations of other Industrial countries via trade. Industrializing countries always, in fact, turned out to be net importers. Control of raw material–producing regions could, it is true, earn an imperialist industrializing power some discount on imported goods under its control—this was almost certainly true for British imports of Indian cotton, for example—but the costs of imperialist wars and administration must be set against such discounts, making any net gain over simply trading questionable. German industry, for instance, despite miniscule "imperial discounts" from Germany's late and non-lucrative empire, grew faster than British industry from the 1880s on. Thus, *perceived* needs and the culturally based clash of network-hierarchy management styles were far more important than the actual profits (if any) of imperialism in generating conquests. In other words, network causes were really cultural causes.

Hierarchy Dynamics

The structural dynamics of hierarchies can be seen as culturally constructed even more easily. Only one true, non-cultural material factor drove some imperial expansion: the need for steam-powered imperial navies to have access to friendly coaling stations. Of course, steam-powered navies were necessary because of the scattered nature of imperial holdings, including coaling stations. So in some sense this material factor was circular, except perhaps for the British, whose far-flung empire preceded steam power and had to be converted on the fly. It was first as a coaling station halfway to India that British interest in South Africa arose; vast piles of diamonds were serendipity.

The other "hierarchy factor" was unequivocally cultural: the race for empire, especially in the "scramble" phase of 1885 to 1914, was driven by nationalist-inspired competition. Having a big empire became a point of

FIGURE 21.3 HMS *Dreadnought*. Force projection in the age of coal.

national pride, with the gendered analogy of manhood and size competition both obvious and apt. Envy of the vast British Empire influenced French imperialism and became a point of obsession in German policy under Wilhelm II in the two decades before World War I, inspiring not just attempts to build up German African territory but also, ominously, to attempt to rival the British Royal Navy. The nationalist chickens of imperial competition came home to roost disastrously in 1914.

Cultural Dynamics

If both network and hierarchy causes of imperialism were really cultural, other cultural factors also played a role directly as justifications of imperial adventures, though not everyone in imperialist countries accepted these rationalizations.

Justifications

Three justifications of imperialist adventures proposed at the time stand out. First, what is often referred to, after the Rudyard Kipling poem, as "The White Man's Burden." That is, imperialists justified their conquests as necessary to bring "civilization" to the ignorant and backward peoples of the world. Real material accomplishments in imperial colonies might be cited in support of such a "burden," including the dissemination of new scientific knowledge, especially medical discoveries and treatments, and, as in British India, the construction of railway networks. The attractions of such things to some of the colonized are, furthermore, undeniable. Ruhammon Roy, a British-educated Indian, argued to Parliament in the 1830s against continued education in Sanskrit for Indian youth, for example, because in his view all useful knowledge was the province of English. But in 1871, Dadabhai Naoroji, in a London speech assessing the pros and cons of British rule in India, summed up British rule as a "knife of sugar": sweet, but ultimately still wounding. Vast extraction of wealth and impoverishment of the population was his chief charge against the imperial power. British rule in India, moreover, arguably lay at the benign end of imperial rule globally.

The obvious additional factor behind imperialist motivations laid bare by Kipling's title was racism: the White Man's Burden was an undisguised expression of a belief in racial superiority that justified imperial conquest. Non-Europeans, after all, were, in the view of many Europeans, incapable of really ruling themselves in a Progressive way, as evidenced by their static, unchanging, and ahistorical history of "oriental despotism" and backwardness. In this view, conquest could not help but be good for them. This view expressed itself not just in racist terms, but also in terms of age and gender. Ideologies of imperialism often presented native peoples as childlike or childish, depending on whether it was their charming naïveté or their petulant refusal to obey their European parents that needed to be emphasized at any particular point—"new-caught, sullen peoples, Half-devil and half-child," as Kipling himself put it in "The White Man's Burden."

The appeal to images of savage children who needed to be taught civilized ways was a fairly straightforward justification of imperialism. More subtle—and appealing more to European male self-images—were constructions of native peoples, especially their men, as feminized: weak, in need of guidance, lacking in initiative and strength.

In this view, imperialism became both test and proof of European manliness as well as justification of European control.

Finally, a third category of motivation and justification presents a more ambiguous picture. Christian missionaries (who in the nineteenth century were more Protestant than Catholic, a reversal of the Late Agrarian pattern) often both preceded and followed imperial conquests, with mistreatment of missionaries sometimes providing a pretext for imperial conquests. Many, if not most, missionaries held the same racist and "civilizational" views of colonized populations. But their religious motivations were less directly imperial—missions not only preceded imperialist expansion but also outlasted it. Christian missionizing was less a rationale for imperialism than its corollary.

Counter-Voices

The ambiguities of imperialist-era missionary work are a reminder that, as we have noted many times before, no culture is monolithic. If the great tide of imperialist sentiment in late nineteenth-century Europe was capitalist, nationalist, and racist, some voices protested the rush to conquest. Political divides over imperialism tended to reflect the main political divisions discussed in the last chapter. Liberals, because of their close ties to capitalist and free market ideologies and their belief in "Progress," usually supported imperialism strongly. Opposition came from both ends of the political spectrum. Conservatives questioned the costs of overseas commitments and claimed that national policy should be concerned solely with the nation itself. Socialists, on the other hand, asserted the universality of Enlightenment rights—the Rights of Man proclaimed during the French Revolution—to highlight the immorality of imperialism. Jules Ferry, premier (prime minister) of France in 1883 who annexed Tunisia and parts of Vietnam, rejected both sorts of arguments. For him, "a policy of peaceful seclusion or abstention is simply the highway to decadence!" As for the rights of man, he said that "superior races have rights over inferior races. . . . They have the duty to civilize inferior races."

A Broader View

We can look at the arguments for imperialism in another way, in the light of our periodization of world history. We noted above the mutual understanding of Late Agrarian relations between hierarchies, an aspect of the maturity of the Late Agrarian world that was a central theme of Chapters 15 through 17. That mutual understanding evaporated as the nineteenth century progressed. It was replaced by a set of relationships in which the strident voices of European imperialists dominated almost all discourse, confidently asserting their own correctness, both factual and moral, and ignoring, dismissing, or silencing opposition, especially opposition arising from colonized peoples. What accounts for this change of tone? How did Europeans forget what they seemed to know in the eighteenth century?

If we remember that the nineteenth century in our chronological scheme is the *Early* Industrial Era, an answer suggests itself that is not visible from the perspective of traditional periodization that views the period 1500 to 1800 as the "early modern" age and thus sees the nineteenth century, necessarily, as a direct continuation of the

Imagining the Colonized

"Adolescent modern" Europeans proceeded from a heroic self-image, represented by the British lion holding the "key to India" (i.e., the Suez Canal), purchased from the Egyptian government (top left). This self-image led them to project images of colonized people as unruly, lazy, and ungrateful children who needed to be educated by their obviously superior rulers in order to reach "civilized" status. Examples here show education in French West Africa (top right), Uncle Sam following John Bull in bearing "The White Man's Burden" (bottom left), and Uncle Sam as schoolteacher to the Philippines, Hawaii, Puerto Rico, and Cuba (bottom right).

"early modern" and so fully "modern." We have mostly avoided the term "modern" in this book because it is a subjective and moving target (every age has been its own "modern"). But if we equate, for the sake of argument, "modern" with "Industrial," then instead of calling the nineteenth century, especially in Europe, the Early Industrial Era, we might just as accurately call it the Adolescent Modern Era. Suddenly, the intellectual tone of European culture makes more sense.

Reborn, in effect, with the Industrial Revolution, nineteenth-century Europe bore the genetic stamp of its Late Agrarian ancestor, but it was a new entity. A quick childhood up to 1850 gave way in the second half of the century to full-blown adolescence. Filled with the self-assurance of "Progress," dismissing the wisdom of their elders as outmoded, confident in their own immortality as world dominators (what could go wrong with Progress, after all?), and armed with weapons that let them be the world's playground bullies, European men happily asserted their superiority over one and all as a scientific fact. Adolescent Modern scientists nodded their assent, publishing scientific studies based on cranial shapes proving the evolutionary superiority of the white race over, in descending order, yellow, red, brown, and black races. Is it a coincidence that Friedrich Nietzsche, master of the snide dismissal of earlier thinkers and the profound-sounding aphorism, is the favorite philosopher of teenage boys? ("'God is dead'—dude, that is so *deep!*") European

FIGURE 21.4 Plumbing Depths. Friedrich Nietzsche (1844–1900), German philosopher.

cultural leaders had become teenage boys, and it is crucial to note that the gendering of that assertion is deliberate and echoes the tone of the times.

This Adolescent Modern European cultural context is what gave the various arguments for imperialism—capitalist, nationalist, racist, civilizational—such force. There were alternate voices, as we've seen, but bullies like Jules Ferry felt justified in shouting them down while bragging about the size of their empire as the admiring crowd applauded. This Adolescent cultural context also accounts for why the process of decolonization since 1975 has involved not just attempting to overcome the material and structural effects of imperialism but also trying to escape the Adolescent mind-set of imperialism (see the Issues in Doing World History box for more on this topic).

Tools of Dominance

Of course, all the will in the world would not have created world-encompassing empires had not late nineteenth-century European powers deployed a range of tools that allowed them to put their ideas into practice. These tools, like the causes of imperialism, may be analyzed in terms of the three parts of our model: network,

FIGURE 21.5 Europe in South America. Plaza de Mayo, Buenos Aires (1861), one of many new global cities that showed heavy European influence.

hierarchy, and cultural tools all played their role. But, as we mentioned in Chapter 19, demographics underlay the impact of all these tools. People of European descent constituted about 1 in 5 of the global population in 1800; by 1900 that proportion was 1 in 3. (In 2000 it was back to 1 in 5.)

Massive population growth gave European economies a huge weight in terms of being both producers and consumers of goods. It accounts for the seemingly insatiable demand for raw materials and food that prompted imperialist grabs for productive lands, while also explaining why the search for overseas markets was largely an illusory misperception. European political leaders were not unaware of the importance of demography: especially in the era of competitive mass conscription after 1871, generals and statesmen alike became obsessed with birth rates. The most important effect of demographic growth, however, came in the exporting of Europeans.

Massive European emigration—over 50 million emigrants in the second half of the nineteenth century—made possible the growth of industrialization in the United States, which otherwise would have been seriously short of labor. Major waves of immigrants, first from northwestern Europe, later from southeastern Europe, also "whitened" the United States significantly, bringing the proportion of African Americans in the population from almost a third to less than 10% between 1865 and 1910, when the number of Native Americans also reached its historical low. By the latter date, US oppression of its African American and Native American populations reached its post-slavery nadir. Similarly, Germans and Italians flooded into Argentina, where the detrimental impact was also felt by the native population. South Africa, Australia, and Canada received huge numbers of British immigrants, resulting in the creation of "new Europes," places where European immigrants came to dominate the politics and culture of colonies. Finally, many Italians and Maltese joined the movement to tropical lands and plantation labor. Concentrations of Europeans were lower in colonies such as India, Kenya, Vietnam, and Egypt, but even here, European population growth allowed the full staffing of imperial administrations at the top levels of rule, directing lower levels staffed by natives co-opted into service. It was this fundamental demographic context that gave other tools their potency.

Network Tools

Two tools of imperialism operated basically in network terms to facilitate imperialist expansion: rapid communication and wealth. The development of means of rapid communications eliminated the slow communications that had always constrained the expansion or cohesion of Agrarian empires. Steamships led the way, speeding ships to their destinations, no longer dependent on the weather, and carrying goods, troops, and communications. Similarly on land, the spread of railway networks connected inland agricultural and mining centers with ports and ships. The railway networks thus connected peripheries, colonial producers of raw materials, to industrializing imperial cores. In turn, railways also connected the teeming populations of these Industrial cores with the labor markets and available land of colonies. Such forms of rapid transportation of goods and people made both direct and indirect imperial rule possible, and it helped make the economic benefits of empire look potentially profitable.

Added to ships and trains came the telegraph. Cables laid along ocean floors connected British policy makers almost instantaneously with their administrators in India, for example—and made control of the Suez region, where the cable passed from the Mediterranean to the Red Sea, even more vital to British global strategists. Telegraph connections also helped to globalize markets, conveying supply, demand, and price information at speeds that Agrarian merchants such as Abraham bin Yiju (Chapter 8) could not have dreamed of. In short, imperial powers had advantageous access to rapid global information flows.

The other sort of network tool was wealth itself. It could create leverage where direct political intervention was not an option, such as in the Americas. Capitalists,

THE LAYING OF THE CABLE---JOHN AND JONATHAN JOINING HANDS.

FIGURE 21.6 Uncle Sam and John Bull. Cartoonist's version of the impact of the Transatlantic Telegraph Cable (1866). (The Granger Collection, New York)

initially mostly British, invested the capital created by industrial production in banks, railroads, mines, and other concerns in other countries. In places that shared the British/European cultural frame values of rule of law and private property, and that were politically stable and white-run, such as the United States, such investment resulted in the spread of locally owned industrialization. In places missing some aspect of that set of preconditions, such as much of Latin America, capital bought not only business investment, but a stake in the political status quo (as a surrogate for stability and law), the cooperation of local officials, and thus influence over policy. Wealth and the promise of trade could also buy favorable treaties with local leaders in more politically fragmented regions such as parts of Africa, providing an entryway into local politics.

Hierarchy Tools

Entry into local politics allowed imperial powers to bring the tools of hierarchy to bear. Chief among these was Industrial military power. The armed forces of the Industrial imperialists usually could deploy two varieties of military advantage. First, flowing from their network advantages, imperial powers were capable of moving ships and troops around rapidly, which let them multiply the impact of the small numbers of troops they felt free to commit to imperialist ventures. (The overwhelming majority of European troops remained in Europe, as rival powers eyed each other warily.) Railroads were less useful in this regard than steamships, and of the latter, smaller gunboats capable of steaming up and down rivers often proved the most useful, allowing forces to strike deep into non-coastal areas and supply isolated outposts, a capability the British used very effectively in the First Opium War.

Second, the small forces that the imperial powers deployed could almost always defeat far larger local forces because of their advantage in firepower. The range and accuracy of late nineteenth-century breech-loading rifles were far superior to the smoothbore muskets still in use in much of the world, never mind against the spears and arrows used by some indigenous peoples encountering European arms for the first time. The invention of the machine gun and increasing use of light, mobile, and accurate field artillery multiplied imperial firepower even more. European armies were not invariably victorious, but when they got into trouble it was almost always when they overreached and got themselves into deep logistical (supply) trouble in bad terrain against foes who decided to fight guerrilla style rather than head-on against overwhelming firepower. This characterizes several British expeditions into Afghanistan, for example.

European medicine supported European armies. Expeditions into the tropics by any Eurasian temperate zone peoples had never gone well in previous eras of world history. Tropical diseases and the low agricultural productivity of most tropical lands made for an environment that killed off invaders before they could do much. Malaria, in particular, was a killer. But the discovery that

FIGURE 21.7 Rifles versus Spears. British forces defeat the Sudanese at the Battle of Omdurman in 1898.

quinine, an extract of the bark of a South American tree, alleviated the symptoms of malaria, gave Europeans the possibility of exploiting the tropics more fully. (Quinine is bitter tasting, but brewing it into water to make a tonic that could be mixed with gin and a twist of lime made it more palatable—gin and tonic, the drink of imperialists.) More generally, advancing knowledge of germs and disease vectors helped more Europeans survive in tropical lands.

Finally, the professionalization of the state in Industrial European hierarchies carried its own advantages, making imperial occupation and exploitation of conquered regions more efficient. When a branch of a European state was placed atop a traditional Agrarian hierarchy, the pay and opportunities for influence and prestige that it offered often attracted the service of second-tier local elites who could leapfrog their way past established first-tier elites. Such local cooperation proved vital in establishing working colonial administrations.

Cultural Tools

It was not just pay and opportunities to climb the ladder of local power that attracted some elements of native populations into cooperation with imperial powers. As the example of Ruhammon Roy cited above shows, European advances in learning could attract the interest of educated elites in colonized regions. Especially powerful in this regard were science in general and medicine in particular. If weaponry conveyed the potential destructive power of Industrial science, medicine held out its humanist promise not just to educated elites but to commoners as well. Motives for local elites to learn European languages and train at European schools varied. Some genuinely admired all aspects of the new knowledge and desired to lead the "westernization" of their own culture; others saw the opportunity to learn the skills of the colonial masters and in turn use them to end imperial rule. At least in the short run, either path facilitated European control.

Among the scientific disciplines called into service in support of European control was history itself. The disparities of wealth and technology that separated the Industrial imperialist powers from the rest of the world in the late nineteenth century made it easy to construct history as the story of the inevitable rise to dominance of the superior European races. Europeans, according to this view, were the only peoples with "true" history, that is, history in which fundamental change and development happened. Such positivist history, taught in colonial schools, removed agency from colonized peoples and promoted the inevitability of European rule. Unweaving the patterns of such historical narratives without abandoning the professional standards of doing history that also arose in the nineteenth century, as we saw in the last chapter with respect to nationalism, has proven an intellectually tricky task (see the Issues in Doing World History box), since respect for scientific knowledge itself was gradually becoming a nearly global frame value.

FIGURE 21.8 Yes, Ma'am. Colonialist-style schooling in Alaska. (ullstein bild / The Granger Collection, New York)

ISSUES IN DOING WORLD HISTORY

Post-Colonial Theory

The intellectual context of late nineteenth-century imperialism left its mark on the profession of history almost as strongly as nationalism did. Only in the last thirty years or so—effectively, since decolonization and the growing signs that the period of "Western" dominance in world history is not guaranteed to be permanent—has much of the professional historical establishment begun to abandon the ideas about world history imprinted on the profession by the era of imperialism. We have noted some of these ideas already. They include variations on the notion that industrialization was bound to happen in Europe because of some inherent (racial or cultural) European advantage (this book's account of the origins of industrialization as highly contingent and globally networked runs deliberately counter to such ideas); that only European history showed real change, or at least that European history was the pattern by which other histories should be measured; and the very notion of "westernization" as the process that industrialization initiated (see the Issues in Doing World History box in Chapter 22).

The history profession has begun to abandon such ideas not simply because the contemporary context is changing. New theoretical perspectives have pushed the profession in new directions.

Post-colonial theory is one of these. (Post-colonial theory is often grouped together in a vaguely defined "post-modern" category of theories that include deconstructionism and the so-called "linguistic turn" in cultural history. These approaches have influenced literary and cultural studies even more than the field of history.) As developed by various scholars, spearheaded by Indian academics studying the history of British rule on the subcontinent, the central point of post-colonial theory is to rewrite, or perhaps more accurately, unwrite the intellectual assumptions imprinted on historical studies by imperialism. In practical terms, this has meant an emphasis on the agency of the colonized in responding to imperialism, and on recovering the voice of the "subaltern"—those historical actors silenced by the dominant discourses of imperialism. This has, by post-colonial theorists' own accounts, often involved a somewhat paradoxical attempt to use the intellectual traditions shaped by imperialism to undo those very traditions.

Thus, post-colonial theory is both testament to the lasting impact of imperialism on the history profession, and one of the contributors to newer, more global and less Eurocentric approaches to world history.

The most powerful cultural tool working for the imperial powers was not any particular screen image, such as the attraction of medicine, the awesomeness of weaponry, or the inevitability of history, but rather the disorienting challenge to indigenous frame values that Industrial imperialism itself posed. This is another way of restating the claim at the beginning of the chapter that Europeans benefited from the element of surprise. Nobody knew how to deal with the sudden appearance of gangs of gun-toting Industrial adolescents who were ignorant, willfully or not, of traditional rules of diplomacy. Often, the Europeans even surprised themselves, since European science had not necessarily fostered European wisdom. In a world whose global network was being strengthened by industrialization, however, surprise could only last so long.

Imperial Interactions

Imperialism in a highly networked world was bound to create exactly the sort of reciprocal relationships between colonizers and colonized that post-colonial theory (see the Issues in Doing World History box) has helped to emphasize. Put another way, the imperialist world that emerged in the late nineteenth century was created by exchanges, by a dialogue that went both ways, within a context of structural advantage for Industrial over Agrarian hierarchies. Just as with the causes and tools of imperialism, we can look at the patterns of imperial interactions through the three parts of our model.

Imperialist Hierarchies

Although the global network was vital in shaping the overall trajectory of imperialism, in examining imperial interactions we may start with the view from hierarchies because imperialist political relationships reproduced and extended the pattern of Agrarian hierarchy in which politics, or power relationships, dominated economic relationships. Indeed, in the inconsistency between the structure of Industrial hierarchies, in which economics shaped politics, and the structure of Industrial imperialism, in which politics (both structural and cultural) took priority over economics, lay one of the seeds of the end of imperialism. In the meantime, the intersection of imperialist interests and local conditions and responses brought about a variety of types of imperial influence and control. Although the boundaries between the types presented here were fluid, with every case effectively an ad hoc response to local conditions, several major types can be outlined.

Free Trade Imperialism

"Free trade imperialism," as it has been termed, was arguably the first to emerge (outside the anomalous continuation of British rule in India) and preceded the scramble for more direct political control in Africa and parts of Asia. This form emerged chiefly in Latin America after the end of its wars of independence in 1830, where direct political takeover was diplomatically excluded but where Industrial imperialists, chiefly Britain and later the United States, could assume a common legal and philosophical cultural frame around business transactions. While proclamations of Enlightenment principles of human and property rights by leading Latin American revolutionaries such as Simon Bolívar made such assumptions plausible, the difference in economic conditions and social structures between Latin American countries and the Anglo-American imperialists meant that this commonality was more screen image than frame reality. Still, the image shaped economic and thus political relations.

The chief mechanisms of free trade imperialism were two. The first was insistence by the industrializing powers on the principle of free trade—that is, that Latin American countries not impose tariffs on the importing of British (and later US) manufactured goods. In exchange, the Industrial powers bought Latin American raw materials. The second mechanism facilitated the first: investment in Latin American transport infrastructure, for moving raw materials to port, and banking, to help finance trade. In the process, certain segments of Latin American society, basically those already in political power, profited right along with the Industrial capitalist corporations doing the trading and investing. These mechanisms usually led to informal but effective political influence by the Industrial country, whose diplomacy and law backed up the property rights of the Industrial capitalist corporations. The coercive side of this arrangement stemmed from the fact that trading raw materials for manufactured goods tended to lead the raw material producer into economic dependency and debt (debt financed by Industrial corporate-owned banks), whose terms gave the Industrial power leverage over state policy in the debtor country. But coercion remained mostly an implied threat, since investment also aligned the economic and cultural interests of the Latin American rulers with those of foreign Industrial capitalists.

Thus, this form of economic imperialism saw interactions and influence mediated through the corporate sphere of the Industrial hierarchy, removing states (and overt political imperialism) by one step from the equation (see Figure 21.9). (As we shall see in Chapter 28, the corporate sphere might well exercise such indirect control in *both* directions, threatening to become an entity independent of hierarchies.)

Semi-Sovereign Enclaves

A second form of imperialism emerged in China in the wake of the Opium Wars. Here, the Chinese hierarchy was still too large and powerful to be taken over directly by Industrial powers. Nor did the Industrial powers really want to take on the vast expense and administrative burden of attempting to rule China: they wanted Chinese goods and access to Chinese markets (such as they were) for Western goods. But they could (and did) defeat Chinese forces in individual wars. This allowed first Britain, then others following the British model, to negotiate agreements whereby China granted specific ports and territories to Industrial powers as exclusive trade zones, within which the merchants and other inhabitants of that power would have freedom to carry on trade and would be subject not to the laws of China but to the laws of the Industrial power.

Such arrangements extended an old Chinese technique for managing the intersection of their hierarchy with the network: foreign merchants had long been confined to certain ports through which they were forced to trade. This arrangement therefore allowed the Chinese to maintain at least a screen image of their own sovereignty (though the reality was acknowledged in the fact that such agreements were referred to as "unequal treaties" both in China and elsewhere). But the grant of what was, in effect, diplomatic immunity to all foreign inhabitants of such zones carved out semi-sovereign enclaves within China that were strange dual spaces: Chinese with respect to Chinese people, but pieces of Britain, France, the United States, and so forth with respect to the particular foreigners whose space it was—an arrangement that was called "extraterritoriality," as the enclaves were effectively beyond the territory of China at the same time that they were inside China. Within those enclaves, the frame and screen values of the Industrial country applied, especially principles of free trade and private property in their Western rather than Chinese forms.

FIGURE 21.10 That's My Pie!
Cartoon depiction of imperial powers dividing up China. (The Granger Collection, New York)

Like free trade imperialism, extraterritoriality was a form of imperial control rooted in network relations and the extension of the Industrial hierarchy's corporate sphere. But the lack of a shared cultural frame, real or fictive, between the Industrial

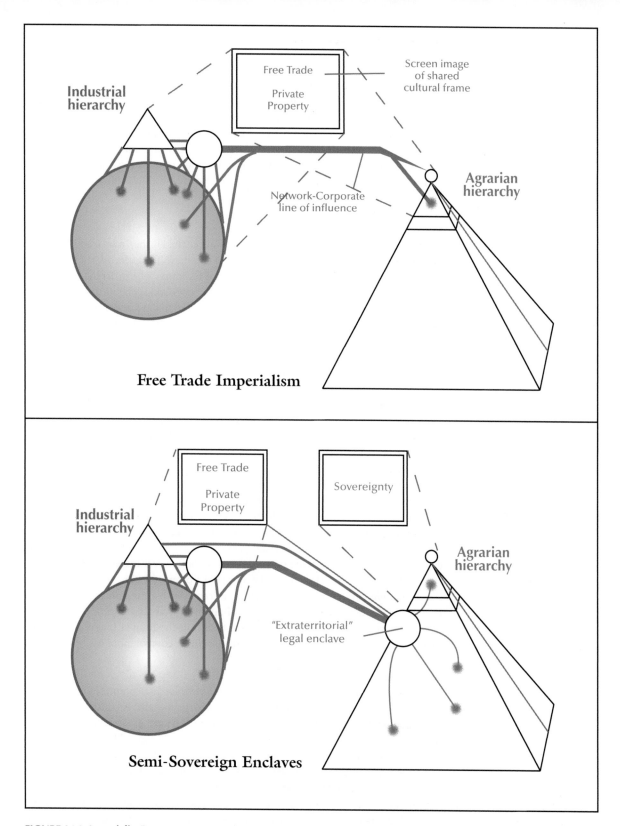

FIGURE 21.9 Imperialist Structures 1. (Top) The structure of free trade imperialism. (Bottom) The structure of semi-sovereign enclaves.

PRINCIPLES AND PATTERNS

How reality looked to people through their cultural frames mattered as much as what reality "really was."

and Agrarian hierarchies led to greater state involvement on the part of the Industrial hierarchy, working on behalf of its corporate sphere, to carve out a cultural space within which the corporations could operate in their accustomed way. Thus, screen images were negotiated between two different cultural frames, with the result interpretable in ways that were acceptable, if different in emphasis, within each frame. (The Chinese considered themselves magnanimous in granting trading *privileges,* while the industrialized powers felt they had received Chinese concessions to legal and free trade *rights* claimed as universal.)

Indirect Rule

In the next two forms of imperialism (see Figure 21.11), the Industrial hierarchy's state played a more direct role in managing colonies. These forms therefore bear more resemblance to Agrarian forms of empire building. The differences, however, are significant. Distant connections across the network still lay behind these forms of hierarchy-to-hierarchy coercion, whereas most Agrarian empire building, especially before the maritime empires of the Late Agrarian Era, had involved expansion into adjacent lands. The typical Industrial Era partnership between the state and the corporate sphere, moreover, characterizes nineteenth-century imperialism, whereas in the Agrarian Era states acted through their warrior and other elites. The exceptions were the experiments of the British and Dutch East India companies beginning in the seventeenth century in India and Indonesia, respectively, and these contributed to the emergence of the new models of imperialism.

The less common of these semi-traditional forms of imperialism was the exercise of imperial rule indirectly, through a cooperative local partner. This sort of arrangement tended to emerge in areas where local hierarchies were small, weak, and numerous, making the complexities of negotiating political and economic relationships easier for a political actor from the area who could take advantage of his knowledge of local culture, rivalries, and so forth. The imperial power provided an implied or real threat of military force to back up the negotiating demands of their local agent, and in return used him to collect and pass on the economic produce of the region, either under the guise of trade or as a system of more direct taxation.

The problem was that since the imperial power and the local agent shared material interests but not a common cultural frame, such arrangements tended to be unstable. They proved most useful to the imperial powers in binding the whole set of local powers into a single system, thereby laying the foundations for creating a single hierarchy over which they could exercise direct control more easily.

Direct Rule

Direct rule became by the late nineteenth century the most common form of imperialism, as most of Africa, much of Southeast Asia and the Pacific, and scattered colonies elsewhere (such as Korea, which came under Japanese rule) fell to (mostly) European powers in the "scramble" phase of colony-grabbing. Thus, direct rule affected regions ranging from long-standing, well-organized hierarchies such as Vietnam to parts of Africa lacking state-level societies. The former, despite a well-organized war of opposition, lost to the superior firepower and organization of French forces; in some of the latter cases, European forces stepped in as "peacekeepers" when systems of indirect rule broke down, though direct conquest also played a part, as in the

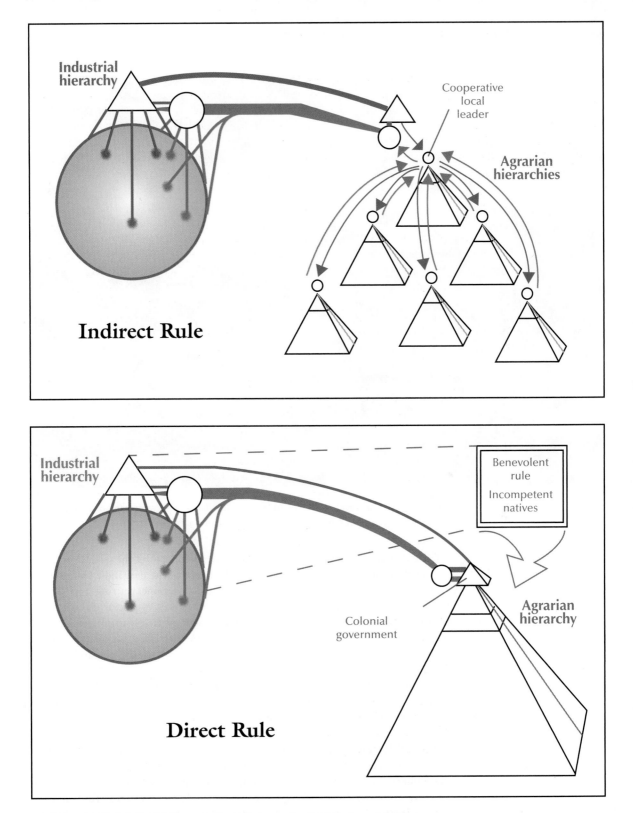

FIGURE 21.11 Imperialist Structures 2. (Top) The structure of indirect imperial rule.
(Bottom) The structure of direct imperial rule, very much like a traditional conquest society.

FIGURE 21.12 The Great Mutiny of 1857. Sepoys, Indian troops trained and officered by the British, rebelled against British rule. Other sepoys helped suppress the revolt.

Belgian Congo. Britain also imposed direct rule in India after the Great Mutiny of 1857, removing control of the colony from the hands of the East India Company.

Direct rule was state run, with the colonial government acting as a distant branch of the professionalized Industrial state. In this way, by placing its own structure atop an existing Agrarian Pyramid, direct rule most clearly resembles Agrarian Era forms of imperialism, with the distinctly Industrial Era twist that the wealth drawn up through the coercive structure was then funneled, in large part, through an adjunct corporate sphere. At least for a while, the imperial power also tended to dominate, though not monopolize, the cultural screen of the colonized society, projecting an image of themselves as benevolent rulers bringing civilization to natives obviously incapable of ruling themselves.

Imperial Networks

The progression from free trade imperialism to direct rule accompanied a shift in emphasis on the part of the imperial powers from trade with non-European areas toward more direct extraction of raw materials from colonies. Trade did not decline during this time, but grew significantly, and some of that flowed through extraterritorial enclaves in China and in other places that granted the merchants of particular Industrial countries monopoly access to the markets in their enclaves. The British, for example, negotiated an exclusive concession on the sale of cigarettes in Persia in the early 1900s. (This case actually backfired, as Persian religious leaders organized a smoker's strike in a country of heavy smokers, forcing renegotiation of the terms of the concession.) But it was trade between the Industrial countries that really boomed, facilitated by a gold-based monetary system that made currency conversion relatively simple and driven by the fact that the richest consumer markets were in the Industrial countries. Growing industrial production to serve these markets meant growing demand for raw materials. Raw materials that could be obtained at an "imperial discount," that is, at politically determined extractive rates rather than a price set in a competitive market, could give a country's industries a competitive advantage.

The extractive regimes that resulted from these pressures appeared most strongly in Africa, where imperial rule was imposed during the competitive "scramble" phase and where the impact on the patterns of local peasant economies was the strongest, though similar effects appeared wherever imperial powers imposed direct rule.

Peasant Economies

The first sort of extractive regime involved the transformation and exploitation of peasant economies. This was the common form in the relatively rich agricultural lands of West Africa. Here, peasants generally kept their land, though significant parts of French West Africa saw the introduction of large plantations in place of small peasant holdings. In either case, village settlement patterns continued from pre-imperial times, and imperialists aimed to extract surplus agricultural production in a fairly traditional way. The problem with this from the extractors' perspective was that traditional peasant subsistence crops, above all yams, had little value for Industrial economies. What did have value were previously marginal cash crops such as palm oil, indigo, and the like. They had been marginal because the cash economy of West Africa was fairly small.

Imperial rule shifted incentives deliberately. Taxes were imposed, payable only in the currency of the rulers. This forced more farmers into growing cash crops in order to pay their taxes. Failure to pay often resulted in imposition of forced labor duties, again focused on cultivation of cash crops. Widespread cash cropping had several further effects on peasant life. In many cases, not enough subsistence crops were grown to continue to feed the population, forcing even more cash cropping to generate money to buy imported food. This made such regions dependent on continued access to imperial-controlled network flows. Furthermore, pre-imperial peasant cultures had usually assigned prestige based on production of subsistence crops. Cash cropping therefore upset traditional local hierarchies and created new ones grounded in market success and cooperation with

FIGURE 21.13 African Colonial Economies. Women carrying bales of cocoa for export from the Gold Coast, ca. 1900. African farmers had initiated the cultivation of cocoa in the late precolonial period and its expansion was encouraged by British colonial officials. Cocoa remains Ghana's primary export, a legacy of the colonial emphasis on cash crops.

the foreign rulers. Market success often went with acquiring some European education and positions in the imperial administration. All this created rivalries between
traditional elites and new emerging elites that fragmented African populations.
Compounding this effect, cash cropping fed into the more pervasive network connections, and this in turn heightened local ethnic rivalries, which imperial rulers
often exploited and worsened by playing "divide and rule."

Raw Materials

Such exploitation appears mild, however, compared to the brutality of imperial rule
in the Congo. Here, rubber trees and copper were the valuable commodities.
Leopold II, king of Belgium, came out of the Berlin Conference of 1885 with the
vast majority of the Congo basin as his privately owned colony—he was the sole
owner and shareholder in a dummy corporation set up to explore and colonize the
region, the Association Internationale Africaine. This supposedly non-governmental
organization legitimized Leopold's private control of a vast region of Africa. This
shows that while international capitalism as a system of economic organization was

FIGURE 21.14 Labor Control. Atrocities in the Belgian Congo, as depicted in the modern
painting *Colonie Belge 1885–1959* by the artist Tshibumba.

not necessarily a leading cause of imperialism, capitalism as the cultural frame of much network activity heavily influenced the forms of imperialism.

The initial exploration was expensive and only loans from the Belgian state kept the enterprise afloat, but by the mid-1890s rubber and copper extraction turned the corporation immensely profitable. The problem was that the profit came from brutal forced labor. Entire villages were conscripted into Leopold's labor force. Organized into chain gangs, men, women and children were punished for infractions of work rules, failure to produce enough, or sheer whim of the overseers by having their hands chopped off. The subsistence economy collapsed, but since importing food was a drain on Leopold's profits, malnutrition and starvation ran rampant. Conditions in "the rubber system" were so bad that an international commission investigated and created a major scandal in Europe by publishing its findings. Leopold was forced to give up control of the Congo, which became a colony of the Belgian government in 1908. By that time, vast damage had been done to the population of the Congo, though lack of precise records or pre-imperial censuses make an actual count of deaths impossible.

Labor Reserves

A third form of exploitation emerged in South Africa and Kenya, both British colonies. Both areas saw significant European immigration and settlement. In both places, mineral wealth overshadowed the potential profits of agriculture. South Africa in particular had not only gold, but the world's richest diamond mines, and diamonds had value both as gemstones and increasingly for industrial tools. Mining, however, required a large labor force, as the Spanish had discovered in Peru in the sixteenth century.

The British solution was to use a mixture of cash taxes and direct coercion, just as with West African peasant economies, to create a form of industrial labor reserve. Men were attracted or conscripted out of their villages for large parts of each year to work for wages in the privately owned mining corporations under the supervision of salaried European foremen. They lived during that part of the year in mass labor camps. As in West Africa, this disrupted elements of the pre-imperial village economy and social structure: cattle herding had been the basis of village prestige and hierarchy, and keeping cattle became impossible for many when they went to the mines. Furthermore, British appropriations of grazing land undercut this aspect of pre-colonial culture even more. On the other hand, it was almost exclusively men who went to the labor camps, and they returned periodically to their home villages. There, since agricultural production fell outside the view of British economic interests, subsistence farming and traditional patterns of village life, maintained by the women, were able to survive more intact than elsewhere.

Imperial Cultures

Although analysis of patterns of economic exploitation can make late nineteenth-century imperialism seem like a one-sided process, it is important to stress again that this was not the case. Yes, colonies fell under new political and economic systems that entailed sometimes wrenching changes in patterns of everyday life, but colonized peoples responded in different ways, and imperial network connections flowed in both directions, affecting colonizers as well as colonized. Furthermore, especially in discussing imperial cultures, we must bear in mind that no culture is monolithic: responses to imperialism varied in both imperial and colonized countries. We will look in detail at the patterns of response and reaction to imperialism by colonized societies in the next chapter. Here we can note some of the cultural exchanges and screen images that arose from the imperial world.

Exchanges

As had been the case since the beginnings of network exchange, perhaps the key exchange was not of goods but of knowledge. Imperialist relationships between Industrial and Agrarian hierarchies prompted such exchanges perhaps even more intensely than usual, as both sides found themselves, in effect, looking at not just another culture but another world.

On the side of the Agrarian societies, their leading thinkers usually actively sought out knowledge of the strange new world challenging the stability of the world they knew. Obtaining a Western education became a priority, and travel to Europe and the United States for direct experience of the new world powerhouses formed an important part of that education. The focus of this side of the knowledge exchange was on practical applications. Science, mathematics, and organizational theory were vital if colonized countries, or those threatened with colonization, were to build their own industrial infrastructures and the modern armed forces that industry supported, while medicine led the list of imperialist knowledge with immediate humanitarian applications. But more abstract aspects of knowledge, particularly the idea of nationalism, would also prove their practical worth. As we shall see in the next chapter, actually putting to use the knowledge of Industrial societies was fraught with political and cultural issues, but the search for knowledge itself was nearly universal, as Agrarian intellectuals attempted to see into their own society's future.

On the flip side, professional academics in imperialist Industrial societies traveled to Agrarian colonies, and indeed to regions of colonial control where indigenous societies were still practicing pre-Agrarian hunting and gathering ways of life, to discover their own past. It is not an exaggeration to say that anthropology as an academic field was born of imperial encounters across the Industrial-Agrarian divide. Unlike differences among Agrarian societies, this divide was so clear and so new that it seems to have stimulated awareness not just of historical development, which was "Progress" in the eyes of most nineteenth-century Europeans, but of the threatened loss of the living pre-Industrial past as the power of industrialization promised soon to pervade the whole world.

"Scientific" anthropology did not, however, escape the cultural assumptions of the time. Anthropology joined history as intellectual justifiers of a racial hierarchy of peoples and countries. Studies of "primitive" peoples not only documented but confirmed the primitiveness of the people studied, casting these societies as "less evolved" not just in terms of technology and social organization but also the supposedly less intelligent nature of such peoples. (Anthropology, like history, has had its post-colonial adjustments of theory.) In this way, anthropology contributed to the nationalist, racist environment of the times, an environment that expressed itself in screen images from popular culture generated by imperial exchanges.

FIGURE 21.15 Scientific Racism. Nineteenth-century classification of skull shapes, "demonstrating" racial hierarchy.

Imaging the Other

For many in Europe and the United States, imperialism turned much of the world into an imagined space of exotic Otherness, a repository for their own ambitions and fears. India played this role for several generations of Britain's population (while Indian food slowly colonized British tables). Teddy Roosevelt's post-presidential journey to the Amazon and the French impressionist painter Paul Gaugin's residence on the South Pacific island of Tahiti demonstrate that cultural fantasies could play out in many places. But it was Africa, as the least known and perhaps most threatening colonial playground in both natural and racial terms, that became the particular focus of many imperialist fantasies. Common references to "Darkest Africa" inscribed the combination of geographic lack of light (knowledge) and human blackness into the consciousness of Industrial societies.

One particular expression of Africa as imperial playground was the huge rise in popularity of big game hunting. Rich Europeans organized safaris, staffed by African porters and equipped with the latest in camping luxuries, whose tallies of thousands of large animals killed and exotic trophies brought home—elephant-foot umbrella stands and tusks, lion-skin rugs (or tiger skins from India), any sort of head that could be mounted on a wall (though "headhunters" were, of course, African). These trophies affirmed the manhood of the hunters in meeting the challenges of the wild. Published accounts of such safaris joined the fictional tales of authors such as Rudyard Kipling in bringing the exotic experience of the African playground into middle class living rooms.

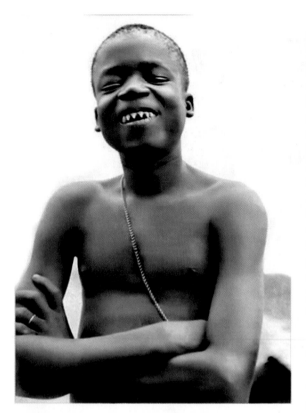

FIGURE 21.16 Racism on the Screen. Ota Benga, who was put on display in St. Louis in 1904 and after that at the Bronx Zoo.

The exotic wilds of the world were also brought home live for public viewing. Public zoological gardens such as the London Zoo got their start during this time, displaying lions, tigers, giraffes, and zebras in cages that ensured the safety of the viewers from the dangerous bits of the world's wilds within. The nature (so to speak) of such zoos is revealed with absolute clarity by the episodes, not infrequent, during which human beings joined the list of wild exotics in the cages. Indeed, entire human zoos, called "ethnological exhibitions" to give them scientific credibility, became wildly popular across Europe from the 1870s. Natives of the Philippines formed an exhibit at the 1904 St. Louis World's Fair, and an African pygmy named Ota Benga was displayed in a cage in the Bronx Zoo next to African and Asian great apes. Protests by local African American clergymen were pointedly ignored by city officials. From our perspective, such displays of people also display the essence of the Adolescent Modern sensibility.

Conclusion

The slow and uneven spread of industrialization created the vast disparities of economic power, political organization, and cultural motivation that made Early Industrial imperialism possible. The meeting of Industrial and Agrarian societies led to various structural arrangements and patterns of economic exploitation, as well as knowledge exchanges. This chapter has focused on the development of imperialism from the perspective of such causes and patterns. But the sudden challenge posed by Early Industrial imperialism to the non-Industrial world elicited its own pattern of reactions and responses. It is to these, and to imperialism from the perspective of the non-Industrial world, that we turn in the next chapter.

FRAME IT YOURSELF

Changing the Frame

The imposition of "adolescent" European values on European imperial possessions, and indeed on the world, shaped the imperial moment in significant ways, as we have seen. Assume that China had industrialized first, as the previous twenty centuries of history might have led one to expect (if one were to expect industrialization at all, which as we have seen, one probably shouldn't). How might Chinese values have translated into a new Industrial context? Would there have been Chinese imperialism? If so, would Chinese imperialism have shaped the world the same way European imperialism did? Would we today conflate "modernization" with "Sinification"?

Further Reading

Headrick, Daniel R. 1981. *The Tools of Empire: Technology and European Imperialism in the Nineteenth Century.* Oxford: Oxford University Press.

Massie, Robert. 1991. *Dreadnought: Britain, Germany, and the Coming of the Great War.* New York: Random House.

Pratt, Mary Louise. 2007. *Imperial Eyes: Travel Writing and Transculturation.* 2nd ed. London: Routledge.

Roy, Tapti. 1994. *The Politics of a Popular Uprising: Bundelkhand 1857.* Delhi: Oxford University Press.

Said, Edward. 1994. *Culture and Imperialism.* New York: Vintage Books.

Spiers, Edward. 2005. *The Victorian Soldier in Africa.* Manchester: Manchester University Press.

For additional learning and instructional resources related to this chapter, please go to www.oup.com/us/morillo

CHAPTER TWENTY-TWO

Imperialism: Reactions and Consequences

Sakuma Shozan.

Introduction

Sakuma Shozan was born in 1811 in Shinshu, in what is today the prefecture of Nagano in central Japan. The son of a samurai, he moved in 1834 to Edo, the capital of the Tokugawa Shogunate that ruled Japan, where he received a classical Confucian education and entered the service of Sanada Yukitsura, a major political leader. The shogun put Sanada in charge of the country's coastal defenses in 1841, just as the First Opium War was ending in China. Sakuma, whose birthplace is about as far from the sea as one can get in Japan, entered a career in which he had to look across the seas to the rest of the world.

The Opium War made the potential challenge facing Japan clear. Sakuma saw that Japan's 200 years of virtual isolation from the rest of the world could not last: Japan would soon have to meet the threat posed by the "Western barbarians" and their steamships and modern weapons. He also saw that the country was woefully unprepared to do so. He immediately took up the study of Dutch (one Dutch ship a year was allowed into Nagasaki harbor to trade; this constituted Japan's "window on the West") and Western sciences. For he was convinced that Japan's only hope of avoiding domination by the barbarians was to adopt their weaponry. He began to advocate this policy openly, publishing a book titled *Eight Policies for the Defense of the Sea* that brought him some notice and a number of students who would later be political leaders after the barbarians did arrive. No mere academic, he applied what he learned in glassmaking and optics to make telescopes. He began studying electricity in 1849 and created Japan's first telegraph several years before Admiral Perry and his US fleet arrived in Tokyo Bay in 1853, bringing a telegraph as a gift and the threat of Western domination as an immediate reality.

One of Sakuma's students tried to stow away on Perry's ship, was caught and arrested, and for his association Sakuma, too, was put under house arrest for eight years. During that time he wrote *Reflections on My Errors*. On reflection, it turned out Sakuma did not think his errors were errors at all. Indeed, he laid out a path for the modernization of Japan. He advocated neither complete traditionalism (which he knew was doomed to fail) nor complete "Westernization"—abandonment of all of Japan's traditions and identity in order to imitate the barbarians. Instead, he said that the wise Japanese leader "employs the ethics of the East and the scientific technique of the West, neglecting neither the spiritual nor material aspects of life, combining subjective and objective, and thus bringing benefit to the people and serving the nation." In short, through "Eastern Ethics, Western Science," Japan could compete and still be Japanese.

Sakuma Shozan's third path, neither traditionalism nor westernization but "modernization," looked simple but turned out to be politically difficult to implement in Japan and elsewhere. Those advocating westernization thought it a half-measure. Traditionalists opposed, sometimes violently, the admission of any Western influence as the thin edge of a wedge leading to loss of identity. They saw Sakuma himself this way, and an assassin cut him down in 1864. Just four years later, his policies would

Framing the Argument

• The economic, political, and cultural challenges traditional Agrarian hierarchies faced when confronted by the challenge of aggressive European expansion

• The different paths of traditionalist resistance, westernization, and modernization that different countries followed in meeting this challenge

• The transformations of cultural identity brought about by the massive human migrations of the nineteenth century

FRAMING Imperialism: Reactions and Consequences

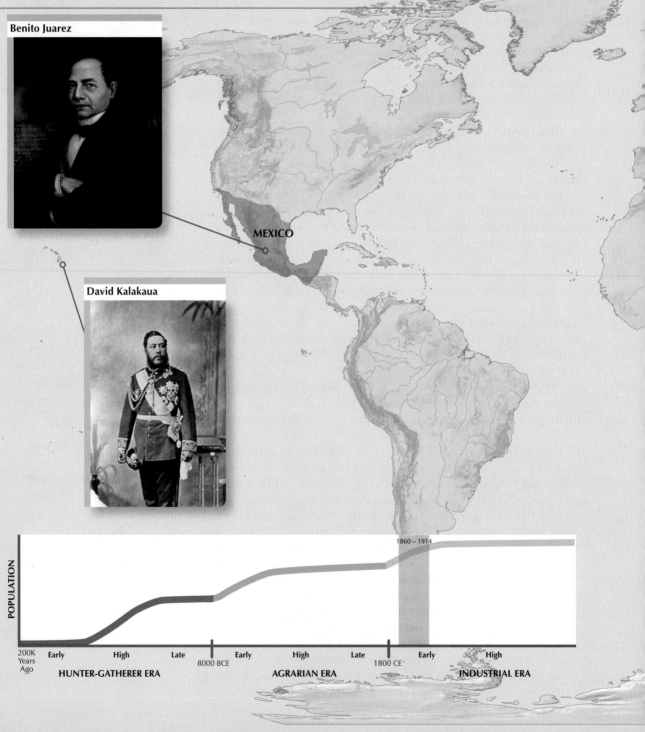

Benito Juarez

David Kalakaua

MEXICO

1860 – 1914

POPULATION

200K
Years
Ago

Early   High   Late   Early   High   Late   Early   High

HUNTER-GATHERER ERA   8000 BCE   AGRARIAN ERA   1800 CE   INDUSTRIAL ERA

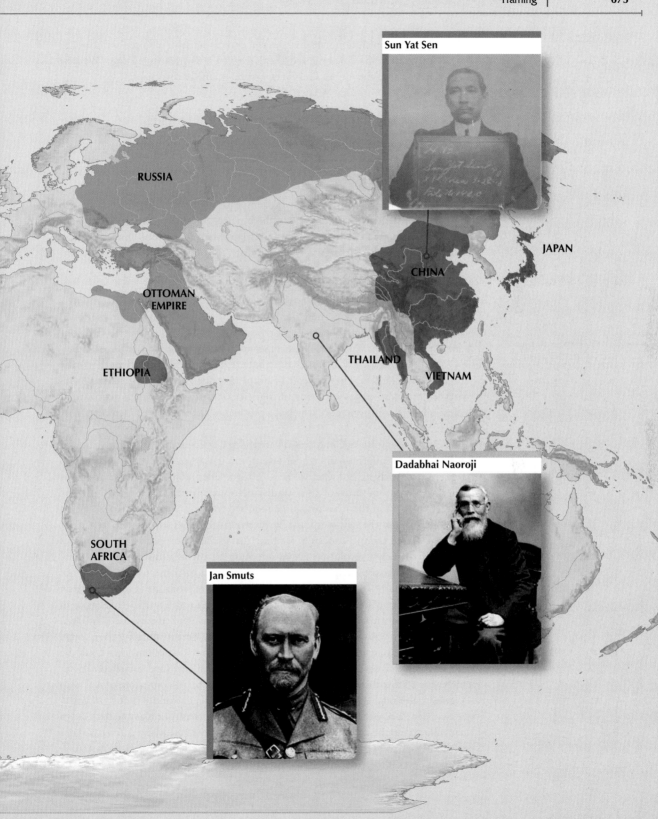

Sun Yat Sen

RUSSIA

JAPAN

OTTOMAN
EMPIRE

CHINA

ETHIOPIA

THAILAND

VIETNAM

Dadabhai Naoroji

SOUTH
AFRICA

Jan Smuts

guide a Japanese revolution. Meanwhile, the choices he saw—choices about policy and identity intertwined—presented themselves to countries facing the "Western barbarians" around the globe. This is the central theme of this chapter.

——— ⊦ ✳ ⊦ ———

The Industrial Challenge

The appearance of Early Industrial imperialist powers from Europe on the global stage from the middle of the nineteenth century onward posed a set of interlocked challenges to the Agrarian societies they encountered. These challenges spanned all three parts of our model.

Network Challenges

The clearest and most immediate threat was the Industrial countries' military effectiveness, flowing across the global network with apparently inexorable force. Nor was this simply a matter of superior weaponry, though that part was obvious to all but mystics and fanatics. (These appeared periodically, as in the Boxer Rebellion in China in the early 1900s, whose adherents believed themselves magically protected from bullets. They weren't.) European armies and their Industrial infrastructure had advantages in terms of logistics, strategic mobility, organization, professionalism, and coherence, the last a product of the nationalist ideologies that inspired them.

Thus, meeting European forces on anything like equal military terms required much more than simply buying modern weaponry if it were available. Soldiers had to be trained to use them. But what soldiers? Warrior elites around the world often saw their elite identity in terms of their traditional weaponry and so resisted both the new technology and the mass discipline required to use it effectively. Conscripting commoners to use the new weapons, however, was equally unacceptable to warrior elites who feared arming a social revolution, just as their European contemporaries did. To avoid such a revolution meant adopting all the administrative and moral mechanisms of mass conscription backed by nationalism. Such mechanisms could not be created overnight—if at all, given the monetary cost of professional administration and the difficulty of deploying nationalism in multicultural Agrarian empires or in fragmented tribal areas. Furthermore, mass conscription implied mass use of modern weaponry, which was difficult to impossible unless they were manufactured at home.

This implied an Industrial infrastructure, again not something that could be built in a day, and something that required economic, legal, and social conditions which were almost always at odds with the social and political dominance of Agrarian societies' traditional elites. On the other hand, the challenge of the Industrial countries' economic power was a major threat in itself, not to mention as the backing of their military might, as free trade imperialism demonstrates. Many Agrarian states could not hope to match the imperial powers bribe-for-bribe among their own functionaries, never mind compete economically in an open market.

This raised the final network challenge: how to manage the suddenly much more powerful—and problematic—intersection between traditional hierarchies and the global network through which the Industrial Revolution was sending its massive power surge. As the Opium Wars (and Admiral Perry in Tokyo Bay) showed, traditional policies of containment and regulation could be blown open by Industrial military and economic power.

Hierarchy Challenges

As the chain of potential responses and their consequences raised by the challenge of European military power shows, any response to network challenges rapidly entailed challenges to the very structure of Agrarian hierarchies. From the perspective of the elites atop any Agrarian hierarchy, the choices appeared particularly stark. If they allowed European merchants in, the resulting transformation of economic practices and culture threatened to totally undermine elites' social and political dominance. On the other hand, the changes necessary to meet the imperialists on their own terms, as the military options showed, threatened to lead down the same path. No wonder that at times the best path seemed to be cooperation with the newcomers—cooperation that might well entail trading the country's independence for the individual security of an elevated if now subordinate position in a colonial administration.

The threat that elites perceived may be illustrated in terms of our model (see Figure 22.1). The basic process was that industrially powered network flows,

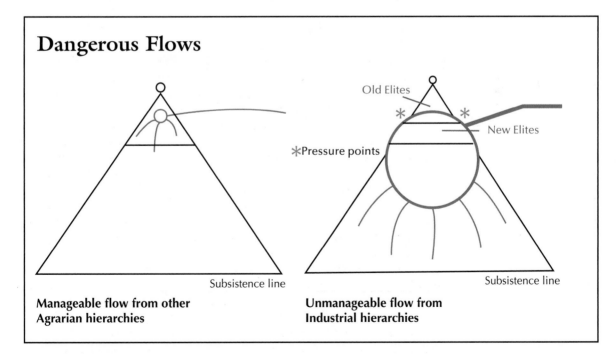

Dangerous Flows

Old Elites

*Pressure points

New Elites

Subsistence line

Subsistence line

Manageable flow from other Agrarian hierarchies

Unmanageable flow from Industrial hierarchies

FIGURE 22.1 **Dangerous Flows.** The industrially powered network pumps its goods and values into a traditional hierarchy.

overwhelming the traditional mechanisms for regulating a hierarchy's network intersection, rapidly recreated the merchant capitalist tumor that had infected many Late Agrarian European hierarchies and that had eventually transformed Britain revolutionarily.

The effect of the tumor was to create a new set of economic elites whose interests lay in cooperating with network flows, both economic and cultural. These new elites were likely to become rivals and thus political opponents of the old elites whose power and prestige lay in the internal, anti-network dynamics of the hierarchy. Thus arose the conflicting interests and competing screen images that made a unified response to the Industrial challenge very difficult to achieve. This in turn made a middle-ground position such as Sakuma Shozan's so politically vulnerable, trapped as it was between traditionalist old elites and westernizing new elites.

A final stage in the process of the Industrial network transforming an Agrarian hierarchy into an Industrial one was possible, but that process was also more contingent. Even when it was achieved, it was often slower to develop, though the long-term trend is arguably inexorable. It was slower and more contingent because neither the Agrarian old elite nor the outside Industrial powers desired the emergence of a new (and potentially rival) Industrial hierarchy (see Figure 22.2).

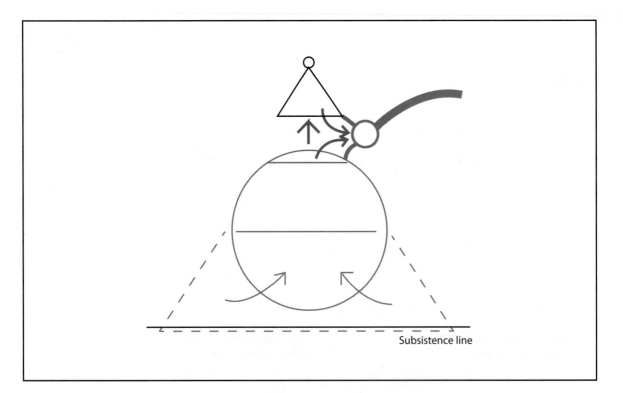

FIGURE 22.2 **Transformation.** The transition caused by network flows from Agrarian pyramid to Industrial state-society-corporate structure.

ISSUES IN DOING WORLD HISTORY

"Modern," "Western," Historical Processes

The distinction between "modern" and "Western" has proven a difficult one, not just for traditionalist Agrarian elites (who wanted no part of either) and their westernizing rivals (who wanted all of both, as they seemed inseparable), but for people ever since, including some historians. This book adopts a straight-forward and materialist definition of "modern": it means "industrialized," which this book usually uses in preference to "modern" because of the ambiguities and moving nature of "modern." "Industrialized" also stands in contrast to "Agrarian." This book has tried to avoid use of the term "Western" except in reference to historical debates that used that term, as it too is a loaded, ambiguous term useful mostly for polemical purposes. Conflating "modern" and "Western" is therefore, from the perspective of historical analysis, problematic.

From the perspective of polemical argument, or politics, on the other hand, such a conflation can be quite useful. European imperialists in the nineteenth and twentieth centuries were happy to define modern-ization in terms of the adoption not just of European Industrial technology but also of European religion and morality. Many British statesmen proclaimed openly the goal of turning Indians into proper Englishmen, even if their skin color was not quite right, and even today many US and European analysts

think that being fully modernized entails adoption of "Western values," which often include the equally conflated trio of democracy, market economics, and capitalism. This is claimed to be useful in terms of promoting human rights, but some arguments for human rights, despite their initial formulation in European medieval and Enlightenment terms, can rely on recent work in evolutionary cognitive science suggesting that key aspects of morality really are universal, even if they get expressed in different cultural terminology, returning us to the Cognitive-Linguistic Revolution with which "modern" (= *Homo sapiens*) history began (see Chapter 1). If we construct human rights as compatible with trans-cultural ethical principles, even if their formulation does reflect their medieval European birthplace, then promoting them runs a lower risk of being culturally chauvinist. (When asked what he thought of "Western civilization," Gandhi replied, "It's a good idea. They should try it sometime.")

If we remove the polemics, the historical point to be made is that "modernization" (industrialization) is a process, and that "modern" (Industrial) societies come in just as many varieties as "pre-modern" (Agrarian or even Hunter-Gatherer) societies came in, and that analysis of their differences is easier if one's analytic terms are not already value-laden.

Cultural Challenges

Agrarian elites perceived the entire set of network and hierarchy challenges, however, not in structural terms such as our model portrays, but in terms of screen images framed by their particular cultural frame values. Thus, the threat of elite loss of social and political power usually showed up on the cultural screen as a threat to the "tradi-tional identity" of the society—an image with broad appeal across the Great Cultural Divide, as "the traditional identity" of the society could be interpreted up and down the pyramid as a threat to stable lifestyles. That the "Western barbarians" showed up speaking outlandish tongues, wearing bizarre clothing, and acting without the least respect for traditional customs made this even more persuasive. As Sakuma Shozan wrote of the Americans, "Their deportment and manner of expression were exceed-ingly arrogant, and the resulting insult to our national dignity was not small." Thus, appeals to "traditional identity" held the potential of creating a more unified response and even opened a possible path to the adoption of full-blown nationalism.

At the same time, it was this very appeal that created the key choices visible in Sakuma Shozan's writings and around the world: traditionalist resistance (maintaining traditional cultural identity is paramount, even if it appears doomed); westernization (traditional cultural identity has failed and must be replaced altogether by Western ways *and values*); modernization (adopting the technology and techniques of the West within the frame of traditional cultural identity is possible and desirable). As the slogan drawn from Sakuma's work put it, "Eastern Ethics, Western Science."

Responding to Challenges: Case Studies

Although modernization was the path that worked for Japan from 1868 on (see discussion later in this chapter), all three paths provide examples of success and failure, at least to some degree. The following set of brief case studies illustrates the variety of paths that different societies followed and the difficulties they faced in meeting the Industrial challenge.

Traditionalist Resistance

Attempts to resist European power without any transformation of a country's political or military structure faced deep difficulties but were not automatically doomed. Maintaining the country's cultural identity was the key goal of traditionalist resistance. The deep connection between that identity and elite power was the root of the difficulty such programs faced.

Vietnam

The period 1528 to 1802 had seen the division of the territory of modern Vietnam between rival ruling families in the north and the south. The various wars between the rival kingdoms and dynastic upheavals within them had provided openings for increasing European influence. Initially, the Portuguese assisted the southern rulers against the Dutch-backed north, with each side selling its ally weaponry and providing advisors and trade connections. Successful missionary activity in the south led to a growing population of Catholic converts. The decline of Portuguese power left a vacuum into which French clerics stepped in the eighteenth century, creating French colonial interest in the region. French advisors even assisted the victor in the final war of the period, Nguyen Anh, who founded the Nguyen Dynasty in 1802.

Anh, despite benefiting from French military advice and trade, was a Confucian-educated traditionalist. Although Anh himself tolerated Catholicism and kept some French advisors at his court, his inclination, fostered by the experience of his own rise to power, was to distrust European influence. His successors, even more traditionalist, went further, persecuting foreign priests and Vietnamese Catholics alike and severely restricting trade with the West in an attempt to exclude foreign influence and secure the

FIGURE 22.3 Vietnam, ca. 1900.

country's cultural traditions. In effect, Vietnam was following the path blazed by Tokugawa Japan in 1640. But times had changed, and the Nguyen Dynasty faced industrializing opponents while deploying less effective military forces than the early Tokugawa shoguns.

Their persecutions of French Catholics in the country provided the French with pretexts for invading. In 1858 an expedition sent by the French emperor Napoleon III attacked the port of Da Nang in central Vietnam, and then captured Saigon in the south, from which base they extended their control over much of the delta of the Mekong River over the next eight years. In 1873 they invaded the north, capturing Hanoi that year, losing it again, but gradually tightening their hold on the area and recapturing Hanoi in 1882. The Sino-French War of 1884–1885 finished the process. All three parts of French Vietnam became part of French Indochina, which also included Cambodia and, after 1893, Laos.

Although guerrilla attacks and ambushes had killed two of the top French commanders during the process of French takeover, French military advantages remained substantial throughout and afterward, as Vietnamese resistance remained channeled in traditional military and cultural paths. The Nguyen Dynasty's heirs and elite supporters continued to organize rebellions against French rule into the early twentieth century, but consistent French success in suppressing them led eventually to recognition that traditionalist resistance was not going to work. It was only then that a new generation of Vietnamese cultural leaders shifted their efforts to modernization efforts modeled on Japan's recent success, starting with official adoption of a Romanized alphabet for Vietnamese writing, aimed at raising literacy rates and involving the common people more effectively. French suppression even of these mostly non-violent movements led to more radical opposition and a bloody twentieth-century Vietnamese history of nationalist and communist anti-colonialism.

South Africa

Unlike Vietnam, which had a long history as both a hierarchy (or, at times, competing organized hierarchies) and a cultural region, southern Africa had a much more complex and less state-oriented history when industrially backed British imperialism began to affect the region. Indeed, southern Africa contained a number of different societies that came into conflict

FIGURE 22.4 Traditionalist Defeat. French colonialists and their collaborators displaying the heads of "bandits," that is, those who resisted French rule. (Rue des Archives / The Granger Collection, New York)

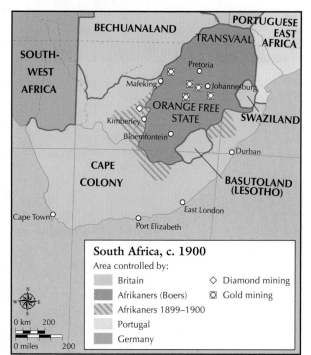

FIGURE 22.5 South Africa, ca. 1900.

FIGURE 22.6 Spears against Rifles. Zulu warriors fighting the British at the Battle of Rorke's Drift, 1879.

with each other as well as with the British, leading to multiple threads of traditionalist resistance interwoven with issues of racial and cultural identity.

The longest-standing inhabitants of the region were Khoisan hunter-gatherers and herders. Two sets of immigrants joined the Khoisan. From as early as 500 CE, waves of Bantu-speaking migrants began to enter the area (see Chapter 11), some of whom mixed with the Khoisan. Then, in the mid-1600s, a small Dutch colony established itself at the Cape. As the settlement grew, some of this population expanded into Khoisan pastoral areas and took up a semi-nomadic herding lifestyle. Largely independent of Dutch control, this population of Trekboers (Wandering Farmers) developed their own language and cultural traditions based in Protestant Christianity, slaveholding, and racial hierarchy. The British took over the colony during the Napoleonic wars, their ownership confirmed by treaty in 1815. British immigration complicated the ethnic-cultural picture even further.

Traditionalist resistance to British rule came from two directions. First, a remarkable leader named Shaka Zulu (ca. 1787–1828) forged a new Zulu Kingdom in the region. Shaka was a brutal but inspired military leader, who forged a disciplined army of spearmen who conquered a vast part of the region, disrupting in particular the pastoral areas of northern South Africa. In the decades after Shaka's death, Zulu expansionism came into conflict both with Boer expansionism and British attempts to consolidate their control of the region. A bloody but historically fascinating three-cornered struggle emerged.

The Zulu Kingdom first clashed with the Boers. Shaka himself had dismissed guns as adequate missile weapons that could be overwhelmed by the fast-moving shock attacks of his spearmen, and initial Zulu successes seemed to confirm his thinking. But a serious defeat against firepower in prepared Boer positions in 1838 restored a rough balance. Fast-moving surprise attacks also dealt the British two major defeats, notably at Isandlwana in 1879, where 20,000 Zulu warriors armed with their stabbing spears overwhelmed a rifle- and artillery-equipped British force of about 1,800. But better prepared British forces rapidly overcame subsequent Zulu resistance.

War then broke out between the Boers and the British in 1880. The Boers were armed with modern rifles, and their guerrilla tactics defeated the British in the First Boer War, but their somewhat decentralized state structures—a result of their individualist pastoral culture—could not compete with British administration and increasing British immigration. They lost the Second Boer War (1899–1902), and a fragile peace was negotiated. Thus, a strong Agrarian state with a traditionalist military culture (the Zulus) and a weak traditionalist Agrarian state with a modernizing military culture (the Boers) both lost to Britain's Industrial state and army. But racial politics created different outcomes in defeat. The Boers reluctantly joined the British colony and used their voting rights to implement the race-based Apartheid system. Blacks (Zulus and other Bantu-speakers) and Coloreds (the growing population of mixed Khoisan, Indian, Chinese, and European peoples), with no voting rights, faced a century of severely restricted rights. Some traditionalism thus survived, for a time, into the Industrial Era of the region.

Ethiopia

The success story of traditionalist resistance is Ethiopia. But both the success and the traditionalism must be qualified, as we shall see.

Ethiopia, though nominally unified in the Late Agrarian period, had entered by the eighteenth century into a period of fragmentation, with rival warlords competing for influence under a figurehead emperor. This coincided with a period of isolation, as a combination of deliberate policy and internal strife cut Ethiopia's network connections to a bare minimum. Gradually, by the early nineteenth century some unity began to reemerge, and by the mid-nineteenth century renewed network flows, which carried the growing threat of European power (especially British interest in the Red Sea area and in Egypt and the Sudan just to the north of Ethiopia), stimulated a revival of central power, although dynastic rivalries continued until Emperor Yohannes IV (r. 1872–1889) gained firm and unrivaled control.

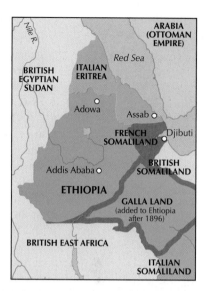

FIGURE 22.7 Ethiopia, ca. 1900.

His path to power contains the first qualification on Ethiopian traditionalism. Emperor Tewodros II had become entangled in a diplomatic dispute with the British, resulting in a British military expedition to the Ethiopian capital in 1868, which resulted in Tewodros's death. In exchange for assisting the passage of the British force, Yohannes received a massive gift of British rifles, artillery, and ammunition. This allowed him to defeat his rival and Tewodros's successor, Tekle Giyorgis II, and become emperor in 1872. Thus, although the Ethiopian state and army retained a traditionalist cultural stance and aristocratic-centered organizational structure, the army could field substantial numbers of soldiers armed with at least some modern weaponry, with both infantry and cavalry forces still prominently armed with traditional Ethiopian spears.

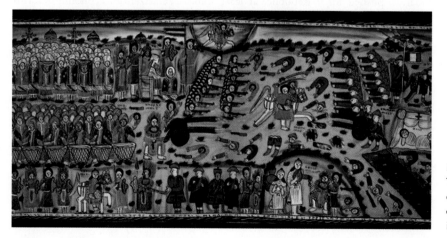

FIGURE 22.8 Traditionalist Triumph. Ethiopian painting depicting the Ethiopian victory over Italian troops at Adowa in 1895.

This semi-traditional force, under Yohannes's successor, Menelik II, kept Ethiopia independent. In the late 1880s, Italy emerged as the key European threat in the area: Italian corporations had bought trading enclaves along the Red Sea that the Italian government then bought out and expanded into Italian Eritrea. Wishing to expand its holdings, the Italians manipulated a trade treaty into a diplomatic crisis that led to war in 1895.

On March 1, an invading Italian army of about 17,000 men fought the Ethiopian army, reported as between 70,000 and 100,000 strong, at Adowa. The Ethiopians crushed the ill-led Italian force. This triumph of Africans over Europeans—and the Ethiopian political independence it defended—became a major symbol across Africa of the possibility for resistance to imperialism. Ironically, however, despite the important role of imported firearms in the battle, the victory also gave the traditionalists in Ethiopia such prestige that the modernization efforts begun under Yohannes and Menelik effectively came to a halt. In 1935 Ethiopia fell to a much more modernized Italian invasion that Benito Mussolini ordered explicitly to avenge the defeat at Adowa, thus qualifying the success of semi-traditional Ethiopian resistance.

Westernization

While traditionalist resistance faced the material problem of how to face European military might, westernizers faced the problem of how to sell the creation of such forces—and all the social and economic transformations they implied—to a population that largely retained a traditionalist cultural frame. This posed a different set of problems for political leaders.

Mexico

Nineteenth-century Mexico illustrates such problems clearly. Mexican independence, as in most of Latin America, arose from the Napoleonic takeover of Spain in 1808. Between that date and 1821, Mexicans fought a confused war for independence that revealed the basic political split in the country between Conservatives and Liberals. Conservatives advocated monarchy, defended the traditional powers and privileges of the Catholic Church and the landowning elite, and they had the support of some indigenous groups. Liberals (who modeled themselves on European Liberals) pushed for a Republic, at least some secularization, economic reforms based on private property rights, and they had the support of some intellectuals and many of the working poor. This view is essentially westernization, with the model of the United States looming ever larger to the north. The fundamental problem facing a successful resolution of Mexico's political problems was the vast inequality in distribution of wealth between landowners and peasantry—in other words, the Agrarian sociopolitical structure was still intact. In addition, there was a lack of a coherent set of frame values that everyone across the socioeconomic divides could agree on.

Thus, from 1821 to 1867, Mexico saw a succession of governments and coups that failed to establish political stability. Conservatives generally held the upper hand until war with the United States broke out in 1847 over Texas, a northern province of Mexico that had received significant US settlement and then declared its independence. The Mexican army, with arms similar to its enemy's, did not perform badly, but lacked unity and consistent popular support, reflecting its society, while the small but relatively effective US army, led brilliantly by Winfield Scott, forced a landing at Veracruz and struck inland, capturing Mexico City in 1848, while other US forces conquered California. Mexico agreed to a treaty in which it sold its northern territories to the United States, and Liberal political forces began to displace the Conservatives who had lost the war. (This allowed the US to project a screen image of capitalist commerce as opposed to military imperialism, a sleight of hand perfected against its own indigenous population as the United States expanded imperially westward.)

The westernizing Liberal resurgence was interrupted between 1861 and 1867 by a French-backed invasion that installed an Austrian prince as Emperor Maximilian I of Mexico. But instead of serving the mineral-extraction interests of his imperial backers in France, Maximilian turned out to be a modernizer who wanted to combine liberal socioeconomic reforms with respect for indigenous cultural traditions. This pleased neither Conservatives nor Liberals, and Maximilian was captured and executed by Liberal forces in 1867.

The Liberals dominated the rest of the century, at first under the elected president and genuine reformer Benito Juárez, then under the dictator Porfirio Díaz. Under Díaz the country experienced its first extended period of peace and rising prosperity. But the Liberal economic program, focused on foreign investment and the buildup of infrastructure, increasingly favored the new capitalist elite. Since Liberalism's foundation in private property prevented meaningful land reform, the disparity between rich and poor and the disconnect between Liberal economics and popular culture both steadily increased. The Liberal westernization experiment ended in the Mexican Revolution in 1911, which constructed a new image of Mexican cultural identity that we will return to in the next chapter.

PRINCIPLES AND PATTERNS
The path to "modernization" was politically vulnerable from both sides.

The Ottomans

The Ottoman Empire had been a great power *in* Europe, if not quite *of* Europe, since the 1400s. The empire's army was still more than capable of holding its own into the eighteenth century, defeating Russia in 1711 (which was itself a pseudo-Western power). But through the rest of the century, Western military developments widened the gap, making the case for reforms of the army pressing, if not for deeper structural reforms, before major industrialization pushed the western European powers even further ahead. Sultan Selim III (1789–1807) attempted to westernize his army, but the challenge this posed to the identity of the long-ineffective but still politically influential Janissary Corps led them to revolt. Selim was killed and reform stalled until Selim's successor, Mahmud II, massacred the Janissaries in 1826. By then, the empire had lost its Greek province to a nationalist revolt and the need for reform went well beyond the military.

The rest of the century saw a complex interplay between efforts at westernizing structural and cultural reforms on the one hand, and cultural complications caused both by conservative resistance and the spread of the (very Western) notion of ethnic nationalism on the other. Nationalism, in the context of a profoundly multicultural empire, proved especially problematic. (See Figure 22.9.)

Mahmud initiated the reform period with the Edict of Tanzimat, or Reorganization, in 1839. The Tanzimat Period lasted until 1876, during which time the Ottoman state managed to reorganize its army along the lines of the Prussian

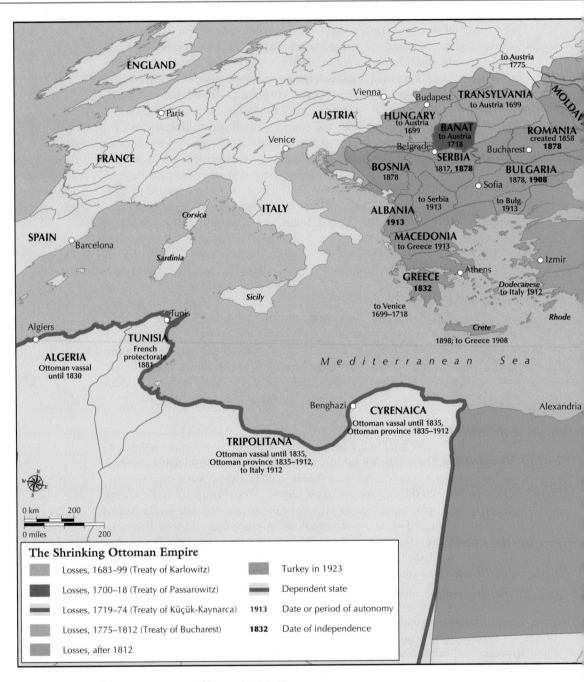

FIGURE 22.9 Decline. Ottoman territorial losses, 1683–1923.

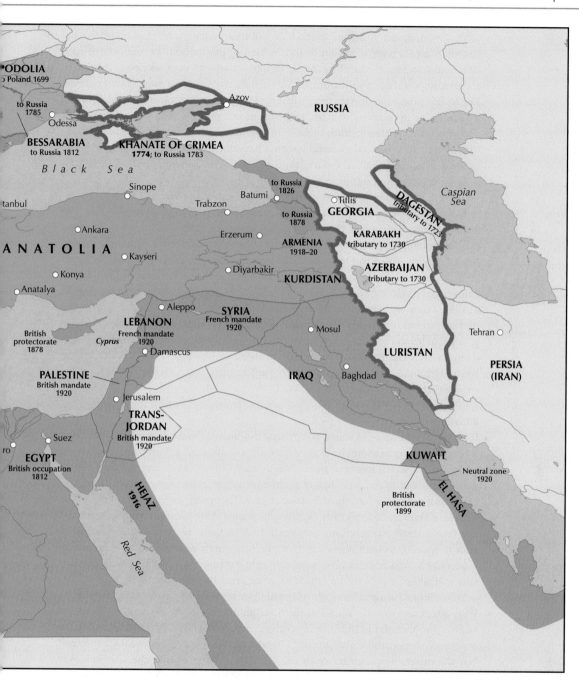

PODOLIA
to Poland 1699

to Russia
1785
○ Odessa

BESSARABIA
to Russia 1812

KHANATE OF CRIMEA
1774; to Russia 1783

Azov

RUSSIA

Black Sea

Sinope

Batumi

to Russia
1826

tanbul

Trabzon

to Russia
1878

○ Tiflis

GEORGIA

DAGESTAN
tributary to 1723

*Caspian
Sea*

○ Ankara

Erzerum ○

ARMENIA
1918–20

KARABAKH
tributary to 1730

A N A T O L I A

○ Kayseri

○ Diyarbakir

KURDISTAN

AZERBAIJAN
tributary to 1730

○ Konya

○ Anatalya

○ Aleppo

SYRIA
French mandate
1920

Mosul

LURISTAN

Tehran ○

British
protectorate
1878

LEBANON
French mandate
1920

Cyprus

○ Damascus

PERSIA
(IRAN)

PALESTINE
British mandate
1920

IRAQ

Baghdad

○ Jerusalem

TRANS-
JORDAN
British mandate
1920

Suez

ro

EGYPT
British occupation
1812

KUWAIT

Neutral zone
1920

British
protectorate
1899

EL HASA

HEJAZ
1916

Red Sea

conscription model, institute a modern banking system, and abolish traditional Ottoman guilds with a nascent factory system of production. In addition to such structural reforms aimed at the state and its interaction with network flows, Tanzimat's efforts also promoted a shift from an Agrarian society toward a more Industrial one. Key to this goal were decrees from 1856 declaring religious toleration and equality, legal equality in the court system, and educational reforms. The reform movement peaked with the promulgation in 1876 of a written constitution that was supposed to create a constitutional monarchy with a parliament. The experiment lasted only two years before Sultan Abdulaziz shut it down. The Tanzimat period came to a close having achieved significant but still limited success.

The constitution had been drafted by members of the Young Ottomans, a nationalist group based closely on similarly named western European movements. The fundamental problem was that nationalism, which in theory should have provided the legitimizing ideology for the state, especially given decrees of religious equality, proved very ill-suited to Ottoman multicultural society. Christian minorities benefited disproportionately from legal and economic reforms because of their better educational levels and concentrations in urban areas, causing resentment among the Muslim majority. Even more divisive, nationalist movements spurred revolts in the Balkans, where Bulgarians, Romanians, Serbs, and Bosnians followed the Greeks in gaining independence from Ottoman rule, though Russian and Austro-Hungarian interests kept the Balkans dangerously unstable right up to 1914. Inevitably, the Young Ottoman movement gave way to the Young Turks, with implications for the empire that played out after World War I.

Russia

If Ottoman reforms were aimed at remaking the empire along western European lines, Russian attempts to meet the challenge of the industrializing powers involved trying to maintain a screen image of themselves as a European power, and this image grew dangerously out of line with reality as the nineteenth century progressed. Ironically, the already established image of Russia as a great European power, itself a result of the success of Peter the Great's early eighteenth-century westernization reforms, made the task facing westernizing reformers more difficult, as the state itself was often hostile to reform. Indeed, Russian politics and society increasingly destabilized as westernizers, modernizers, and traditionalist resisters fought for influence. Nothing went particularly well, although the turmoil made for some great Russian literature.

Nobles and army officers who traveled in western Europe during the Napoleonic Wars attempted to establish a constitutional monarchy in the Decembrist Revolt of 1825. Czar Nicholas I (1825–1855) crushed the revolt and turned to a traditionalist resistance stance under the slogan "Orthodoxy, Autocracy, National Character." But the miserable performance of the Russian military during the Crimean War (1853–1856), in which Russian expansionism toward the Black Sea drew England and France into alliance with the Ottomans, demonstrated the inadequacy of this position. Nicholas's son Alexander II therefore returned to westernization. His key move was to abolish serfdom in 1861, which reduced noble power and opened Russian society to change from below, driven by economic and ideological network flows from the Industrial powers to Russia's west. Pockets of industrialization began, both the middle class and the urban working class expanded, and with that growth came demands for further political reform. By 1881, Alexander was ready to approve a national assembly to propose new reforms when he was assassinated by radical nihilists. (Nihilism, a clear example of the proliferation of self-conscious ideologies discussed in Chapter 20, is not easily characterized as westernizing or modernizing, reminding us that while a good model will make a good deal of information more comprehensible, no model can encompass all of messy reality.)

Alexander's son and grandson Alexander III (1881–1894) and Nicholas II (1894–1917) returned with a vengeance to traditionalist resistance, viewing all Western influence as subversive. But they faced increasing opposition from Liberal Industrial capitalists, nobles, and moderate socialists advocating further westernization, as well as from Marxist socialists under Lenin who pushed for a modernizing revolution that was anti-capitalist. The disastrous performance of Russia's army and navy in the Russo-Japanese war of 1904–1905 (see discussion later in this chapter) revealed the growing hollowness of Russia's "Great Power" status and tipped the political turmoil into a full-blown revolution in 1905. Nicholas, against his will, issued the October manifesto that called for the immediate creation of a national legislature and expanded voting rights and legal reform. This split the Liberals and moderate socialists from the radicals, ending the revolt. But the unproductive balance between traditionalists, westernizers, and modernizers continued. Thus, when Russia's great power status and treaty obligations led it into World War I, it was fully prepared to offer an even more disastrous military performance than in 1905.

FIGURE 22.10 **Bomb explosion at the home of a Russian nihilist in Paris, 1907.**

Modernization

Traditionalist resisters such as those in Vietnam and Ethiopia rejected change as antithetical to their cultural frame; westernizers such as those in Russia and the Ottoman Empire rejected their own cultural frame as antithetical to necessary change. Modernizers, by contrast, attempted to fit change into their own cultural frame. Though subject to political attack from both traditionalists (who thought it went too far) and westernizers (who thought it did not go far enough), modernization programs did achieve at least some success in the few places where modernizers were able to direct policy. It is to those places—China, Japan, and Thailand—that we now turn.

China

China's defeat in the First Opium War in 1842, which we introduced at the beginning of Chapter 21, not only revealed the magnitude of the challenge facing the greatest power of the Agrarian world, it made the challenge more complicated.

The combination of material expense, administrative overload, and humiliation and loss of prestige destabilized the Qing Dynasty's control over China, especially in the south. This was, after all, a dynasty of Manchu rulers who had made it a point to continue marking their ethnic-cultural differences from the Han population, even as they ran a very traditional Confucian bureaucracy. A number of local revolts against Qing rule broke out in the 1840s but were suppressed. Thus, instability in the internal hierarchy compounded the threat posed by European network intrusions.

The most dangerous domestic movement started not as a political revolt but as a religious sect. Hong Xiuquan, a failed candidate in the imperial exams, converted to what he saw as Christianity, though the heterodoxy of his creed is indicated by his own claim to be the younger brother of Jesus, sent to China to rid it of Manchu rule. Hong's sect grew in part by policing their region against bandits and pirates more effectively than Qing officials were able to do. In late 1850, responding to Qing persecution of the sect, Hong launched a full-scale revolt. The Taiping Rebellion, as it came to be known, turned into a massive civil war that lasted for fourteen years. At its height, the Taiping rebels controlled most of the southern third of China (see Figure 22.11). The Qing struggled to contain the rebellion as the European powers maintained neutrality in their coastal enclaves.

The turning point came in 1861, when new Taiping offensives aimed for Shanghai, a key European port of trade. With Chinese domestic instability now threatening their profits, Britain and France supplied officers and troops to the Qing forces. This alliance defeated the Taiping forces at the Battle of Shanghai and then systematically reduced the rebellion over the next four years, though the Qing spent another seven years mopping up pockets of resistance, even after the collapse of the Taiping kingdom in 1864. The Taiping Rebellion was the most costly war of the nineteenth century. Because most of the military operations of the war consisted of sieges of large cities, civilian deaths from starvation and disease were massive: most estimates put the death toll at around 20 million soldiers and civilians. The American Civil War (1861–1864), by comparison, led to around 700,000 deaths, less than 5% of the Taiping total.

The assistance provided by European powers in suppressing the rebellion led them into further constructive arrangements with the Qing in the hopes of propping up the dynasty as a stable and lucrative trade partner. The self-interest of the growing number of Industrial imperialists, however, each of whom competed for trade through unequal treaties and the designated "treaty ports" they created, complicated the political context of Chinese modernization efforts.

For starters, the Qing court itself remained largely hostile to most modernization programs. A combination of inertia, corruption, and not unjustified distrust of foreign motives accounts for some of this hostility. The rest stemmed from the personal inclinations of the Dowager Empress Cixi, who effectively ruled China from 1861 until her death in 1908, acting as regent first for her son the Tongzhi Emperor, then after 1875 for her nephew the Guangxu Emperor. She favored maintaining traditional Qing systems of government and culture, even imprisoning Guangxu when he advocated for more thorough administrative reforms in the 1890s. She did recognize the necessity of modernizing at least the weaponry of the Qing army, a stance possible because Qing identity was not by this time tied to particular weapons

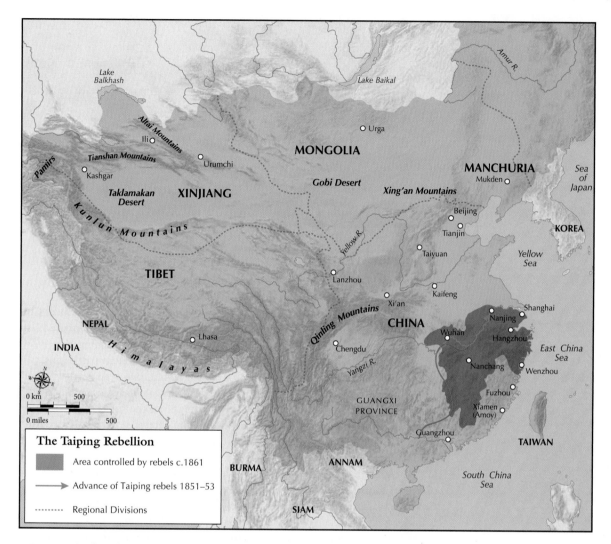

FIGURE 22.11 The Taiping Rebellion.

or tactics. (The Chinese use of gunpowder weapons from the eleventh century is relevant here.) This recognition did not lead to direct action on the part of the government in Beijing, however. Instead, modernization became the project of a small group of talented provincial governors under the Qing. Their program was known as the Self-Strengthening Movement. Its intent, echoing the position adopted by Sakuma Shozan in Japan, was best stated in a book published by one of their leading members, Zhang Zhidong: "Chinese learning for fundamental principles and Western learning for practical application."

The Self-Strengthening governors used state revenues to set up arms factories and shipyards. Foreign advisors were hired to train local workers and organize production. The aim was to modernize the armed forces enough to be able to meet the

FIGURE 22.12 Self-Strengthening Movement. The Fuzhou dock, established by Zuo Zongtang, founder of the Self-Strengthening Movement. (Rue des Archives / The Granger Collection, New York)

Industrial powers on more equal terms and so defend the values of traditional Chinese civilization, still viewed by the reformers as vastly superior to that of the Western barbarians. It is difficult to assess the efforts of the Self-Strengthening Movement. While they did produce modern rifles and some relatively modern battleships, this was in each case at greater expense and time than would have been needed to purchase such items abroad. Their efforts to set up factories ran up against conflicts with the demand for labor from local landlords, highlighting the social transformation necessary to foster industrialization. And as state-run enterprises, they suffered from corruption and inefficiency. Still, by the early 1890s, Qing forces appeared to be making progress.

The great irony is that what undid the Self-Strengthening Movement was the success of another Asian modernization program, namely in Sakuma Shozan's Japan. China and Japan went to war over control of Korea in August 1894. By April 1895, Chinese forces had suffered such serious defeats that Japan not only controlled Korea but also annexed Taiwan. Self-Strengthening was discredited and effectively abandoned. Only in the wake of the anti-foreign Boxer Rebellion in 1905—a classic case of traditionalist resistance that Cixi briefly supported before it was decisively defeated by an Eight Nation Alliance of Industrial imperialist powers—did the Qing court halfheartedly attempt more systemic reforms. These were too little, too late, and the Qing fell in 1911 to a revolution that proclaimed a Republic, ending millennia of Chinese imperial rule.

Japan

The Japanese modernization program that killed the Self-Strengthening Movement constitutes the one case in the nineteenth century of a non-Western (European or US) power successfully escaping colonial domination and joining the Industrial powers as an imperialist itself. How did Japan pull off Sakuma Shozan's program, a path that proved so difficult elsewhere?

At first, it did not look as if Japan would follow the modernization path. The most widespread reaction to Admiral Perry's gunboat diplomacy that forced Japan open to foreign trade under threat of bombardment was strong traditionalist resistance. Riots broke out and foreign merchants who had moved into Japanese port cities were killed. But this merely prompted threats of massive retaliation by the Industrial powers. The Tokugawa Shogunate was forced into further unequal trade treaties and extraterritorial privileges for foreign merchants. Still, the shogunate itself remained stubbornly resistant to change that might threaten its power, just like the Qing court.

Here, however, differences between Japan and China began to become important. Though the Japanese emperor was a figurehead over the shogun, the existence of the imperial house provided a potential focus for a political-cultural appeal over the shogun's head. Furthermore, the structure of the shogunate—a federation of domains dominated by the Tokugawa but not to the exclusion of semi-independent action by other daimyo (domain rulers)—meant that some outlying western provinces not on the main island could initiate some aspects of modernization on their own, as the Self-Strengthening governors had. In the early 1860s, the daimyo of Satsuma and Choshu began importing and then manufacturing modern weapons and raising conscript armies on the Western model. In addition, they advocated restoration of the emperor to full power and the end of the shogunate.

Meanwhile, the sudden opening of the country to foreign merchants had thrown the previously closed economy into turmoil. Bankruptcies multiplied, unemployment rose, and the shogunate's monetary system virtually collapsed. The shoguns found themselves trapped between the rising threat of the southwestern daimyo, which moved them toward at least some military modernization, and the virulent anti-Westernism that such moves prompted from traditionalists, who already blamed the shogunate for rising Western influence. Ultimately, the shogun's army defeated one attempted southwest rebellion, with considerable foreign assistance aimed at maintaining their pliant trade partner in power. But in 1868, with a new emperor and a new shogun having just taken up their offices, the conscripts of the southwest domains defeated an invasion by the shogun's samurai. The Emperor Meiji's decree abolished the shogunate, restoring the imperial house to full power on the model of the German Kaiser.

The Meiji Restoration initiated a period of rapid economic, social, political, and cultural restructuring aimed at modernizing Japan while defending its cultural traditions. The details of the actual restructuring are relevant, as we shall see in a moment, but what really made this program work was the modernizers' successful redefinition of those cultural traditions, that is, the way they appealed to Japanese frame values even amidst change. The emperor himself, revered as a god descended from the Sun Goddess who created Japan and its people, formed the symbolic centerpiece of the program. His picture oversaw every classroom in a new system of universal public education; each day started with a pledge of allegiance to the emperor. Revered as the spiritual "father of the country," his divine descent easily translated into a strongly ethnic nationalism that subordinated individual interest to what the country's leaders decided was the national good (and that was aided by a smaller, more culturally homogenous population than that of many other Agrarian

The Structure of Meiji Japan

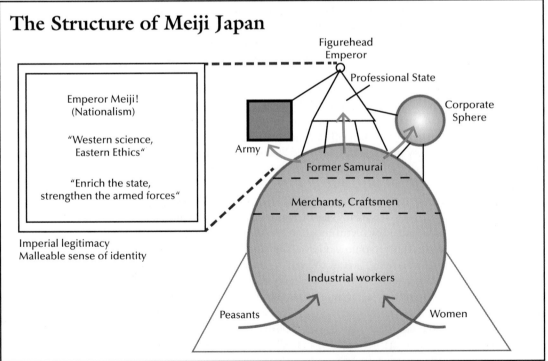

FIGURE 22.13 **Japanese Modernization.** (Top) This picture of Emperor Meiji was displayed in every Japanese classroom and even housed in special shrines on school campuses. (Bottom) The transformation of the structure of Japan from Tokugawa (Agrarian) to Meiji (Industrial).

societies). The early slogan of the modernizers, "Enrich the state, strengthen the armed forces," justified technological and cultural borrowings that could be presented as extending a Japanese tradition of borrowing from China on Japanese terms that dated back into the 800s. In short, the Meiji modernizers invented a set of cultural traditions that constituted a Japanese version of a state-centered Industrial cultural frame. This was the key achievement that underpinned the rest of the modernizing program, creating just enough consent and cooperation to make the coercive measures that the program required bearable.

Meiji leaders, having in effect torn the state off the top of the social pyramid and professionalized it on the fly, set about modernizing the social structure of Japan under a traditionalist guise. The samurai were formally demilitarized and stripped of their special legal and military privileges. Legal restrictions on peasants were likewise abolished and freedom of movement instituted. A powerful screen image of a Confucian-based "family" model of social organization, however, helped keep social relationships heavily paternalistic and authority laden. The combination of this screen image with strong nationalism made for a cooperative and self-sacrificing labor force for Japan's emerging capitalist enterprises.

Social reform provided the platform for rapid industrialization. The Meiji government approached this strategically, studying Europe and the United States to decide what industries to create. Their chief goal was the usual heavy industries necessary for national defense: munitions, shipbuilding, railways, and machinery, built on a strong steel industry. To finance the creation of such industries, the state did two things: it imposed crushing taxation on the agricultural surpluses of the peasantry, and it set up cheap but efficient textile mills to serve the export market, first for silk (building on a traditional Japanese strength), then for cotton, staffed by women and children paid a pittance, justifying the low rates by the Confucian model of social relations. These two strategies provided investment and operating capital, allowing the Meiji government to avoid foreign debt. Once enterprises were a going concern, the state sold them off at discount rates to samurai families to compensate them for their loss of formal status. This co-opted the most educated and managerially experienced class of society into the modernization program and let them set an example to the rest of the population of adapting to modernization.

There was one other structural effect, visible in terms of our model, that was almost as important as the reconfiguration of the Japanese cultural frame to successful Japanese modernization: the creation of Japan's own corporate sphere. This was key in an industrially networked world to successfully managing the network-hierarchy intersection. By generating and then privatizing its industries (unlike China), Japan avoided the usual outcomes illustrated in the models of imperial control in Chapter 21: no corporate sphere at all (e.g., Vietnam and other directly controlled colonies); or one dominated by foreign corporations or investments (e.g., Mexico, the Ottomans).

Japanese modernization worked so well that they were able to renegotiate the unequal treaties with the West, "open up" Korea in 1876 in the same way Admiral Perry had opened Japan in 1853, and defeat China in the battle for control of Korea in 1894. By 1890, under the new Taisho emperor, the modern Japanese identity was secure enough to absorb a new wave of enthusiasm for Western culture—dress,

FIGURE 22.14 Siam Modernizer. King Chulalongkorn, or Rama V, ca. 1890. (ullstein bild / The Granger Collection, New York)

music, art, and so forth. But Japan's actual graduation to Industrial great power status came in 1904–1905, when it took on and defeated a recognized European great power, Russia, crushing the Russian fleet and more than holding its own in land battles. Like Ethiopia's victory at Adowa in Africa, Japanese victory over a "white" nation proved symbolically important within Asia; in contrast to Adowa, the result of the Russo-Japanese War stimulated further Japanese modernization. Japan entered World War I seeing itself as an equal of the European states.

Thailand

We noted above that Japan was the only country to escape colonial domination *and* join the Industrial imperialist powers itself. The Kingdom of Siam (now Thailand), however, achieved notable success in maintaining independence and modernizing the country at least in certain ways. As in Japan, the success of Thai modernization depended in part on a successful transformation of the cultural frame by which Thai cultural identity was measured.

For centuries, through 1850, the Kingdom of Siam had been aggressive, militaristic, and the dominant power in Southeast Asia. But its rulers were already aware of the threat posed by Industrial imperialism before the outcome of the First Opium War drove home the point, and in 1850 British and American ships sailed into Bangkok demanding trading privileges, extraterritoriality for their merchants, and that the kingdom reform its political structure. The brother of the king, a Buddhist monk with some Western education named Monkut, took the throne the next year as Rama IV, and he faced renewed British pressure in 1855. But he actually welcomed this foreign pressure, because it gave him the leverage he wanted with the traditionalist warrior aristocracy, as well as many of the common people, to institute a modernization program. Furthermore, he agreed to British trade demands (soon granted also to other Industrial powers), because he perceived, correctly, that expanded trade was all that the British wanted, whereas the French clearly had territorial designs on all of Southeast Asia. The French were already engaged in Vietnam, and Monkut hoped to win British support against French encroachment.

Although this plan did not exactly work—the British stood by while the French provoked a series of diplomatic crises that resulted in Siam ceding all its non-Thai provinces to the French—ultimately the British did lend a diplomatic guarantee of Thai independence in exchange for a few territorial gains of their own (see Figure 22.15). Meanwhile, Monkut and his European-educated son Chulalongkorn, who succeeded his father in 1868 and ruled as Rama V, engineered a significant modernization program that helped guarantee further independence.

As in Japan, the first key to the success of this program was a reconfiguration of Siam's cultural frame. A kingdom that had been expansionist and militaristic suddenly projected a powerful screen image of peacefulness and non-aggression, an image that rapidly became frame reality and defused British fears for its Burmese and Indian possessions. Chulalongkorn then showed in his personal beliefs that Western technical education could be compatible with continuing devout Buddhism. Finally, these elements were mixed with Thai language and customs to convert traditional Siamese cultural identity to a self-conscious Thai nationalism, a process probably actually assisted by the loss of non-Thai provinces to the French.

Within this new nationalist frame, structural reform became much more acceptable. Chulalongkorn thoroughly modernized the state, creating a professional bureaucracy and government departments, including a budget office, a cabinet, and a new court system. To further the creation of a modern social sphere, he outlawed slavery and virtually eliminated debt bondage. The army, while remaining small, adopted modern weaponry and training. Traditionalist resistance made the pace of reform slow at first, but the success of the frame reconfiguration meant that resistance evaporated with generational change. A true Thai corporate sphere was lacking, reflecting the remarkable fact that Chulalongkorn's modernization came about without creating a significant industrial base. When Thailand entered World War I on the Allied side in 1917, they gained a seat at the peace negotiations, where they won guarantees of their political independence. Thai modernization had worked out in a very different way from Japanese modernization.

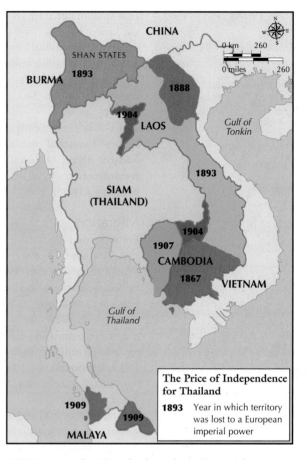

FIGURE 22.15 The Price of Independence. Territorial concessions by Siam, 1867–1909, most of which went to France and England. Siam remained as a buffer between the two imperial powers.

Migrations and Identities

It is easy in narrating the imperial encounters of the late nineteenth century to fall into a nationalist perspective in which the top level of interstate diplomacy comes to represent the experience of the people affected by these encounters. Indeed, the usual term for such diplomacy—"international"—equates top-down political and military maneuvering with the "nations" (as in cultural communities of people) that diplomats supposedly represent. Nationalism, however, was only starting to spread beyond Europe in the late nineteenth century as one of many consequences of

**PRINCIPLES AND
PATTERNS**
*By the nineteenth century,
networks reached more
people in every hierarchy,
reflecting the long-term
growth of network power.*

Industrial imperialism. A nationalist perspective furthermore does not even capture the varied dynamics of diplomatic relations in a world of both Agrarian and Industrial hierarchies of various levels of complexity and organization. Furthermore, even a less nationalist but still state- or hierarchy-centered perspective can lose sight of how much more important network flows were to many individual lives than official hierarchy relations. And in this part of the chapter network flows means movement of people.

The late nineteenth century saw human mobility reach new heights, facilitated by new Industrial means of transport and as yet largely unhindered by political barriers. An age of migrations then created new conditions for the construction and reconstruction of cultural identities both by migrants and by the societies where migrants arrived.

Migration

From the mid-nineteenth century to World War I, industrialization spurred migration in a number of ways that we noted in the previous chapter. Factories drew people from the countryside to the city, initiating an ongoing urbanization of human habitation that is still progressing today. Most of this occurred within countries, but sometimes, as with Irish immigration into British Industrial cities, such migration crossed lines of "national" culture, if not political control. The massive growth in population created by industrialization, concentrated at first in Europe, led over 50 million Europeans to emigrate to various destinations, both to emerging Industrial powers such as the United States and to colonial destinations such as South Africa, Argentina, and Indonesia.

Europe was far from the only source of mobile labor, however. Chinese emigrants, as they had for centuries, moved out along the mercantile routes of the global network, establishing Chinese-population outposts throughout Southeast Asia and the Indonesian archipelago. Though China, unlike European powers, did not take the protection of such emigrant communities as a political necessity, and indeed viewed emigrants as having forsaken the protection of the imperial throne, the informal community of "greater China" remained tied together by strong mercantile and cultural connections. Chinese contract labor also found its way to South Africa and in increasing numbers by the 1890s to the west coast of the United States, where they played a notable role in building railway lines, including the first transcontinental railway. Indian labor, guided by the political connections of the British Empire, moved in large numbers to South Africa, where they contributed to the growth of the "colored" population that complicated the black-white picture of race relations there, and to the West Indies and Caribbean as agricultural labor, making Columbus sort of right about what he'd found, 400 years after the fact. Finally, the vast African Diaspora, most of which occurred during the slave trade of the Late Agrarian Era, continued at least for a time into the nineteenth century.

Even before World War I radically altered the political dynamics of network flows, this vast movement of people had begun to provoke reactions. This was especially true of migrations in which non-European peoples began to move toward the already industrialized powers, such as the flow of Chinese labor to the United States. In the nineteenth century, by contrast, it was Europeans who left for other

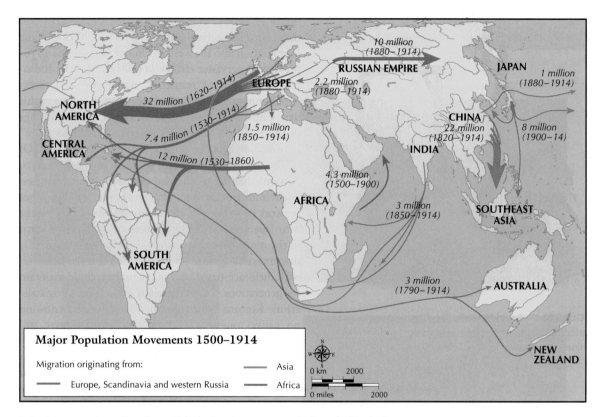

FIGURE 22.16 Mass Migrations. Global migration patterns, which peaked in the late nineteenth century.

countries. The causes of this reversal of the dominant flow of nineteenth-century migration by the early twentieth century are not surprising. First, European population growth slowed and population growth elsewhere exploded, beginning the demographic phase in which ethnic European numbers would drop back down from 1 in 3 to 1 in 5 of the global population by 2000. This made for relative labor shortages in the Industrial countries and growing surpluses in non-Industrial countries, just the opposite of the earlier situation. On top of this, migration from non-Industrial to Industrial countries had become a movement of people from poor economic opportunities to rich ones, also a reversal of earlier European migration that involved a movement from restricted peasant opportunities not just to industrial jobs but often to virtually free land available for more lucrative farming. This kind of move cushioned the cultural shock of migration and took advantage of the migrants' already developed skills. Finally, much of this new migration involved movement from a politically and socially restrictive hierarchy to greater political and social freedom. (See Figure 22.16.)

These underlying economic and demographic dynamics, however, were obscured in the perceptions of many in the Industrial countries that began receiving

Mao Zedong.

PART VII

Crises

1914 to 1989

In 1914, the people who had been marching around in other people's rooms got into a huge fight among themselves over what style of architecture the Industrial mansion should be built in. Between 1914 and 1945, the Early Industrial Era ended and the High Industrial Era began. Part VII covers a century when the mansion suffered crisis after crisis, while the number of its inhabitants increased exponentially.

Chapter 23 explores that first major fight and its effects: how walls were torn down, wiring and plumbing damaged, and room decorating schemes changed drastically. Inhabitants of many rooms began to argue about which wall colors were proper for all rooms. Those arguments hardened when the wiring and plumbing of the mansion suffered a severe power outage. Chapter 24 shows us the fuses that blew and the even larger fight that broke out throughout the mansion in the wake of the outage. The fight drove one school of architects into the mansion's closets. In Chapter 25, we see two remaining schools of architects continuing to argue about how to build future rooms of the mansion, threatening to destroy the whole structure. Meanwhile, people in many of the rooms finally kicked out the people from other rooms who had invaded and tried to repaint their walls.

CHAPTER TWENTY-THREE

"The West" in Crisis, 1914 to 1937

Ernst Jünger, Erich Maria Remarque, and their World War I novels (author photographs courtesy of The Granger Collection, New York)

Introduction

Ernst Jünger was born to a prosperous middle class family in Heidelberg, Germany, in 1895. Erich Maria Remarque was born to a working class family in Osnabrück in 1898. Jünger volunteered for the German army on the eve of World War I. Remarque was conscripted into the army in 1916. Jünger and Remarque both served in the trenches of the Western Front in France. Jünger was injured three different times; after the third injury, he spent the rest of the war in a German hospital. Remarque too was injured, taking shrapnel in several places including the neck, and he, too, then spent the rest of the war in a German hospital.

After the war, Jünger remained in the army until 1923, and he began writing. In 1920 he self-published *Storm of Steel,* a novel based on his experiences in the war, which became a best seller and made Jünger a well-known figure. Remarque also began writing. In 1929, he published *All Quiet on the Western Front,* a novel based on his experiences in the war, which became a best seller and made Remarque a well-known figure. Jünger wrote of war as the ultimate test of manhood: "Hardened as scarcely another generation ever was in fire and flame, we could go into life as though from the anvil; into friendship, love, politics, professions, into all that destiny had in store. It is not every generation that is so favoured." Remarque, while recognizing the intensity of the wartime experience, considered it dehumanizing: "But now I see that I have been crushed without knowing it. I find I do not belong here [back home] any more, it is a foreign world." Thus, both men used art to make their wartime experiences meaningful and to begin constructing new post-war identities for themselves and others. All of Europe, if not the world, faced the same tasks.

Adolph Hitler's Nazis came to power in 1933. They praised Jünger's works and offered him political office, which he refused. They banned Remarque's works; Remarque himself had moved to Switzerland the year before. Jünger rejoined the army when World War II broke out; Remarque moved to the United States in 1939. But Jünger was dismissed from the army in 1944 for association with the plot to assassinate Hitler, the same year that Remarque's sister was executed for subversion. Remarque, by then a US citizen, returned to Switzerland in 1958 with his American movie star wife Paulette Goddard; he continued to write until he died in 1970. Jünger lived the rest of his life in Germany, also writing prolifically. He abandoned politics altogether after the war, wrote critically of Hitler's regime, and experimented widely with drugs: he was friends with the inventor of LSD, whose invention he sampled a number of times. He stood behind everything he wrote, but at a memorial for the World War I battle of Verdun in 1984 he called the German ideology of war a "calamitous mistake." He died in 1998 at the age of 102.

Thus, though in some senses political opposites, Jünger and Remarque also illustrate the complexity of ideology and identity in the wake of the

Framing the Argument

• The growing impact of industrialized, technologically advanced ways of waging war on networks, hierarchies, and culture

• The causes, events, and consequences of one of the stupidest wars in world history

• The ideological and political upheavals that preceded and followed the war, especially the linked rise of communist and fascist states

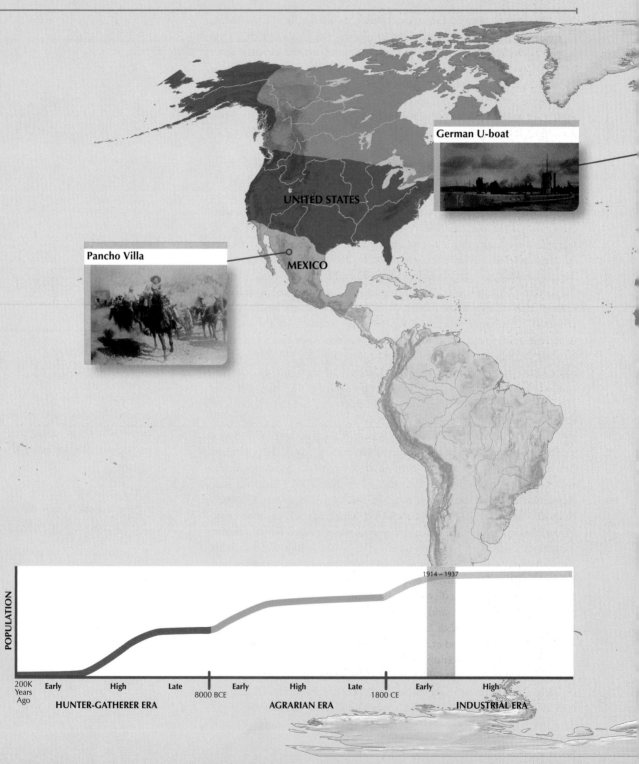

German U-boat

Pancho Villa

UNITED STATES

MEXICO

1914 – 1937

POPULATION

200K
Years
Ago

Early   High   Late

8000 BCE

Early   High   Late

1800 CE

Early   High

HUNTER-GATHERER ERA

AGRARIAN ERA

INDUSTRIAL ERA

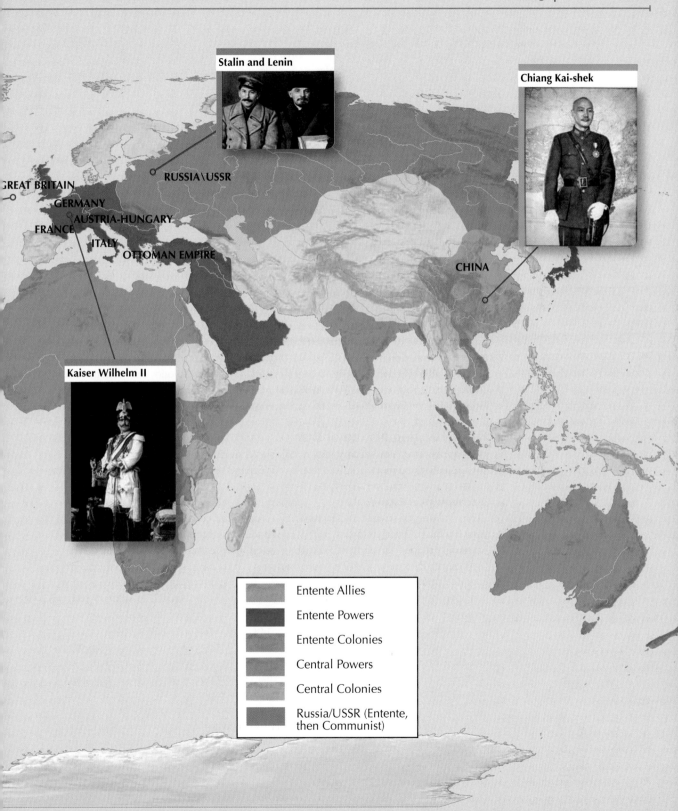

Stalin and Lenin

Chiang Kai-shek

RUSSIA\USSR

GREAT BRITAIN

GERMANY

AUSTRIA-HUNGARY

FRANCE

ITALY

OTTOMAN EMPIRE

CHINA

Kaiser Wilhelm II

Entente Allies

Entente Powers

Entente Colonies

Central Powers

Central Colonies

Russia/USSR (Entente, then Communist)

global cataclysm of World War I. The war exposed in stark relief the contradictions of the Early Industrial Era without solving them, and so that war led to a century of further war, intensified ideologies, and vehemently contested attempts by individuals and societies to shape the new Industrial world by constructing new meanings and identities. We begin the examination of those processes in this chapter.

———— ＊ ————

War and Society since Industrialization

The twentieth century was, in terms of human deaths inflicted directly by the weapons of war, the bloodiest in human history. The Russo-Japanese War of 1904–1905 was the first major conflict in human history in which deaths from combat outnumbered deaths from disease within armies, while World War II was the first in which overall deaths from combat, including civilian casualties, exceeded even the indirect toll of disease and famine in wartime. It is easy to exaggerate the impact of war: all the self-inflicted carnage did not much slow the most massive population boom in human history over the same century. But industrialization did alter warfare, with significant impacts on (and far beyond) the battlefield. It is impossible to understand World War I and the rest of the century without understanding the changing nature of war.

The Changing Nature of War

Warfare became more deadly in two major ways during the twentieth century. First, weapons became more deadly. Second, war expanded vastly in scale and scope.

Technological Change

The wedding of science and technology to capitalist economics that characterized much industrialization meant that, even if underlying economic, social, and cultural dynamics shaped the paths of industrialization, new technologies were its face. This was especially true in war. The outcomes of warfare, even in the Industrial Era, are not determined solely or even predominantly by weaponry technology, which is only one part of the wider technological changes created by industry. New military technologies did have important effects, however, above all on mobility and firepower.

At the strategic level, that is, regarding entire campaigns and armies, we have already noted how steamships and railroads enabled states to move armed forces over much greater distances much more quickly in the nineteenth century than ever before in human history. Later, the internal combustion engine and air transport would increase this ability yet further. But strategic mobility vastly outpaced tactical mobility, which is the ability of armies to move around the country beyond their railheads and ports, especially in proximity to enemy forces. At this level, World War I armies marched on foot and were supplied by horse-drawn carts (indeed, significant parts of World War II armies did the same). It was only with tanks, trucks, and

FIGURE 23.1 Bi-Planes to ICBMs. British World War I Airco D.H.9A light bombers, an early step in taking war beyond the surface of the planet.

later helicopters that the potential for greater battlefield mobility rose. Technology also extended the concept of mobility. Submarines took navies underwater, zeppelins and planes took air forces into the skies, and missiles and satellites eventually took war to space. Satellites also extended advances created by telegraphs, radio, and other electronic communications by enhancing the mobility of military information, as well as the range and mobility of command and control.

The transformation of firepower was just as dramatic. Rifled muskets extended the range of infantry fire, effectively driving cavalry from the battlefield from the 1830s. Breech-loading rifles and smokeless propellants enhanced rates of fire and the ability to fire from cover. Machine guns vastly multiplied rates of fire. Cannons saw such constant improvements in range, accuracy, and types of munitions that artillery accounted for the great majority of World War I combat casualties. Plane- and missile-borne explosives created a whole new vector of firepower, which also illustrates the increasing range of platforms from which firepower could be deployed. In general, the range, accuracy, and destructiveness of military firepower has risen steadily since the Industrial Revolution. The ultimate development along these lines, nuclear weaponry, is so effective at what it is designed to do as to be self-defeating.

The Scale of War

The central effect of industrialization, however, as we have already seen in all spheres of life, can best be described in terms of mass: mass demographic growth, mass production, mass consumption, mass politics, mass culture, and so on. Each of these had a military aspect, the sum of which created the context for using new military hardware. From the mid-nineteenth century far into the twentieth century, armies raised on the Prussian system of conscription and reserves maintained hundreds of thousands of soldiers in peacetime and could mobilize millions of trained men in wartime. Such vast armies could deploy to multiple fronts, which themselves became bigger, which meant not just wider, but deeper as well. The Western Front in World War I stretched from the borders of Switzerland to the English Channel in a continuous line of multiple trenches backed by reserve areas and artillery that could shell targets tens of miles away, and even that front was dwarfed by the Eastern Front in World War II.

Along these fronts, battles got bigger, deeper, and more deadly, as significant improvements in military medicine (an aspect of the improvement of scientific medicine generally) struggled to keep pace with the ability of weaponry to flay flesh and mangle minds. The twentieth-century death toll and war's new ability to out-kill microbes and starvation attest to this transformation. Total Russian deaths in World War II, 20 million, exceeded the total size of all the armies that fought in the Napoleonic wars.

New weaponry did not necessarily bring victory. In the nineteenth century, disparities in weaponry had aided European imperialism. But that effect diminished through the twentieth century: the global weapons network supplied firepower to all consumers, while even older weapons had sufficient range and power to create trouble, as great powers keep relearning in guerrilla wars. In wars between similarly armed major powers, other factors mattered even more.

As a final parallel with the general effects of industrialization, mass armies and the distances over which Industrial weaponry can kill meant that the battlefield became depersonalized, in much the same way that the authority of Agrarian Era priests, scribes, and warriors became depersonalized into Industrial Era institutions, including ideologies, bureaucracies, and military establishments. Seeing individual enemies became a rare event—never mind face-to-face encounters. At the contemporary extremes, remote-controlled drones and computer-aided targeting turn erstwhile warriors into video gamers—except that real people die.

The Widening Effects of War

Larger, more mobile armies with longer range weaponry had the ability to affect human societies more pervasively than before, while raising and maintaining such forces also created challenges for their states and cultures. Generally, war has acted as a magnifying glass, intensifying many of the tendencies built into nationalist and capitalist Industrial societies.

War and Networks

One of the clearest effects of Industrial war is on the network ties between and within different societies. Surface ships and submarines could blockade a country's maritime network connections very effectively. Though the German submarine blockades of Britain receive more attention, the British blockade of Germany in World War I was more effective, resulting in perhaps 800,000 civilian deaths from starvation, while the American submarine assault on Japanese oil imports in World War II starved that country of fuel. Air power promised the ability to disrupt an enemy's internal network, though this promise exceeded the results for most of the century. Even in smaller wars, limitations imposed forcibly on an enemy's network connections, such as trade embargoes, no-fly zones, and other tactics, have become common preliminaries to or accompaniments of war.

The growing importance of network connections in a more pervasively industrialized world, however, has also arguably influenced diplomatic calculations against war, as major trade partners have strong incentives not to go to war with each other. Network connections can also be used actively to promote alliance and peace. Probably the most successful instance of this was the rebuilding of Germany and Japan after World War II by the United States, an effort that involved the network transfer not just of material wealth but of political and cultural values as well. The vast international arms trade, however, is a destabilizing force in global politics.

War and Hierarchies

Industrial warfare affected societies both directly and indirectly. The range of modern weaponry and the depth of fronts and battles meant that more of a country's civilian population could come under fire, even if accidentally, though often intentionally, as is common in strategic bombing campaigns. Most populations perceived this as a more serious violation of the line between military action and civilian life, and this perception was partly a result of the success of Industrial Era hierarchies at drawing that line more clearly (by more widely disarming and policing civilians and thus reducing everyday violence) than their Agrarian predecessors had done. Agrarian societies, inadequately policed and thus prone to "self-help" (feuds and vendettas), constructed a less clear line between war and peace in terms of violence and much less disparity in the types of weapons used in each.

Even when war did not strike directly, the mobilization of social resources in major war efforts often reinforced the effects of Industrial capitalism by "churning" the fluid social sphere, that is, by breaking down old cultural norms, particularly norms of employment and public participation in economic activity. Thus, major war efforts, especially those that rose to the level of what is sometimes called "total war" such as the World Wars, forced societies to draw on every resource possible, and so saw the increased movement of women and discriminated minorities into industrial jobs to replace workers who joined armies. This effect varied according to the levels of preexisting social mobility (as well as ideologies about social mobility), but cultural norms were nevertheless relaxed widely.

States necessarily led efforts at total mobilization, and so Industrial warfare added to the growth in state power that is such a marked theme of the Industrial Era. War efforts justified state intervention in economic activity through Industrial policy and new taxation required to fund expensive Industrial wars. State regulation of production (setting quotas and placing orders), of the workforce (prohibiting

FIGURE 23.2 Network Stranglers. Submarines proved most useful at destroying merchant shipping during wartime, threatening the network connections that a modern Industrial economy relied on.

FIGURE 23.3 Warning.
President Dwight Eisenhower giving his televised farewell address in 1961, during which he warned of the dangers of "the military-industrial complex" influencing policy.

strikes in strategic industries), and of consumption (rationing), even if they did not outlast wartime conditions, accustomed people to a larger state role. Total mobilization was necessary, at least in wars between major Industrial powers, again with the World Wars as the major examples, because they tended to become wars of attrition to some extent, that is, wars in which a basic measure of power could be calculated from the combination of a country's population and industrial production. This equation became clear enough that in wars that pitted seriously unequal opponents against each other, as in many of the post–World War II wars of decolonization, the weaker side resorted rapidly to "unconventional" or guerrilla warfare, avoiding as far as possible direct confrontation with the better equipped conventional force.

The cooperation necessary between the state and the corporate sphere in major war efforts also increased the power of the latter—or in state-run economies, such as those of the mid-twentieth-century communist powers, represented a further aspect of growing state power. This cooperation easily extended to preparations for war, creating the conditions for permanent, powerful arms industries whose interests might sway state policy—the "military-industrial complex" that Dwight Eisenhower warned of in his farewell address at the end of his term as US president. The actual impact of large defense industries on the domestic economics and politics of particular societies is open to debate, but there is some evidence that the unproductive nature of military investment can slow economic growth. Less debatable is the destabilizing effect of international arms sales noted above. The arms trade is therefore a possibly significant exception to the usual rule that war is bad for business and thus that capitalist network flows tend to reduce war.

War and Culture

The debate over the impact of military-industrial complexes is one piece of evidence for the powerful impact of Industrial warfare on culture. The toxic mixture of nationalism and militarism that pervades much twentieth-century history is the most visible aspect of what is clearly a reciprocal relationship: nationalism promotes war, and war reinforces divisive nationalistic views. This relationship need not be permanent, however: this mixture is a cultural construct, a screen image, and it can be challenged by other screen images. Analyzing current trends in historical perspective is difficult (see the Issues in Doing World History box in Chapter 25), but the last third of the twentieth century saw, in at least some areas of the world—especially in many of the most industrialized countries—a reduction in militarism and a recognition of the folly of past militarism, as Ernst Jünger's remarks at Verdun in 1984 remind us. Why has this been so?

The simple answer is that humans are capable of learning from experience, and the cost of the World Wars was so vast as to cause a reaction. While there is certainly some truth in this, it is too simple; otherwise, World War II should not have followed World War I, especially in Europe, which was already so traumatized. A more complex answer has many interlocked elements. In addition to reactions to the costs of the World Wars, the wars themselves restructured global network relationships and politics—one of the central themes of this and the next chapter—in ways that raised the costs of war even further (to nuclear levels) and eventually reduced the incentives for major wars. At the same time, at the societal level, it seems that the richer societies get, as industrial development continues to advance, the less willing the citizens of such advanced societies are to make the huge sacrifices required by a major war. This seems especially true of democracies. Furthermore, the spread of democracy seems to have created an additional effect beyond mere reluctance about the costs of going to war: two democracies have not fought each other, unless one counts the American Civil War as between two separate democratic states. (The capitalist-network culture variation on this observation is that no two countries each with a McDonald's have gone to war.) More generally, widening access to the cultural screen means that more images are projected, both for and against war, meaning that no single image dominates as much as state-sponsored nationalist militarism did from the mid-nineteenth century until well after World War II.

War has influenced culture in many other ways—images of war are a major part of popular culture. One important influence is that war can be a pervasive metaphor for many sorts of struggles. The use of this "warfare paradigm" is intended to indicate the urgency of the task, even if the metaphor is not appropriate: the "Cold War" (really a constant threat of war), the "War on Drugs" (substances don't fight), and the "War on Terror" (nor do abstract nouns). Such metaphorical screen images of fighting real wars can also, however, justify increased state power and the suppression of opposition. We will return to many of these themes in later chapters.

World War I

Although essentially a European civil war, World War I took place within a network of global connections, including those shaped by industrialization and Industrial imperialism, and it certainly had global consequences. It deserves the name "World War" and marked a significant turning point in the development of the Industrial world. It also initiated nearly a century of struggle over what shape the maturing Industrial world system would assume.

The Causes of the War

Like many historical events, especially political-military ones, World War I resulted from a combination of deep structural conditions that made the conflict possible, perhaps even likely. But the war was not inevitable. Individual choices within that combination of conditions triggered the outbreak of war.

Structural Causes

The essential cause of World War I, in terms of our model, was the radical transformation of the world brought about by industrialization and its effects. Such transformation was only partly underway by 1914, and focused on the industrializing countries that were to be the major players in World War I. The complex of changes resulting from industrialization was nevertheless already so significant and so rapid and had such far-ranging implications that it was disturbing, disruptive, and difficult for many groups in these newly Industrial societies to adjust to it.

This was especially true for the traditional elites of such societies whose power and status were most challenged by the rise of Industrial economics and mass politics (and the accompanying decline of Agrarian sources of wealth and prestige). Among the major powers in World War I, most were conservative monarchies—Germany, Austria-Hungary, Russia, the Ottomans—and among the democracies, democratic mechanisms and liberal values were firmly established only in Britain (and the US when it entered, under the slogan of "making the world safe for democracy"). France had a checkered nineteenth-century history of revolution and reaction; Italy had a shallow experience of democratic processes complicated by serious regional tensions.

The extreme discomfort of royal-aristocratic rulers with the transformations under way in their societies contributed to the pervasive militarism and nationalism that characterized European politics in the decades leading up to the war. Large conscript-reserve armies, as we have noted before, were training grounds not just for military skills but for nationalism and a particular order-taking, obedient form of citizenship. They can be read as conservative rulers' attempts to impose military discipline on the growing mobility and assertiveness (aka "disorder") of the working classes.

What might be called a "myth of continuity" in European culture complicated efforts to deal with Industrial transformation in non-destructive ways. This "myth of continuity" was an inevitable corollary of the culture of "Progress," the self-satisfied European view that the military and scientific power they now wielded resulted from the "natural" development of their racially superior "Western" culture. According to this view, if industry were the result of continuity, then this justified the continued power of kings and aristocrats, and the recruitment of aristocrats as the officers of the new conscript armies instantiated this view. In short, old and new existed in delicate and uncomfortable balance in 1914, holding conflicting views of what "Progress" meant.

All of this was multiplied and complicated by ethnic nationalism as a fundamental frame value through which all analysis was filtered, making nationalist competition a basic fact of inter-country politics. We have already seen this as a factor encouraging imperialist adventures in the decades before 1914. When the war broke out, even the various European socialist parties reacted with nationalist fervor rather than internationalist idealism. When these socialists were faced with what was, in their own terms of analysis, a war for the benefit of capitalists that, again in their own terms, should have demanded a "workers-of-the-world-unite" resistance to war, every one of them voted overwhelmingly (where they had a parliamentary voice) for war on nationalist lines.

Meanwhile, these long-term structural inducements to war, especially militarized nationalism, created a further set of short-term structures that enhanced the chance of a war breaking out on a large scale. The first of these involved the planning and transport necessary to mobilize armies of millions of men. Not only had every European power but the British copied the Prussian conscript-and-reserve system of raising armies, they had also copied the German General Staff system for managing them. A key aspect of that management was creating the railway schedules that would take troops from where they gathered by rail to the front where they would march into enemy territory (see Figure 23.4). Since an advantage of even a few days in mobilizing might prove decisive in the early stages of a war, all the great continental powers' armies were on hair-trigger alert for mobilizations that were almost impossible to stop once started. The necessities of war planning therefore severely constrained diplomats' room to maneuver in a crisis.

Complicating this was the fact that all the major and minor powers had become tied together in a system of alliances. The foundations for this were laid in 1890 when Kaiser Wilhelm II abandoned the policy established by his father's chancellor, Otto von Bismarck, of maintaining friendly relations with Russia, which was designed to avoid the threat of a two-front war against France and Russia. In response to this change in policy, France and Russia then formed an alliance that Germany countered with an alliance with Austria-Hungary, Russia's rival for influence in the Balkans. The Ottomans also allied with Germany. These alliances were structured such that if any one power went to war with another, every possible ally and enemy was drawn automatically into the war. And this ultimately happened when Austria-Hungary declared war on Serbia, which triggered Russian entry, which brought in Germany and France. It also brought in Britain. Shortly before the war, Britain had abandoned its century-long policy of remaining neutral, which had enabled it to play a balance-of-power role in European diplomacy. Additionally abandoning a historical rivalry with France, Britain joined the Franco-Russian alliance.

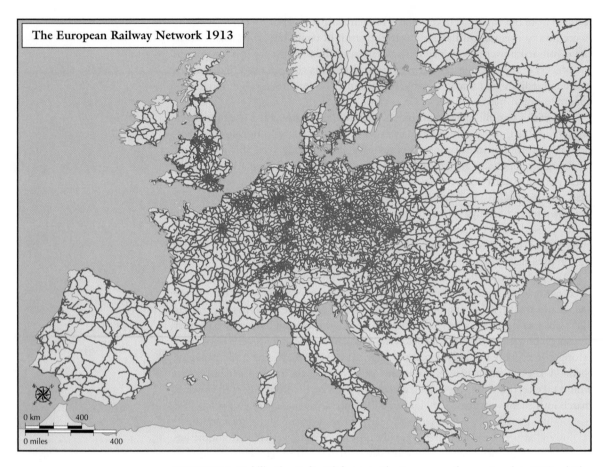

The European Railway Network 1913

0 km   400

0 miles   400

FIGURE 23.4 Mobilization Rules Diplomacy. The European railway network in 1913, which shaped complex mobilization plans, thus constraining diplomatic options.

Finally, mobilization plans, alliances, and nationalist rivalry contributed to a growing cultural acceptance of the inevitability of war, and this acceptance was based partly on this history of swiftness and decisiveness of the Prussian wars against Denmark (1864), Austria (1866), and France (1870–1871) that had unified Germany. This view was further enabled by military analysis that paid far too little attention to warnings about the nature of war offered by non-European conflicts such as the American Civil War and the Russo-Japanese War, among others. After all, only Europe mattered.

Individual Responsibility

This account of the structural causes of the war may make it seem as if the war were inevitable, with a depersonalized "Europe" led into war by vast impersonal forces. In addition, the approach of this book, with its model that highlights impersonal structures and systems, emphasizes this style of explanation. But the key concept in

PRINCIPLES AND PATTERNS

"Structures" do not make decisions, people do. Structures are the patterns of accumulated individual actions.

our model of cultural frames and screens reminds us that while structures did indeed emerge from the actions of many individuals, those same individuals, shaped by their cultural and structural environment, are also in turn reshaping those very cultures and structures. The causes of World War I offer a particularly apt example of the interaction between impersonal structures or patterns and individual decisions and actions, and this reminds us that nothing in history was inevitable: contingency, as we have seen repeatedly (and which was introduced in the Chapter 2 Issues in Doing World History box), lurks everywhere in historical interpretation and analysis.

Focusing on individuals within their environment can also sharpen our focus on causation. The above analysis of structural causes of the war tends to spread responsibility for the war broadly across all the participants, laying only a bit more at the feet of the more conservative, militaristic monarchical powers, who had a more uncomfortable relationship with Industrial capitalist transformations than did the more liberal democracies. There is some element of truth in that impression, but ultimately such a view is somewhat misleading. A much larger share of the responsibility can reasonably be assigned to Kaiser Wilhelm II of Germany.

It was Wilhelm, as we have already seen, who destabilized the diplomatic situation by abandoning friendly relations with Russia. His decision to push Germany

FIGURE 23.5 Kaiser Wilehlm II. The individual most responsible for World War I.

into a naval building program, though, was even more important. A large navy served little strategic purpose for Germany, whose main military concerns were land-based and within Europe: its few African imperial possessions had small economic value in case of war. Instead, Germany's naval buildup merely antagonized Britain, the world's top naval power, and inserted Germany above France as the chief threat to British interests, especially after the Japanese removed the Russian fleet from the equation in 1905. It was this that moved Britain closer into cooperation and then alliance with France and Russia, which further increased the strategic threat to Germany of a two-front war, which in turn encouraged even more aggressive German war planning.

Why did Wilhelm pursue this policy? It is not totally clear. Perhaps he underestimated Britain's ability to respond in a naval arms race. Battleships were also powerful symbols of national strength, an image Wilhelm wished to project. But most historians also see Wilhelm's lifelong obsession with the British, whom he seems to have both despised and envied, as a driving psychological motivation for his policies: he had a difficult personal relationship with his English mother (and he was the grandson of Queen Victoria of England). Ultimately, Wilhelm seems to have wanted a war, both to aggrandize imperial Germany and to take the British (as well as the traditional French enemy) down several notches. He and Germany must therefore bear much responsibility for the war.

This leads us to a final set of observations about the causes of World War I. We can analyze and to some extent understand how the conditions that made war possible evolved, and we can even understand at some level Wilhelm's disturbed motivations that pushed those conditions over the edge. But stepping back a bit, World War I remains one of the more mystifying wars in history. The major European powers who fought it did themselves and their position in the world terrible damage in the process, and they had, from any reasonable perspective, nothing to gain and everything to lose from launching a war. Open network connections among them were enhancing the wealth of all of them, and they sat atop imperial possessions that spanned the globe.

That this group of playground bullies could not find the entire globe large enough to accommodate all of them thus stands as the pinnacle (and endpoint) of Adolescent Modern stupidity. Wilhelm II's psychological obsession through his mother with the British, whose larger fleet and empire seemed to challenge Wilhelm's manhood, thus stands as a quintessentially adolescent trigger for a war that need not have happened.

The Course of the War

German troops poured into neutral Belgium at the beginning of August 1914, aiming to sweep around Paris and the flank of the French army massed on the Franco-German border. They almost succeeded, which might have fulfilled the promise, repeated on both sides, that the troops would be home by Christmas. But after initial disasters, the Allies improvised an effective counterattack at the Marne, and the Western Front rapidly evolved into a trench-based stalemate from Switzerland to the English Channel. Four Christmases and millions of deaths would pass before the British and French, ultimately backed by the United States, would survive a war of attrition against the Germans that finally ended in November 1918, with the final peace not signed until June 1919, during which time the British blockade of Germany continued, resulting in over 200,000 additional civilian deaths. (See Figure 23.6.)

The Eastern Front, where Germany and Austria-Hungary faced Russia, remained somewhat more fluid because the ratio of men to space was much lower, and because both the Austrian and Russian armies proved susceptible to periodic collapse. When the Germans focused on this front in 1917, the final Russian collapse was political: revolution broke out in November, Czar Nicholas and his family perished, and a provisional government negotiated peace with Germany in early 1918 as the country devolved into a civil war from which the communists, led by Lenin, would emerge victorious.

The great majority of the fighting took place on the Western and Eastern Fronts, but other fronts saw action. Austrian and Italian forces created their own trench-based stalemate along their mutual border. A badly executed British amphibious attack on the Ottomans at Gallipoli resulted in more trench-based stalemate and

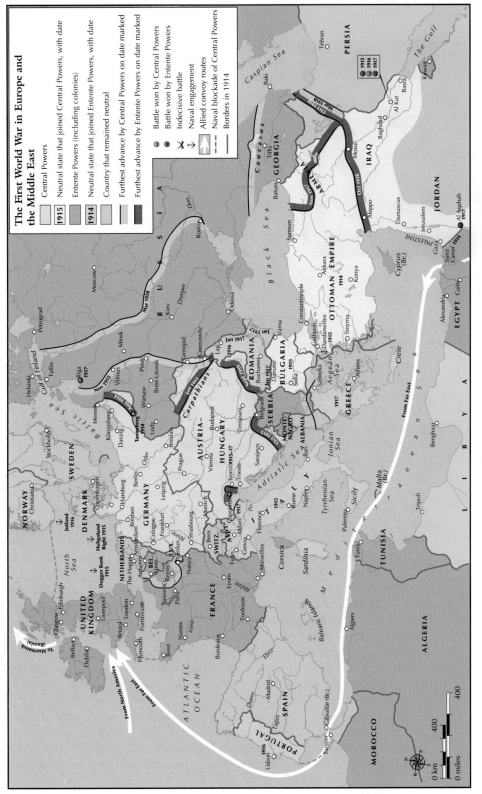

FIGURE 23.6 World War I. The crucial theaters of World War I in Europe and Southwest Asia, pitting the Allied Powers against the Central Powers.

FIGURE 23.7 The Empire Helps Out. The famous Gurkhas with their deadly kukries (knives) near Neuve Chapelle, France, ca. 1916.

British withdrawal, but elsewhere in Ottoman Palestine, British forces operated more successfully. Small-scale operations characterized the fighting between British and German colonies in Africa, while Japan joined the Allies in picking off German colonial possessions in the Pacific. The war was also global in drawing resources into the main European theaters. Troops came from all over the British and French empires, including not just Canadians and Australians but Indians and Africans, and they served on the Western Front. Imperially controlled raw materials and food assisted the Allied cause, and eventually, the agricultural and industrial resources of the United States proved decisive for the Allies.

The major naval theater of operations was the North Sea and the North Atlantic. The Germans challenged the British blockade that strangled German network connections only once, at Jutland in 1916. A battle that was essentially a draw tactically was a major strategic victory for the Allies, as the blockade remained intact and the German surface fleet spent the rest of the war confined to port. The German counter-blockade of Britain using submarines, after initial successes, faltered in the face of effective convoys and counter-submarine tactics. The major result of the submarine campaign was the entry of the United States into the war on the Allied side—and this result was disastrous for Germany.

The Experience of War

It is even more true of World War I than of most wars that a bare narrative of what happened on different fronts at the political-military level fails to capture the impact of the war. On all the major fronts, especially the Western Front (which was most visible to the world because of British and French network connections), the war was not a matter of maneuvers, battles won or lost, and visible progress. It was an entrenched hell of barbed wire, massed artillery, machine guns, and poison gas, a world hospitable only to steel and mud, where flesh and nineteenth-century visions of glory and "Progress" went to die. Given pre-war expectations, this experience of World War I came as a great shock.

By 1914, firepower had far outpaced mobility on the battlefield, meaning that the only way to attack was for men to march forward into a hail of small arms and artillery fire, while defenders buried themselves in the earth against the attackers' guns. Once a front stabilized, new attacks were advertised by easily detected massing of reserves and announced by preliminary artillery bombardments, all of which might gain several hundred yards of cratered ground, but not more, and at the cost of several hundred thousand lives. Bloody attritional stalemate set in: warfare as stupidity.

Attempts to break the entrenched deadlock looked first to technology. Poison gas first appeared in 1915. It made hell even more hellish, but failed to create usable breakthroughs, especially once gasmasks became standard equipment. By 1917, British engineers had created the first tanks, which indeed created such an unexpected

FIGURE 23.8 Inhuman Conditions. (Top) Old meets new: a cavalry lancer wearing a gas mask. (And the horse will breathe . . . how?) (Bottom) British machine gunners, also in gas masks, in 1916.

breakthrough at Cambrai that the British were unprepared to exploit it and the moment passed, though there was promise for more effective use of the tanks if they could be made more reliable. The Germans achieved impressive results with new infantry infiltration tactics in the spring of 1918, consisting of sudden surprise attacks without artillery bombardment that bypassed strongpoints and tried to get into the enemy rear. But the specialist units wore down rapidly, and by then Germany had no reserves left to sustain the offensive. Airplanes appeared at the front early on, but these were useful mostly for observation. A pilot throwing a hand grenade from the sky could not possibly break a deadlock that even a million rounds of high explosive artillery failed to blast through.

Effective combinations of infantry, artillery, armor, and airpower that restored mobility to the battlefield would appear in the next war. But World War I remained attritional. Armies did not lose vast battles, they broke: the French army mutinied in 1917, the same year that the whole Russian war effort collapsed. Arguably, the "weapon" that ended the war was tins of American corned beef, whose smell when they were heated up convinced the German army it was not going to win.

Total War

It was the effort required to win a war of attrition at a countrywide scale that forced the invention of industrially based total war, the basics of which we outlined above. Conscription increased, industries converted to munitions production at government direction, employment patterns shifted, and supplies were rationed as relatively recently industrialized hierarchies put everything they had into the struggle. Naval blockades and other restrictions on trade assumed major importance because these hierarchies were more dependent on network connections than ever before. This aspect of the war created an important advantage for the Allies given that, as we have noted, the British and French had at their disposal significant naval power and imperial resources, to which US forces were added in late 1917.

The aspect of total war mobilization that had perhaps the most lasting influence was cultural mobilization. In order to persuade their populations to continue to support massive losses and sacrifices, states had to turn to more intentional projection of screen images than ever before, or in standard terms, to propaganda. As the war dragged on, cultural appeals evolved, as the posters in the "Images on the Screen" exemplify. Initial appeals were nationalist, emphasizing the viewer's duty and the virtues of the home country. This reflected a nationalist world despite the fact that the ideological differences between the various European powers were not in fact terribly large. In the terms we introduced in Chapter 12, World War I began as intracultural warfare, a war within a cultural area whose participants understood each other and the rules. But as the struggle became more desperate, it devolved into a subcultural war, with enemies demonizing each other and cultural differences emphasized, as posters of the menacing subhuman Hun—the demonizing British term for the Germans—show clearly. The cultural atmosphere created by such propaganda inevitably made a successful peace settlement much more difficult to achieve.

Enemies on the Screen

As World War I evolved into a horrible war of attrition, it took on the character of a sub-cultural conflict, with each side demonizing the other in an effort to justify the costs of war and maintain home morale. A common theme of such demonization, illustrated here, was portraying the enemy as less than human. Top left: US poster depicting the Germans as a brutish ape. Bottom left: The proud German eagle faces the threat of the British spider. Top right: An Italian poster warns of the vicious German snake. Bottom right: The subcultural conflict spreads: a White Russian poster shows its hero slaying the red dragon of communist forces in the Russian civil war that broke out after Russia withdrew from World War I.

Consequences of the War

The first and most basic impact of the war was demographic. About 17 million people died in the war, made up of close to 10 million military personnel and over 6 million civilians. Almost 60% of the military casualties occurred on the Allied side. Combat caused more military casualties during the war than disease, continuing a new trend established by the Russo-Japanese War. But in terms of overall deaths, this is true only because the Spanish influenza epidemic of 1917–1920 is not counted as part of the war. It killed between 50 and 100 million people globally, vastly out-killing the Great War. But because it was global, scattered, and hard to recognize as a global phenomenon at the time, as well as being a *natural* disaster, it was not the traumatic event that the war undeniably was. Cultural perceptions matter as much as material realities. The epidemic seemed random; the war invited interpretations of its meaning that continue to this day.

It was not that the material effects of the war (or the epidemic) were unimportant, however. Between the war and the epidemic, between 3 and 6+% of the world's population died in a six-year period. Even if the explosive population growth of the century rapidly made up for and even exceeded the losses, such losses of life consti-tuted a shock to the global network of exchange: from an economic perspective, the world lost a vast number of producers and consumers. The fact that the war concen-trated the casualties disproportionately in the Industrial imperialist countries of Europe mattered as well. Europe's population was at the time the world's richest concentration of consumers. The producers who most missed those extra consumers were the non-Industrial world's growers of raw materials. The prices of their com-modities were lower than they would have been, so that slower economic develop-ment blunted the political impact of the war in potentially loosening imperialist influence (in free trade areas) or control. Within European hierarchies, the demo-graphic loss was felt as the absence of a "lost generation" and accelerated the slow-down of European population growth while the rest of world began to speed up in the wake of the flu epidemic.

The blow to the global network was compounded by the changes the war brought to the culture of economic exchange. The late nineteenth-century growth of industrialized trade had been lubricated by all the major Industrial powers' adherence to a standard of monetary exchange based on gold, which reduced the transaction costs of international trade. This particular mechanism of exchange became more rigid and less useful, however, due to a combination of factors that sucked some of the lubrication out of the network's operations. There were the costs of war themselves, along with the evaporation of some countries' gold reserves, and there was the subsequent economic turmoil. This turmoil was further compounded by the imposition of vast reparations payments on the losers of the war in the peace treaties and by economic distrust, an aspect of the general cultural distrust and of rising ideological barriers that resulted from the subcultural nature of the last phase of the war.

Thus, World War I re-exposed the fundamental tension between network flows and the stability and identity of individual hierarchies that has been a consis-tent theme of this book and that our model highlights. The global dominance of a limited number of culturally related European hierarchies had to some extent

PRINCIPLES AND PATTERNS

The tense intersection of networks and hierarchies has been, in forms specific to different eras, a key engine of much historical change.

disguised this tension for much of the nineteenth century. The inherent conflict between international capitalism and nationalism, industrialism's version of the
merchant dilemma, was already visible in its early form
in the nineteenth century and in the buildup to 1914,
but after World War I this tension was developing into
its full form. The ideological conflicts of the twentieth
century that World War I unleashed were, in fundamental ways, conflicting attempts to address this
tension.

Cultural Consequences

World War I's most profound effects were cultural, as
the contrasting reactions to the war and the flu epidemic, as well as the damage to the nineteenth-century
culture of economic exchange, demonstrate.

FIGURE 23.9 Post-War Trauma. This Poster by German
artist Käthe Kollwitz reflects the deep shock to European
notions of "Progress" and optimism created by the horrors
of World War I.

Within Europe, the immediate impact of the carnage on entrenched front lines was to shatter the com-
placent vision of uncomplicated Progress that was a
dominant theme of 19th-century European cultural
outlooks. This view of Progress rested on the scientific
and technological advances that had made the Industrial powers of Europe rich and
globally dominant and that promised an ever-improving world. At the front lines of
World War I, however, science and technology created industrialized death. The
tools of human advancement had suddenly become the tools of destruction. Belief
in Progress was not totally destroyed, but the costs of Progress in terms of dehumanization, environmental degradation, and the possibilities for self-destruction
suddenly became much clearer. The culture of Adolescent Modernism took a beat-
ing so serious that it gave way to post-adolescent cynicism among many European
intellectuals, to uncertainty and to a search for new answers among others, topics
we will return to later in this chapter and in Chapter 24.

The obvious costs of Progress and the obvious stupidity of the war Europeans
had gotten themselves into damaged the moral underpinnings of imperialism.
Europeans did not let go of their possessions. Indeed, Britain gained influence
and some territories in the Mideast at the expense of the dismembered Ottoman
Empire, and the Allies also divided up former German imperial colonies among
themselves, though Japan failed to receive what it saw as its just share of German
Pacific possessions, fueling its distrust of Western powers. While colonized peoples were as yet unable to challenge European military dominance, they grew
more ideologically restive and witnessed many new examples of European
mortality.

The cultural changes brought about by the war were reflected in the peace treaties that followed. Shock at the costs led the Allies to impose massive reparations
payments, especially upon Germany, and these complicated economic recovery from
the war. The aftereffects of subcultural demonization of enemies during the war
served to entrench nationalism even more deeply as a naturalized frame value of

FIGURE 23.10 Nationalism Triumphant. Kemal Atatürk, the leader who helped transform the remains of the Ottoman Empire into the secular, nationalist state of Turkey.

hierarchy construction. Thus, the principle of "national self-determination" guided the demolition of the Austro-Hungarian Empire and the Russian possessions it had given up in its separate peace with Germany. Poland re-emerged as an independent state after more than a century. The core of the dismembered Ottoman Empire reconceived itself under the leadership of Kemal Atatürk into the secular, nationalist state of Turkey.

A whole host of new states such as Czechoslovakia, an independent Hungary, and Yugoslavia occupied central Europe and the Balkans. The plethora of "micro-nationalities" in the Balkans, however, defied strict application of the principle, made the creation of economically viable hierarchies difficult, and fostered further nationalistic grievances. In short, a stupid peace followed a stupid war, making further conflict likely. "The West" remained in crisis, and the crisis would spread globally.

Political Upheavals

By undermining the idea of Progress and exposing the myth of continuity associated with it, World War I reshaped the ideological landscape of global politics. With old ideas discredited and with a variety of countries, old and new, looking to explain the meaning of the war and to construct (or reconstruct) national identities, heightened ideological competition—a more intense battle of "isms"—spread from Europe to more and more areas of the world and came to characterize twentieth-century politics. In other words, the myth of European continuity no longer disguised the scale of the transition from an Agrarian to an increasingly Industrial world. Instead, the transition was acknowledged, and the competition became one focused on defining the shape that the Industrial global system would take.

This competition called for ideologies that could do two different things. First, people needed analytic tools that would help them understand what the new Industrial world was really like (and for the many societies not yet industrialized in 1918, how to join the Industrial world most efficiently). Second, people wanted ideologies that told them who they were in the context of the new Industrial world. The problem was that few if any of the ideologies on offer in the early twentieth century could convincingly perform both functions at once.

Pre-War Revolutions

This problem had shown up even before World War I in some parts of the world affected by colonialism. Nearly simultaneous revolutions in Mexico and China presaged the wider ideological struggles to come.

FIGURE 23.11 Modernizing Screen Image. *History of Mexico: From Conquest to the Future,* a fresco in the National Palace in Mexico City, painted by Diego Rivera from 1929–1935, sums up the Mexican Revolution. Note the top center, where Karl Marx points out the future to indigenous workers in front of the Aztec past. (© Banco de Mexico Diego Rivera Frida Kahlo Museums Trust . Mexico D.F. / Artists Rights Society (ARS), NY)

The Mexican Revolution

The Liberal capitalist and increasingly dictatorial rule of Porfirio Díaz in Mexico came to an end with a disputed presidential election in 1910. Díaz declared himself the winner of an obviously fraudulent vote, but Francisco Madero, the supposed losing candidate, called for the overthrow of the Díaz government, and by 1911 the country was at war. Madero made promises of land reform that appealed to Mexico's poor peasants, long ignored by Díaz's capitalist-focused modernization program, but he failed to follow through and the conflict widened, becoming multi-sided and confused. Although most fighting ended in 1920, the true shape of the Revolution took longer to emerge. It was under the presidency of Lázaro Cárdenas (1934–1940) that the promise of the Revolution was largely implemented, cemented by Cárdenas's peaceful transition out of power and Mexican support for the Allies in World War II.

The ideological settlement of the Revolution addressed the needs for analysis and identity in different ways. In terms of political economy, a mixture of socialism and pre-capitalist agrarianism attempted to build on and spread more equitably the foundations of modernization laid during Díaz's regime. Land reform redistributed farmland to the peasantry as communal property. On the socialist side, many foreign firms were nationalized, including the oil industry, and state planning came to dominate attempts at economic development. Although elements of Liberalism and democracy continued as screen elements in this ideological mix, the reality for the rest of the twentieth century was one-party rule under the Institutional Revolutionary Party and a state-dominated economy.

Meanwhile, revolutionary leaders representing the poor and largely Indian population of the countryside contributed to a new ideology of Mexican identity, *indigenismo*. This celebrated the mixed Spanish-Indian identity of Mexico, in contrast to the European focus of Liberalism. Although *indigenismo* had political implications, it served mostly to establish a new and powerful screen image of Mexican national identity.

The Chinese Revolution

Rebellion against the decrepit Qing Dynasty broke out in October 1911, and in February 1912 millennia of monarchical rule ended with abdication of Emperor Puyi and the declaration by Sun Yat-sen, a Western-educated nationalist, of the Republic of China. The declaration disguised the still divided nature of the country, however, and various Chinese groups struggled to find either an ideology of analysis or a coherent concept of Chinese identity, never mind put them together as the Mexican Revolution had eventually done.

One problem was that Sun's nationalism was a largely empty vessel on both counts. It had no real plan for economic and social modernization, which invited criticism from the emerging Chinese Communist Party, while its historically based notion of Chinese identity constrained the possibilities for either kind of modernization while inviting reactionary and monarchist revolts. One traditional response to the end of a dynasty—warlordism—became rampant.

The most powerful of the new warlords, Chiang Kai-shek, emerged in the 1920s as the leader of a nominally nationalist government that tended toward military dictatorship. It almost immediately began fighting a civil war with the Communists, whose vision of modernization necessitated an improbably deep transformation of Chinese identity. Their conflict was interrupted by the Japanese invasion that started World War II, and China's difficult path to modernization continued only after that conflagration ended.

Ideology and Politics

The prominent role of the Chinese Communist Party, supported from the newly communist Soviet Union based in Russia, brings us to a consideration of the main political ideologies of the post–World War I world that attempted to provide analysis and identity.

Liberalism in Crisis

Liberalism, the dominant nineteenth-century ideology most associated with the idea of Progress and the myth of continuity (known in British terms as the Whig view of history), suffered most in the new ideological environment, though major elements of it survived more robustly in the United States, which had suffered much less in the war and saw itself as exceptional anyway. In the European democracies, however, Liberalism was in crisis, and democratic socialists assumed the main political opposition to mainstream Conservatives. But the lack of enthusiasm generated either by democratic socialists or Conservatives (who took up some of the limited state, pro-capitalist tenets of Liberalism) was reflected in the rise of more extreme choices further out on the political spectrum.

Communism

Communism, the political ideology based on Karl Marx's copious writings on history, purported to provide a "scientific" analysis of the development of Industrial society that pointed toward a diagnosis of and permanent solution to its ills. In Marx's dialectical view of historical development, human relationships with the environment had produced class distinctions; class conflict was the engine that drove history. Ancient master-slave economies had given way to feudal lord-serf relations. This lord-serf conflict of feudalism (in its Marxist sense) had given birth to the bourgeoisie, or capitalists, who both overthrew feudalism and called into being their own subordinate class, the proletariat. The endpoint of this sequence was to be the triumph of the proletariat, the end of class distinctions, and an industrially supported humanistic utopia.

Communism was avowedly against nationalism (class was the most important division, thus "workers of the world unite"), against imperialism (which it saw as a natural result of international capitalism), and against discrimination based on gender or race (the American Communist Party worked vigorously against Jim Crow laws in the United States). While also avowedly democratic, however, it recognized that elimination of capitalist interests would require a stage of development called "the dictatorship of the proletariat," led by the professional analysts of the Communist Party, before the stateless communist utopia could be realized.

It was this loophole that allowed the Communist Party in Russia to justify its triumph after the Revolution of 1917. Russia, which was overwhelmingly under-industrialized and which lacked any real capitalist class, was, in Marx's own view, an unlikely place for the communist revolution to begin. (Indeed, a careful reading of Marx suggests that the entire world needs to be fully Industrial before the historical dialectic can lead to the

FIGURE 23.12 Beyond Marx. Vladimir Ilyich Lenin (1870–1924), the Russian Revolutionary leader who created political Marxism.

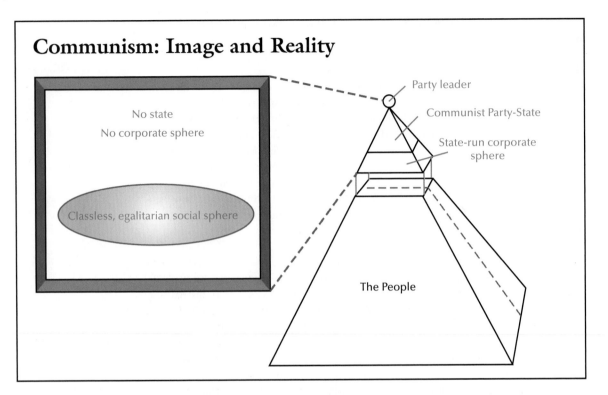

Communism: Image and Reality

No state

No corporate sphere

Classless, egalitarian social sphere

Party leader

Communist Party-State

State-run corporate sphere

The People

FIGURE 23.13 Communism: Image and Reality. The practical reality of communist societies in the twentieth century, contrasting with the communist screen image ideal of fully Industrial, post-capitalist society: a flattened social sphere, running itself without a state or corporate sphere, providing for all from the productive power of industry.

proletarian utopia—a condition nowhere near true, even today.) But Lenin and his followers decided that they could force the pace of history, although this would necessitate an extended period of Party-led proletarian dictatorship to develop communism and defend it against the reactionary forces of global capitalism. The Chinese communists would face an even more pressing need to redefine the path of communist world history, putting Agrarian peasants in the forefront of the revolution. Indeed, because communist theory offered a path to modernization for countries disadvantaged in the context of Industrial capitalist network connections, almost all communist countries were significantly underdeveloped at the start. Thus, starting in Russia (the new Union of Soviet Socialist Republics, or USSR), the practical character of communist governments throughout the century assumed a more familiar shape, summarized in Figure 23.13.

A professionalized, Industrial state, subsuming its own "corporate sphere," sat atop a society whose traditional shape resulted both from industrial underdevelopment and from rigid political control by the ruling party. Ironically, however, as communist societies developed industrially, they also developed their own version

ISSUES IN DOING WORLD HISTORY

Marxism and History

Karl Marx's analysis of history was the foundation of political communism, as we have seen. It also became an influential force in the development of the modern history profession. Academic history in the nineteenth century, as we have seen in previous Issues in Doing World History boxes, was dominated by perspectives that stressed nation-oriented political and military history led by "Great Men." By the early twentieth century, with the transformations created by industrialization becoming much more widespread and obvious, history began to have to catch up with reality. Styles of history thus emerged that dealt more with economic developments and the social history of mass society. In this atmosphere, Marx's own analysis came into its own, providing new perspectives and tools to new generations of historians.

Marxist analysis stimulated several lines of historical thought. First, it was explicitly and assertively materialist in outlook. That is, it located the most important motivations for historical change in the relationship of humans to their environment and in the systems of economic production that those relationships created. This was by contrast to the emphasis in nineteenth-century history on the power of abstract ideas. Second,

it was therefore an early and powerful version of social history. This was the history of common people, not of Great Men, an outlook produced partly by Marx's materialist view, but also driven by his belief in the humanity of everyday workers—a humanity that he saw capitalism stripping from them. Finally, his analysis was inherently transnational and even global, since he saw the same class-based processes operating everywhere. Marxist history was, potentially, world history, not nationalist history.

Not that Marx (and subsequent Marxist historians) necessarily got it "right." Class conflict turns out not to be a very good concept for analyzing pre-Industrial societies, for example, and Marxist globalism, having arisen from analysis of European societies, has a hard time avoiding Eurocentrism. And Marxist history is burdened with the ahistorical problem of Marxist teleology—the predicted socialist utopia—even outside the orthodoxy of official Marxist history in communist countries. But no history gets it right, and in the process of constant revision that is doing history, Marxism asked difficult questions and posed challenges that non-Marxist historians had to meet.

---

of the "merchant capitalist tumor" that had exploded Agrarian societies exposed to capitalism. Not only did industrialization create social groups who chafed under rigid political constraints, just as merchant capitalism had done, but those groups' dissatisfaction was exacerbated by the disjunction between the image of communist ideals and the reality of communist rule. In part, this is because communism proved better at analysis than at providing identity. We will return to these topics further in Chapter 27. In another irony, the more industrialized communist societies became, the more they took on the character of the other major reaction to Industrial capitalism, fascism.

Fascism

Unlike communism, fascism has appeared almost exclusively in countries that were already industrialized or well along in industrializing. This is because fascism does not promote the transformations from Agrarian Era structures to those inherent to industrialization, as communism does (in theory), but is instead a reaction against those changes. Fascism is in fact a continuation and ideological intensification of the nineteenth-century conservative reaction to industrialization.

As a reminder, Industrial capitalism creates mass society, mass politics, and new classes and class conflict, threatening the stability of traditional authority. The tendency of capitalist economics is also to undermine traditional values via commodification: traditional social and gender relationships succumb to the economic logic of commodified labor, and traditional moral restrictions (on commerce and then by extension on cultural expression) surrender to the all-encompassing marketplace. This, too, threatens traditional authority structures. Finally, the pace of change in Industrial society is vastly greater than in Agrarian society, which in itself can be upsetting to some. Fascist leaders appeal to and exploit fear of these transformations to gain and keep power.

The problem for fascism is that its program is inherently contradictory, because the other thing fascist leaders want is industrial and military power backing their political power. How could they have that without the social transformations that necessarily accompany them? It is this contradiction that accounts for the key characteristics of the politics of fascist states.

First, fascists have always been virulently anti-communist because communism promotes the very transformations fascism wishes to suppress. This leads to a fascist political economy in which private ownership of capital is necessary ideologically; fascism thus works, to some extent, with capitalism and has a separate corporate sphere, unlike communism. But fascist states also tend to feature at least some elements of state planning consistent with a wartime economy.

This is because fears about national security and war, or the threat of war, are powerful tools for the promotion of state and military power and, at the same time, for suppressing dissent, which is necessary if social transformation and unrest are to be resisted. To heighten the existential threat implied by "national" security, particular groups of fascists ground their identity in extreme nationalism—fascism is again the reverse of communism in being better at creating identity than doing analysis. Fascist nationalism posits a mystical, collective sense of the nation (not an individualist, democratic one), backed by appeals to mythical, pre-capitalist national history. This almost always entails some notion of "racial purity," which is almost always xenophobic, anti-immigrant, and in different cases anti-Jewish, anti-black, essentially anti-"racial enemy," thus creating an immediate domestic threat as a "fifth column" of foreign threat. This further justifies the suppression of dissent. Fascists promote cultural conformity (including the maintenance of traditional gender roles) and try to eliminate all forms of "class conflict," from labor unions to the political voices of socialists, communists, or even promoters of democracy (which is far too open to subversive influences to make fascists happy). This often buys them the support of capitalist interests, for whom fascism provides a docile, pliable workforce.

In short, fascists want the state and military power created by industrialization without the social transformation also created by industrialization. This disjunction can also be shown in terms of our model, as in Figure 23.14.

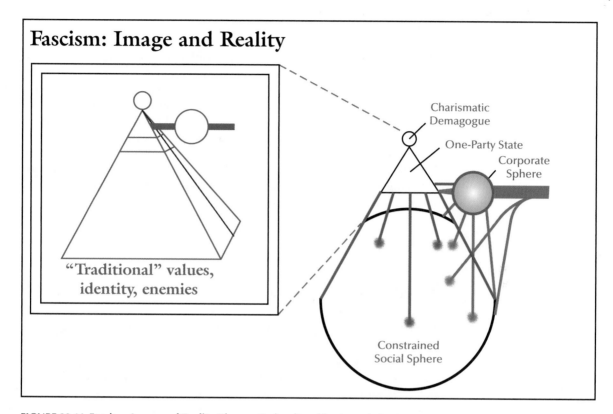

FIGURE 23.14 **Fascism: Image and Reality.** The practical reality of fascist societies, set against the fascist screen image ideal of an ordered, disciplined, and harmonious traditional social structure with modern corporate power.

Italy from 1920 under Benito Mussolini was the first avowedly fascist state—the name "fascism" comes from the "fasces," the bundle of rods symbolic of the might of the classical Roman army that Italian fascists adopted as their party symbol. Mussolini famously "made the trains run on time," a quintessential symbol of *ordered* Industrial society. In the troubled economic times of the 1930s, which we will explore in the next chapter, Adolph Hitler's Nazi Party came to power in Germany, Francisco Franco led his Spanish fascists to victory in the Spanish Civil War, and Japan's military leaders led it down a fascist path. (Charismatic demagogic leaders are often but not always a feature of fascism.) Fascist Germany, Italy, and Japan were defeated in World War II, but fascism has by no means disappeared as a form of resistance to the sometimes troubling transformations brought about by industrialization. This, too, is a topic we shall return to in Chapter 27.

FIGURE 23.15 **Faces of Fascism.** Benito Mussolini and Adolph Hitler, the iconic faces of charismatic fascist leadership.

Conclusion

World War I brought the world of the nineteenth century to a bloody halt, deeply damaging European prestige and shaking the foundations of imperialism. The political upheavals that preceded and then accompanied the war initiated a period of intense ideological competition over the emerging shape of an Industrial (and predominantly capitalist) world system. Communism and fascism took center stage in the decades after World War I, but democratic values, though shaken, continued as an alternative to both. Global politics, poisoned by an unsatisfactory settlement to World War I and brought to a boil by global economic crisis, led to an even vaster and truly global war as the struggle to define the world system continued. This is the story of the next chapter.

FRAME IT YOURSELF

Extending the Frame

World War I may have been primarily a European civil war, a fight among the playground bullies of the late nineteenth century, but it drew many non-Europeans into its melee. One prominent way this happened was that imperial European powers, especially the British and French, drew on their colonies for manpower. Indians fought in the British army, Moroccans fought in the French army, and so on.

Investigate one of these cases. What network and hierarchy mechanisms did imperial powers use to recruit and transport such troops? Perhaps even more important, what cultural screen images did the imperial powers project to their colonies to justify using colonial troops on their behalf? Was "because we can" the only reason they gave, or were there other justifications? What imperial frame values shaped these screen images?

Further Reading

Beckett, Ian. 2001. *The Great War 1914–1918*. London: Longman.

Fitzpatrick, Sheila. 2008. *The Russian Revolution*. 3rd ed. Oxford: Oxford University Press.

Fussell, Paul. 1970. *The Great War and Modern Memory*. Oxford: Oxford University Press.

Gonzales, Michael J. 2002. *The Mexican Revolution: 1910–1940*. Albuquerque: University of New Mexico Press.

Grasso, June M., J. P. Corrin, and Michael Kort. 2009. *Modernization and Revolution in Modern China: From the Opium Wars to the Olympics.* 4th ed. Armonk, NY: M. E. Sharpe.

Neiberg, Michael S. 2005. *Fighting the Great War: A Global History.* Cambridge, MA: Harvard University Press.

For additional learning and instructional resources related to this chapter, please go to www.oup.com/us/morillo

CHAPTER TWENTY-FOUR

The World in Crisis, 1929 to 1945

Albert Einstein before he became a screen image.

Introduction

Albert Einstein's image loomed large on the world's cultural screen during the twentieth century. His name and face—shaggy hair and mustache, basset-hound eyes animated by a humorous twinkle—symbolize intellectual genius, and his screen image is captioned by the most famous mathematical equation of the century, $E = mc^2$, the key that opened the door to atomic weaponry and then nuclear weaponry and energy generation. His was the image of science's first global superstar, a fitting heir to the image of Isaac Newton, star of European Enlightenment science.

Amazingly, Albert Einstein was also a real person, born in Ulm, Germany, in 1879, to a non-observant Jewish family. His education culminated in a doctorate from the University of Zurich, Switzerland, in 1905, the same year that he published fundamental papers on photoelectricity, the Brownian motion of particles, special relativity, and the equivalence of mass and energy (the source of the famous equation). These contributions vaulted him into a leading role in the revolution in physics taking place at the beginning of the twentieth century, and by 1914 he was a research professor at the University of Berlin. In 1917 he published his general theory of relativity, which reconceptualized space-time and gravity. He won the Nobel Prize for Physics in 1921.

His fame by then was such that the rest of his life was played out on the global cultural screen, laden with symbolic gravity. He left Germany in 1933 when Adolph Hitler's Nazis rose to power, moving to the United States and becoming a citizen there in 1940; thereafter, Einstein's Jewish identity became more important to him. He also joined the NAACP and worked against racism in the United States. Previously a pacifist, once in the United States he renounced pacifism, joining other scientists in warning President Franklin Roosevelt of the danger that Hitler's Germany might develop an atomic bomb and urging that the United States do so first. When the Manhattan Project produced a successful bomb, however, Einstein argued against dropping it on Japan.

Meanwhile, his scientific work continued, but with more fame than success. He was never comfortable with the statistical and probabilistic nature of some of the key pieces of quantum mechanics, arguing to Niels Bohr, the Danish physicist who helped develop quantum theory, that "I, at any rate, am convinced that He [God] does not throw dice." His own work focused on an unsuccessful attempt to find a "unified field theory" that would unite gravitation and electromagnetism. He died in 1955.

Einstein's life was therefore woven into the main themes of this chapter. Science became a major player in the search for understanding and meaning that the crises of the early twentieth century provoked, but findings in science itself, especially quantum mechanics, undermined the

Framing the Argument

• How economic collapse in the context of intensifying ideological competition brought the Industrial world system to a new and more intense peak of crisis

• The ambiguous role of science in the global search for understanding and meaning: how it created new technology but also came to undermine its own promise of certain knowledge

• The causes, events, ideological frames, and consequences of World War II

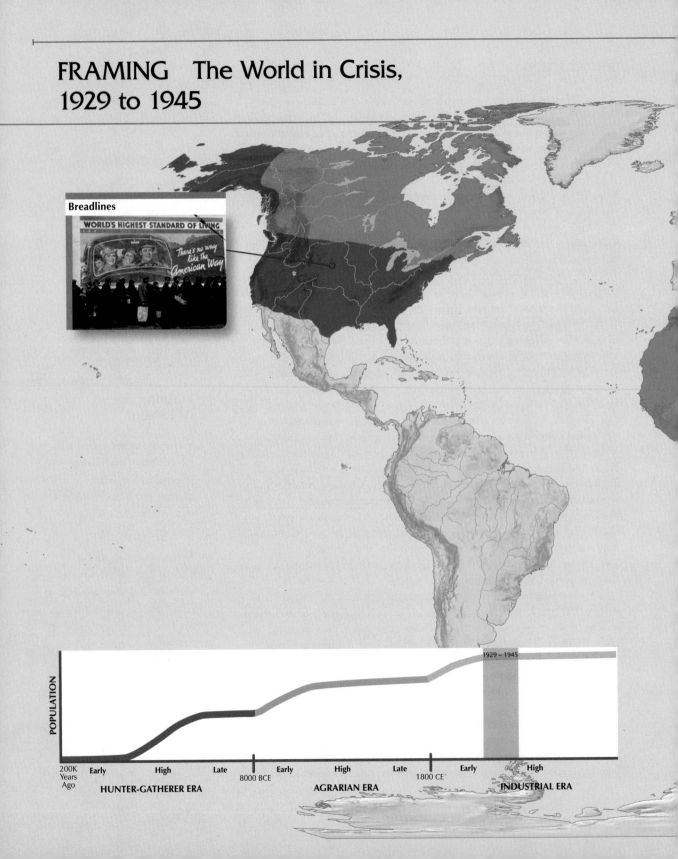

FRAMING   The World in Crisis, 1929 to 1945

Breadlines

WORLD'S HIGHEST STANDARD OF LIVING

There's no way like the American Way

1929 – 1945

POPULATION

| 200K Years Ago | Early | High | Late | 8000 BCE | Early | High | Late | 1800 CE | Early | High |

HUNTER-GATHERER ERA   AGRARIAN ERA   INDUSTRIAL ERA

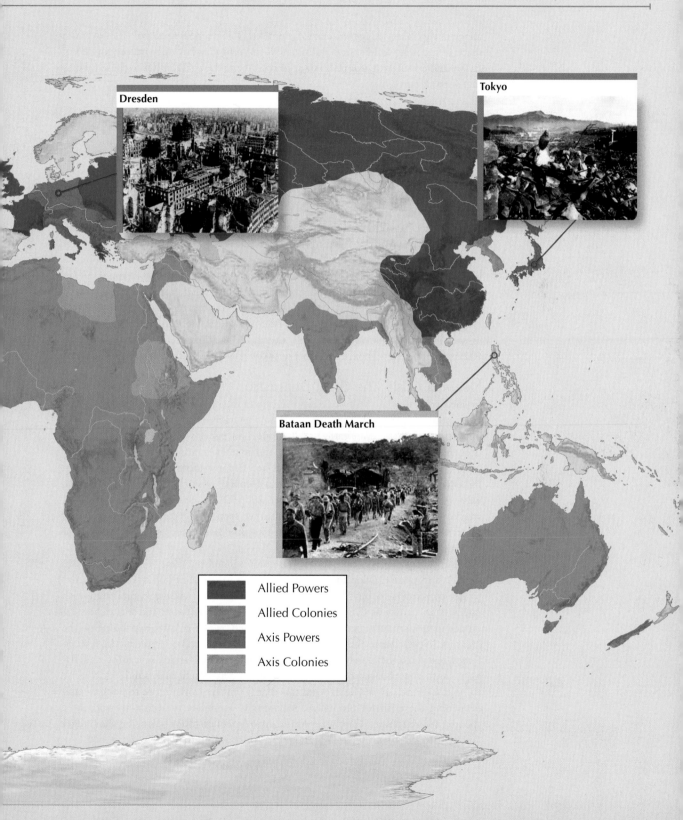

Dresden

Tokyo

Bataan Death March

Allied Powers

Allied Colonies

Axis Powers

Axis Colonies

image of sure knowledge that science promised. The deepening global crisis over the shape of the new world system culminated in World War II, which was entangled in racism and ended with atomic blasts at Hiroshima and Nagasaki. It is to these themes that we now turn.

---

*

The Growing Global Crisis

The global community attempted a "return to normalcy," in the words of US president Warren Harding, after World War I. But the nineteenth-century world could not be rebuilt. The new presence of a communist regime in Russia from November 1917 led to a wave of revolts and uprisings through 1923, though none succeeded in creating a further communist state. Fascism appeared with Mussolini's government in Italy from 1921. War reparations kept the German Weimar Republic unstable, as Germany began paying its debt to France and Britain, essentially with American loans. Still, the global economy recovered and through 1929 grew strongly. Then, the global network itself went into crisis.

Network Crisis: The Great Depression

Economists today are still debating the causes of the Great Depression, but a few main points seem firmly established. Financial crises—the bursting of speculative bubbles causing the evaporation of huge piles of paper wealth—had been regular occurrences since stock markets began, and market economies produce a regular cycle of expansions and contractions that had become more rapid and visible since industrialization had taken hold. The Great Depression started in the United States, with the stock market crash of October 29, 1929, a classic financial crisis that triggered an economic downturn as consumer spending decreased in the wake of the crisis. This was "normalcy," though of an unpleasant sort, and was expected to be temporary.

But policy mistakes of several kinds compounded the crisis. The United States passed the Smoot-Hawley Tariff in 1930, raising the price of imports in an attempt to get consumers to buy American goods. Many other countries retaliated with tariffs of their own as the traditional tension between network and hierarchies exploded in modern form, and world trade collapsed by 50% to 80%, depending on the measure. At the same time, the Federal Reserve, the central bank of the United States, restricted the money supply when it should have expanded it, leading to deflation and further reduced consumer spending (in deflation, it makes individual sense to hold your money in the expectation that it will be worth more tomorrow) and deepening the crisis for producers. Attempts to stimulate the economy with state spending were too small and were constrained by concerns for balancing the budget and by the rigidity of the Gold Standard in constraining state monetary policy.

FIGURE 24.1 Image and Reality of Poverty. Mother and her children during the Great Depression in the US, a photograph by Dorothea Lange, 1936.

The power and pervasiveness of the global network were demonstrated by the spread of the contagion. US loans to Germany dried up, ending reparation payments to Britain and France, and collapsing US consumption and production, as well as tariff wars, brought the Depression rapidly to most of the world. Industrial production declined by perhaps 30%, but primary producers—farmers, miners, and loggers— were hit hardest, whether in non-Industrial countries as a whole or in those economic sectors in Industrial countries. Unemployment soared to around 25% in the United States, Britain, France, and elsewhere, and it was over 30% in Germany in 1932. Though the world economy began to recover slowly in 1933, the Depression lingered in many places until World War II replaced the Depression with a different sort of crisis.

Crisis and Hierarchies

The length and severity of the Great Depression varied according to the different policies countries pursued, with different political consequences. Perhaps the worst thing about the Great Depression for global politics is that the freest countries suffered the most.

Depression and Democracy

An economic downturn as broad and deep as the Depression placed serious strains on democratic societies. The worst threat in such a situation is that economic disparity threatens to tear apart the underlying consensus—the frame values—upon which successful democracy must be based. In other words, if there is too great a divergence in the interests and material circumstances of rich and poor, the peaceful resolution of policy differences becomes impossible. Under the strain of Depression, new and shallowly rooted democracies collapsed across Latin America, in Germany, and in Japan, almost always to reactionary, fascist-leaning, or openly fascist governments that promised to keep order against "communist inspired" subversion, a political position that conflated calls for social-democratic amelioration of the effects of the Depression with the symbolic threat posed by the mere existence of the Soviet Union.

КОМСОМОЛ-УДАРНАЯ БРИГАДА ПЯТИЛЕТКИ

FIGURE 24.2 Image of Prosperity. 1930s Soviet propaganda poster celebrating socialist prosperity.

In fact, where democracy survived, it did so because new social programs and state intervention in the economy worked well enough to prevent the misery of 25% unemployment from becoming social unrest. The creation or expansion of unemployment insurance schemes, public works projects, state pension systems, and so forth not only stimulated economies in the short term, they also projected an image of long-term security on the cultural screen that calmed fears of collapse. Franklin Roosevelt's New Deal is the most famous, though also one of the most limited, of such policy packages. Thus, by increasing the role of the state in the economy, such policies maintained political freedom—a result that is more readily visible if we separate the notions of democracy, free markets, and capitalism (as this book did in Chapter 19). Indeed, free markets suffered worse damage from "nationalist capitalism" (tariffs) than from "state socialism" (which was basically aimed at ameliorating the effects of capitalism). Put another way, the Depression exposed the tensions between democracy and capitalism more clearly than prosperity ever could.

Communism: Stalin's Soviet Union

That tension was exposed particularly explicitly with the comparative economic success of the Soviet Union during the 1930s. A series of Five Year Plans begun by Josef Stalin created significant economic growth in the Soviet Union, especially in terms of heavy industry production, just when the capitalist economies fell into the worst of the crisis. Soviet leadership amplified this success by trumpeting Soviet worker-friendly policies—universal employment, guaranteed health care, "cradle to grave security"—to distressed workers everywhere. The communist alternative to capitalist economics never seemed more attractive.

Communism of course promised a worker's paradise and was, as we saw in the last chapter, grounded in humanist values, unlike fascism. But the Soviet economic success of the 1930s is explicable without reference to Marxist theory. For starters, the Soviet Union was largely isolated, by its own choice and by the policy of capitalist countries, from the global network, insulating it from being infected by the Depression. Furthermore, remarkable *rates* of growth were easier to achieve when starting from the much lower base of industrialization in Russia than obtained in the more mature Industrial powers. Also, the rates were achieved by what can be seen as an extreme form of state-sponsored economic stimulus of the sort that also worked, at lower levels, in the democracies.

Finally, however, the same network isolation that insulated the USSR from the Depression also hid from the world the real costs of Russian economic growth. Peasants were forced into collective agricultural enterprises by the millions, entailing the deaths of millions, especially from the most prosperous class of landowning peasantry, who were labeled "class enemies." This was merely part of a larger process, as rapidly industrializing an entire political-economic system required massive levels of political coercion, purges, and mass executions. Only as a screen image can Stalin's Soviet Union be seen as a happy, prosperous place. It certainly wasn't free, politically or economically.

Fascism on the March

The tension between democracy and capitalism was further exposed by the relative economic successes of some of the countries that turned to fascism. This did not include Italy, fascist through the 1920s. The alliance between Mussolini and Italy's major capitalists seems neither to have helped nor hindered economic growth until the Depression. The Depression hit hard, however, and recovery was hindered, despite massive spending on armaments as Mussolini sent Italian forces into Abyssinia and Ethiopia in 1935–1936, by a new nationalist-fascist emphasis on economic self-sufficiency that kept Italian trade limited. Italy entered World War II almost entirely unprepared industrially.

Germany was hit extremely hard by the Depression, as we have seen, which contributed substantially to the success of the Nazi party in the 1933 election that brought Hitler to power: Germany had also stopped paying reparations in 1932. Hitler played not just on economic misery and the potential for social disorder that threatened to accompany it, but also on resentment toward the terms of the Treaty of Versailles and the outcome of World War I. (The purported threat of social disorder was often put into practice by the Nazi's own brown shirts, gangs of uniformed thugs who intimidated opponents and made trouble that was then blamed on left-wing subversives.) Hitler played up the myth of the "stab in the back," the notion that it was not the German army that had lost the war but rather the civilian government that had betrayed the army by surrendering when the Kaiser abdicated. He therefore combined economic populist rhetoric with appeals

FIGURE 24.3 Mass Politics. But not democratic politics. Mass Nazi rallies such as this one created the image of popular government under a dictatorship.

to both capitalist and military interests. In short, a carefully crafted screen image of a proud Germany reclaiming its rightful place in the sun largely substituted for defined policy.

Policy was not long in coming. With the Depression already easing when he took office, Hitler stimulated the economy by ramping up military spending in a rearmament program that was at first secret, as it violated the terms of the Treaty of Versailles, but by 1936 became more open. Hitler also shut down opposition, initiated anti-Jewish measures (ensuring that Einstein would stay in the United States, among many other consequences), and created a fascist dictatorship where the fragile Weimar Republic had stood. Hitler used ethnic nationalism to justify not only internal "ethnic cleansing" but also territorial expansion, as Germany demanded territories in Czechoslovakia that had substantial German-speaking populations. The Western democracies, preoccupied with their own problems and hoping desperately to avoid a new war, allowed Hitler to march Germany on the road to a new war.

Japan, too, suffered from the Depression, as its economy shrank by almost a tenth between 1929 and 1931. But the Japanese finance minister devalued the currency and initiated large state spending programs, aimed mostly at expansion of the armed forces, as in Germany, and Japan recovered quickly, emerging from the Depression by 1933. But the same finance minister, concerned now with the threat of inflation posed by an expanding economy, attempted to rebalance the budget by cutting military spending. Nationalists and the army itself protested, and the minister was assassinated in February 1934, in an uprising that, despite being suppressed, led to increasing military influence over the government. Deficit spending on rearmament led to impressive industrial growth, but also to continued inflation and restricted economic freedoms for consumers. As in Germany and Italy, the major capitalist interests in Japan had no real problem accepting life in a nondemocratic society, allying the state and corporate spheres at the expense of the social sphere.

Network Mechanisms and Recovery

Japan's currency devaluation points to a final factor in recovery from the Depression around the globe. The earlier a country abandoned the restrictive old gold standard and let their currency float on international markets, the earlier and more fully it recovered from the Depression. The cultural shift involved in abandoning the gold standard and its associated national gold reserves was one more step in the infiltration of network values and mechanisms into the operation of hierarchies. The intersection between hierarchies and the network was becoming ever more complex and market-driven.

Crisis and Culture: Science

At the beginning of the twentieth century, "Western" science was already exhibiting a level of cross-cultural appeal unprecedented for any other system of thought, even the major salvation religions that emerged after the Axial Age. The self-correcting method of scientific inquiry, theoretically unaffected by culture (more accurately, affected by culture but with cultural distortions also subject to self-correction when practiced cross-culturally), opened its knowledge to anyone. Even participation in science was theoretically open to anyone with the proper training, though in practice this meant that science remained everywhere a largely male preserve, with notable exceptions such as Marie Curie, and the preserve of whites in the United States and European countries. (The extent of the Jewish academic community was a sore spot for the Nazis, who purged German universities of all their Einsteins.) The practical applications of science proved the utility of science and carried their own cross-cultural appeal.

Advances in medicine had the most popular appeal around the world and contributed to population growth. Industrial chemistry had applications from cloth dying with new synthetic dyes to weapons manufacturing. Before World War I, scientific advances spread rapidly within Europe and beyond, as new inventions and processes were patented but almost automatically licensed to firms in other countries. Even military technology, such as new ways of making stronger plate armor for battleships, spread rapidly under a network-based culture of knowledge sharing. World War I, however, brought weapons and other research under much closer nationalist scrutiny; and from that time forward, weapons advances became state secrets, exemplified above all by the Manhattan Project that produced the US atomic bomb, and corporations began taking greater advantage of patent monopolies.

Nevertheless, the cross-cultural appeal of science remained powerful. World War I and the subsequent period of spreading global crisis in fact added to that appeal. In addition to the utility of its practical applications and the openness of science to practitioners from different cultures, even the abstract findings of science seemed to promise a more objective, "real" knowledge of the world than other systems of thought, a kind of certainty backed by experimental proof in understanding how the universe worked. It is not surprising that in the search for understanding that followed the shock of World War I, especially in Europe, more people looked to science for understanding and even some notion of identity. Some of this became tied up with political ideologies. As we saw in the last chapter, Marxism claimed to present a "scientific" understanding of history and human social dynamics, while fascists ironically but gleefully appropriated distorted notions of evolution, especially Social Darwinism, to bolster their ideas

PRINCIPLES AND PATTERNS

The development of modern science joined Axial Age philosophies and the salvation religions as a major landmark in human cultural history.

FIGURE 24.4 The Appeal of Science. Modern medicine's efficacy was attractive to people everywhere. Here, European doctors run a clinic in the Mideast.

victory at Midway that destroyed four large Japanese carriers in turn wrecked the Japanese ability to go on the offensive. Industrial capacity then took over, as the United States added carriers steadily while Japanese shipyards could not even replace the navy's losses.

As in World War I, submarines also played a major role. The more well-known aspect of this was the German U-boat campaign in the North Atlantic, which was designed to strangle Britain's network connections. Technological improvements to subs since World War I had made them more dangerous: snorkels allowed them to cruise below the surface, making them harder to spot, while improved torpedo guidance systems made their attacks more reliable. But the key improvement was, once more, in communications: radio allowed groups of German U-boats to operate as "wolf packs," combining against groups of merchant ships so effectively that for a time in 1940 British shipping losses rose to alarming levels. But the British rapidly re-adopted the convoy system created in World War I and reinforced their anti-submarine fleet with large numbers of destroyers "borrowed" from the United States under the Lend-Lease program even before the United States entered the war. The British also fitted convoy ships with newly invented sonar and put together air cover across the North Atlantic from bases in Greenland and elsewhere. Losses came under control. Submarine warfare really paid off in the Pacific, where US subs preyed on the Japanese merchant marine in the Sea of Japan, targeting oil tankers in particular with spectacular success. Incomprehensibly, the Japanese never implemented either convoys or effective anti-submarine warfare, and the home islands gradually ran out of fuel.

Air Warfare

We have noted the role of air power in both land and naval warfare already. In land warfare, tactical air support involved direct attacks against enemy troop formations and fortifications, but even more important, the interdiction of supply lines, lines of communication and reinforcement, as well as the disruption of headquarter units in the rear of battle. The Luftwaffe, the German air force, was designed to handle these tasks, and it proved adept at doing so. Similarly, the Russian air force also focused on such tasks and outdid the Germans in tactical air assaults (again, an effective but expensive technique that only the Russians could realistically implement). The British and American air forces, which saw themselves as arms for strategic bombing, had greater difficulty coordinating tactical air support with their armies and developed an effective tactical support plane only after they equipped fighters with bombs, making them precision fighter-bombers. Pure bombers had previously proved woefully inadequate at taking out bridges or other tactical targets.

Allied strategic bombing campaigns, did, however, play a significant part in the war effort, whereas the Luftwaffe had little success in its "blitz" against London in late 1940. Every air force that attempted strategic bombing found it more expensive than its proponents had promised, nor did it cause the collapse of civilian morale that they had predicted. In fact, bombing campaigns seemed if anything to stiffen civilian resolve. Furthermore, the imprecision of bombs dropped at night by the British (to lessen their own losses) and even during the day from high altitude by the

United States meant that it was much harder than antici-pated to take out specific industrial targets. Even such target facilities as ball bearing factories proved easy to decentralize, limiting the impact of strategic bombing on industrial production in Germany or Japan. What fi-nally worked in Germany was the strategic bombing corollary of the US submarine campaign against Japan. Allied bombers began targeting German oil refineries—huge, immobile, and highly flammable targets—in June 1944. By December of that year, the German military had effectively run out of fuel. The impact of earlier targeting of refineries remains one of the great "what ifs" of the war.

Strategic bombing also caused massive civilian ca-sualties, lowering the bar between attacks on military and civilian targets and highlighting the moral quanda-ries of engaging in total war. The United States always wished to maintain the idea that it only attacked mili-tary targets, but both they and the British ended up using incendiary bombs on urban areas with horrific results, the best-known examples of which are the fire-bombings of Dresden and Tokyo, where separate fires joined into unstoppable firestorms. The morality of stra-tegic bombing came into sharpest focus, of course, with the US dropping of atomic bombs on Hiroshima and

FIGURE 24.11 The Atomic Age. The mushroom cloud over Nagasaki, August 9, 1945.

then on Nagasaki in August 1945. Interestingly, the debate usually focuses on the first, which was arguably defensible. Nagasaki remains a much more problematic afterthought.

Ideology, Race, and War
The feature of World War II that marks it as a major stage in the struggle over the shape of the Industrial world system is not its technological modernity nor even its global scope and impact. Instead, the intense ideological dimensions of the war show that this was not just a set of power games and territorial disputes, as World War I had appeared to be when it began, but rather a fight over the future paths of indus-trialization, social structure, and the way the meanings of the industrial world would be constructed. This is reflected in how the war is often named. If World War I was for western Europe "the Great War," World War II was for Britain and the United States "the Good War." Whatever moral ambiguities arose in practice—and there were inevitably many in a war so large and fiercely fought—World War II remained for the Allies a totally justifiable fight against fascism, its associated racist ideologies, and aggression. It was not, like World War I, a stupid war.

The Holocaust and Race War
The central event of the racial aspect of the war is the Holocaust, though during the war the full extent of the Nazi war against the Jews and other minorities was not

visible. More than 6 million Jews died during the course of the war, some of whom the German army massacred directly as it advanced into enemy territories (part of a broader German military assault on civilians that we will return to in a moment), but millions more were taken to labor camps, where they were worked to death while their labor benefited German capitalist corporations, and, ultimately, to death camps fitted with gas chambers. The Holocaust's industrialization of death is thus the quintessential result of the fascist ambivalence toward the process and consequences of industrialization itself, as the Nazis used state-directed industrial capabilities (with the complicity of private corporations) to exercise genocidal control over society, in particular over a racially identified segment of society demonized as the cause of the social "disorder" created by industrialization. The (considerable) extent to which the German people were also complicit in the program of genocide therefore resulted not just from successful Nazi manipulation of historical German Christian anti-Semitism. Rather, complicity also resulted from the (interim) success of the

FIGURE 24.12 Labor and Death Camps. Nazi concentration camps: the industrialization of death in support of racial purity, a quintessentially fascist combination.

Holocaust as part of the wider fascist screen image of defending German identity (itself cast in terms of racial "purity") against racial, class, and foreign enemies. The importance of this program is indicated by resource allocation: while German army units were running out of fuel and supplies on the Eastern front in late 1944, the death camps were given all the transport they needed.

As crucial to Nazi ideology (and Hitler's personal worldview) as extermination of the Jews was, however, it was only part of a larger racialized approach to war on the part of the German fascist state and the German army. The training ground for this had been German colonial policy in Africa in the first decades of the twentieth century, where suppression of the Maji Maji Rebellion and related uprisings in German southeast Africa had ingrained the idea of racial enemies and the genocidal use of military force against entire civilian societies into German military practice. The direct extension of this was that German soldiers reacted especially brutally when faced by African French soldiers in both World War I and World War II, as for example when they massacred 3,000 captured French African troops in 1940. Thus, when Hitler sent his armies into the Soviet Union, Nazi propaganda and German military history combined so that the German army became not just a proficient military tool for attacking the Soviet army, but a willing partner in genocidal warfare against Slavic populations.

Though neither as systematic nor as focused as the German ideology, the Japanese worldview was also deeply racialized. "Racial purity" and superiority had long been an element in the construction of Japanese collective identity. This showed up in Japanese actions in China, especially the infamous Nanking Massacre in December 1937, where the patriarchal side of fascist "traditional values" was made especially clear by the systematic rape by Japanese soldiers of between 20,000 and 80,000 Chinese women. It also showed up in the Japanese attitude toward Americans, whom the Japanese viewed as a "mongrel" race that was tainted in particular by its significant African American population. Nor was the United States free of racism in its own society: popular images of the Japanese in the American press often depicted them as subhuman, monkey-like creatures. The effect such images had on the actual conduct of war in the Pacific, which has been called a "war without mercy" because of such racist demonization, remains, however, a disputed topic among historians. It does seem that, unlike the fascist powers (for whom all wars were inherently subcultural), Britain and the United States tried hard at the official level to fight World War II as an intracultural war (based on at least militarily mutually comprehensible cultures).

FIGURE 24.13 The Rape of Nanking. Race War in Asia: Chinese troops entering Nanking in December 1937. Infamous mass rapes and massacres followed. (ullstein bild / The Granger Collection, New York)

Thus, they "demonized" their opponents only to the extent of accurately characterizing how bad they really were and kept the blame on leaders rather than on the people, perhaps with an eye already toward post-war tensions with their communist ally.

Ideology and Home Fronts

Ideology also affected how different powers handled the potentially transformative effects of conducting another "total war." Here, too, the fascist powers found themselves handicapped by their own traditionalist ideology. While the democratic and communist powers saw significantly increased participation in industry by women, who replaced men headed off to the front, this was exactly the sort of social change that fascism was designed to resist, and so German and Japanese women did not join the labor force in nearly the same way—indeed, Hitler's regime encouraged German women to stay home and have children, the "natural" role for females in an ideology based on racial competition. Women in the democracies did not hold on to all their gains after the war ended, though French women did gain the vote after the war. Returning soldiers reclaimed their jobs, and during the decade and a half just after the war something of a traditionalist reaction against changing gender roles took place in the changed context of the Cold War showdown with communism. Communist support for gender and racial equality, at least ideologically, rendered democratic support for both open to suspicion from conservatives.

FIGURE 24.14 Stirring the Social Sphere. The democratic powers in World War II facilitated the socially transformative impact of the war. By contrast, the fascist powers preferred maintaining traditional gender roles to mobilizing for war efficiently.

The explicitly racist ideologies of the fascist powers also made for notable domestic discomfort in the racially segregated and discriminatory United States, an issue made even worse by the government's internment of Japanese Americans during the war. This obvious contradiction led African American political leaders to question how the United States could oppose racism abroad yet defend it at home, a question for which there was no good answer. Blacks, whose loyalty (unlike Japanese Americans') was never questioned, had increased economic opportunity during the war just as (white) women did, and many served in the armed forces. They, too, questioned what exactly it was they were defending. And though there was a similar traditionalist reaction toward race issues as toward gender issues in the 1950s United States, the war fatally weakened the grip of Jim Crow. Baseball began integrating itself two years after the war, President Truman integrated the US armed forces the next year, *Brown v. Board of Education* ended the law of "separate but equal" in 1954, and the Civil

Rights movement grew thereafter. The racial history of the United States remained ugly, but the contrast with the Holocaust and with Japanese treatment of Korean "comfort women" is clear.

The other clear effect of the war on home fronts was to end decisively any lingering remnants of the Depression. Under total war conditions, economic production soared with the huge stimulus of government deficit spending. The fact that most of that spending went (necessarily) to military procurement, however, was not without problematic long-term consequences, a topic we will return to in Chapter 25.

Consequences of the War

A war so vast, destructive, and global was bound to have vast and global consequences. One thing the war did not do, at least immediately, was settle the struggle over the shape of the emerging Industrial world system. It repudiated, at least for a time, the openly reactionary, repressive, and anti-"modernizing" position that Nazism and Japanese ultra-nationalism advocated, but the war did not settle the struggle between the competing "modernizing" visions of communism and capitalism, nor did it clarify the relationship between democracy and capitalism, despite the conflation of the two encouraged by anti-communism. Indeed, it didn't even eliminate fascism itself (or its reactionary view of modernization), only the major openly fascist states.

But in eliminating those, the war set the global stage for the Industrial world system to take shape in a competition between capitalism and communism that would last for almost 50 years beyond the end of the war. Though they had managed to cooperate admirably during the war, the Allies began to split almost before the war was over, and it did not take long for their relationship to turn into the Cold War that will be a major subject of the next chapter. In China, Japanese surrender did not even bring that much respite, as Chiang Kai-Shek's nationalists and Mao Zedong's communists immediately resumed the civil war they had been fighting when the Japanese invaded, though Mao's forces were now in a much stronger position than before. These global tensions shaped the re-industrialization of Germany and Japan with the help of their former enemy the United States. Capitalist versus communist competition also shaped the spread of industrialization, with consequences we will explore in Chapters 26 through 28.

War, Memory, and Identity

For half a century World War II shaped the screen images that the major participants projected of themselves out of the war. Historical memory of the war became a crucial aspect of many societies' understanding of the Industrial world system—and of their place in it.

On the losing side, there is a clear contrast between how Germany and Japan have handled the historical memory of the war. Both post-war Germanies—democratic West Germany and communist East Germany—were open about the Nazi period, a tradition that has continued into unified Germany. The construction of German identity through this historical self-criticism has been consciously directed not only at repudiating that past but at changing the direction and image of

German historical trends. By contrast, Japan has been much less open about historical knowledge of its World War II history. The Nanking Massacre is often not even mentioned in Japanese history textbooks, and the history of militarism and ultra-nationalism that led up to the war rarely receives critical public examination. Japan has assumed a non-militaristic identity since the war, but this has been a matter of making a virtue of necessity, because the US-imposed post-war constitution severely limited the size and operational scope of Japanese military forces.

Views of history matter, as is evident in the post-war politics in these two societies. Though East Germany was, of course, under a Soviet-backed dictatorship until unification, it has since joined West Germany in what was, since shortly after the war, a vigorous multiparty democracy willing to debate public issues. The German state has also been willing to restrict open expression of neo-Nazi political positions (while recognizing that there are issues of free speech involved in doing so). Japan largely swept its ultra-nationalist past under the rug and had one-party rule by the conservative Liberal Democratic Party for more than fifty years after American occupation rule ended in the early 1950s. Ultra-nationalist political groups enforced political conformity by assassinating those who openly expressed leftist political views, and this limited investigations into Japan's past.

Among the winners there has been a similar range of reactions, though none perhaps quite so conflicted as Japan's and almost all much more openly debated. France is most complex, because its early exit and long occupation, including the cooperation with Germany offered by the rump Vichy state that ran southern France under German direction, have led to competing historical screen images of both heroic resistance and shameful collaboration. The effect of this on French politics has been shifting and ambiguous. China saw little real historical debate about its role and which of the nationalists and communists should receive credit for effective Chinese resistance, given that the competition between those two parties was fought out not in the classroom but on the battlefield.

For Britain, the war became the focus of national pride, focused especially on "their finest hour" during the Blitz, the German air assault on Britain, when Britain faced the Nazi threat alone (except, of course, for the support of their imperial possessions) after the collapse of France and before the Nazi invasion of the Soviet Union. But in some ways, the political effect of this historical memory of heroism and triumph itself caused difficulties because it was so increasingly at odds with Britain's actual post-war power in the world. India, the

FIGURE 24.15 Nationalist or Communist? World War II Soviet recruiting poster that proclaims, "The Motherland Is Calling." Not much communist ideology visible.

"crown jewel" of the empire, obtained its independence in 1947, and the rest of the empire ceased to be imperial, either by fighting for independence or by being converted peacefully into the autonomous nations of the British Commonwealth over the following two decades. It also became increasingly clear that in the Anglo-American alliance that was the cornerstone of the democratic world's diplomacy during the Cold War, Britain was the junior partner. Thus, history comforted Britain while at the same time complicating its transition to a new world order.

The Soviet Union faced an interesting dilemma after the war in terms of its identity. Under the grip of Soviet rule and its official historiography, the emphasis of public historical memory was on communist triumph and the Marxist progress of history, and the Cold War competition with the United States only heightened this emphasis. But during the war, the failure of communist ideology to inspire had already been revealed, as the state appealed openly to Russian nationalism and the war was remembered in society as "The Great Patriotic War," fought in defense of Mother Russia. The tension between the two images remained until the fall of communism in 1989.

ISSUES IN DOING WORLD HISTORY

World War II and Video Culture

World War II was the first major war that was captured to a significant degree on film. The accessibility and immediacy of footage of the war, especially with the rise and spread of television technology, brought to the fore, especially in the United States, the tension between academic and popular history. Visual histories of the war could reach mass audiences and contributed to the construction of popular images of what the war was about. They have also helped keep the war as the most popular topic of military (and, arguably, world) history in mass media of all sorts and as a major topic in popular culture.

The demands of mass audiences also shaped such histories, of course, in ways that have come to be debated and examined by historians. Television shows such as the US series "Victory at Sea," which detailed the Pacific campaigns, aimed at accuracy but presented US footage about US accomplishments to a US audience. Different sorts of unintentional distortions could afflict even less nationalistically focused video histories. In the early days of the History Channel,

a cable television channel dedicated to exploring history (something many professional historians found simultaneously gratifying and horrifying), their motto seemed to be "All Nazis, All the Time." There was no intention of glorifying the Nazi regime, but disproportionate coverage can create its own distorting effect.

Even more interesting but problematic issues arise in popular fictional accounts of World War II. Did *Hogan's Heroes*, a weekly situation comedy set in a Nazi prisoner of war camp, trivialize fascism—"oh, those silly Nazis!"—at the height of Cold War tensions? (Obvious answer: "Well, duh!") What message does *Saving Private Ryan* have about the war? Or, even more enigmatically, *Inglourious Basterds*, with its totally counterfactual history? The range of popular culture makes generalizations here difficult—the lesson for students of history is that the images projected on different cultural screens are complex, and those images may be about many things at once. They certainly repay close study.

Finally, US memory of the war fit harmoniously but still problematically with its self-image as the world's great bastion of democracy and freedom, and the "Greatest Generation" that grew up in World War II assumed leadership of the United States for nearly fifty years afterward. The image was not entirely out of line with reality and seemed appropriate for what was clearly the world's greatest power after the war—economically, militarily, and perhaps morally. But the moral certainty of that image contributed to heavy-handed post-war US politics, internally and externally, which threatened to undermine the good the United States had achieved. We will return to these themes in the next chapter.

Conclusion

The global crisis initiated by World War I and heightened by the Great Depression came to a head in World War II. Though it did not settle the fundamental issue underlying the entire period of crisis, World War II did create the framework within which the issues behind the crisis could evolve in a slightly less globally traumatic way. The crisis—the struggle over the shape and meaning of the developing Industrial world system—entered a period of more patterned, almost institutionalized conflict. This was embodied both in the Cold War and in the decolonization movements that intersected so messily with the Cold War. It is to these topics that we turn in the next chapter.

FRAME IT YOURSELF

Frame Your World

The Holocaust continues to resonate as a powerful image on the world's cultural screens. What depictions of the Holocaust are you familiar with? Who projects them? Why do they do so? That is, what propositions about identity and the meaning of the world do images of the Holocaust attempt to create? What conditions in today's world make for the continued resonance of such images?

Further Reading

Bergen, Doris L. 2009. *War and Genocide: A Concise History of the Holocaust*. 2nd ed. New York: Rowman & Littlefield.

Bowler, Peter J., and Iwan Rhys Morus. 2005. *Making Modern Science: A Historical Survey*. Chicago: Chicago University Press.

Eatwell, Roger. 1997. *Fascism: A History*. New York: Penguin.

Glantz, David M., and Jonathan M. House. 1998. *When Titans Clashed: How the Red Army Stopped Hitler*. Lawrence: University Press of Kansas.

Murray, Williamson, and Allan R. Millet. 2000. *A War to Be Won: Fighting the Second World War, 1937–1945*. Cambridge, MA: Harvard University Press.

Service, Robert. 2010. *Comrades! A History of World Communism*. Cambridge, MA: Harvard University Press.

For additional learning and instructional resources related to this chapter, please go to www.oup.com/us/morillo

CHAPTER TWENTY-FIVE

Crisis Institutionalized and Transformed: 1945 to 1989

| Indira Gandhi meeting Nikita Khrushchev.

Introduction

In 1971, Indira Gandhi, the first (and so far only) female prime minister of the independent democracy of India, led her majority Hindu country into a thirteen-day war with Muslim Pakistan. Some fighting took place along the disputed border of Kashmir between northwest India and what was then West Pakistan, but in the key campaign Indian forces defeated the Pakistani army in East Pakistan, which thereby gained its independence as Bangladesh. Prime Minister Gandhi then negotiated a successful peace treaty with Pakistan that left the situation in Kashmir flexible.

Indira, born in 1917, was the granddaughter of Motilal Nehru, a prominent nineteenth-century Indian nationalist, and daughter of Jawaharlal Nehru, a leader of the Indian independence movement who became India's first prime minister when India achieved independence from Britain in 1947. She attended Oxford University, where she met and married Feroze Gandhi (no relation to the other great figure of the Indian independence movement, Mahatma Gandhi). Returning to India in 1941, she served unofficially in her father's Congress Party government after 1947. When Jawaharlal Nehru died in 1964, Indira officially entered Parliament and became prime minister in 1966.

Economic development was her chief focus. Her "Green Revolution" agricultural policies succeeded in turning India from a net importer to a net exporter of food, and the poverty rate fell from 65% to 45% during her first two terms in office from 1966 to 1977. She also guided India's foreign policy, both in the 1971 war and by initiating India's nuclear program in 1967. This resulted in a successful underground bomb test in 1974, in a move designed to counter China's program and to steer India between the great Cold War powers of the United States and the Soviet Union. A conviction for violating election laws led her to declare martial law in 1975; when she called new elections in 1977, she and Congress were swept out of power. But she returned in 1980. Finally, having ordered the army to attack Sikh rebels inside one of the holiest Sikh temples in the Punjab in 1984, she was assassinated by Sikh members of her own bodyguard.

Indira Gandhi's career encapsulates the themes of this chapter. Her family led the largest and most successful decolonization movement of the age. India's stormy but still successful experiment in democracy illustrates the challenges that newly independent countries faced. Her foreign policy had to negotiate the tensions of the Cold War, and India became a leader of the nations who tried to opt out of the pervasive bipolarity the Cold War imposed on the period. Her domestic policies reflected the renewed centrality of global network connections and economic development in the post–World War II world. Finally, the nationalism upon which the Congress Party was founded, the partition that divided India from Pakistan (and then split Pakistan in 1971), and the religious tensions that led to her assassination all remind us that constructions of cultural identity (and the post-colonial politics often built around those identities) were not confined to Cold War paradigms. It is to these themes that we turn in this chapter.

Framing the Argument

- How the recovery of the global network after World War II intersected with the "bipolar" world of Cold War hierarchies

- The causes, patterns, and consequences of the Cold War, including the complications that the rift between the Soviet Union and Communist China caused in Asia and elsewhere

- The causes and course of decolonization, or the dismantling of nineteenth-century imperialism, and the problems newly independent nations faced in nation-building

FRAMING Crisis Institutionalized and Transformed: 1945 to 1989

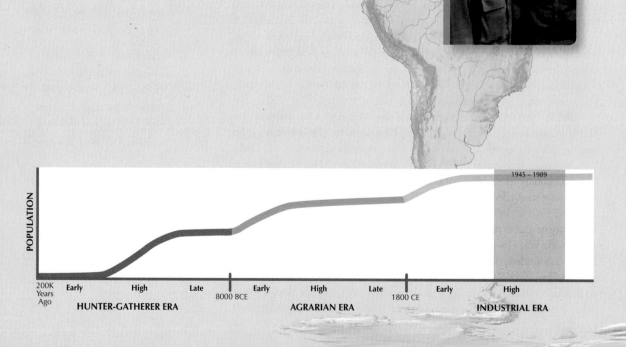

Che and Castro

POPULATION

| 200K Years Ago | | | | 8000 BCE | | | | 1800 CE | | | |
| Early | High | Late | | Early | High | Late | | Early | High | |

HUNTER-GATHERER ERA

AGRARIAN ERA

INDUSTRIAL ERA

1945 – 1989

Kim Il Sung

Ho Chi Minh

Idi Amin

NATO Countries

NATO Allies

Warsaw Pact

Other Communist Countries

Nonaligned Countries

Decolonized Countries

The World of 1945 to 1989

World War II may not have settled the struggle over the shape of the evolving Industrial world system, but it had eliminated fascism's organized resistance to the socially transformative effects of industrialization. The war also profoundly transformed the contours of global economic and military power.

The Global Network Recovers

The first thing that became clear as the war ended was that the United States stood unchallenged as the world's greatest economic power. World War II had reinvigorated the depressed US economy, and its inherent industrial strength, already the world's most productive after World War I, now had few if any rivals. Indeed, the US economy stood in need of partners, and US policy makers went about rebuilding the global network itself and the economic foundations of the hierarchies that it considered its allies. These allies included US allies from the war, especially in Europe, and its former enemies in western-occupied Germany and Japan. The European effort was spearheaded by the Marshall Plan, named for US Secretary of State George C. Marshall, which aimed to rebuild western European economies and so to strengthen democratic societies and states against further communist inroads. The United States also funded a large-scale investment in Japan. The network-directed efforts included, through the Bretton Woods Agreement, the creation of new mechanisms to regulate and facilitate global financial transactions. By contributing to the creation of the International Monetary Fund and the World Bank, the United States provided institutionalized mechanisms of trans-hierarchy network management. These US efforts were aimed at spreading market economics and capitalist economic organization through the global network. These economic efforts were complemented by attempts to build a global system of political cooperation, instantiated in the United Nations.

This set of policies proved among the most spectacularly successful global initiatives ever. By 1970, the United States and its Japanese and western European allies dominated global economic output probably even more thoroughly than the handful of major Industrial powers of the late nineteenth century (see Figure 25.1).

Such growth attested to the successful reinvigoration of the economic flows of the global network and provided a solid foundation for increasing globalization of other sorts of exchanges, especially cultural ones. On the other hand, these policies had most success in reindustrializing formerly industrial countries and fostering economic growth in already rich countries. The spread of industrialization and rising standards of living was slower in poorer areas of the world, including Latin America, much of Asia, and almost all of Africa. This was partly a result of imperfect understandings of the mechanisms of economic development and thus various ill-conceived policies. But even more, until 1989 the global operation of the economic network was hindered by the political division of the world between capitalist and communist powers. The communist world, under the leadership of the Soviet Union, actively resisted the US economic program, which it viewed as a tool of capitalist imperialism, and indeed, the very disparities in wealth created (in part) by the operations of capitalism and market exchanges provided fuel for communist critiques. The capitalist powers, in turn, responded with policies that sometimes sacrificed economic development in favor of

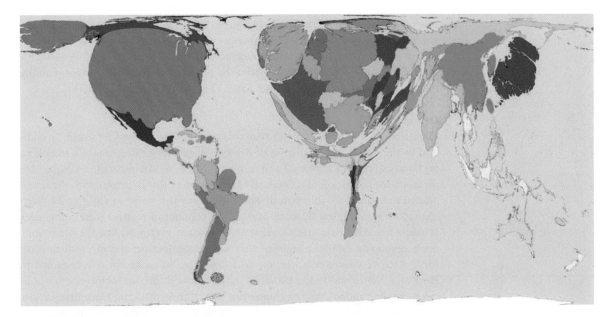

FIGURE 25.1 Size Is Money. The world in 1970, with countries represented in size proportional to their total gross domestic product, or GDP. The dominance of the United States, Japan, and Western Europe is evident.

political security, resisting anything that could be construed as socialist or communist, whether or not such labels were accurate. This political division, though not absolute or totally pervasive, nevertheless colored economic development strongly through the early 1970s and continued as a significant factor through the collapse of communist regimes in most of the world in the early 1990s and the subsequent abandonment of communist policies even in nominally still-communist countries.

Hierarchies Dividing the Network

Thus, the second major feature of the world of 1945 to 1989, after US economic dominance and the recovery of the global economic network, was the bipolar Cold War division of the world's hierarchies. This bipolarity was a very real division, but it was often more dominant as a screen image than it was in practical reality.

Bipolarity

The division was most clear politically and militarily in Europe, where the major powers lined up in two mutually opposed alliances, the North Atlantic Treaty organization (NATO), headed by the United States, and the Warsaw Pact, headed by the Soviet Union. Such treaty organizations were the formal framework within which the ongoing global crisis that had begun in World War I and continued in World War II now became institutionalized.

What the division was based on, however, was somewhat unclear (in part deliberately so). Nominally, the division was between communist countries and capitalist countries, pitting two economic systems against each other. It was also, however, supposed to be a division between communist countries as *undemocratic, dictatorial* states against liberal democracies. This aspect of the division arose from the deliberate conflation of capitalism and democracy on the part of the leading capitalist powers. (Further confusion was fostered by the habit of communist states naming themselves "Democratic Republics," which they clearly weren't.)

Or Not

The reality was far more complex than this stark bipolar view of the world. In addition to the misleading conflation of democracy and capitalism, whose tensions we began to explore in Chapter 23 and to which we will return in detail in Chapter 26, there was the conflation of theoretical Marxist-communist principles with the actual practices of almost all communist states, which we also noted in Chapter 23. Such conflations were evident on both sides. Many communist regimes were communist in name but effectively traditional state-dominated pyramids. On the other side, many nominally capitalist regimes were also undemocratic and often dictatorial, while some very solid democracies, as in both the Scandinavian countries and in Jawaharlal Nehru and Indira Gandhi's India, followed socialist socioeconomic policies more thoroughly than any communist power. Indeed, all the major democracies pursued social-democratic, if not fully socialist, domestic policies to some degree.

The real departure from the bipolar image of the world, however, came not from the complexities of politics and socioeconomic policy within each camp, but from the fact that the two camps were far from comprehensive in including all the world's hierarchies. Many hierarchies, from their own perspective and compared to a bipolar perspective, were either non-aligned or mis-aligned. This was widely recognized enough at the time that this set of hierarchies was often referred to as "the Third World" countries. From the perspective of the "first two" worlds, they were "non-aligned" (a term that was grounded in the expectation of alignment) in the sense that their allegiance had yet to be decided or won. But from their own perspective, non-alignment was usually the result of a conscious choice to opt out of the restrictions imposed by bipolarity. Indira Gandhi's India is the prime example of this, and India consciously attempted to assert a sort of leadership role among non-aligned nations. But their role and the meaning of non-alignment was challenged by China, which, although communist from 1949, was from the early 1950s seriously at odds with the Soviet Union and therefore played the "non-aligned" role with regard to the US-USSR bipolarity from a different angle.

Or Maybe So

The meaning of "the Third World," however, reveals something else significant about the post–World War II world and the evolution of the Industrial world system. The term came to mean not just "politically non-aligned," but "economically underdeveloped." From this perspective, the US-USSR bipolar world offered a choice of paths of economic development—different models of how to industrialize and thus "modernize." These models dominated thinking about economic development, such that even attempts to create a "third way," such as Nehru and his daughter attempted in India, involved borrowing bits from both, more than anything outside those two boxes. We will return to the question of economic development later in this chapter. For now, we may recognize the "sibling rivalry" aspect of US-USSR bipolarity: both sides offered visions of industrially based modernization that acknowledged and accepted (at least theoretically) the socially transformative effects of industrialization. This was the real legacy of World War II and the defeat of the fascist powers for the evolution of the Industrial world system.

Cultural Screens

The notion that the world of 1945 to 1989 was politically and economically bipolar is thus a distorting lens, a dominant screen image that usually obscures more than it reveals for the purposes of historical analysis. But we cannot simply dismiss it, for it was a distorting lens at the time, as much as it is for historians looking back on the period now: it affected people's perceptions and actions at the time. In other words, the image of bipolarity was strong enough that it assumed its own reality, and the disjunction between people's perceptions at the time and what "reality" looks like to us now must form part of our historical analysis of the period. The "bipolar" lens only evaporated in the early 1990s, and so it forms part of the historical memory of many people alive today. They remember the notion of bipolarity, and their memories of the period are still filtered through the lens. This complicates the historian's problem (see also the Issues in Doing World History box below).

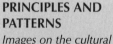

PRINCIPLES AND PATTERNS
Images on the cultural screen have as much "reality" in shaping people's actions as material conditions do.

FIGURE 25.2 Underdevelopment. Slum area in Nairobi, Kenya. The poor in such areas not only lack resources, they often lack legal title to the property they occupy.

Crisis Part III: The Cold War

Even if the bipolarity of the entire world was simply a dominant and influential screen image that did not match perfectly with reality in all places, the Cold War itself was certainly real, and its importance was magnified by the image of bipolarity. We now turn to an analysis of this sibling rivalry over the evolving shape and meaning of the Industrial world system.

Causes

Rather than viewing the origins of the Cold War as a structural problem involving competition over the world system, one can see it as a diplomatic failure to turn the victory in World War II into a peaceful framework for the evolution of that world system. In this view, the central question asks who was to blame for the rapid transition of World War II into a Cold War, and answering this question has been a matter of a long and contentious debate among historians. In fact, the history of Cold War historiography mirrors the history of the Cold War itself, because much of the history was written while the conflict was still in progress, raising problems explored in the Issues in Doing World History Box.

Histories of the Cold War through the early 1970s stressed and reinforced the ideological divisions between the two sides. This meant that US historians placed the blame squarely on Soviet aggression as part of a master plan for worldwide communist domination, aggression that in turn necessitated an active US defense of the free world. Conversely, official Marxist historians in the Soviet Union, as well as some Western historians (American and European, especially French), placed greater blame on American aggression, which the Marxists argued was carried out not just militarily but economically, through the mechanisms of predatory imperialist capitalism. This line of interpretation drew a sharp distinction between capitalism and democracy and emphasized US support for the former, often at the expense of the latter. In this view, the US atomic bombing of Nagasaki did not so much reinforce the message to the Japanese sent by Hiroshima as it warned the Soviet Union of new US capabilities.

This sort of analysis led, especially from the mid-1970s through the end of the 1980s, to a school of analysis that de-emphasized ideology and instead emphasized power politics, casting both the United States and the Soviet Union as large, neo-imperial powers operating largely in terms of "rational," state-centered self-interest. This proved especially helpful in interpreting many of the civil wars and conflicts where minor powers acted as proxies for the two major powers. On the other hand, it probably downplayed ideology at the highest level too much, because ideology of a bipolar struggle remained a powerful screen image, as noted earlier.

One aspect of this less ideological analysis that has retained value connected the domestic political conflicts and competing agendas within each great power to their foreign policy stances. This sort of analysis pointed to the US rearmament that began in 1947, after a year of largely disbanding the forces that fought World War II, as motivated not so much by a real Soviet threat as by fear of a return to Depression. The Soviet threat became a convenient pretext for new investment in the military to keep the economy going, and it was accompanied by a Red Scare atmosphere in which dissent could be stifled more effectively. President Eisenhower's farewell address in 1961 fueled such interpretations by warning of the danger of an overly influential military-industrial complex.

Capitalism versus Communism

Though the reality was more complex, the image of a bipolar struggle between capitalism and communism, between the United States and the Soviet Union, dominated cultural screens in the 1950s and into the 1960s. Top left: An advertisement that appeared in *Better Homes and Gardens* seeking donations for Radio Free Europe (Advertising Archive/Everett Collection). Top right: A Soviet poster depicting "The Road of Talent," first in capitalist countries, second in socialist countries. Bottom left: Another Soviet poster proclaims that basic goods are only for the rich in capitalist countries, but are for everyone in socialist countries. Bottom right: Comic books pitched in: "Captain America . . . Commie Smasher" makes the world safe from communist traitors.

Since the Cold War ended, the ideological passion has dissipated to some extent, and multiple strands of the above analyses have been integrated, enriched by the opening of previously unavailable Soviet archives and the declassifying of more US material. Blame for the Cold War can probably be assessed on both sides, and it is clear that neither side understood the other fully.

The mutual mistrust and at least partial mutual misunderstanding that initiated the Cold War began almost before World War II was over. In 1946, George Kennan's "Long Telegram," sent back to the United States from Moscow in February, analyzed the Soviet Union in terms of its uncompromising plans to spread communism everywhere. In November, a corresponding "Novikov Telegram" to the Soviet Union from Washington, DC, portrayed the United States as driven by militaristic capitalism to foment a new war and seal its own world domination. Both telegrams contained elements of truth and exaggeration. President Truman the next year declared the Truman Doctrine of containing communist expansion, as well as the Marshall Plan. When Marshall Plan funding began the reindustrialization of the western-occupied zones of Germany in 1947, including their sectors of Berlin, the Soviets responded by blockading western-held Berlin in early 1948, leading to the Berlin Airlift. That same year the Soviet-led coup that overthrew the democratic government of Czechoslovakia, which was in Soviet-controlled Eastern

FIGURE 25.3 Chocolate Bombers. Plane coming in as part of the Berlin Airlift, one of the first crisis points in the Cold War. West Berliners referred to the planes as "chocolate bombers" for the sweet supplies they carried.

ISSUES IN DOING WORLD HISTORY

The Problem of Contemporary History

The historiography of the Cold War is a perfect example of the problem of doing contemporary history, which we have now entered with this chapter and which will only become more pressing in the next three chapters that form the last section of this book.

History, as we explained very early on in this book, is a way of understanding who we are and how our world got to be the way it is. When we do more distant history, this goal often sits in uncomfortable tension with the goal of understanding past societies on their own terms, without reference to contemporary issues. When we do contemporary history, that kind of tension dissolves: the past is near enough and similar enough to the present that the lines of influence are direct. But in losing this tension, one necessarily acquires a different one.

When we do distant history, understanding how our world got to be the way it is can be understood in a very broad, generalized way. Investigating how the origins of trade among hunting and gathering tribes grew and developed might, for example, tell us something (or at least will be interesting) because we live in a highly and globally networked world. But in doing contemporary history, the way our world is now takes on a much more precise and contested meaning. In

effect, the "endpoint," the now, is constantly moving, and thus historical analyses move with it. When there seems to be relative stability and continuity, as it seemed for most of the Cold War, histories emphasize the factors creating and reinforcing continuity, so that if the continuity is a tense or contested one, as the Cold War was due to ideology and the nuclear shadow, the "lesson" drawn from such histories is likely to be one of why a tense stalemate will continue or how it will end in war.

The sudden, total, and largely peaceful collapse of Soviet communism across the Soviet Union and Eastern Europe starting in 1989 caught everyone by surprise—not just historians, but intelligence analysts, futurologists, political scientists, and the general public. We will leave aside the question of whether the sudden collapse of the Cold War enemy necessitated (or made space for) the creation of a new threat with which to replace it, at least for some political factions. The sudden collapse in any case suddenly made all previous Cold War histories obsolete. This is the problem of contemporary history: we're at the constantly moving endpoint, and so we've got no perspective. We almost certainly don't know "how it turned out" yet.

Europe, cemented the hard lines of the Cold War. But meanwhile, developments in Asia were about to expand and complicate Cold War geopolitics.

Asian Complications

Conflicts and developments in Asia complicated the politics of US-USSR bipolarity from early in the Cold War. China was the key player.

The Chinese Revolution

Chiang Kai-shek's nationalists had resumed fighting Mao Zedong's communists immediately after the Japanese surrender and withdrawal. The war had allowed Mao to build up his forces, so the struggle was evenly matched through much of 1947. But communist victories in Manchuria and northern China secured a strong base for Red Army forces,

FIGURE 25.4 Corrupt Leadership. Chiang Kai-Shek, leader of the Nationalist side in the Chinese Civil War, inspecting troops in 1945. The troops wore straw shoes while generals got rich on American aid.

and the nationalist situation rapidly deteriorated as a result of bad generalship, corruption, and increasing defections. In 1949, Chiang's forces withdrew to Taiwan, where, protected by US naval forces, they established a nationalist dictatorship. Mainland China became the People's Republic of China under the rule of Mao and the Communist Party.

This development was a major gain for world communism and a huge setback for containment. US politicians asked each other, accusingly, "Who lost China?," and the focus of Cold War tensions shifted to the Pacific rim. The communist triumph in China hastened the end of the US policy of reforming and democratizing occupied Japan in favor of reindustrialization and rehabilitation of much of Japan's pre-war political and economic leadership to provide a secure ally in the region. In 1950, the region's tensions broke out into the Cold War's first hot conflict.

The Korean War

The Korean Peninsula had been partitioned between the United States and the Soviet Union along the 49th parallel after World War II, and autocratic dictatorships had emerged in both halves by 1948, the northern state communist and supplied by the Soviet Union, the southern supported by the United States. Neither side was happy with the partition, and in 1950 North Korea launched a surprise attack on South Korea. South Korean units retreated in disarray, but they defended just effectively enough to allow US troops to arrive from Japan, spearheading a UN-sanctioned intervention. (The USSR, by boycotting the Security Council, could not veto the resolution authorizing UN involvement.) Establishing a defensive perimeter around Pusan, US forces under Douglas MacArthur then broke out and drove the North Koreans all the way to and beyond the 49th parallel, with an amphibious landing behind North Korean lines playing a key role. But the pursuit carried so far into North Korea that China then intervened. (See Figure 25.5.)

The element of surprise, the ability of lightly armed Chinese infantry to move quickly through rough terrain without mechanized transport, and the scattered positions of US forces let the Chinese army in turn drive US forces back in a rout. MacArthur's response was to call for a widening of the war. He wanted to blockade the Chinese coast, to receive permission to pursue Chinese aircraft into Manchurian air space, to bring nationalist Chinese troops into the war either in Korea or in a direct assault on China itself, and ultimately to use atomic weapons against China. Truman refused, as the US Joint Chiefs of Staff thought expansion would lead to Soviet intervention and a nuclear World War III. When MacArthur made his disagreement with the decision public, Truman dismissed him from command. New leadership helped stabilize the situation on the ground, and by late 1951 the war had become stalemated near the original border along trench lines that were reminiscent of World War I.

The Korean War introduced some of the new dynamics of war under the threat of atomic and nuclear weaponry. The US policy of containment implied wars with limited aims that might not be won outright without risking far too great a cost. But as a US threat to deploy atomic bombs had seemed to play a part in finally bringing about a truce in 1953, the war also brought such weapons further into the calculations of Cold War rivalry, helping spur an arms race (see discussion later in this chapter). At the same time, North Korean aggression reinforced the perception that containment was necessary, and debate within the democracies shifted from whether containment was the right goal to how containment should be implemented. This in turn led to peacetime conscription, permanently higher force levels, and significant rises in military expenditures.

Thus, the Korean War played a key role in moving the Cold War from its early phase of mutual ad hoc crisis management reactions to a subsequent phase of more institutionalized forms of conflict. Institutional conflict took the various forms of military spending, economic investments, and manpower allocation, and all of these were informed by a permanent crisis mentality on both sides, which in effect institutionalized the bipolar view of the world discussed earlier. The fact that the Korean War has not yet formally ended—the fighting ceased with a truce that has remained in place since, but not with a formal peace treaty—thus symbolizes the elevation of the Cold War during the Korean conflict to the status of a real war that was expected to be, if not permanent, at least very long lasting.

China Gets Complicated

Management of the Korean conflict on the communist side, however, exposed and exacerbated tensions between the Soviet Union and Communist China that rapidly developed into a full-scale rift, as Mao had no intention of playing the role of obedient servant to Soviet grand strategy. Some of this was expressed in terms of official doctrinal disputes that resembled the sorts of doctrinal religious disputes of Agrarian Era hierarchies (not coincidentally, given the traditional-looking power structure of each country), akin to, for example, the 1054 schism between Orthodox and Catholic Christianity. These disputes focused in particular on the role of the peasants in communist society. In "orthodox" Marxist-Leninist theory, the peasantry were viewed as backward-looking reactionaries (Marx's *Communist Manifesto* refers to "the idiocy of rural life"), but Mao, given the structure of Chinese society and its lack of a real industrial bourgeoisie, necessarily had to assign a revolutionary role to the peasantry in his theoretical writings, no matter how illusory that role turned out to be in practice.

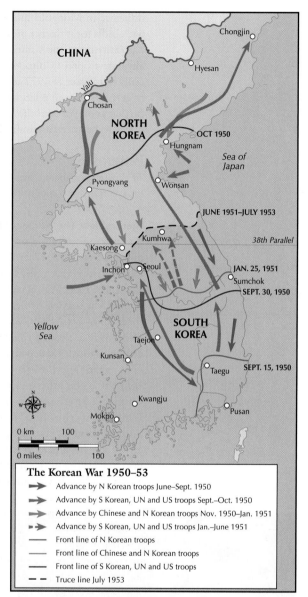

FIGURE 25.5 **The Korean War.**

The result of this split was that, although the Soviet Union and China continued to cooperate on some things and would make a show of ideological unity against the capitalist world when necessary, they pursued different agendas. Their common border in the north of China became a militarily tense one, and they competed for influence in Mongolia and elsewhere. China came to identify itself as a competitor with India for influence among "Third World" nations. Though the distorting lens of bipolarity made the United States slow to recognize and exploit this schism, eventually it developed a China policy separate from its USSR diplomacy. This became especially significant in 1972 under US president Richard Nixon, when the United States largely normalized relations with Communist China (which, however, introduced a further complication: the United States now had to carefully shape its "Two China" policy to balance Communist China and Nationalist Taiwan).

Patterns

The institutionalization of the Cold War that the Korean conflict stimulated developed into patterns of competition and periodic crisis that we can examine thematically.

Hierarchies: The Nuclear Shadow

The most important characteristic of the Cold War was that it generated the threat of nuclear warfare that could have obliterated Industrial human societies, if not humans altogether. This threat developed as the result of an arms race that was central to the Cold War. The United States saw atomic weapons as part of their ability to deter the massive Soviet army from invading western Europe, but their monopoly lasted only until 1949, when the Soviets successfully completed their own atomic weapons test, though this was at a very high cost to the devastated post-war Soviet economy. Both sides converted from atomic (fission) weapons to nuclear (fusion) ones in the early 1950s and developed larger and larger stockpiles of such weapons, each citing the other's capabilities as necessitating a response. Britain, France, and China added atomic capabilities in 1952, 1960, and 1964, with Indira Gandhi's India joining the "club" ten years after China. Nuclear proliferation was then confined to these six powers until after the end of the Cold War, at least officially.

The arms race involved not just the bombs themselves, but their means of delivery. In fact, the most important turning point in the arms race was not the shift to nuclear technology, but the development of intercontinental ballistic missiles, spurred on by the Soviet Union's successful launch of *Sputnik,* the first artificial satellite, into orbit in 1957. Rocketry could deliver warheads far faster than strategic bombers such as the United States' B-52s, deployed in 1955, and rockets could not be shot down. Suddenly, the entire United States was vulnerable to Soviet missile strikes, and the arms race entered outer space. Pressure to deploy launch systems that were invulnerable to a first strike, such as missile silos, then led to the development of submarine-based missiles, first deployed by the United States in 1960, two years after their first successful ICBM test. Specially built nuclear-powered subs armed with missiles then became a mainstay of both sides' deterrent forces. The potential of missile attacks led to the Cuban Missile Crisis of 1962, when both sides came right to the edge of launching a nuclear exchange before the Soviets, in President Kennedy's words,

FIGURE 25.6 Détente. Chinese premier Chou En Lai and US president Richard Nixon during the latter's trip to China in 1972, when relations between the two countries were normalized.

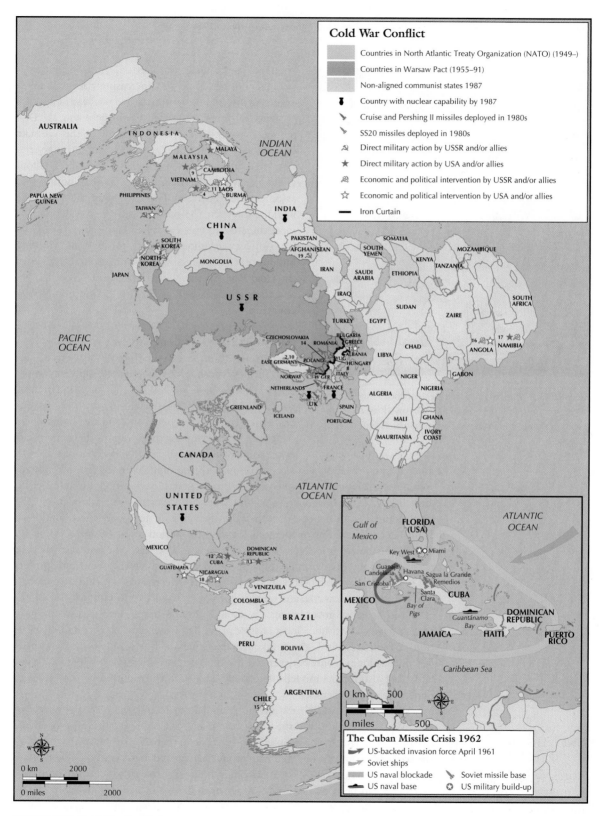

Cold War Conflict

Countries in North Atlantic Treaty Organization (NATO) (1949–)

Countries in Warsaw Pact (1955–91)

Non-aligned communist states 1987

Country with nuclear capability by 1987

Cruise and Pershing II missiles deployed in 1980s

SS20 missiles deployed in 1980s

Direct military action by USSR and/or allies

Direct military action by USA and/or allies

Economic and political intervention by USSR and/or allies

Economic and political intervention by USA and/or allies

Iron Curtain

AUSTRALIA

INDONESIA

MALAYSIA

MALAYA 3

CAMBODIA

VIETNAM 9

PAPUA NEW GUINEA

PHILIPPINES

LAOS 11

BURMA 4

TAIWAN 6

INDIAN OCEAN

INDIA

CHINA

SOUTH KOREA 5

NORTH KOREA

JAPAN

MONGOLIA

PAKISTAN

AFGHANISTAN 19

IRAN

SOMALIA

SOUTH YEMEN

KENYA

MOZAMBIQUE

TANZANIA

SAUDI ARABIA

ETHIOPIA

USSR

IRAQ

TURKEY

EGYPT

SUDAN

ZAIRE

SOUTH AFRICA

PACIFIC OCEAN

CZECHOSLOVAKIA 14

ROMANIA

BULGARIA

GREECE

ALBANIA

YUG

HUNGARY 8

ANGOLA 16

NAMIBIA 17

CHAD

LIBYA

GABON

2,10

EAST GERMANY

POLAND

NORWAY

W GER

ITALY

NIGER

NIGERIA

NETHERLANDS

FRANCE

ALGERIA

UK

SPAIN

GREENLAND

ICELAND

PORTUGAL

MALI

GHANA

MAURITANIA

IVORY COAST

CANADA

ATLANTIC OCEAN

UNITED STATES

MEXICO

DOMINICAN REPUBLIC

12 CUBA

13

GUATEMALA 7

NICARAGUA 18

VENEZUELA

COLOMBIA

BRAZIL

PERU

BOLIVIA

CHILE 15

ARGENTINA

Inset map:

Gulf of Mexico

FLORIDA (USA)

ATLANTIC OCEAN

Key West

Miami

Guanajay

Candelaria

Havana

Sagua la Grande

Remedios

San Cristobal

MEXICO

Santa Clara

CUBA

Bay of Pigs

DOMINICAN REPUBLIC

Guantánamo Bay

JAMAICA

HAITI

PUERTO RICO

Caribbean Sea

0 km 500

0 miles 500

The Cuban Missile Crisis 1962

US-backed invasion force April 1961

Soviet ships

US naval blockade

US naval base

Soviet missile base

US military build-up

0 km 2000

0 miles 2000

FIGURE 25.7 Cold War Conflicts.

FIGURE 25.8 Mutually Assured Destruction. Launch of an intercontinental ballistic missile (ICBM). Anywhere on earth was now vulnerable to an attack against which there was no defense.

"blinked" and disaster was averted. The continued development of better missiles, increasingly accurate guidance systems, and more destructive warheads created a "balance of terror" described by the acronym MAD—mutually assured destruction—that was the ultimate expression of institutionalized crisis. An entire generation grew up aware of the location of nuclear fallout shelters, having practiced drills on what position to assume under their school desks to await the end of the world. Moreover, the nuclear arms race was only the most threatening warhead on an entire arsenal of Cold War military technologies and conventional military buildups that consumed vast resources on both sides of the Cold War, for the United States, the Soviet Union, and their allies, as well as for the leading non-bipolar countries.

Networks: Economic Competition

The resources poured into the Cold War arms race highlight the networked, economic side of Cold War competition. This competition had in effect been initiated by the United States' Marshall Plan, in which the Soviets prohibited the eastern European countries in its sphere of influence from taking part. Thus, the communist conception of industrialization and economic growth was put into a head-to-head competition with the capitalist one. This actually involved two different aspects of economic production. First, it pitted privately owned, capitalist systems of production against state-run industries as ways of producing manufactured goods. Second, it put the dynamics of free-market economics up against central planning as methods for the distribution of goods and services. Of course, this description draws a sharper distinction between the two systems than really existed, especially on the capitalist side, since many of the democratic powers ran significant parts of their economies on a state-directed basis, including nationalized industries such as coal and transport in countries such as Britain, which periodically had socialist governments. It should also be noted that massive military procurements constitute a form of state planning of economic activity and distribution of resources. Still, the fundamental distinction holds and formed the basis for competition not only between the major powers on either side of Cold War bipolarity, but also for the models of economic development exported by both sides to underdeveloped societies.

While nuclear war thankfully never broke out to test the hierarchy aspect of Cold War competition, and the "winners," if any, of Cold War cultural competition (see discussion later in this chapter) can be debated, there is no doubt which side won the economic competition. State-run production proved inefficient; even more, state planning could not come close to accomplishing what the global network of market exchanges had been refined to do over four millennia of increasingly global trade.

PRINCIPLES AND PATTERNS

Screen images matter, but so does material reality.

The capitalist and market economies also started with a huge initial advantage, constituting as they did almost all the major industrialized countries of the nineteenth century, while the communist world consisted of barely industrialized economies such as the Soviet Union's and a lot of not-even-industrializing economies such as China's. The communist powers were not only unable to close the gap, they fell farther and farther behind. Eventually, it was, simply, the ability of the capitalist, market economies to out-produce the communist ones that won the Cold War. The communist political systems of the Soviet Union and Eastern Europe collapsed under their failure to provide butter with their guns as the non-communist economies could do. "Communism" survived the Cold War, in name but not in substance, only in Castro's isolated Cuba and in China, which converted its economy to the capitalist, market-driven model while keeping the Communist Party in power. We shall return to this development in Chapter 27.

Cultural Competition and Costs

If the free market, capitalist economies won the Cold War, both sides arguably lost the cultural competition the war fostered. In what was, again, really a sibling rivalry between alternate but related versions of an industrially modern vision of the global system, each side put forth a huge cultural effort to demonize the other. This was because both sides conceived of the struggle as a long-term variant on total war, a view strongest in the 1950s and fostered by the growing threat of nuclear calamity as the arms race proceeded. To maintain support among their populations for the high expenses of constant military buildups and the human costs of the periodic hot wars, the United States and the Soviet Union acted much as the major powers of World War I, also a war of sibling rivals, had done (but as the United States and Britain had largely avoided doing in World War II). The Cold War thus became a classic subcultural conflict, in which the "soul" of the global system was purportedly at stake and compromise positions became culturally ruled out.

This cosmic bipolarity had effects on global diplomacy that complicated the process of decolonization and inflamed other regional struggles for decades. Cosmic-level bipolarity, however, also could not help but have damaging effects for the domestic politics of both sides. A war with supposed cosmic significance against an enemy wielding weapons that could destroy civilization seemed to require unquestioning obedience from the societies involved to their respective states, for example. In the Soviet Union, this only reinforced and entrenched the rigid authoritarianism (or "dictatorship of the proletariat") that the Communist Party had imposed from the moment it had gained power, against the grain of Marxism's humanist roots. But in the United States, Red Scares, McCarthyism, and other movements to suppress dissent, uncover "traitors," undermine civil liberties, and impose ideological conformity in the name of a vague but all-encompassing notion of national security ran against the very ideals upon which the country was founded and for which it supposedly was fighting. Such domestic damage was highlighted by US support for many brutal right-wing dictatorships simply on the basis of their claims to be anti-communist. In short, both sides maintained a permanent wartime economy, promoted the idea of permanent enemies, and used the presence of that enemy to restrict the range of domestic political expression. There were differences

FIGURE 25.9 McCarthyism. Senator Joseph McCarthy's witch hunts epitomized the Cold War–inspired repression of dissent; McCarthy is here satirized as Simple J. Malarkey by cartoonist Walt Kelly in his comic strip "Pogo." (The term "McCarthyism" was invented by another cartoonist, Herblock.)

of degree, to be sure. But here, then, was the sad irony: by engaging in Cold War with each other, both sides became more like the fascists they had jointly defeated in World War II.

The Cold War had other cultural effects, as well. The United States and the Soviet Union engaged in a paramilitary Space Race, and in symbolic wars for Olympic medals in a hyper-nationalized sports environment. But the renewal of the militarized culture of the nineteenth century was the most damaging aspect of the Cold War: its culture of war has carried over decades past the end of the Cold War, as we will see further in Chapter 27.

Détente, Dénouement

The tension of the Cold War eased in the mid-1970s when US president Nixon linked the winding down of the Vietnam War (discussed later in this chapter) to détente, first with China, then with the Soviet Union. Treaties limited nuclear weapons. Tension rose again in the early 1980s, with the Carter-Reagan military buildup, Reagan's rhetoric about the "Evil Empire" (a re-emphasis on subcultural demonization), and the Soviet war in Afghanistan. But just when all this made the institutionalization of Cold War bipolarity seem ever more intractable, the internal economic weakness of the Soviet position became clearly visible. From 1985, the reforming

Soviet leader Mikhail Gorbachev's attempts to open up the economy led to demands for political reform, and in 1989 communist regimes across eastern Europe collapsed without much of a struggle. The Soviet Union itself broke apart and abandoned communism in 1991, and the Cold War was suddenly and unexpectedly over.

The Cold War did not end the struggle for the shape and meaning of the Industrial world system. It removed communism as an ideological player in that struggle. That left two major ideological forces standing: capitalism and democracy. Just as the end of World War II exposed the great divide between the Allies who had fought fascism together, the end of the Cold War began to expose the contradictions between these somewhat uncomfortable allies in the fight against communism. And the collapse of communism as the major anti-capitalist ideology opened space on the political stage for the re-emergence of various forms of neo-fascist anti-modernism, a theme we will return to in Chapter 27.

Transformations: Decolonization and Beyond

If the Cold War represented the institutionalization of the struggle for the shape of the Industrial world system among the great Industrial powers and their associated ideologies, the process of decolonization, the breakup of the European empires built up in the late nineteenth century into newly independent countries, transformed that struggle. Though complicated at times by the imposition of bipolar Cold War politics, decolonization was more about the maturing of the Industrial world system and the end of an anomalous century of European hegemony created by the specific starting point and uneven spread of industrialization. Thus, a number of causes, both deep and more immediate, came together to bring the age of European imperialism to an end almost as rapidly as it had begun not quite 100 years earlier. (See Figure 25.10.)

> **PRINCIPLES AND PATTERNS**
>
> *The century from 1850 to 1950 was the anomaly in the last 22 centuries of history. Seeing this is one benefit of doing world history.*

Causes

The European imperial grip would have begun loosening simply because of the reversal of the demographic pattern of the nineteenth century. From 1900 (or perhaps 1914) on, the number of Europeans in the world was in relative decline, from their high of one-third of the globe's population around 1900 back toward what had been their historical share of about one-fifth. This meant that there were fewer Europeans to rule colonies and that the colonies were capable of deploying greater resources on their own behalf than when Europeans had first colonized them. Compounding this basic demographic trend, the changes in network flows that imperialism brought to colonies, especially European goods (including weaponry and military training for local police and armed forces), knowledge, and ideologies eroded the advantages Europeans had deployed earlier. It did not take long for a familiar dynamic to emerge: the colonized came to know their masters better than the colonizers understood those they ruled.

Against this background, it is evident that the damage the Industrial imperialist powers did to each other in the World Wars weakened the hold of imperialism even more. This was not just a matter of reduced resources in manpower and productive capacity. Indeed, both surpassed their pre–World War II levels in the major imperialist countries, especially Britain and France, soon after World War II. US investments via the Marshall

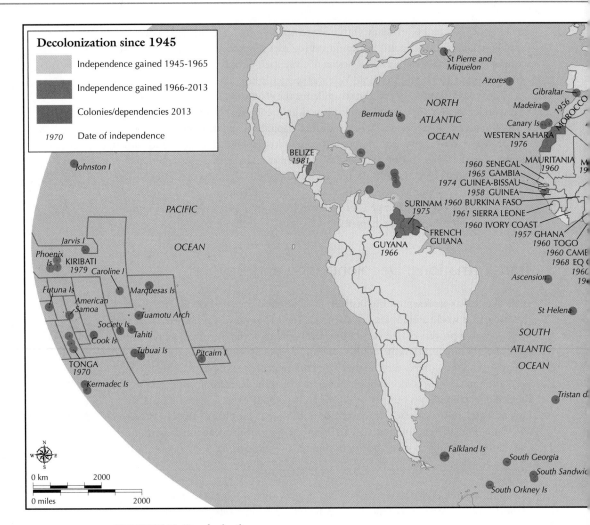

FIGURE 25.10 Decolonization.

Plan assisted the recovery, though resources had to stretch further, given greater resistance in the colonies. The defense of imperial dominance had to compete with Cold War containment commitments for military resources. World War II had also demonstrated again that non-Europeans could fight effectively against Europeans (the Japanese reinforcing the lesson they'd first demonstrated in 1905 against Russia) while the experience of the war reduced the willingness of European societies to make further large sacrifices.

Above all, World War II had made the moral task of defending imperialism complicated. It had been a fight against fascism and aggression, and for democracy and freedom. Defending imperial rule did not fit comfortably with either ideal, and indeed the United States pushed for decolonization after the war, at least until some independence movements became associated with Marxism and thus Cold War bipolarity. The contradictions between defending freedom against fascism but denying it to colonies was visible both to colonial societies and to the societies of the imperial powers,

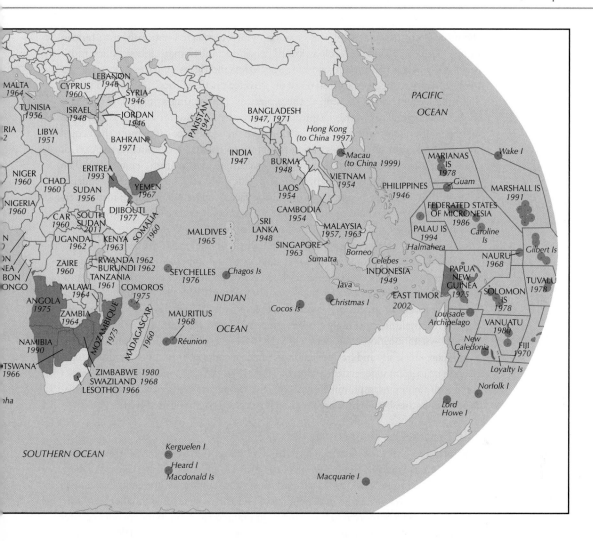

motivating protests in both. The imperial powers justified their rule by increasingly emphasizing it as "training" their colonies for independence, a variation on the older "white man's burden" rationale for seizing empires. This position acknowledged the eventual necessity of decolonization but fell back on arguing that the time had not arrived, an argument paralleled in the United States among some opponents to the Civil Rights movement. Colonial independence leaders responded in much the same way civil rights lawyer and eventual Supreme Court justice Thurgood Marshall did to such gradualist arguments: "Seems to me 100 years is pretty damn gradual."

The ideologies of independence movements, on the other hand, drew strength from the war and its aftermath. Three main ideological strands appeared in varying mixtures in almost all independence movements. First, democracy and conceptions of universal human rights were restated forcefully at the end of the war in the charter of the United Nations. Second, the power of nationalism continued and carried with it the principle of national self-determination, which connected nationalism to human rights. The connection was a bit awkward, as democratic human rights applied to individuals, whereas nationalism constructs societies (and rights) in terms of groups, and many colonies turned out to contain many possible "nationalities" (ethnic, linguistic, and tribal groupings), complicating the project of constructing a "national" nationality (see discussion later in this chapter and in Chapter 27). But for as long as there was an imperialist enemy still in control, nationalism proved a force often more than equal to democratic principles in motivating resistance to colonial rule. Finally, the explicit anti-imperialism of communism, as well as its critique of capitalism, which offered an explanation of the poverty of many colonies, made it attractive to many independence leaders. This was even before factoring in the fact that the major imperialist powers were democracies and thus open to charges of hypocrisy, and the fact that the conflation of democracy and capitalism, perhaps useful in a Cold War context, made both concepts vulnerable to communist (or nationalist) critique in colonial arenas.

Finally, the reinvigoration of the economies of the imperialist powers and of the global network itself, especially under the influence of US free trade policy and the promotion of capitalism, began to alter the perceptions of imperial leaders regarding the economic benefits of imperialism. The growth of international capitalism was making open political imperialism increasingly obsolete. Imperial powers recognized that the operations of their own multinational corporations (MNCs) could extract resources from around the world more efficiently and freely than direct imperial control. This helped motivate imperial powers to grant independence without a fight in some cases and then, as in the case of the British Empire most prominently, to rebrand the empire as a commonwealth of independent countries bound by shared trading privileges, as well as shared culture.

The Process of Decolonization

The interaction of these factors led to different patterns. The British, intimately tied to the United States in the image of World War II, and with a long history of both imperial glory and global trade, released most of its empire without a fight between 1947, when India gained its independence, and the early 1960s. Smaller, less connected powers were more reluctant. Belgium granted the Congo independence after much international pressure and the beginnings of armed revolt in 1961. But that same year, Portugal refused to grant Angola independence, and a war began that lasted until Portugal finally gave up control in 1975. For the French, colonial power represented a more glorious past than the immediate history of World War II could offer, and they attempted to hold on to their possessions, but this failed in both Southeast Asia and North Africa. The conflicts that arose in these two parts of the French empire illustrate well some of the difficulties of violent decolonization.

Vietnam: Decolonization Meets the Cold War

The French reoccupied Indochina after World War II ended, much to the dismay of Vietnamese nationalists, who expected to receive independence. The occupation went against the policy of US president Franklin Roosevelt, expressed near the end of World War II, but the transition from the Japanese occupation of Vietnam, delegated by the Allies to Chiang Kai Shek's China, was confused, and French forces wrested control from a provisional government set up by Vietnamese nationalist leader Ho Chi Minh. Despite issuing a declaration of independence modeled on the

United States' 1776 Declaration, the Vietnamese could not get US support in their quest for ending their colonial status. Instead, worried about the Marxist leanings of Ho Chi Minh, the United States backed France, which prompted both the Soviets and the Chinese communists under Mao to back Ho Chi Minh. Marxist ideology came to dominate the resistance. Despite a major effort, the French could not defeat the insurgency, and after a significant defeat in 1954 at the Battle of Dien Bien Phu, rising domestic resistance to the war in France made the war untenable and the French withdrew. Vietnam was now independent, and the story might have ended there as a successful case of decolonization.

Vietnam was partitioned at the end of the French-Indochina war, however, with a communist government in the North and a US-backed government in the South. The partition, as in Korea, suited neither side, and communist insurgents in the South, with backing from the regular forces from the North, began trying to undermine South Vietnamese stability in late 1955. The United States responded, first by sending in military advisors, then gradually sending in combat troops to support the South. The American commitment rose rapidly in the 1960s, reaching a peak of 541,000 troops stationed in Vietnam in January 1969. The major motivation was Cold War containment, with the US government concerned that the fall of South Vietnam would lead, in what was called the "domino theory," to the subsequent fall of other Southeast Asian states.

FIGURE 25.11 Crumbling Empire. A 2009 exhibition at the Museum of Vietnamese Revolution in Hanoi, Vietnam, celebrates the 55th anniversary of the 1954 victory at Dien Bien Phu over the French.

In Vietnam the United States faced the problems of limited war even more starkly than in Korea. US strategists assumed that inflicting high casualties on the North Vietnamese army would break the North Vietnamese will to fight, but they miscalculated both the level of Vietnamese commitment and the coercive powers of the communist state. Since, as in Korea, the United States had no wish to provoke a direct intervention by either China or the Soviets, it could not invade the North directly, nor did strategic bombing cow the enemy. Instead, in what became a war of attrition, the United States also came to face powerful domestic dissent. The South Vietnamese regime proved increasingly corrupt and inept, and the war seemed not only pointless but unending. Furthermore, US attempts to interdict, by secret bombing missions, North Vietnamese supply lines through the borderlands of Laos and Cambodia destabilized both of those countries and in turn led to their takeover by communist insurgencies.

By 1972, however, the security of Thailand, the major US ally in the region, seemed assured, and a communist insurgency in Indonesia was defeated, defusing the "domino" threat. The United States negotiated its way out of the war in 1974, and the following year Saigon, the capital of South Vietnam, fell to Northern forces, ending the war. The complexities of Cold War politics in Vietnam were not over, however. By 1978, pro-Soviet Vietnam was at war with Communist China. In all, Vietnam's wars for independence, complicated by the Cold War, cost the lives of between one and three million Vietnamese people, in addition to hundreds of thousands of Cambodians and Laotians and almost 60,000 US servicemen and women.

Algeria: The Complexities of Decolonization

Algeria was one of France's oldest colonies, and it was even governed not as a colony but as a department of France. French settlers had moved to Algeria, and by the early 1950s this population of *colons* numbered more than a million. They dominated the politics and society of Algeria, discriminating against the native population of more than 8.5 million Muslims, with the backing of the government in France.

In 1954, a revolt began on a small scale, mostly restricted to terror bombings, under the direction of the Front de Libération Nationale (FLN). But with the loss of Indochina fresh in the minds of French policy makers, the insurrection drew a disproportionate response. France sent 65,000 reservists to suppress the rebels. Savage search-and-destroy operations launched against suspected FLN strongholds killed as many loyalist Muslims as rebels, because the French could not easily tell the groups apart. Once again, the asymmetry of colonial knowledge became an important factor in a decolonization struggle. The rebellion spread and increased in the scale of its activity. France responded by sending more troops—up to 390,000 in 1956—now including conscripts, a highly unpopular move in domestic French politics. Tactics on both sides became more brutal and caused more civilian casualties. By this time, relations between the *colons* and the native population had

FIGURE 25.12 More Crumbling Empire. French soldiers facing FLN guerillas in Algerian urban warfare.

become hostile as well, and French troops faced the dual task of chasing guerrillas and trying to protect *colon* settlements.

Despite never losing a battle to the rebels, the French army could not eliminate the FLN, and the heavy attritional toll of the war alienated the French electorate. Charles de Gaulle, elected president in 1958, began working toward a political solution, which put him at odds with both the *colons* and the French military leadership in Algeria, who were against any negotiations with the FLN. De Gaulle suppressed attempts to seize power in Algeria by both the *colons* and part of the army in 1960 and 1961, but the war had now become a three-cornered one between Gaullists, *colons,* and Muslims, leading to much more slaughter before a final independence agreement was finalized in 1962.

Post-Colonial Transitions

Violence sometimes accompanied even peaceful transitions to independence. Britain partitioned its Indian empire into the separate countries of India and Pakistan just before granting them independence in 1947, leaving several principalities to decide for themselves which part they would join. Muslims and Hindus then fought each other in widespread rioting, with vast numbers of refugees fleeing in both directions, Muslims to Pakistan and Hindus to India. The countries actually went to war briefly the same year over the border in Kashmir, and would return to fight each other several more times, including the 1971 war under Indira Gandhi's leadership.

Hierarchy Building

This illustrated that, despite the claims of the imperial powers to have been "training" their colonies for independence, many colonies were left woefully unprepared to create effective governments, working civil societies, or coherent cultural identities when their former imperial rulers left. Furthermore, factionalism, Cold War complications, and the often violent conditions under which independence was achieved contributed to the difficulties in establishing successful hierarchies with viable network connections and coherently framed cultural screens. Nor could establishing these elements of a working modern country be approached one by one, for as our model shows, all three parts are interconnected and affect each other.

Creating effective mechanisms of governance—never mind just or democratic ones—was the most obvious problem many former colonies faced. Angola, for example, having fought the Portuguese from 1961 to 1975 for independence, then witnessed a brutal civil war from 1975 to 2002 between the two leading organizations that had fought for independence. Each was based in different ethnic groups within the borders of the country—the tendency of colonially drawn borders to include different ethnic groups in one colony and to divide some ethnic groups between different colonies proved, especially in Africa, to be a major roadblock on the road to stability. Though both started out professing mildly socialist policies, after independence one identified itself as Marxist and received support from the Soviet Union, the other as "anti-communist" and received support from the US. A third independence organization sat out the civil war. Having received support from Communist China during the fight for independence, this group then received significant US support after independence. A fourth organization of militant separatists, representing yet another

FIGURE 25.13 Angola

FRAMING   The Modern Global Network: Environment and Economy since 1970

FRAMING MAPS. Maps shape how we see the world. This "Framing the Chapter" feature in the first 25 chapters of *Frameworks* has presented world maps using a fairly standard projection that emphasizes geographic relationships. In the last three chapters, the maps stretch our imagination to see the world in different ways. A composite view of the earth at night, taken from satellite imagery and transformed to reflect population levels, frames the environmental and cultural themes of Chapters 26 and 28. A map that shows land mass proportional to military expenditures provides a visual exclamation mark to the hierarchy-based themes of Chapter 27. As you can see, maps have perspectives in the same way that written histories do.

Exxon Valdez oil spill

Amazon Deforestation

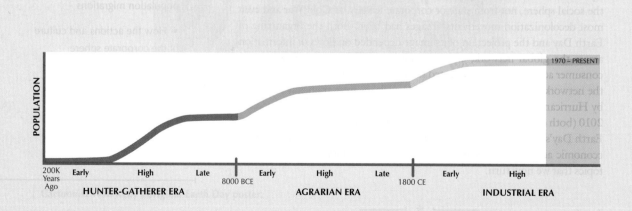

POPULATION

200K Years Ago	Early	High	Late		Early	High	Late		Early	High
				8000 BCE				1800 CE		
	HUNTER-GATHERER ERA				AGRARIAN ERA				INDUSTRIAL ERA	

1970 – PRESENT

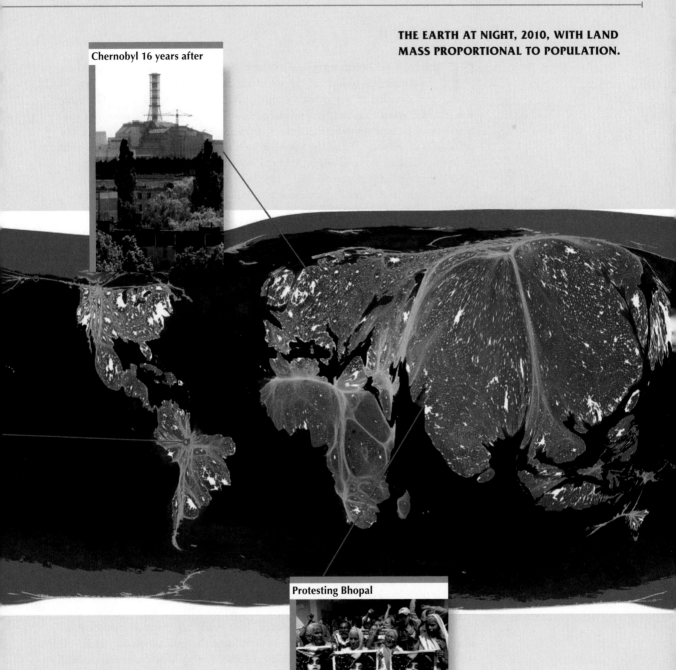

Chernobyl 16 years after

THE EARTH AT NIGHT, 2010, WITH LAND MASS PROPORTIONAL TO POPULATION.

Protesting Bhopal

Environment

This book's examination of human history began with the natural world and the environmental context of the structures and systems of human history. Its periodization of world history into three broad eras, the **Hunter-Gatherer Era**, the **Agrarian Era**, and the **Industrial Era**, is grounded in the changing relationships of human communities to their environment at the most basic level: the economics of subsistence and the resulting total human population of the earth. In addition, the sheer number of people in the world in the Industrial Era also matters, especially given industrial technology's capability to significantly multiply the impact of human numbers. What do these graphs (see Figure 26.1) mean in the present?

More People

We will return later in this chapter to the various impacts that more than 6 billion people (which will rise to around 10 billion by mid-century) have on the global environment. For the moment, looking at the arithmetic graph from the perspective of our model, we can remember that a basic trend of human history has been that rising population has in the long term consistently produced stronger network connections among different human communities, more extensive and inclusive hierarchy organization of those communities, and greater capacities for collective cultural memory and inventiveness. The current global network, which includes organizations such as the European Union at the regional level and the UN and the World Bank at the global level, and global Internet culture certainly conform to that rule.

Current demographics even supplies a mechanism for the increased pace of change in the Industrial Era. The year 2008 was the first in which more than half of the world's population lived in urban environments. By adding density to numbers, cities have historically been the engines of historical change. Cities are where networks and markets work most efficiently, where mass political organization is easiest, and where cultural creativity most thrives. (Cities can sustain mass transit systems, cleaner than suburban or rural private cars, and the world's urban poor are better off than the rural poor.) The trend toward greater urbanization is continuing as total population keeps rising.

The first graph in Figure 26.1 reminds us explicitly, however, that population from a different perspective is leveling off: indeed, it already has in many rich countries. This trend has a number of consequences and poses its own challenges, especially for individual countries. For starters, with richer populations producing fewer children and with global life expectancies at an all-time high and rising, the widely predicted phenomenon of "graying societies" has already begun in some places. Populations with proportionally large numbers of (older) retired people in relation to (younger) working people face issues about the affordability of pensions and medical care. Of course, this issue is in part created by the division of the global population into politically separate states and cultures—or, more accurately, by the cultural lens created by nationalism—as there is currently no shortage of young workers globally. The immigration of labor to rich economic areas has kept some countries' retirement systems (including the United States') solvent, whereas countries such as Japan with very restrictive immigration policies are facing the "graying" problem much sooner.

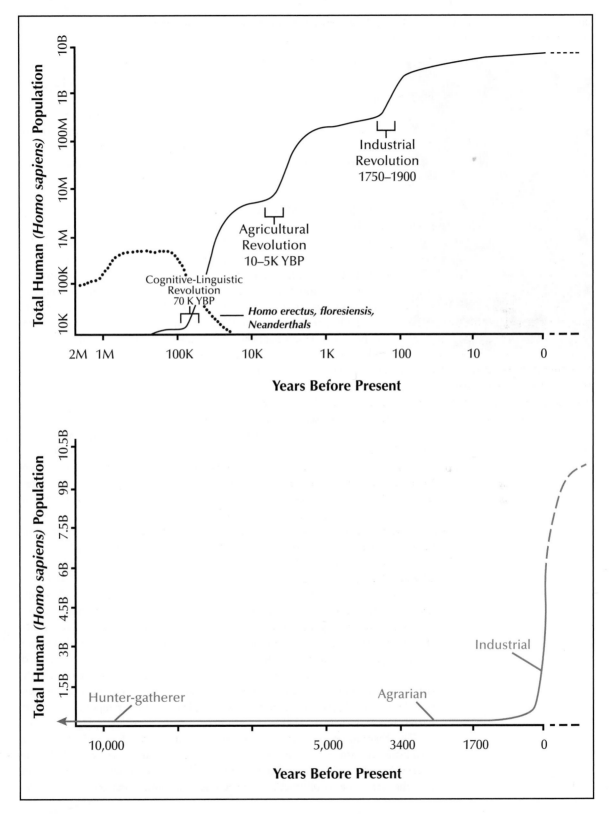

FIGURE 26.1 Demographic History.

FIGURE 26.2 An Urban World. The Forbidden City in Beijing during a long holiday week in May 2007. Cities cram crowding and creativity together.

The even harder issue to imagine is how capitalist economics, which is predicated on growth, will operate under conditions of static global population. Rising population stimulates economic growth under Industrial capitalist conditions, whereas it sometimes outran the capacity of Agrarian economies to support rising numbers, leading to famines and other population catastrophes. It may well be that population growth is not strictly necessary for economic growth, but some adjustments of expectations may be necessary.

The Next Revolution?

This issue of growth combined with the shape of the second graph in Figure 26.1 inevitably poses an additional question: What if there's another revolution that will allow human population to increase happily once again? (Perhaps the "happily" part is most contingent.) The historian's answer (or at least this historian's answer) is that maybe there will be one (though its shape is as opaque to us now as advanced Industrial conditions were for any Agrarian Era person), but that this isn't a question of historical interpretation because it hasn't happened yet, and so I don't have to answer it. The prudent answer is that we can't count on one, and so we must plan for what we can at least reasonably foresee.

Issues and Constraints

What we can see and foresee is a world of between 6 billion and 10 to 12 billion people over the next century, accompanied by continual technological change that will be, from the perspective of our log graph, non-revolutionary. (We will disregard constant claims by advertisers that the latest invention changes the world, and note that none of the claims for the revolutionary power of the Internet, for example, has a massive demographic component.) Humans have always altered their environment in intentional and unintentional ways. This number of people with Industrial technology, as powerful as it is, has made those alterations globally significant.

Climate Change

The most prominent and dangerous of these alterations has been to the global climate itself. In two hundred years of burning fossil fuels to power the Industrial Revolution and the ongoing world it created, humans as a species have accomplished what the earliest oxygen-producing single-celled life forms took more than a billion years to do: changed the global climate. The microbes' change was more drastic, of course, since oxygen is a caustic, reactive gas, and most subsequent life outside the earth's now rare anaerobic environments has had to adapt to living with oxygen. What humans are apparently trying to do is simply change the temperature settings on the current oxygen-based climate for life.

The basic mechanisms are well-known. Burning fossil fuels releases carbon dioxide into the atmosphere. As one of the major greenhouse gases, extra CO_2 traps more solar energy, warming the global climate. The fossils making up fossil fuels are from the vast amounts of vegetation, including fern forests, that covered the earth before and into the age of dinosaurs, when the earth's climate was much warmer and wetter than it is now. Thus, releasing the carbon that vegetation trapped naturally threatens to recreate the age of dinosaurs far more pervasively than Jurassic Park genetics could. With the spread of industrialization and its demands for power for production, lighting, transport, and so forth, production of CO_2 and other greenhouse gases has steadily increased over the last 200 years; by 1970, the effects on global climate started to become visible (at least in retrospect).

In one sense, a warming global climate is nothing new. The earth's climate has been through many dramatic periods of cooling and warming. Remember, the last Ice Age ended only 13,000 years ago. This means that modern humans as a species have lived through several cycles of cooling and warming. But since the end of the last Ice Age, the species has made massive investments in styles of civilization predicated on roughly the climate we've had since 11,000 years ago. Civilization has adapted to several "mini-Ice Ages," or periods of slightly colder climate, the most recent of which reached its depths around 1600, and corresponding periods of warming, though not without some regions of state-level societies collapsing, as we have seen several times. If global warming over the next century is in the range of 1–2° C, similar adaptations, aided by better technology, will likely be possible. Some already warm regions may suffer as deserts advance; some cooler regions may become more temperate and grow more of the world's food. Even this level of warming will create problems, however, for the worst affected areas of the world are also its poorest.

The trouble is that warming of 1–2° C is at the very low end of estimates of what may happen. Some models show warming of as much as 6–10° C at the other extreme. The problems such warming would create would be much more drastic and difficult to deal with. For starters, even the lowest levels of warming will mean a rise in the global sea level, both from thermal expansion of the oceans and from the melting of polar ice caps and glaciers in Greenland and elsewhere, some of which has already happened. Since global network activity has made coastal locations some of the most favored for the location of the world's great cities, a rise of several feet would be problematic; with temperature rises over 3°, sea levels could rise ten or twenty feet (or more), flooding vast coastal areas—all of Bangladesh would go under, as would New Orleans, among innumerable other examples.

Further complicating the problem of adapting to climate change is that global climate and weather is a chaotic, non-linear system. Thus, while adding 1° of warming would probably just make everything somewhat warmer, with fairly predictable results (including stronger hurricanes), adding 2–3° of warming could tip the dynamics of global climate into a much more chaotic pattern featuring sudden extremes of heat and cold, much more severe weather of all sorts, and largely unpredictable shifts from one to the other. Huge and constant weather catastrophes would, obviously, be much harder to adapt to than incremental change. It is this prospect that has prompted global efforts to reduce greenhouse emissions and keep the scale of warming manageable.

These efforts have so far been halting, disputed, and relatively small because of several factors. One is that the still uneven spread of industrialization makes efforts to curb emissions seem to some less industrialized countries like an attempt by the fully

Nor are population growth and industrialization the only possible factors in increasing production of waste. As an example that explains the impetus behind the original Earth Day, between 1945 and 1970 the population of the United States rose 40%. The US gross domestic product (GDP) over the same period rose 50%, which meant that people were getting richer per capita. Basic consumption per capita of food, clothing, and housing did not rise at all. And yet the amount of pollution produced over that period rose between 200 and 2000%. Why?

Over that same period, throwaway containers replaced returnable ones, synthetics replaced natural materials (nylon instead of cotton, detergent instead of soap), and energy-wasteful products replaced energy-efficient ones (cars got much larger and more powerful, synthetic manufacturing requires heavy energy usage). There was no real advantage to the new products in terms of performing the functions they were designed for: a soft drink pours out of a returnable bottle just as well as out of an aluminum can. But in every case, the environmentally more wasteful product was more profitable. The old products were phased out and their replacements sold as "new and improved" versions, a classic illustration of the power of screen images (literal screens, as in TV, in many of these cases) to shape people's perceptions. In other words, the capitalist culture of the network contributed to increasing rates of pollution. (This is no plea for communist state-run production, however, which has proven even worse at environmentally sound practices, since states will regulate themselves even less readily than they regulate private corporations and are less subject to market demand for greener products.)

Indeed, the successes of Earth Day and other environmental movements in slowing (and in a few cases reversing) this aspect of the problem were founded in counter screen images that created a demand for more environmentally sound products and packaging and that helped craft politically viable legislation designed to protect the environment. Corporations have responded in two ways: first, by providing more environmentally sound products; second, and arguably more pervasively, by providing more environmentally friendly screen images of themselves and their products while not actually changing their practices or products much at all. Sadly, it is often difficult for the environmentally concerned consumer to tell the difference.

Nor is it clear that as much real progress has been made on dealing with solid waste as with air and water quality. Overall production has continued to grow with global economic growth, and hyper-packaging (such as individually wrapped servings of food) is more prevalent now than in 1970. The most visible testaments to the problem of solid waste disposal are not the vast landfills that future archaeologists (if there are any) might find grimly horrifying or unbelievably hilarious. Instead, it is the Great Pacific Trash Vortex that shows how far humans are from figuring out how to live without soiling their own nest (and the nests of others). The Vortex is a gigantic island of floating plastic trash, by some estimates more than twice as large as the state of Texas, that collects in the mid-North Pacific because of the circular wind and current patterns of the ocean there, bringing plastic junk from beaches in North America and Asia as well as waste dumped directly into the ocean. In its densest regions, it far outweighs the biomass of plankton in the water; the water itself contains toxically high levels of dissolved plastic. This festering sore on the surface of the sea is a reminder that only 1% of the plastic produced in the world each year ends up being recycled. The rest is incinerated, buried, or heads for a swim.

Thus, pollution results from the number of people in the world multiplied by Industrial production, a formula disturbingly similar to our estimate of the ability of a country to wage total war. Except in this case, as Walt Kelly's Pogo Possum said, the enemy is us.

The basic problem of mass production is compounded further by certain forms of market failure (as in overfishing) and by the profit-driven, short-term outlook imposed on production by the capitalist culture of the global network. This contributes not just via wasteful products, noted earlier, but by encouraging corporations to off-load the environmental costs of doing business, especially when those are long-term and dispersed, onto the general population. Thus, businesses that dump toxic wastes into the environment rarely pay any of the public health costs associated with increased rates of cancer and other illnesses caused by those wastes. Corporations will dispute their responsibility for such long-term costs (see the tobacco industry for a paradigmatic example), but rarely pay even when the costs are immediate and the responsibility is direct, as with the British Petroleum oil spill in the Gulf of Mexico, which will also have long-term impacts.

Biodiversity

We could multiply specific examples of environmental threats to human health for the rest of this chapter and beyond. But humans are not the only creatures affected by human-produced environmental degradation and change. Extinction rates for other species are already up massively across the globe, such that the human-induced disappearance of species going on right now is, according to some biologists, already at levels that will make it noticeable at geological scales. In other words, humans are not only vying with early oxygen-producing microbes as changers of the world's climate, but are in the same league with the meteor strike that killed off the dinosaurs, as well as other catastrophic die-offs of life-forms that have struck the earth periodically. Semi-deliberate exterminations via hunting—a modern, technologically empowered version of the impact humans began to have on animal populations soon after the Cognitive-Linguistic Revolution—have played some role in this, especially if the poaching of endangered species, such as elephants for ivory, is included. The major problem, however, is habitat loss, as encroachments of human settlement and its extensions in terms of logging, mining, and agriculture keep expanding with growing population and industrial production.

This loss of biodiversity may be viewed in two ways. First, and more abstractly, different forms of environmental ethics recognize either the rights of other species to share the earth with humans or some sort of moral obligation on the part of humans to be responsible stewards of the planet over whose environmental future they have come to have significant control. Interestingly, this is an area in which animal rights activists and some Christian (and other religious) ethical traditions have converged, from very different premises, on the notion of "stewardship."

FIGURE 26.7 Pollution Enters the Cultural Screen. Earth Day protests, April 22, 1970 (top row, in New York City; bottom left, in Berkeley, CA) and an anti-nuclear protest in Japan, 2012.

The Christian premises of this notion, grounded in human superiority over as well as responsibility for nature, lead to the second, often more practically effective, strand of thought about loss of biodiversity: that it is actively bad for the future of humans themselves. One set of arguments along this line points out the yet-undiscovered medical and economic benefits hidden in the genetics of rare or undiscovered species. Along similar lines, the eco-tourism benefits of wildlife protection are advanced as economically more valuable than alternatives that threaten extinction. Another line of argument points to the very real dangers of a world of virtual monocultures. That is, the range of major human domesticates, especially in terms of large meat animals and especially cereal crops, is very restricted—compounded by the fact that the genetic stock of most major cereal crops has been further narrowed by selective breeding and genetic modification. Furthermore, most of the resulting genetic stock is owned, with patent protection, by a few major corporations, whose crops sometimes will not grow properly without application of their own fertilizers. Setting aside the ethics of this use of patents until later in this chapter, the huge genetic monocultures that this economic model of agriculture has produced may well be vulnerable to devastating epidemics: genetic variation has always been a front line of defense against micro-parasitic infestations. A new virus that could kill a vast proportion of the world's corn crop would make the nineteenth-century Irish potato famine look insignificant by comparison.

Responses

How to fix environmental problems is the subject of much public policy debate. From the perspective of our model, solutions tend to be of two sorts. Hierarchy-based approaches involve regulations, prohibitions, and standard setting followed by detailed administrative enforcement. Such approaches have had significant successes, especially in the areas of air and water quality, but have also aroused the most direct opposition from Industrial capitalist interests. Opposition arises despite the fact that the economic impact of regulation is far from one-sided: it encourages innovation and makes possible new businesses that can meet the demands created by regulation. This reveals how the innovation-encouraging culture of a market-based network sometimes conflicts with the vested interests of established industries in the corporate

FIGURE 26.8 Harvesting Intellectual Property. A field of corn whose genetic code is owned by Monsanto.

sphere, a pattern that extends far beyond environmental issues, as we will explore further below. Hierarchy-based approaches can be enacted within individual hierarchies or more widely by international treaty agreements.

Network-based approaches inevitably involve hierarchies as well, but attempt to make market mechanisms substitute for direct state regulation in terms of implementation. This involves one or more hierarchies setting goals—usually some overall amount of allowable emissions—and then establishing a market by which companies can trade their shares of that total. This allows the market to distribute emissions most efficiently while still meeting the overall goal. As we noted above, network-based responses can also involve "selling" environmentally sound policies—both state-based and those involving changes in individual behavior—in the marketplace of ideas.

This, however, becomes a matter of competing screen images and frame values, and highlights the fact that the reception and success of either hierarchy- or network-based approaches also depends on the screen images and frame values though which they are viewed. If corporate profit trumps a healthy environment culturally, no amount of regulation or market-based solutions will be very effective. Cultural competition in environmental issues, moreover, is not just a matter of corporate interests versus environmental ones (as we have noted, some businesses can profit by providing environmentally helpful goods or services). It also pits the administrative and cultural divisions of the global network—the administrative borders of individual states, but even more the cultural borders of nationalism—against the globalism of environmental issues. The only cultural frame that will bring environmental issues—and their possible solutions—into focus is one that recognizes the inherent interconnectedness of all environmental issues and that "national" interests cannot be separated from global processes. (See Figure 26.9.)

Forecasting?

Environmental issues are a new reminder of a factor in human history that has been there since the beginning: that the natural world sets constraints on human activity, a reminder that will become more forceful the greater the impact humans have upon their own environment. Failure to live within those constraints (or to overcome them—which has effectively happened only twice, with the inventions of agriculture and industry) can lead to the collapse and even disappearance of whole societies. The early Indus River societies of Harappa and Mohenjo-Daro may well have succumbed to environmental change, and state-level societies disappeared from Mayan society for reasons that included environmental overreach and endemic warfare.

As the Mayan example shows, environmental catastrophe is more likely to lead to the collapse of state-level societal organization than to the disappearance of humans altogether. And the scientific and organizational resources of modern societies are deeper and more powerful than those available to earlier Agrarian Era societies. Thus, it is possible for us to understand, forecast, and act upon such forecasts far more effectively than previous societies could. The goal of sustainability is certainly reachable, at least in theory. But should current policies fail and the world

PRINCIPLES AND PATTERNS

Humans have been deliberately altering their environment since the Cognitive-Linguistic Revolution.

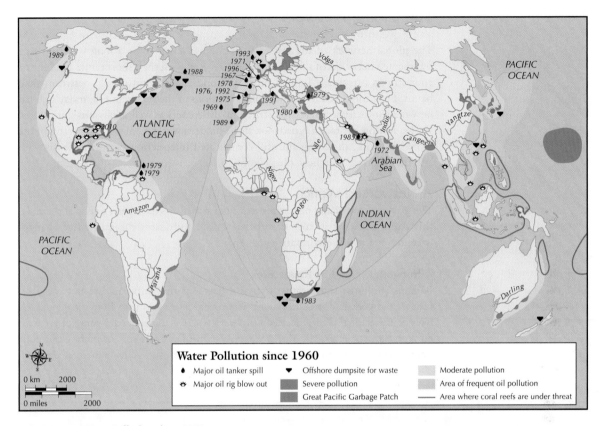

FIGURE 26.9 Water Pollution since 1960.

be struck by environmental disaster(s) within the next hundred years, does our model tell us anything about what the results might be?

Of course, outright collapse of state-level societies is certainly possible if the disaster is bad enough. But short of that? Ignoring for the moment that forecasting is not the historian's job, several key factors stand out. Remember that the basic constraints on the political organization of Agrarian Era societies were low productivity and poor communications, the constraints exploded by industrialization. It is not hard to imagine climate change producing disturbances powerful enough that these constraints reappear, and if not exactly in their Agrarian form, then at least relative to contemporary conditions. This suggests that one danger of environmental catastrophe would be conditions unfriendly to the continued exercise of democratic government: "low and slow" tended to produce restrictive hierarchies. If we also remember that warfare seems to have been invented in part in response to environmental stresses and the resource shortages those stresses created, the picture begins to look even grimmer. Perhaps it is best to try to avert catastrophe.

The Global Network

The global network of the last forty years has clearly come a long way from the fragmented networks of the Hunter-Gatherer Era, with their short range and limited connections carrying a limited range of goods, ideas, and people between small bands. Even compared to the network operations of the Agrarian Era, today's global network shows some interesting structural differences as well as obvious similarities. In this section, we take a broad look at the modern world from the perspective of the global network, including the still-complicated intersection between the network and the world's hierarchies. (See Figure 26.10.)

A Networked World

The growing power and pervasiveness of network flows have been a central theme of this entire book. It is now time to step back and assess the qualitative changes wrought by gradual quantitative growth.

A Network Divided by Hierarchies

Perhaps the most significant difference between the Agrarian Era network and today's network is how deeply and pervasively it reaches into individual people's lives compared to hierarchies. For ancient societies, and indeed for most people in all Agrarian societies, the world was made up of various sets of hierarchies connected by various networks. Their experience of their hierarchy came first. Indeed,

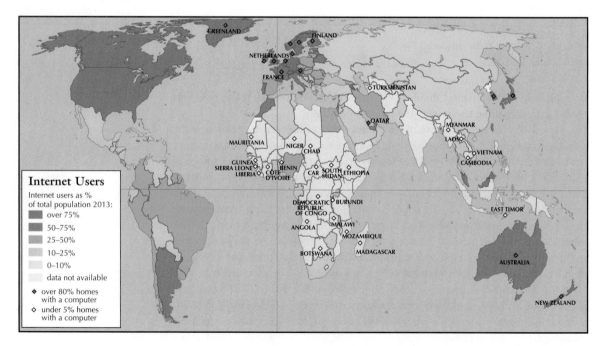

FIGURE 26.10 Global Internet Use.

for most people, the primary influences on their lives were even more restrictive. They lived their lives in their birth community, likely a nearly autonomous place in economic and cultural terms, with very attenuated network connections. Even for more cosmopolitan elites, long-distance network connections provided mostly exotic luxury goods.

By contrast, today's world is a single network divided by hierarchies. That is, the experience of an increasing number of people in today's world, materially if not fully consciously, comes first from the global network, mediated secondarily by the hierarchy they live in. An inhabitant of the United States, for example, is likely on any particular day to be wearing a shirt sewn in China and shoes manufactured in Vietnam, to drive a Japanese car, to use a Swedish or Finnish cell phone, to eat Chilean grapes, and to use a Taiwanese-assembled computer to check news of a tsunami in Japan. And compared to an inhabitant of The Netherlands, even that experience is relatively insular. One may think of oneself as "American," for example, but modern nationalist notions of identity are constructed consciously in opposition to (or at least in the context of) the cross-cultural connections of a global community. The balance of network and hierarchy influence may be closer in areas such as rural southwest China or parts of sub-Saharan Africa, but the tentacles of the global network reach such places directly (for example, through cell phone networks, even if the cell phone is shared across an entire village) and indirectly through network influences on the economic policies of individual hierarchies, among other channels.

This shift in the balance of power between networks, which have become a single global network, and hierarchies accounts for the movement in some regions toward political agglomeration, with the European Union being the most prominent example. At a purely practical level, the political division of the network introduces inefficiencies into the market operations of the network in terms of such things as tariff barriers, labor mobility, and currency exchanges that political agglomeration is designed to reduce. (We will examine the tension between this tendency and the tendency toward nationalist-inspired fragmentation in the next chapter.) One of the economic advantages the United States has enjoyed for over a century is having a continent-sized economy and network under a single hierarchy. China and India have the potential for similar economies of scale, geographically and demographically.

Network Connections and Societies

The shift in the balance of power between network and hierarchies is also gradually decentering political power within and among hierarchies. In the Agrarian world, the regions with the densest local networks were usually also the ones with the greatest concentrations of political power, as power attracted network connections and dense local networks funded the building of powerful hierarchies. (The periodic power of steppe nomad confederations is a partial exception to this rule. But the largest confederations grew from relatively robust steppe networks, and the fragility of steppe polities reflected their less firm network foundations.)

Today, dense local networks are increasingly pervasive. While this partly provides resources for hierarchy building to an increasing number of societies, the refusal of dense local networks to conform to established political borders also undermines those borders and complicates the ability of states to regulate and

wealth can be controlled by a tiny elite, much less free), economic development and levels of freedom are clearly related, though in complex ways that include cultural and historical influences.

Complications

Focusing purely on the influence of market economics may paint too simple a picture, however. The capitalist and corporate culture of the network of the world's corporate spheres does not necessarily reinforce market forces. As we have seen, one of the central effects of capitalism is to concentrate wealth, introducing greater disparities of wealth even in the context of rising overall prosperity. This can, as we have also noted, stretch or break the common frame values uniting very rich and very poor, undermining the ability of a democracy to function effectively. An advanced capitalist economy can also threaten to substitute consumerism for democratic participation in a society's frame values.

Concentration of wealth in corporations further extends the complications that corporate capitalism introduces into democratic governance. Here we come back to seeing corporations as a class of immortal individuals participating in what was designed as a game for mortal humans to play. Corporate wealth certainly buys political influence—remember that "one dollar, one vote" is the governing principle of corporate governance—while corporate efforts to escape regulation by hierarchies set examples that can undermine the ideals of cooperative citizenship. The corporate capitalist (and even the market's) cultural focus on competition can obscure the much more necessary cooperation that makes both market economics and collective government possible at all.

Cultural focus on competition also obscures the fact that corporations and capitalism are perfectly comfortable operating in unfree markets (monopolies are a natural result of capitalism, as we have seen) and in unfree hierarchies. Sometimes, given the restrictions on labor rights and political discourse generally in non-democratic states, they operate more comfortably in such states than in strong democracies. The strong economic growth of China since the 1980s, when the Chinese Communist Party gave up being communist and instead became essentially fascist, demonstrates this clearly. (Following our definition of fascism in Chapter 23, note "Communist" China's combination of capitalist private property, at least in the most important sectors of the economy, with suppression of dissent and a strong emphasis on nationalism built on appeals to China's imperial past.) Whether the much stronger global market influences that have come with Chinese economic development will overbalance the current corporate-capitalist-fascist structure of the Chinese hierarchy remains an open question, and carries warnings about possible trends in corporate-capitalist-democratic hierarchies.

Nationalisms Resurgent

Corporate influence may complicate the operations of democracy, but in terms of the cultures of the world's networked hierarchies, the ideological competition for democratic ideals since 1989–1991 has come much more from the resurgence of various expressions of nationalism. Why is this, and what tendencies does this resurgence create?

Reasons for Resurgent Nationalisms

The ongoing transformation of the world by industrialization is the underlying reason for the resurgence of nationalism. Transformation means change, and change, though welcomed in theory and promoted by those who will benefit from it, is usually disruptive to the status quo, whether that status quo is Agrarian or an already established version of Industrial society. Since the economic structure and culture of the Industrial Era promotes continual change—the opposite of the stability and resistance to change that Agrarian hierarchies were built for—disruptions and the resistance they spawn are a constant aspect of the Industrial world. Constant change can certainly become its own large-scale status quo, but it still generates disruptions that some people find uncomfortable.

Specifically, and given the still-incomplete industrialization of the world, the inequalities of wealth and power created by the capitalist aspect of the global network have often become a focus of discontent with disruptive change. As we have seen, such inequalities occur both between different societies and within individual societies. In practical terms, inequality can mean a lack of economic opportunities for some societies or for groups within societies. Underemployment and no hope for a better future, or even a future as secure as the past might have been, create problems, especially for young males, the group most likely to turn to violent expressions of discontent.

Many people affected by such circumstances quite naturally look for an ideology that can focus and make coherent their discontent with their lives. Such ideologies can perform several functions. They can explain why life is terrible. Explanation can then lead to a prescription for action to bring about change. Ideologies can provide an identity to the ideology's adherents, especially when the ideology's explanation of conditions involves blaming some other group for the world's troubles, creating an Other for the purpose of focusing in-group identity. There is no requirement, of course, that the explanations ideologies provide be accurate. Indeed, explanatory subtlety is often inversely related to emotional appeal.

At least from the mid-1800s, one of the key ideologies opposed to capitalism was communism, which offered an analysis of the capitalist version of industrialization that had academic, "scientific" plausibility. From 1917 it had a home base in the world community of hierarchies in the Soviet Union, a base that expanded significantly after 1945. Thus, for most of the twentieth century, communism dominated the field of anti-capitalist ideologies, and did so in a way that was deliberately anti-nationalist. This division was expressed through the Cold War. But the collapse of European communism in 1989 and the Soviet Union in 1991 effectively discredited communist ideology: neither poor and isolated Cuba nor communist-in-name-only China provided evidence to the contrary.

When communism collapsed, many people still felt the need for an ideology to oppose capitalism and blame somebody for its effects. Democracy was either unavailable or too tainted by association with capitalism to provide a clear alternative. Thus, nationalism moved back into prominence on the world stage. Nationalism, as we have seen, is naturally opposed to the disruptive changes brought about by industrial capitalism, a quality that also let it play a role in undermining communist rule in eastern Europe. It creates divisive Others. Its lack of intellectual coherence, in the

FIGURE 27.6 Communism Crumbling. The Berlin Wall falling in 1989.

hands of skillfully demagogic leaders, enhances its emotional appeal and flexibility, as new enemies can always be plugged into the nationalist equation as necessary to enhance a nationalist leader's appeal and power. Finally, because nationalism is a widely accepted screen or even frame value in global politics, at least in some forms, nationalist protests can gain an almost automatic level of legitimacy when they first appear.

Types of Nationalism

The usual form of nationalism is the one associated with the ideal of the nation-state, where the "nation" is a people whose identity arises from a common history, language, and culture, a mythical but powerful mixture dependent on constructions of the past. It is expressed regularly at, for example, international sporting events such as the Olympics, where the display of flags and the playing of national anthems (whose nineteenth-century style of European orchestral arrangements, even for non-European countries, betrays the historical context for the birth of nationalism) proclaim the identity of the athletes, even if the legal rules of naturalization and citizenship make a hash of the ethnically "national" character of many teams.

Lurking just below or beside this sort of "patriotic" nationalism are its more selective and considerably less flexible variants. "Ethnicity," a concept as culturally constructed as nationality, has always been one of the key markers of traditional nationalism, except perhaps in cases such as the United States, a multi-ethnic "nation of immigrants." Still, the history of the United States bears the scars of ethnic nationalism's sibling, racism. Ethnic nationalism has been a strong and visible force in the fragmentation of eastern Europe, especially the Balkan Peninsula, since 1989, with the breakup of Yugoslavia into many constituent parts as the centerpiece of that

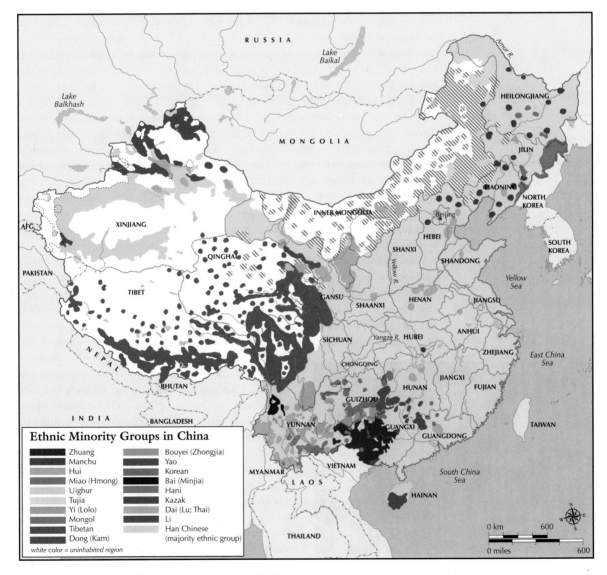

Ethnic Minority Groups in China

Zhuang
Manchu
Hui
Miao (Hmong)
Uighur
Tujia
Yi (Lolo)
Mongol
Tibetan
Dong (Kam)

Bouyei (Zhongjia)
Yao
Korean
Bai (Minjia)
Hani
Kazak
Dai (Lu; Thai)
Li
Han Chinese
(majority ethnic group)

white color = uninhabited region

FIGURE 27.7 Diversity. Ethnic minority populations in China.

story. But conflicts between, for example, different peoples in Indonesia, between Han Chinese and various minority groups especially in the south and west border regions of China, and even the Chechen conflict with Russia also show the tendency for ethnicity to become a significant and sometimes violent line of cultural division. While language and culture play the crucial roles in identifying ethnic groups, many ethnic nationalist appeals assume, implicitly or even explicitly, a "genetic" component to the divisions among ethnicities. (See Figure 27.7.)

A second component of the mythic stew that makes up nationality has often been religion. Expressions of what might be called religious nationalism are also visible in any number of conflicts since 1991. The nationalist emphasis on identity here focuses less on ethnicity, especially in any sort of pseudo-genetic way, and more on religious belief and community as the markers of a "nation." The Zionist ideology that pushed for the creation of the state of Israel is a prominent example of this sort of nationalism. Its assumption of a common Jewish identity has been tested by significant Russian-Jewish immigration since 1991, prompted in part by more openly expressed anti-Semitism in post-Communist, nationalist Russia. Another example is the Bharatiya Janata Party (BJP), a Hindu nationalist political party in India whose ideological roots trace back to the "Hindutva" movement of the 1920s that defined Hindu nationalism. But arguably almost every religious fundamentalist movement of recent decades, including Muslim groups such as the Muslim Brotherhood and even Al Qaeda, as well as Christian fundamentalists in the United States claiming that the United States is a "Christian country," are as much, if not more, variations on nationalism as they are modern versions of traditional religious belief. This is because their focus is more on the groups' creation and identity than on theology and doctrine, areas in which they often lie well outside the mainstream of the larger religious communities to which they supposedly belong.

Finally, we can classify all these variants of nationalism under the heading of what anthropologist Brian Ferguson has called "identerest politics," that is, politics (usually divisive and destructive politics) based on some constructed notion of identity that pits one such constructed group against its Others. That neither race, ethnicity, nor religion need be a central component of identerest politics is illustrated by the violence engendered in Rwanda by conflict between Hutus and Tutsis. Rwanda's borders are among the few in Africa that predate colonialism. Rwanda contains only a single "ethnic group" by traditional definitions: all Rwandans share a single language, religion, and culture. But historical and social differences between Hutus and Tutsis marked pre-colonial Rwandan history, resulting in one-sided colonial administration and post-colonial tension. This provided plenty of ammunition for a Hutu separatist movement and, in 1990, led to a civil war. This led to the Rwandan genocide of 1994, when Hutu extremists killed between half a million and a million Tutsis and Hutus who were "too moderate" before being defeated militarily. Identerest politics is thus an even broader category than nationalism, strictly

FIGURE 27.8 Nationalism and Religion. A Bharatiya Janata Party rally.

speaking, but the historical prominence of nationalism makes it a label worth retaining, with identerest politics as an analytical tool for understanding it. What the concept of identerest politics does is put the focus on the exploitation of difference as a way for leaders and groups to gain and keep power, which is the key to nationalism.

Tendencies of Nationalist Politics

The tendencies that nationalist politics create are in some ways as contradictory and incoherent as the various sorts of nationalism themselves. On the one hand, one obvious result in some places has been the division of existing countries along "national" lines, as noted above. Especially when nationalist-inspired separatist movements offer the promise of protecting ethnic minorities oppressed by a hostile majority, this tendency has often gained the approval and sometimes even the support of the global community of countries, reflecting the continued importance of nationalism as an accepted frame value in the cultural construction of hierarchies.

One problem that arises from this tendency is that since "nationality" is a cultural construct, the subdivision of countries could theoretically be taken to absurd lengths. The absurdity arises from the networked context in which hierarchies exist, discussed earlier in this chapter: at some point, unless the new fragment country is willing to surrender a good bit of their newly won sovereignty to some supra-national organization, it will face the difficulty that smaller countries are usually less

FIGURE 27.9 Orphaned by the Rwandan Genocide.
Identerest politics taken to extremes.

viable economically than larger ones. Thus, one feature of modern hierarchies is the tension between the nationalist elements of their cultural frames and the practical incentives of their networked world. This marks the continuing tension between networks and hierarchies highlighted by the dilemma of the Chechen separatists.

Another problem woven into this tension often leads to the second main direction of nationalist politics, which is to stimulate counter-nationalisms and fascist tendencies. Fascist tendencies are built into the nature of nationalism anyway: nationalism is built around emphasizing differences, which easily bleeds into emphases on exclusion, competition, and therefore conflict between "national" groups. In such competition, the control over the powerful mechanisms of modern states becomes both the focus of competition and the tool with which the "winners" (perhaps temporary) can hammer their foes. This means that nationalists generally want a strong state, as long as it is their own and opposition to their use of it can be suppressed. This is a classic incoherent fascist goal: a strong industrial-military state without the social disruptions inevitable to industrialization. Also leading in fascist directions is that nationalist movements often focus around charismatic leaders, whose exploitation of nationalism heightens their own personal power.

Thus, nationalist-inspired separatist movements inevitably encourage nationalist responses from the dominant groups they wish to separate from, as the Chechen revolt spurred Russian nationalist opposition. This is because the nationalist frame of separatist movements also frames the response, and because separation would weaken the majority state (note the Russian concern for the oil infrastructure located in Chechnya). Nor is this tendency restricted to the dominant group. While both sides committed atrocities, it was the out-of-power Hutu rebels who conducted the Rwandan genocide in 1994, for example. Genocide and "ethnic cleansing" represent the cultural frame of ethnic nationalism applied to the extreme.

The terrorism conducted in Moscow by the Chechen rebels is another example of the sorts of tactics both sides in a nationalist-fascist competition tend to resort to. Terrorism also reminds us of the complexity of the types of nationalism and nationalist politics. Religious nationalism can exist within individual hierarchies, as the periodic violence between Hindu nationalists and Indian Muslims attests. The religious nationalism of the Afghan Taliban is another example. But given the trans-hierarchy reach of most major religions in today's highly networked world, religious nationalism can also transcend hierarchy borders. Al Qaeda's brand of religious fascism certainly does so, though it is worth remembering that while Al Qaeda certainly opposes the United States and all it represents about industrial modernity, its other ultimate target is the Saudi Arabian monarchy (with the United States targeted as its supporter). Al Qaeda at root is, in other words, a Saudi religious-nationalist group.

Extreme nationalist politics, whether ethnic, religious, or identerest generally, also appear below the level of separatist movements and outright civil wars, often as an element of open, pluralist democratic politics, though an element ultimately in conflict with openness and pluralism. (The openness and pluralism of democracy is one expression of the constant change and potential disruption of Industrial mass politics, and so is a natural target of nationalist-fascist attack.) This can be seen clearly in the assassinations by ultra-nationalist Japanese groups that have suppressed discussion of Japan's role in World War II. But it also shows up in anti-immigration and anti-immigrant policies, which almost always fall back on essentialist notions of national (dominant group) identity, and in ethnic and racial politics more generally. The same traditionalist, essentialist notions of identity, clothed in religious rather than strictly ethnic terms, can inspire opposition to women's rights movements, gay rights movements, and workers' rights movements. In the latter case, identerest politics may even be an emotionally powerful cover for pro-corporate capitalist interests.

All of this is evidence that the transformations of industrial capitalist society are certainly easy to perceive as disruptive (i.e., evil), and that stability and order have an emotional appeal for many people that cannot be reduced just to the defense of vested interests. And given the broad acceptance that nationalism has in mainstream global politics (remember flags and national anthems), opposition to nationalist politics requires not just appeals to higher principles of universal human rights and the

FIGURE 27.10 Who Belongs? Immigration, naturalization, identity: issues contested on the cultural screen.

unity of humanity (as for instance in global environmental contexts), but different, inclusive, and democratic screen images of "national" history that can give flags and anthems different symbolic readings.

Varieties of Modern Conflict

Hierarchies, brought into ever closer contact by the power of the global network within which they exist and put under tension by the ongoing transformations of the Industrial Era, continue to generate violence and armed conflict of various sorts around the globe. Complicating matters, variations on nationalist politics often turn peaceful disputes warlike and heighten the intensity of already violent clashes. At the same time, the end of the Cold War has shifted the frequency of types of wars away from large-state conventional wars and toward the sorts of conflicts variously referred to as sub-state, unconventional, irregular, or asymmetrical. We may approach this variety of conflict through our model.

ISSUES IN DOING WORLD HISTORY

Is a Global Perspective Possible?

World historians have increasingly claimed to see the world from "a global perspective." (This book makes the same claim.) These claims reflect a number of truths about the development of world history as an academic field over the last thirty years. They are, to start with, a reaction against the Eurocentrism that colored accounts of world history since the birth of the modern historical profession in nineteenth-century Europe. It also reflects the growing scholarship about non-European parts of the world, much of it created by scholars from and working in those parts of the world. This work can be drawn on to synthesize a picture of global history. More source materials are now available from a variety of societies, though the linguistic barriers to any one scholar drawing upon a truly global range of primary sources remain close to insurmountable. Finally, the attempt to deploy global perspectives recognizes the fact that many world historical patterns and processes, for instance the operations of the global network of trade, cultural exchange, and environmental degradation, are more clearly visible from "above" national boundaries than from within them. But do these developments allow a global perspective? What does such a claim really mean?

Let us start with the fact that every historian has a particular *perspective*. Just like a photographer,

a historian must stand in some particular place to take a picture of the past. This "place" is made up of the historian's life experiences, which as a whole produce a particular cultural frame from within which the historian views the world. A perspective is both inevitable and not necessarily problematic, because perspective is not the same as *bias,* which is the intentional use of a particular perspective to distort the picture—like a photographer shooting a movie set façade and claiming it's a real building. Indeed, the more the historian is aware of and explicit about her own perspective, the more she can compensate for the limits of her own perspective and make her history less subject to bias.

But can such compensation ever allow the creation of a global perspective? For any individual historian, probably not. Hypothetical "views from space" must remain hypothetical, since no beings from space are writing human history, and the hypothetical perspective chosen will reflect the earthly origins of the hypothesizer. But for the profession as a whole, the accumulation of many individual historians' perspectives, like a vast photomontage, can gradually approach the effect of a global perspective. Doing world history is, after all, a globally collective enterprise.

Conventional Wars

The "normal" sort of war between two (or more) hierarchies of (roughly) equal military capability has not disappeared from the post-1970 world. The India-Pakistan War of 1971 (see Chapter 25), the Arab-Israeli Wars of 1967 and 1974, and the long, destructive Iran-Iraq War of 1980–88—the largest and most costly war of the modern era—are the most prominent examples. Both the First Iraq War (1991) and the Second (2003) looked in advance to be serious conventional wars, but proved in the event to be pretty asymmetrical in favor of US organization and technology, though the second devolved into a seriously different sort of conflict after its initial stages. For now, however, conventional inter-hierarchy war has become less frequent. We have noted some of the reasons for this already: the growing influence of network connections in discouraging costly inter-hierarchy war; the gradual cementing of hierarchy borders in international law; and the influence of the spread of democracy

Conventional War between Hierarchies

FIGURE 27.11 Conventional War Between Hierarchies. (Top) Conventional war in model
form. (Bottom) Scene from the Iran-Iraq War of 1980–1988.

FRAMING   Networked Frames and Screens: Culture since 1970

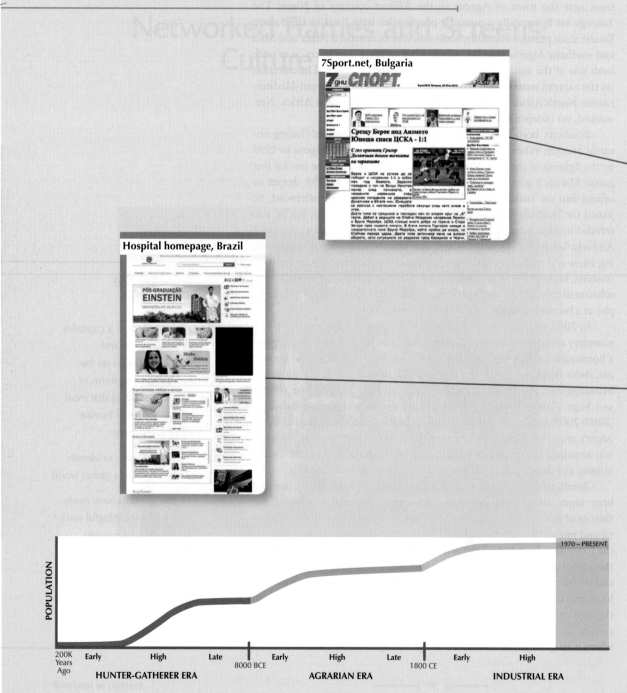

7Sport.net, Bulgaria

Hospital homepage, Brazil

POPULATION

200K Years Ago

Early   High   Late   Early   High   Late   Early   High

8000 BCE   1800 CE

HUNTER-GATHERER ERA   AGRARIAN ERA   INDUSTRIAL ERA

1970 – PRESENT

THE EARTH AT NIGHT, 2013, WITH LAND MASS PROPORTIONAL TO POPULATION.

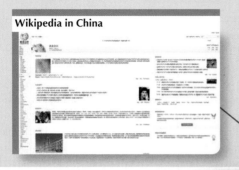

Wikipedia in China

United Arab Emirates homepage

Revisiting the Cognitive-Linguistic Revolution

We may start by briefly revisiting the Cognitive-Linguistic Revolution introduced in Chapter 1. As we discussed there, the evolution of human cognition proceeded through several stages. The last stage, which produced symbolic culture, was made possible around 70,000 years ago when our species, *Homo sapiens,* began to produce speech that associated discrete sounds with discrete objects, actions, and concepts, and to link those sounds (words) together with syntactic rules. This sort of language, unlike earlier forms of primate communication, linked humans' social intelligence to their biological, physical, and technological intelligences and turned the world, from the human perspective, into a vast and ongoing drama, not just lives lived but lived self-consciously, narrated (verbally, musically, artistically, performatively), and given lasting identities and meanings.

It was the capacity of language and the associated forms of symbolic expression it spawned (or, in the case of music, that co-evolved with it and gained power from its association with words) to endow the world with symbolic meaning—as well as the fundamental fact that variations of the new form of communication could be translated from one to another, unlike the older form—that created the foundations for networks and hierarchies, the basic structures of world history that we have modeled starting in Chapter 1. Networks were no longer weakly constituted by episodic moments of biological exchange (isolated human groups trading mates), but strongly and continuously constituted by the idea that goods (especially goods with symbolic value, including the symbolic value we think of as economic exchange value) and ideas could be traded, had been traded, and would be traded again. Symbolic meaning made differentiation of economic roles, gender roles, and social status possible, and so made hierarchically organized societies possible. And as we have seen, it was symbolic culture that, over the subsequent millennia of developments in networks and hierarchies, mediated the tense, creative intersection between those two structures.

Finally, the emergence of symbolic culture posed its own new challenges: How would humans understand and navigate a world alive with symbolic meaning, intentionality (apparent and real), and the self-consciousness of mortality? The search for meaning in an intentional world was thus the path to religion and origin stories, as well as to more recent manifestations of the similar impulses to understand and explain, including academic history and modern science.

This led us to the final part of our model. Every individual sees the world through a cultural frame, a set of cultural understandings of how and why the world works. The collective and shifting sum of these individual frames forms the different cultural frames of separate human communities. And the collective arguments, conflicting self-understandings and projections of identity, and interpretations of meaning that arise within any society form the images that each society projects on the cultural screen enclosed by its cultural frame. As we have seen, the reciprocal relationship of cultural frames and screens with the material structures of networks and hierarchies—cultural perceptions shaping social structures,

FIGURE 28.1 Symbolic Status. Opulent burial goods symbolize hierarchy, even in death.

social and economic developments affecting culture—has been central to understanding the patterns and developments of world history. We have been examining culture all along, in other words. But we may now turn to examples of this complex reciprocal relationship generated by our contemporary world.

Dynamics of Culture

The particular patterns of modern culture are deeply affected by the context of the global network. But deeper patterns of cultural history are evident in the oldest form of networking by *Homo sapiens,* the use of language. We shall take each of these in turn.

Culture, Capitalism, and Networks

Since we looked at the political cultures of hierarchies in the last chapter, we will focus here, in terms of the contexts and influences on patterns of cultural production and distribution, on the relationship between cultural products and the global network. Both the network of global markets and the capitalist structure of most network operations have significant impacts on the contemporary culture.

Culture and Commodification

The central impact of an advanced capitalist environment for culture is that culture is now a commodity—indeed, *the* commodity. This means many things. At the simplest level, and not even counting items of subsistence and material culture such as staple foods, clothes, or cars as such, commodities are cultural expressions. People often buy not food, clothing, and cars, but cuisines, fashions, and lifestyles—all part of a broader culture of consumerism that we will return to later in discussing the functions of culture. This observation may seem so obvious as to reveal almost nothing, but we may observe several aspects of the commodification of cultural objects that are historically significant.

First, we should remember that the buying and selling of cultural artifacts, although as ancient as networks themselves (remember that items that could convey symbolic prestige, such as feathers and shells used in ritual display or the ochre pigments used in body painting, constituted one driving force in long-distance exchanges long before agriculture was invented), have not always been the dominant mode of acquiring either utilitarian or status items. Coercive taxation, elite patronage of skilled labor (often binding to the point of slavery), military plunder, and theft were, during the long Agrarian Era, often more significant than trade, and created values that shaped the trade that did exist. The accumulated wealth of Agrarian elites was hoarded, consumed (often conspicuously), and most significantly given away as cultural-political investments in power: gifts, as we have noted many times, created obligations and displayed the power and generosity of the giver. The accumulated wealth of capitalist elites is hoarded, consumed (often conspicuously), and invested in order to generate more wealth—a reflection of the basic inversion of the relationship between wealth and power brought about by industrialization: before, power led to wealth; now, wealth leads to power. The cultural corollary of that political

PRINCIPLES AND PATTERNS

In the Agrarian Era, power led to wealth. In the Industrial Era, wealth leads to power.

inversion is that in the Agrarian world, cultural objects might at times be commodities; in today's world, commodities might sometimes be cultural objects.

Second, the combination of capitalism and markets makes a vast range of cultural choices available to mass populations (though arguably the choices are often more apparent than real). Almost all luxury trade before industrialization was conducted on behalf of wealthy elites (that's what made it luxury trade!), who therefore dominated the conscious construction of cultural identity via consumption. For the great mass of most Agrarian Era populations, cultural choices were limited and inherited, at least in terms of material consumption (which in any case was more dominated by basic subsistence). But industrialization has opened up the field of identity construction via consumption to the mass market. Producers recognize this aspect of commodity consumption and, in accordance with the advertising rule that one "sells the sizzle, not the steak," market their products accordingly, with identity (or the image of identity, which is even easier to market) foregrounded. Thus, to use an example connected to Bombino, the car manufacturer Volkswagen names its Sports Utility Vehicle (a category designed to keep as many identity choices open as possible) the Touareg, using the French spelling. Buy one, and you, too, can experience the freedom of the desert nomad, but without the risk of being shot by Niger's military. It will even come with a sound system on which you can play Bombino's music, bringing you one step closer to true Tuaregitude.

The commodification of objects, however, barely scratches the surface of the vast range and power of capitalism to create commodities of almost anything. We noted some of this in Chapter 20. Want to commodify an emotion or a concept? Thrills and chills can be sold at an amusement park, and if love is harder to sell, sell the image of love on Valentine's Day or at your local jewelry store. Want to sell freedom? Well, there's an SUV whose name will give you the freedom of . . . oh, right, we already mentioned that.

Even more important, the fundamental human expressions that arose with the Cognitive-Linguistic Revolution have become the commodities of the global entertainment industry. People, as a necessary function of who we are, tell stories, make music, and make art. Technically, the medium that carries the expression may be the commodity, but it is the expression itself that is really sold: nobody says, "Look, I have a DVD!" They say, "Look, I have a DVD of Ridley Scott's *Bladerunner!*" It's the content that counts. Commodifying that content may be simply a matter of making commercial the sorts of human gatherings at which stories and music have been performed since the Cognitive-Linguistic Revolution (and in more limited ways before): live theater, live music, and live comedy are village events with tickets (though with one important difference we will come back to later). Or it may involve printing a book, filming a movie, or distributing Bombino's song "Tar Hani" digitally, in which case the medium has become almost as abstract as the message.

FIGURE 28.2 Nomadic Mobility. Or at least modern mobility with a nice screen image of nomadism.

The capitalist structure of such commodification also leads to producers trying to set limits on distribution and unpaid use, however—this is where we see the possibility for conflict between creativity and profits that led to the creation of "intellectual property" (IP), a topic we introduced in Chapter 19 with James Watt and explored further in Chapter 26. IP has since taken on a life of its own and has become the cutting edge of contemporary commodification. Through patents, copyrights, and trademarks, genes, stories, songs, names, words and phrases, and concepts ("one click shopping") have become the commodified property of some person, though most likely an immortal and fictive corporate person endowed with the legal rights of a real person.

Globalism

What happens to all these commodities? Thanks to the power of the global network of exchange, they can themselves spread globally, becoming elements of a sort of shared global culture. Some of these products encode their own subset of network connections—for example, the music of the Los Angeles–based band Dengue Fever. That story starts in Southern California in the 1960s, with the surfer music of the Beach Boys and similar bands, which found its way to Cambodia, where local musicians made it their own, with Cambodian lyrics and an infusion of local melodic riffs. Tragically, almost all the artists and musicians in Cambodia died in the Khmer Rouge's brutal genocide of its own people (roughly 6 million dead) in the 1970s, a side effect of the Vietnam War. But records of the music survived to be discovered by two brothers from Los Angeles, who put together a band to play in that style in the early 2000s. They were joined by the top new Cambodian female singer, who was detained by the US immigration services and had to find a job. Their music is a kind of history of their network.

Similar "mosaic" aspects of elements of global culture can be seen in restaurants around the world, whether Indian restaurants in London, Thai restaurants in Indianapolis, or McDonald's restaurants in Paris. Some elements are even more global. Two levels of clothing are prime examples: blue jeans and the "Western" business suit, which was invented in London in the early 1800s and has since become the near-universal cultural symbol for "man with serious business to do," undoubtedly either capitalist or nationalist business, at that (or else he'd be wearing blue jeans). It is these nearly universal elements, most of which have come out of the northwestern European and US cultures that have been Industrial capitalist longest in the world, that raise fears (or hopes) in some quarters about cultural imperialism or the homogenization of global culture. Nor are such fears necessarily groundless. For one thing, every industrialized society shares both structures and patterns of culture that are more similar to those of other Industrial societies than they are to the structures and cultures of that society's own Agrarian past. But there is cultural variation among Industrial societies, within those common patterns, just as there was cultural variety among Agrarian societies.

FIGURE 28.3 Dengue Fever (the Band). Members include brothers Ethan and Zac Holtzman, who recruited Cambodian singer Chhom Nimol.

As we noted in Chapter 22, "modernization" and "westernization" are not the same thing. We will discuss a second, more serious sort of linguistic evidence for cultural imperialism below.

Localism

Just as nationalism and local politics act as countervailing forces in politics to the agglomerating influences of the global network and capitalism, however, local tastes and identities are not simply helpless victims of the tendency toward global cultural homogenization created by the same operations of the capitalist network. Instead, they create countervailing possibilities for the survival of local cultures.

Indeed, our discussion of globalization of culture has already included one such pathway. Seeing various aspects of the global cultural mix as elements in a mosaic presupposes the separate existence of different local cultures that can contribute tiles to the mosaic. Thus, global cuisine does not consist just of some universally marketed set of foods and drinks, McDonald's hamburgers washed down with Coke or Pepsi notwithstanding, but of the choice of different cuisines that are attractive because they are different. Thus, a sort of "niche marketing" dynamic serves both to spread local products more widely and to serve local tastes with their traditional fare. Variety can be maintained even under somewhat globalized, apparently homogenizing structures. McDonald's in India does not serve beef hamburgers, for example, since eating beef is a Hindu taboo (and Muslims will not eat pork). Instead, it serves patties made from ground chicken or veggies. Burgers in Pakistan are often made from a mixture of ground lentils and lamb. The global tourism industry is built around selling local difference as an exotic commodity.

There is a limit to what the exploitation of market niches and the capitalist structure of the network can accomplish in preserving local cultures, however. The local "product" must be marketable to remain protected—a dynamic that limits market-based approaches to the preservation of endangered species, as well: people may pay to see lions and tigers in the wild, but a small, undistinguished looking fish endangered by a hydroelectric dam project is harder to market. Furthermore, there is the problem that commodification tends to sell appearance much more than underlying reality—the sizzle, not the steak. Thus, just as the commodification of "hippie" symbols from 1960s politics as fashion statements denatures their political message, or as marketing angry protest music to a mainstream audience sucks the anger and the protest out of it, marketing exotic places threatens to turn them into parodic images of themselves. This is because mass marketing requires that exciting difference be wrapped in a layer of comfortable familiarity. This dynamic is certainly visible in tourism, where organized tours to strange foreign places not only understandably avoid really dangerous spots, but view the localities they do visit from hotels that conform to a global standard of comfort and amenities—hotels that are the colonial outposts of global homogenization in the wild jungles of local diversity.

FIGURE 28.4 Comfortable Anywhere. The view from a room in an underwater hotel in Dubai.

Mosaic Projections

The modern world of universal commodification produces fascinating mosaics of identity projection. (Top left) Chinese punk rockers, for whom Mao Zedong and Che Guevara are identity commodities. (Top right) The near-universal reach of American "food" commodities: an Afghan boy consumes Pop Tarts to show off who he is. (Bottom left) Cell phones and traditional dress on the streets of Toulouse proclaim the identity of their users and wearers. (Bottom right) Prince Charles visits the Australian Outback, where indigenous identity itself is the commodity on offer.

FIGURE 28.7 Worshippers. Members of the Church of Manchester United during a ritual gathering.

They model the culture of the capitalist workplace: they run according to carefully defined, legalistic rules; their activities are regulated or measured by a clock (baseball being a significant exception to this rule); and a specialist class of managers supervise the workers, who are themselves specialists of the highest order. But for purposes of identity construction, it is not the members of the industry but their customers who are worth examining.

For in many ways, modern sports have assumed many of the functions usually handled by religion in the Agrarian world. Sports affiliations create and define communities, from the international to the local levels, in the way that religions, sects, cults, and shrines defined pre-Industrial communities. A sports team's ritual events (games) take place at venerable sacred grounds (think Wrigley Field, though building a new, bigger, better cathedral is also an option—public funding of shrines to please the gods is a truly ancient practice, after all). The faithful gather together at these venues to worship their local saints (in the case of professional football in New Orleans, literally Saints), wearing the insignia and regalia of their sect. The regalia (caps, jerseys, and so forth) can also be displayed outside formal services—your author is wearing one of his St. Louis Cardinals T-shirts as he writes this section. Indeed, doing so assists members of the faith in identifying co-religionists they might not otherwise know, providing a hook on which to hang cultural bonding in any location.

The allegiances expressed through attendance and regalia wearing are not trivial, as the bitterness of some rivalries attest—or as the passion of a fanatical Little League parent can show. Soccer started a war between El Salvador and Honduras in 1969. "Fan," the word for a sports supporter, is, after all, short for "fanatic." And these allegiances really can build a communal identity otherwise riven with division: witness the impact on India of their 2011 victory in the Cricket World Cup, which completed the deification of their leader, the great batsman Sachin Tendulkar. This bonding effect is widely recognized and even promoted within that pervasive global frame value, nationalism. See, for example, "Cardinals Nation" and "Red Sox Nation," among others.

Meanwhile, the mythic power of a few religious saints and heroes—Pele, Michael Jordan, the denizens of a higher plane of existence—is such that they transcend national boundaries. And sports teams can become the repository of existential meaning for their communities: Cubs fans know the meaning of suffering, the Saints' first Super Bowl victory redeemed a post-Katrina city.

Capitalist business structures can complicate this picture. Team owners are anomalies: Does the team belong to the owner or the community? (The community-owned Green Bay Packers demonstrate the strength of an alternative model.) If an owner moves a franchise, the abandoned community can be devastated. And stars who sign with other teams are seen as apostates, heretics, embodiments of evil, even while it is acknowledged that "it's just a business," after all. This is why some

FIGURE 28.8 Immortal Batsman. Sachin Tendulkar adds to his career run total.

worshippers prefer more localized, less capitalist shrines, such as college or high school sports, as foci for their chosen identities. The conflict here is that while the temple itself may be more pure (and that's a big maybe in terms of big-time college sports), or at least more attuned to local interests, with the saints more under community control, the saints are correspondingly less powerful, a dilemma that would have been familiar to the adherents of many local cults and shrines, pagan or salvationist, from earlier times.

The point of this extended—and quite serious—comparison is that the constructed nature of sports-based identities is obvious. People mostly know that they choose teams to root for (some do inherit their allegiances via that basic conduit of all forms of the cultural construction of identity, the family), that they can change their allegiances, and that their display of allegiance is a matter of consumer choices provided by the capitalist structure of sports. Some sports atheists don't like sports, uncontroversially demonstrating the very choice of being a fan. At some level, in other words, most sports fans will acknowledge the "artificiality" of the sports-based aspect of their personal and communal identity. And yet, those identities still matter; they are in fact not artificial, but real.

They've just been very obviously made real by culture, not by nature or some supposed transcendental, supernatural force.

The same, however, is true of all forms of cultural identity. It's just that apparently biological "facts" such as skin color, or belief in Truth or gods, obscures the perception of this fact in the cases of identities—racial, religious, even gender—that people think of as somehow more fundamental.

Making Meaning

This discussion of identity brings us to the other function of human culture since the Cognitive-Linguistic Revolution: making the world meaningful.

Communication and Community

As with our discussion of identity, we may start first with an analysis of basic context for making meaning, the history of forms of communication themselves and their impact on cultural expression.

Oral Culture

Language, the fundamental product of the Cognitive-Linguistic Revolution, was at first and is usually still an oral-aural form of communication, sign languages in deaf communities and the considerable communicative value of the facial expressions and body language that accompany speaking notwithstanding. For the first 65,000 years or so after the Cognitive-Linguistic Revolution (which this books dates hypothetically at roughly 70,000 years ago), language was exclusively oral-aural and produced human

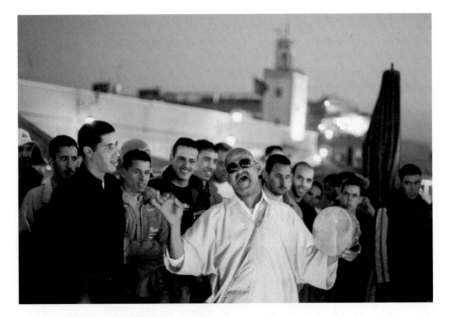

FIGURE 28.9 **The Power of Story.** Crowd gathered around a popular storyteller and musician performing on the central square of Djemaa El Fna in Marrakesh, Morocco.

communities with oral cultures. In such cultures, cultural meaning is constantly constructed and reconstructed orally, or at least with oral communication as the center of gravity around which other arts such as music, painting, pottery, and architecture revolve and through which they are interpreted.

Such cultures usually characterize themselves as very traditional—that is, they think of their culture as unchanging, as it is passed on from one generation to the next without conscious change. Memorization and apprenticeship are the key cultural tools for the transmission of oral culture; reliance on memory contributes to the self-perception of an unchanging culture. Oral cultures do change, of course, constantly, but in small evolutionary ways that largely go unnoticed. Even more important, oral cultures generally make no distinction of social status in cultural expressions. There may be some traditions, sometimes expressed in the form of memorized stories or oral poetry (which is not memorized, but re-composed with each performance), that are more sacred than others, but there is no distinction between "high" and "low" (or elite and popular) culture in oral societies, because everyone shares the same communications system.

Scribal Culture

The distinction between high and low emerged with the invention of writing and the creation of scribal cultures. In scribal cultures, some forms of culture are committed to writing, which in its various forms is both the graphical representation of oral language and a device for off-loading human memory from the brains of individuals to various forms of external storage. Much early scribal culture consisted of transcriptions of oral forms (this is how we have Homer's poems), not just because they were the known tradition, but because oral forms and personal testimony had more prestige than the new, potentially unreliable medium of communication. (How can you trust a text if you cannot interrogate its author in person, judging not just his words but his facial expressions, which give many subtle clues about trustworthiness, and know his reputation?) But in every culture that made the transition from oral to scribal, at some point the social context of writing and the characteristics of scribal communication elevated written culture over oral culture.

In terms of characteristics, the key is that writing makes words permanent: linguistic cultural products could outlive their producers. The products themselves then took on the role of cultural beings. This exposed them to extended analysis and, inevitably, criticism and theorizing, which could also be extended to other non-written forms of culture. In other words, scribal cultures became more self-conscious. This in turn encouraged innovation and the recognition of change, giving scribal cultures a different self-image from oral cultures, even if change was conceived in a backward-looking, traditionalist form. Writing allowed conversations with the great teachers of earlier times, not just memorization of their words. In terms of social context, in all scribal cultures reading and writing tended to be specialized skills, available only to those with enough wealth and leisure to devote to learning these skills. Put in terms of our model of Agrarian societies, literacy was an elite skill, limited for the most part to the top part of the pyramid (and often to the male half of that top).

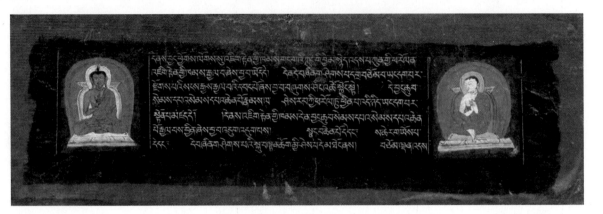

FIGURE 28.10 Permanent Words. Manuscripts convey ideas through words and pictures that outlast their creator.

Elite literacy in turn changed language itself. Studies of both ancient Akkadian (the second written language of the early Mesopotamian empires after Sumerian) and Early New High German in the period when printing and literacy spread between 1500 and 1700 show that writing made language syntactically more complex. Writing also allowed the creation of "classical models" of diction and style that could persist for centuries, which further distinguished written from oral expression and the language of elites from the dialects of the masses.

All of this produced the distinction common to scribal cultures between elite and popular (or, from the perspective of the elites, high and low) culture. High culture was written (or written about), permanent, self-conscious; low culture was oral, transitory in its expressions even if lasting in its collective existence, and unreflective. These distinctions are captured in the cultural aspects of our model of Agrarian societies, especially where input into cultural frames and screens came from and in the presence of the Great Cultural Divide. (See Figure 28.11.)

Print Culture, Agrarian and Industrial

The specialized skill of literacy and the low productivity of handwriting—a crucial aspect of the "low and slow" constraints on the structure of Agrarian hierarchies—meant that the information capacity of scribal cultures remained limited and its products relatively expensive, which reinforced the elite nature of the written side of scribal cultures. The invention of printing, especially movable type printing, changed these dynamics somewhat. The productivity of printing is much higher than that of handwriting, even without steam-powered industrialization behind it. This made books and other forms of printed material such as pamphlets and broadsheets cheaper and more accessible, and so created print cultures. Agrarian print cultures saw a significant expansion of the amount of cultural production committed to paper, while the greater information storage and production capacity of print allowed an expansion of the scope of human knowledge. It also encouraged a slow but steady rise in the number of people with access to written (printed) words. It is also sometimes asserted that print increased the fidelity of human "external memory," as it

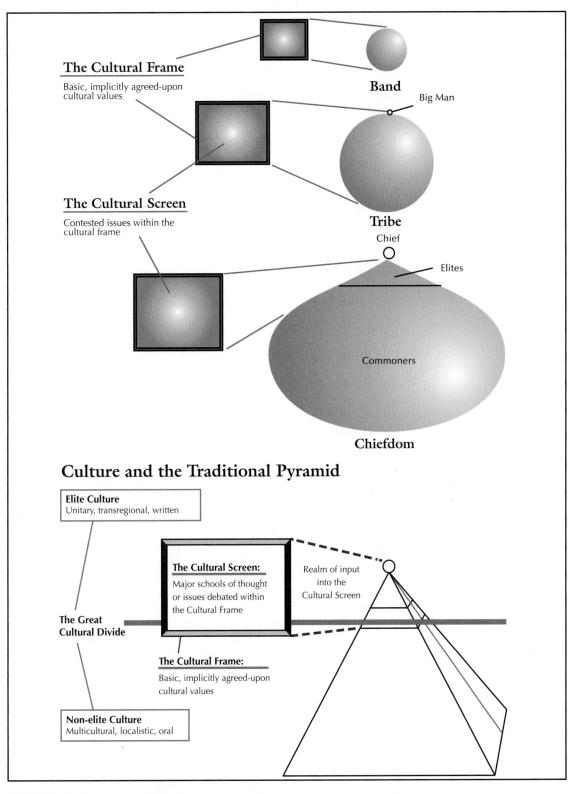

The Cultural Frame

Basic, implicitly agreed-upon cultural values

Band

Big Man

The Cultural Screen

Contested issues within the cultural frame

Tribe

Chief

Elites

Commoners

Chiefdom

Culture and the Traditional Pyramid

Elite Culture
Unitary, transregional, written

The Cultural Screen:
Major schools of thought or issues debated within the Cultural Frame

Realm of input into the Cultural Screen

The Great Cultural Divide

The Cultural Frame:
Basic, implicitly agreed-upon cultural values

Non-elite Culture
Multicultural, localistic, oral

FIGURE 28.11 Structures of Culture. Input into cultural frames and screens, from band to state, and the emergence of the Great Cultural Divide.

reduced the copying errors that plagued manuscript production. While in the long run this is probably true, in many cases print made some errors harder to correct, as the error could now exist not in one or a score of copied manuscripts, but in hundreds or thousands of printed copies.

As the example of typographical errors in texts emphasizes, print's greater productive capacity reinforced the permanence of linguistic cultural products, which continued, now even more strongly, to distinguish them from the oral cultures of illiterate portions of society. Thus, although print under Agrarian conditions of production may have lowered where the Great Cultural Divide bisected society, it did not erase it.

Industrialization, however, did begin to undermine the conditions under which a Great Cultural Divide could exist, as we discussed in Chapter 20. Not only did industrialization, applied specifically to printing technology, vastly raise the productivity of printing beyond Agrarian levels, making printed products even cheaper, but the material benefits of industrialization made mass society richer. Thus, what the combination of industrialization and printing seemed to promise to do was to make print cultures *pervasively* print-based, down through almost all levels of society and in new areas such as sheet music. This, in fact, still did not truly erase the fundamental cultural division that had created the Great Cultural Divide, however; it just moved it even further down and made it fuzzier as a boundary.

Electronic Culture

It was the Industrial world's constant inventiveness that erased the Great Cultural Divide. Starting with Thomas Edison's phonograph and continuing through tape recording, movies, videotape, and then the conversion of all such forms to digital formats, the communications technologies of industrialization revolutionized the production of culture and helped reshape the communities that use them. For the key effect of these new technologies was to do for all forms of ephemeral culture what writing had done for speaking: made them (potentially) permanent. Today, we have access not just to the thoughts of Albert Einstein, but to the acting of Charlie Chaplin, the sports skill of Red Grange, the voice of Enrico Caruso, the Delta blues of Blind Lemon Jefferson, and the desert guitar of Bombino. In effect, such technologies, while not making oral culture written, have erased the only meaningful difference between oral and written culture. (See Figure 28.12.)

As a result, there is no longer a defensible distinction between "high" and "low" culture. There is mass culture, and there are constructed distinctions between elite and popular culture based on claims about "quality," or level of self-conscious theorizing, or opacity (difficulty of understanding), or other screen images of screen images, as we characterized this development in Chapter 20. And the same technologies constitute a significant part of the mechanisms of the global network, a network that makes mosaic pieces out of bits of cultural expression from around the world, offers menus of identity choices, and creates a new, global community and context for the making of meaning through culture.

Answering Big Questions

The academic approach to the human quest for meaning has usually centered on philosophical attempts to formulate that quest as a set of formal questions and then

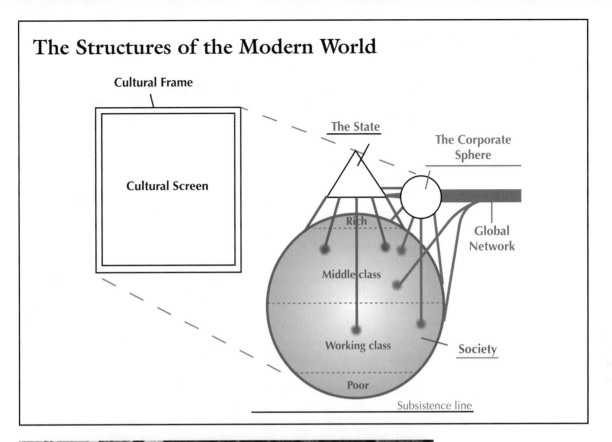

The Structures of the Modern World

Cultural Frame

Cultural Screen

The State

The Corporate Sphere

Rich

Global Network

Middle class

Working class

Society

Poor

Subsistence line

FIGURE 28.12 Good-bye Great Cultural Divide. (Top) The structures of the modern world, with no Great Cultural Divide, and input into the cultural frame and onto the cultural screen from all of society—just as happened in bands and tribes, but on a far vaster scale—thus the "global village," though it is a far more complex and contested village than the phrase usually conveys. (Bottom) The ephemeral actions of Charlie Chaplin made permanent on film.

try to answer them—a very self-conscious, "high culture" view. This path emerged fully, as we saw in Chapter 4, with the philosophies and religions of the Axial Age, many of which are still perceived as foundational to modern philosophical and religious traditions. The Big Questions raised then about the place of humanity in the cosmos, about social order, and about individual ethical action within cosmic and social order are still relevant today. But modern approaches to these questions have tended to split and specialize, reflecting the influence of the Axial Age Greek emphasis on method over content that informed the scientific revolution of the seventeenth century and the latter's evolution into modern science.

Science, Religion, Ethics

Thus, science has come to dominate, in one sense, explorations of humanity's relationship to the cosmos and place in the physical world, because this question can easily be formulated as a set of "how?" questions (How did life arise? How did simple life-forms produce us? and so forth) that science is built to answer, even if it cannot produce all the answers yet. The beginning part of the first chapter of Volume 1 of this book, from the Big Bang through the evolution of life-forms through the Cognitive-Linguistic Revolution, is grounded in what science can currently tell us about these questions. Science has been vastly productive in answering such questions, and in spewing out fun technologies as it has done so, but for many people, posing the cosmic question as a "how?" question ducks the central issue—which scientists readily admit. Science may be able to show that we seem to be a very contingent product of evolution on a small, perhaps unusual planet—an accident on a speck of dust in an unimaginably vast universe—but it cannot answer the "why?" question about this finding: Why should this be so? What does it *mean*?

Traditional religious doctrines continue to provide answers to this question for many people, as well as to possibly related questions about proper social order and individual ethics. Problems sometimes arise when science's "how?" answers seem to conflict with literal interpretations of a religion's "why?" stories, but most scientists and religious thinkers seem content to live with separate, complementary realms. Problems also arise when literal interpretations of religious answers to social order and individual ethics, formulated for the hierarchical conditions of the Agrarian world where most major religions arose, seem to conflict with the different conditions and tendencies created by industrialization. Here, too, however, the flexibility of the human ability to make meaning can finesse such issues. In addition, the global network offers a virtual marketplace of religious ideas, of possibilities for negotiating any perceived disjunction between doctrine and science, life, or whatever.

Nor is religion the only possible approach to the "why?" questions that science cannot answer. Atheist and existentialist views of accidental creatures in a vast uncaring universe see such a picture precisely as freeing those creatures to make their own meaning. Most modern philosophical theories of social order and ethics are non-religious (as some always have been: ask Confucius). The view that the universe has no inherent transcendental meaning is implicit in the one science that does, in a way, deal in meaning. Psychotherapy, especially of the "talking cure" sort, attempts to get people to tell their own stories in such a way as to reconstruct the meaning of their lives in a more satisfying way.

Arts and Science

Indeed, people generally make their lives meaningful in the same way they have since the Cognitive-Linguistic Revolution: by telling and listening to stories, including stories about their own lives and stories about the lives of others that resonate with them. Interpreted broadly, this is what art is—not just the art of gossip, but storytelling in the form of books, poetry, songs, movies, TV shows, sports, YouTube videos. Stories are everywhere. Visual arts and music without words can tell more abstract stories, which are heard at emotional levels of our cognitive systems before they are processed in linguistic ways. Thus, Bombino's music creates and binds community and tells stories, verbal and musical, that give that community identity and meaning.

Finally, in a fascinating bit of recursion, one of the "how?" questions that science has made major strides in answering in the last twenty years is how the human

> **PRINCIPLES AND PATTERNS**
> *People make meaning by telling stories, including stories cast as history.*

FIGURE 28.13 Multimedia Stories. Words and pictures combined in the Sandman series by Neil Gaiman.

privileges of corporate-capitalist intellectual property should not be allowed to strangle all but the most private expressions of democratically participatory culture.

History and Meaning

Finally, we can't end this history of the world without noting again that history, too, is a form of storytelling, a way of understanding the world and making it more meaningful. The "plot" of this story has involved networks, hierarchies, cultural frames and screens—in other words, a lot of somewhat abstract concepts. But it has also told stories about individuals, from the Ice Man in Chapter 2 to Omara "Bombino" Moctar. Ideally, the structures help explain the individual stories, while the stories make the structures come alive, reminding us that they are the product of the aggregate actions and beliefs of all the world's people. The combination, I hope, has made both the great sweep of past events and the complex twists and turns of today's news more comprehensible. And ideally, through understanding, comes a greater ability for you not just to give the world meaning for yourself but to make it better.

Conclusion

Contemporary global culture, like the global world of hierarchies and the global network of the previous two chapters, is necessarily an unfinished story. That is why these chapters have concentrated on thematic analysis rather than narrative of ongoing events. If these themes and the analytic tools this book has developed since the first chapter have value, then this book does not need to carry on various narratives. People since the Cognitive-Linguistic Revolution have had the ability to learn language, to perform music, and to be historians. History is a collective enterprise that benefits from multiple perspectives. Pick up some tools—these, or others you find more useful—and join the fun. Do history.

FRAME IT YOURSELF

Frame Your World

Really. Do history. Frame your world.

Further Reading

Chau, Adam Yuet. 2011. *Religion in Contemporary China*. New York: Routledge.
Geary, David C. 2004. *The Origin of Mind: Evolution of Brain, Cognition, and General Intelligence*. Washington, DC: American Psychological Association.

Harrison, K. David. 2008. *When Languages Die: The Extinction of the World's Languages and the Erosion of Human Knowledge.* New York: Oxford University Press.

Root, Deborah. 1996. *Cannibal Culture: Art, Appropriation, and the Commodification of Difference.* Boulder, CO: Westview Press.

Smith, Bonnie. 2000. *Global Feminisms since 1945.* London: Routledge.

Stearns, Peter. 2006. *Consumerism in World History: The Global Transformation of Desire.* 2nd ed. London: Routledge.

For additional learning and instructional resources related to this chapter, please go to www.oup.com/us/morillo

Periodization Terms

- ◉ Hunter-Gatherer Era (before 8000 BCE) Chapter 1
- • Early Hunter-Gatherer (before ca. 70,000 BCE)
- • High Hunter-Gatherer (ca. 70,000 BCE to ca. 20,000 BCE)
- • Late Hunter-Gatherer (ca. 20,000 BCE to 4000 BCE)
- ○ Agrarian Era (8000 BCE to 1800 BCE)
- • Early Agrarian (8000 BCE to 700 CE) Chapters 2–7
- • High Agrarian (400 to 1500) Chapters 8–14
- • Late Agrarian (1500 to 1800) Chapters 15–18
- ○ Industrial Era (after 1800)
- • Early Industrial (1800 to 1945) Chapters 19–24
- • High Industrial (1914) Chapters 23–28
- • Late Industrial (the future?)

Cognitive-Linguistic Revolution
(ca. 70,000 years ago)
Agricultural Revolution
(ca. 8000 BCE)
Industrial Revolution
(ca. 1800 CE)

Hunter-Gatherer societies
Agrarian societies
Pastoralist societies
Industrial societies

The Model: General Terms

Model	Hierarchies	Cultural frame
Structures	Culture	Low and slow
Networks	Cultural screen	

Network Terms

Network flows	Inner circuit Eurasia	Dense local network
Network circuits	Outer circuit Afro-Eurasia	Network crisis

Hierarchy Terms

Simple societies	Commoners	Nomad-Sedentary cycle
Bands	Class power	Warfare
Tribes	Top and bottom layers of the Pyramid	Intracultural warfare
Complex societies	Gender power	Intercultural warfare
Chiefdoms	Front and back faces of the Pyramid	Subcultural warfare
State-level complex societies	Industrial hierarchy	Reactions to imperialism
Agrarian Pyramid	State	Traditionalist resisters
State	Social sphere	Westernizers
Society	Corporate sphere	Modernizers
Unitary political leader	Conquest societies	Identerest
Elites	Fragment societies	Kleptocracy

Terms Relating to the Intersection of Networks and Hierarchies

Merchant dilemma	Worldly travelers	State-private dichotomy
Cores	Spheres of maritime activity	War-peace dichotomy
Peripheries	Naval sphere of maritime activity	Official-unofficial dichotomy
Wise practitioners	Merchant sphere of maritime activity	Navies of imperial defense
Informed officials	Pirate sphere of maritime activity	Predatory sea peoples

Cultural Frame and Screen Terms

Frame values	Cultural screen images	Great Cultural Divide

Glossary

Agrarian Era The era between the Agricultural Revolution (8000 BCE) and the Industrial Revolution (1800). Characterized by the dominance of Agrarian societies. (Hunter-gatherers survived through the Agrarian Era and into the Industrial Era.) Divided into Early, High, and Late Agrarian.

Agrarian Pyramid The shape in our model for state-level Agrarian societies.

Agrarian societies Societies whose main source of subsistence and wealth production was agriculture.

Agricultural Revolution (ca. 8000 BCE) The domestication of plants and animals.

Band The smallest, simplest of simple societies. Usually under a hundred people, mostly related.

Chiefdoms Complex societies, usually consisting of several thousand people, led by a chief and a hereditary elite, but lacking the institutional organization of a state-level complex society.

Circuits *See* **Network circuits**.

Class power The political, coercive power exerted from the top down in Agrarian Pyramids that drew resources up to the top.

Cognitive-Linguistic Revolution (ca. 70,000 BCE) The emergence of modern word-and-syntax speech and the metaphorical thought that

speech made possible and expressed. This revolution also entailed the emergence of music as a separate realm of communication. Laid the foundations for the creation of networks, complex hierarchies, and cultural frames and screens.

Commoners Non-elites. The lower part of the Agrarian Pyramid.

Complex societies Societies with permanent hierarchical divisions within the society.

Conquest societies A society ruled by a foreign elite or state that is unconnected to the society.

Cores Political-economic regions that exert control over the politics and economics of peripheral regions.

Corporate sphere In Industrial hierarchies, the sphere of activity in which corporations operate. Sits at the link between the network on one side and both the state and society on the other.

Cultural frame The metaphorical frame around an individual's or society's cultural screen. The frame represents the limits within which the society projects images. These limits are created by mostly unconscious, assumed ideas about what counts as possible or "natural."

Cultural screen images The ideas, political positions, cultural arguments, and so forth that individuals or groups argue about

consciously and so project onto their cultural screen.

Cultural screen The metaphorical screen (like a movie screen) upon which individuals and societies project images that represent conscious ideas about their identity and the meaning of the world.

Dense local network A region of a network where connections and the exchange of goods and ideas are particularly robust.

Early Agrarian Era From 8000 BCE to 700 CE (see Chapters 2–7). Includes Axial Age (Chapter 4) and Age of Empires (Chapter 5).

Early Hunter-Gatherer Era From before the Cognitive-Linguistic Revolution (ca. 70,000 BCE).

Early Industrial Era From 1800 to 1945 (see Chapters 19–24).

Elites The upper layer of the Agrarian Pyramid; those with power and status; aristocrats, non-commoners.

Fragment societies Societies formed by the migration of only a fragment of another society. The result is a society that is often more egalitarian than the original society.

Frame values The largely unspoken or assumed cultural beliefs that make up an individual's or society's cultural frame. Values taken by that individual or society to be "natural" and that therefore don't need to be consciously defended.

Front and back faces of the Pyramid
The front-back division of the
Agrarian Pyramid that represents the
gendered public/male (front) and
private/female (back) realms of
society.

Gender power The political coercive
power that drew resources from the
private-female realm of the Pyramid
to the public-male realm (and from
there via class power toward the top).

Great Cultural Divide In Agrarian
hierarchies, the division between
elite culture and the culture of the
common people.

Hierarchies Individual human
societies, all of which are
characterized by being organized by
vertical structures of power.
Common forms include kingdoms,
empires, city-states, nation-states,
and so forth.

High Agrarian Era From 400 to
1500 (see Chapters 8–14).

High Hunter-Gatherer Era From the
Cognitive-Linguistic Revolution to
ca. 20,000 BCE.

High Industrial Era Since 1914
(see Chapters 23–28).

Hunter-Gatherer Era The era
before the Agricultural Revolution
(8000 BCE). Characterized by
hunter-gatherer societies Divided
into Early, High, and Late Hunter-
Gatherer (see Chapter 1).

Hunter-gatherer societies Human
societies that made a living by
hunting animals and gathering fruits
and vegetables.

Identerest Form of politics that makes
some claim about group identity
a central political interest.

Industrial Era The era since the
Industrial Revolution (1800).
Characterized by the dominance of

Industrial societies. Divided into
Early, High, and Late Industrial.

Industrial Revolution (ca. 1800)
The invention of mechanized means
of production powered by means
more powerful than muscle, wind,
and water.

Industrial hierarchy The shape in the
Industrial Era of state-level complex
societies, consisting of three parts:
state, social sphere, and corporate
sphere. Industrial equivalent of the
Agrarian Pyramid.

Industrial societies Societies whose
main source of wealth production is
mechanized industry.

Informed officials In network-
hierarchy intersections, informed
officials were members of hierarchies
who supervised, regulated, or
otherwise exploited network flows.
Customs officers are an example.

Inner circuit Eurasia The subcircuit
of the Eurasian network in the High
and Late Agrarian Era that included
the nomadic, pastoralist societies of
the central Asian steppes and the
major hierarchies immediately
adjacent to the steppes.

Intercultural warfare Warfare
between two groups whose cultures
(especially of warfare) are not just
different but unknown to each other.
Such warfare tends to be
characterized by pragmatic
opportunism on both sides.

Intracultural warfare Warfare
between two groups who share a
culture (at least of warfare). Such
warfare operates by known rules and
conventions.

Kleptocracy Literally, "rule by theft."
Another way of saying that Agrarian
Era hierarchies were coercive in
nature.

Late Agrarian Era From 1500 to
1800 (see Chapters 15–18).

Late Hunter-Gatherer Era From
ca. 20,000 bce to 4000 bce, ending
in the Agricultural Revolution.

Late Industrial Era The realm of
science fiction writers. Future
historians will know it in hindsight.

Low and slow Shorthand for "low
productivity and slow
communications," the two basic
constraints that shaped Hunter-
Gatherer and Agrarian societies, with
emphasis on the latter. The Industrial
Revolution largely eliminated these
constraints.

Maritime spheres of activity A model
of the relationship of the three major
sorts of maritime actors, navies,
merchants, and pirates.

Merchant dilemma The problem for
Agrarian state-level hierarchies that
their rulers desired the goods
merchants made available but did not
trust merchants (or network flows
generally). This led to a variety of
techniques for regulating such flows
and controlling the potential that
merchant (network) values had to
subvert hierarchy values.

**Merchant sphere of maritime
activity** One of the three maritime
spheres of activity, merchant shipping
of goods.

Model For our purposes as historians,
an explicitly worked out
generalization of patterns and a
theory of causation. In our case, the
model is presented in visual terms.

Modernizers A type of resistance to
European imperialism that advocated
adopting imperial technology but
retaining traditional culture.

Naval sphere of maritime activity
One of the three maritime spheres of

activity, the operations of state-run navies.

Navies of imperial defense The main model of Agrarian naval organization, designed to defend a hierarchy at sea and to police network flows.

Network circuits The subdivisions of a network. Also called *subcircuits*. Networks can be divided geographically as well as by sorts of flows. A circuit primarily devoted to trade in copper lamps differs from a circuit primarily devoted to the spreading of Buddhist holy texts, for example, both in the sorts of goods and ideas they carry and in the kinds of people (merchants versus monks, in this case) who carry them. Circuits can overlap or be totally separate from each other.

Network crisis A major breakdown in network flows. A modern example is the Great Depression.

Network flows The movement of goods, people, and ideas across networks.

Networks The horizontal connections between different human societies. Goods, people, and ideas move across networks.

Nomad-sedentary cycle The cyclical pattern of relations between central Asian steppe nomadic pastoralists and their sedentary Agrarian neighbors, characterized by periodic conquest of sedentary areas by the nomads, followed by redivision of the nomadic and sedentary parts of the combined hierarchy.

Official-unofficial dichotomy One of the three ways to divide maritime spheres of activity. This unites navies and merchants against pirates.

Outer circuit Afro-Eurasia The set of High and Late Agrarian Era hierarchies that lay in a ring around inner circuit Eurasia. They were generally smaller than the major hierarchies of inner circuit Eurasia and were connected by a set of largely maritime subcircuits.

Pastoralist societies Societies whose main source of wealth production was herding domesticated animals; a subset of Agrarian societies.

Peripheries Regions that are controlled or heavily influenced in political-economic terms by a core region.

Pirate sphere of maritime activity One of the three maritime spheres of activity, the activity of pirates.

Predatory sea peoples A form of naval activity halfway between navies and pirates.

Priests Elites whose authority derives from their religious role. One of the three types of elites in Agrarian hierarchies, along with scribes and warriors.

Scribes Elites whose authority derives from their specialized knowledge, usually of written texts and documents and the ability to produce them. One of the three types of elites in Agrarian hierarchies, along with priests and warriors.

Simple societies Societies with no or minimal hierarchy. Examples include bands and tribes.

Social sphere In our model of Industrial hierarchies, the sphere that represents the non-state, socioeconomic activities of the population. Connected to both the state and the corporate sphere.

Socioeconomic structure A social structure whose organizing principles are built on economic relationships. Examples include networks or the social sphere of Industrial hierarchies.

Sociopolitical structure A social structure whose organizing principles are built on political (i.e., coercive, power-based) relationships, for example the Agrarian Pyramid.

State-level complex society A society that has a formal state and multilayered social gradations of status; the most complex form of hierarchy. *See* **Agrarian Pyramid, Industrial hierarchy**.

State-private dichotomy One of the three ways to divide maritime spheres of activity. This unites merchants and pirates against navies.

State The organization that wields formal power over a society. In Agrarian hierarchies, it is usually congruent with the informal social power of elites. In Industrial hierarchies, it is the professional managerial organization that regulates the social and corporate spheres.

Structure In this model, a network or a hierarchy.

Subcultural warfare Warfare in which the two sides share a broad culture but are divided within that culture. Subcultural enemies tend to demonize each other and aim at mutual annihilation.

Top and bottom layers of the Pyramid In the model of Agrarian hierarchies, the division of the Pyramid into elites (top) and commoners (bottom).

Traditionalist resisters A type of resistance to European imperialism

Volume 2

Credits

Index

Note: Page numbers followed by *f* and *t* indicate figures and tables, respectively; page numbers in *italics* refer to unnumbered photos in the Images on the Screen features; page numbers preceded by S refer to the Summary chapter in Volume 2.